Policing Today and Tomorrow

MICHAEL L. BIRZER

Wichita State University

CLIFF ROBERSON

Washburn University

PEARSON

Prentice
Hall

Upper Saddle River, New Jersey 07458

Library of Congress Cataloging-in-Publication Data

Birzer, Michael L.
Policing today and tomorrow / Michael L. Birzer, Cliff Roberson.
  p. cm.
Includes bibliographical references and index.
ISBN 0-13-119068-7
1. Police—United States.   I. Roberson, Cliff—II. Title.

HV8139.B57 2007
363.2'3'0973—dc22

2005052312

Executive Editor: Frank Mortimer, Jr.
Associate Editor: Sarah Holle
Marketing Manager: Adam Kloza
Managing Editor: Mary Carnis
Production Liaison: Brian Hyland
Production Editor: Janet Bolton
Director of Manufacturing and Production: Bruce Johnson
Manufacturing Manager: Ilene Sanford

Manufacturing Buyer: Cathleen Petersen
Design Director: Cheryl Asherman
Senior Design Coordinator: Miguel Ortiz
Cover Design: Michael Ginsberg
Cover Art: iStockPhoto
Electronic Art Creation: Integra
Composition: Integra
Printing and Binding: Hamilton Printing
Copy Editor/Proofreader: Maine Proofreading Services

Pearson Education LTD.
Pearson Education Australia PTY, Limited
Pearson Education Singapore, Pte. Ltd.
Pearson Education North Asia Ltd.
Pearson Education Canada, Ltd.
Pearson Education de Mexico, S.A. de C.V.
Pearson Education—Japan
Pearson Education Malaysia, Pte. Ltd.
Pearson Education, Upper Saddle River, New Jersey

10 9 8 7 6
ISBN 0-13-119068-7

Contents

CHAPTER
11

POLICE ORGANIZATION AND MANAGEMENT   306

CHAPTER
12

CRITICAL ISSUES IN POLICING   341

CHAPTER
13

POLICING AND TERRORISM   359

APPENDIX
A

HAWAII POLICE DEPARTMENT—DRUG TESTING GENERAL ORDER NO. 529   375

Preface

Albert Einstein once stated: "Wisdom is not a product of schooling but the lifelong attempt to acquire it." This is a message that we need to convey to our future police officers—that learning is a lifelong attempt to acquire knowledge.

Policing Today and Tomorrow examines both the present and future state of policing. The text takes an active and future view of policing—what law enforcement students need to know. For example, we have provided coverage on the implications for the police of policing an ever-changing and pluralistic society. The text examines many other topical areas that are usually given minimal attention in other texts, such as women and minorities in policing and police recruitment and selection. The latter topic isn't just a review of the current selection methods utilized but the development of a profile of the desired police officer of the future based on both changes in society and changes in police strategies (such as community policing and problem solving). *Policing Today and Tomorrow* is designed in a manner that emphasizes not only the written text but also the visual aspects of learning with pictures, graphs, charts, interactive text, and other visual aids. Other pedagogical features include pertinent Web resources, which will be listed at the end of each chapter so that students may query additional information on a topical area.

Chapter Organization and Overview

Chapter 1 discusses myths and realities of policing, consequences of the crime-fighter image, and roles and functions of police. In Chapter 2, we examine modern police systems and include discussions on jurisdiction, police accountability, styles of policing, scope of the law enforcement industry, and different types of law enforcement agencies. We conclude that chapter with sections on international policing and private police. In Chapter 3, community-oriented policing concepts and issues are discussed; problem-oriented policing, evaluations of community policing, and the future of community-oriented policing are covered in the chapter. Chapter 4, whose subjects include police brutality, police culture, varieties of police misconduct, and the Rampart case study, examines police culture, misconduct, and deviance. Chapter 5 looks at the legal issues in policing, including the legal authority of police, the concept of due process, the role of our courts, constitutional rights of citizens, the police officer as a witness, and police liability. In Chapter 6, we discuss the problems and issues involved in policing our diverse society. The human resources aspects of recruitment and selection are covered in Chapter 7: the recruitment process, selection issues, and innovative approaches to the recruitment and selection of police officers. Training, development, and education of police officers are looked at in Chapter 8, and Chapter 9 examines the role of and the issues involving women and minorities as police officers. Police operations—including patrol functions, patrol methods, evaluations of patrol, types of police investigations, and evaluations of criminal investigations—are covered in Chapter 10. In Chapter 11, we look at police organization and management issues; subjects we discuss include the definition of an organization, the traditional police organization, organizational structure, the military model, organizational terminology, levels of management, and organizational change. Critical issues in policing, including police stress and burnout, police suicide, and police alcoholism and drug abuse, are found in Chapter 12. Chapter 13 examines policing and terrorism; the chapter defines terrorism and threat assessment, examines the effects of terrorism on police operations, discusses homeland security, and concludes with a section on the future of policing.

Acknowledgments

The book draws on the talents and resources of many people. A "thank-you" is due to our friends and colleagues who have so graciously assisted us in this project. The Prentice Hall team, which includes Frank Mortimer, Jr., Sarah Holle, and Janet Bolton, deserves special thanks. The manuscript reviewers, Dana C. DeWitt, Chadron State College, Chadron, NE; David Graff, Kent State University—Tuscarawas, New Philadelphia, OH; William Nardini, Indiana State University, Terre Haute, IN; William Parks, University of South Carolina—Spartanburg, Spartanburg, SC; Arnold Waggoner, Rose State College, Midwest City, OK, are also due a special thank-you for their guidance, advice, and recommendations. We are grateful for the assistance of the Honorable Marc H. Morial, President and Chief Executive Officer, National Urban League; Janet Zobel, National Urban League; Angeli Frasure, Kansas Highway Patrol; Sergeant Kevin A. Barrick, Virginia State Police; Colonel Paul D. McClellan, Superintendent, Ohio State Highway Patrol; Tim Weaver, History Department, Ohio State Highway Patrol; Gregory Shipley, Director of Media Communications, Maryland State Police; Albert Ortiz, Chief of Police, San Antonio, Texas, Police Department; James Corwin, Chief of Police, Kansas City, Missouri, Police Department; William Bratton, Chief of Police, Los Angeles Police Department; Norman Williams, Chief of Police, Wichita, Kansas, Police Department; and Rafael Pineiro, Chief of Personnel, New York City Police Department.

To my loving wife Gwynne, and my precious son, Michael Jr.
—*Michael Birzer*

The Role of Police

Key Terms

Bobby
Bow Street Runners
Community policing
Constables
Cops
Crime fighter
Kefauver Committee
Mutual pledge
Peacekeeping
Pendleton Act
Police
Police functions

Policing
Praetorian guard
President's Commission on Law
    Enforcement and Administration
    of Justice
Professionalism
Questers
Role of police
Sheriff
Vigiles
Volstead Act
Wickersham Commission

Outline

Introduction
Factors Shaping the Role
    of Police
Myths and Realities of Policing

Crime-Fighter Image and Its
    Consequences
Roles and Functions of Police
Implications of Change

Learning Objectives

After reading this chapter, you should be able to:

1. Identify the influence of history on the modern-day police agency.
2. Discuss the myths of policing.
3. Describe the various roles of police.

4. Identify the concepts of community policing.
5. Discuss the role of the public in preventing crime.
6. Identify the present-day functions of policing.
7. Explain why America is a nation of small, decentralized police forces.
8. Discuss the role of politics in shaping American policing.

INTRODUCTION

This chapter examines the current role of police in the United States. As is true for most of our other public institutions and agencies, policing (in its current role) is shaped to a great extent by its history. To understand why the majority of police functions in the United States are handled by local independent police departments and there is no national police force, we need to examine the historical evolution of policing in the United States.

What does the term "**police**" mean to you? There are many books on policing, but few make any attempt to define the term.[1] It is defined in one dictionary as: "The governmental department of a city, state, etc., organized primarily for keeping order, enforcing the law, and preventing, detecting, and prosecuting crimes."[2] The problem with that definition is that historically most policing has been done by organizations that are not a department of government and the police are not always primarily concerned with keeping order, enforcing the law, and preventing, detecting, and prosecuting crimes. The definition also fails to point out the most important difference between police and other organizations—the ability of the police to use coercive force.

The National Advisory Commission on Criminal Justice Standards and Goals advocated that if the many different purposes of police were narrowed to a single focus, it would emerge as the obligation to preserve the peace in a manner consistent with the freedoms secured by the Constitution.[3]

While the police have the highest and most visible role in overcoming the threat and fear of crime, it does not follow that the police alone bear this responsibility. The responsibility is shared with each individual and each level of government. As Sir Robert Peel, who is credited with founding the

---

Fictional or (Partially) Realistic Situation?

More and more I was finding it difficult to do this job. All I saw was human wreckage. Even when I succeeded in dong something that felt right, more often than not, I'd been cursed for it. People didn't want cops around. Even my victories produced confusion. I had been fighting these feelings by not thinking about them, pushing them aside like bad food, knowing that if I ate much more, it would soon make me sick. But you can't run from moral dilemmas, and I knew my days in law enforcement were numbered unless I found an answer. [Fictional detective Shane Scully in Stephen J. Cannell's, *Vertical Coffin* (New York: St. Martin's Press, 2004), p. 12.]

POLICING IN ACTION

Cops

The slang term for British police officers is "**bobby.**" They were dubbed that after their founder, Sir Robert Peel. The American slang for police is "**cops.**" The origin of that term is not as clear as the origin for the term "bobby." One source suggests that the word is short for "copper," which means to capture. Another thinks that the word emerged as slang because the early police officers wore uniforms that had large copper stars on them, and a third suggests that the word "cop" originally meant "constable on patrol."

British police system, stated: "The police at all times should maintain a relationship with the public that gives reality to the historic tradition that the police are the public and the public are the police."[4]

FACTORS SHAPING THE ROLE OF POLICE

To understand our present police force, it is necessary to understand its antecedents. It has been stated that the modern-day police forces are prisoners of their history. Policing started as a private matter: Individuals were responsible for protecting themselves and maintaining an orderly community.[5] Organized police departments did not appear until the 14th century in France. One of the earliest reported efforts in policing was in the 6th century B.C.E. when unpaid magistrates in Athens were given the authority to adjudicate cases brought before them by citizens. It was the responsibility of citizens to arrest the wrongdoer, bring him or her before the magistrate, and then punish the offender. Citizens frequently banned together in towns and formed watches that operated during the hours of darkness; in addition, citizen groups patrolled the town borders to protect the town against invaders.

About the 5th century B.C.E., **questers** (trackers of murders) were established as one of the earliest known specialized investigative units. Later, Emperor Augustus, who ruled the Roman Empire at the start of the Christian era, established the **praetorian guard,** which is considered by some as the first police force. The praetorian guard's duty was to protect the emperor and the palace. Augustus also established the **vigiles,** who patrolled Rome's streets both day and night. The vigiles were known for their brutality and are considered by many as the first civil police force designed to protect citizens.

During the 1st century C.E., public officials called licors were used in Rome to serve as the magistrates' bodyguards. They were also responsible for bringing prisoners before the magistrates and for carrying out the punishments imposed by the magistrates.

The modern police department's origin can be traced to Alfred the Great of England when during the 9th century he structured his kingdom's defenses to prepare for a Danish invasion. For internal security purposes, Alfred instituted the system of **mutual pledge.** This system organized the country into groups of 10 families. The groups of 10 families were called tithings; 10 tithings were then grouped together into 100 families called constables. The **constables** in each geographical area were combined to form administrative units called shires (later called counties). Each shire was governed by a shire-reeve, the forerunner of our present **sheriff.**

Night watches were established in the urban areas of England in the 13th century to protect the streets during the hours of darkness. The night watch is considered the first rudimentary form of metropolitan policing. From the 13th century until the 17th century, there was minimum development in the area of policing. During that period, the concept in England was that each citizen had a duty to enforce the laws of England, but in actual practice, law enforcement was almost nonexistent.

In 17th-century England, the chief law enforcement officials were the magistrates, who presided over the courts, ordered arrests, called witnesses to investigate criminal activity, and examined prisoners, and the parish constables, who had only limited authority to arrest and whose authority was confined to small districts. In the rural areas, the shire-reeve was responsible for maintaining law and order among the tithings. Some of the constables in the urban areas had assistants called beadles; the beadles were used primarily to clear the streets of vagrants.

Development of the London Police Department

Robberies were flourishing in England during the 16th and 17th centuries. In 1693, Parliament passed an act providing for a reward of 40 pounds for the capture and conviction of any highwayman or road agent. As a result of this act, the English thief-takers emerged. Thief-takers were private individuals who were paid by the government on a piecework basis. They had no official status and only the authority of private citizens to arrest. They received rewards in return for the apprehension of criminals; in addition, on conviction of a criminal they got the criminal's property unless former property owners could prove that the criminal had stolen it from them. During serious crime waves, Parliament would increase the bounty reward for certain crimes. The origin of the American West bounty hunters can be traced to the English thief-takers.

Many of the thief-takers were criminals themselves. As the ranks of the thief-takers grew, a class of professional thief-takers developed. The system probably created more crime than it prevented. The thief-takers would in many cases encourage individuals to commit crimes and then arrest them for the rewards. There were also reported cases in which innocent people were framed by the thief-takers, who planted stolen property on them in order to collect a reward.

By 1829, there were over 3,000 uniformed constables in the city of London. Henry Fielding, a novelist who wrote *Tom Jones*, was appointed a

---

Want Ad on a British Poster in the 1750s

All persons who shall for the future suffer by robbers, burglars, etc., are desired immediately to bring or send the best description they can of such robberies, etc., with the time and place, and circumstances of the fact to Henry Fielding, Esq., at his house in Bow Street.

---

magistrate in Westminster, near London. His office was located on Bow Street. He established a relationship with the local pawnbrokers and requested that they notify him when someone tried to pawn stolen property. He ran advertising in the local newspapers inviting anyone who was the victim of a crime by robbers or burglars to immediately send or bring to his Bow Street office a description of the property stolen and of the criminal. He formed a small group of unofficial investigators. This group was nicknamed "**Bow Street Runners.**" They were not salaried and received their money under the standard thief-takers' reward system. Later the government provided financial support for the Bow Street Runners.

When Henry Fielding stepped down as magistrate because of poor health, he convinced the government to appoint his brother John as the magistrate. John Fielding was blind and was referred to as the "Blind Beak." ("Beak" was at the time a slang word for judge.) John received government funds to establish a civilian horse patrol of eight men to patrol the streets of London. After less than a year, the patrol was disbanded. A new horse patrol was later established, and the men were outfitted in red vests and blue jackets and trousers. One of the promises made by John Fielding was that the individuals would wear distinctive uniforms to ensure that they were not used as spies and that people who gave information to a constable would know that the individual was a constable.

In 1829, Sir Robert Peel, England's Home Secretary, convinced the Parliament to pass the Act for Improving the Police In and Near the Metropolis. This act established the first permanent police force for London. This police force was composed of over 1,000 men and was structured along military lines. The men were required to wear distinctive uniforms and were under the supervision of two police commissioners, one a lawyer and the other a military officer. At first, they were known as the "new police"; later they became known as "bobbies" in reference to Sir Robert Peel's nickname.

The basic tenets of the act that established the bobbies were as follows[6]:

- The police must be stable, efficient, and organized along bureaucratic lines.
- The police must be under governmental control.
- The best evidence of the efficiency of the police will be an absence of crime.
- The distribution of crime news is essential.
- The policeman should have a perfect command of his temper and a quiet and determined manner.

PIONEERS IN POLICING

Sir Robert Peel

Photo courtesy of the Library of Congress

In 1822 Robert Peel became Home Secretary of England. As Home Secretary, Peel created the Metropolitan London Police in 1829, leading to the nicknames of "Bobby" (which still endures) and "Peeler" for London's police officers. In 1829, Robert Peel's Metropolitan Police Act was passed; this provided permanently appointed and paid police constables (the Peelers). The first thousand of Peel's police, dressed in blue tailcoats and top hats, began to patrol the streets of London in September 1829. The Peelers were issued a wooden truncheon carried in a long pocket in the tail of their coat, a pair of handcuffs, and a wooden rattle to raise the alarm. By the 1880s this rattle had been replaced by a whistle. The Metropolitan Police Act proposed a number of reforms for policing in London. One of the principles of the Reform Act commonly quoted today, especially in community policing literature is, "The police are the public and the public are the police; the police being the only members of the public who are paid to give full time attention to duties which are incumbent on every citizen in the interests of community welfare and existence." Peel is considered the father of the London Metropolitan Police.

- Good appearance commands respect.
- The proper selection of persons and their proper training were the root of efficiency.
- Police headquarters should be centrally located and easily accessible to the police.
- Police should first be hired on a probationary basis.
- Police records are essential to the necessary distribution of police strength.

Unfortunately, the new police were not well received by the English public. Often open battles ensued between the bobbies and the citizenry.

The London Metropolitan Police introduced some new concepts to policing that exist today. They included the requirement for a stated mission of the police, the military organizational structure of the police, and the need for continual presence of the police.

Emerging Police Departments

America is a nation of small, decentralized police forces.[7]

When the colonists settled in America, they brought the English law enforcement structure with them. America was mostly rural and was

Lt. George Mingle with his 1934 Chevy patrol car. Lt. Mingle later served as the Superintendent, Ohio State Highway Patrol, from 1944 to 1957, the longest tenure of any Ohio State Highway Patrol Superintendent.

Photo courtesy of the Ohio State Highway Patrol

policed by those in the offices of constable and sheriff. Under the mutual pledge system, the constables were responsible for law enforcement in the towns and sheriffs were responsible for policing in the areas of the counties outside the towns. Originally the Crown-appointed governors appointed the constables and sheriffs, but after the American Revolution, they were elected by popular vote. In the larger cities, the English constabulary-night watchman system was adopted. By 1636, Boston had a night watchman and a military guard; soon both New York and Philadelphia established similar night watch systems. The New York night watchman system was referred to as the "Rattlewatch" because the men sounded rattlers during their rounds to announce their watchful presence.

Probably the first modern police force in the United States was the slave patrols established in the South. The slave patrol was a distinctly American form of law enforcement intended to guard against slave revolts and to capture runaway slaves. The Charleston, South Carolina, slave patrol had over 100 officers and at the time was probably the largest police force in America.[8]

In the 19th century, the Industrial Revolution reached the colonies. The American cities and towns grew in size, and constables were unable to handle the increasing social disorder caused by the migration to the urban areas. One historian described the lawlessness in America in the mid-1800s with these words:

> New York City was alleged to be the most crime-ridden city in the world, with Philadelphia, Baltimore and Cincinnati not far behind.... Gangs of youthful rowdies in the larger cities...threatened to destroy the American reputation for respect for law....Before their boisterous demonstrations the crude police forces of the day were often helpless.[9]

Philadelphia was one of the first American cities to develop an organized metropolitan police force. In 1833, a wealthy philanthropist died and left in his estate funds to establish a competent police force in the city. Using these funds, the city government established a 24-man police force for day work and a 120-man night watchman force. The force was disbanded less than two years later. Boston in 1838 created a day police force to supplement its night watch, and other cities soon established similar forces. The establishment of the police forces was not a break with the past. It was more like a consolidation and modification of existing institutions—day and night watches, constables, and sheriffs.[10]

In 1844, New York State passed legislation that established a unified day and night police force for New York City and abolished its night watch. In 1854, Boston consolidated its night watch with the day police. Other cities, using the New York model, developed their own unified police forces during the 1850s and 1860s. By 1870, all of the nation's largest cities had full-time unified police forces; by the early 1900s, almost all cities had established unified forces. The police forces were generally under the control of a chief or commissioner who was appointed by the mayor, often with the consent of the city council. The mission of the early police departments was merely to "keep the city superficially clean and to keep everything quiet that was likely to arouse public ire."[11]

Politics and Policing

The salaries of the new police officers were among the lowest in local government service, and the low salary precluded attracting sufficiently qualified candidates. To meet staffing requirements, personnel standards were compromised. Many unqualified personnel were appointed as police

Early police officer taking a bribe during the Prohibition era.

Photo courtesy of U.S. Library of Congress

officers. Illiteracy, poor health, chronic drunkenness, and criminal records were not barriers to police employment.

The chief requirement for appointment appeared to be the proper political connection. Promotions within the police forces were often based on politics rather than ability. For example, Chicago police officers in the 1850s were expected to kick back a regular portion of their salary to the local controlling political party. After the 1880 elections in Cincinnati when a new political party gained control of city administration, 219 of the 295 police officers were summarily fired; six years later when a different political party assumed power, 238 of the 289 patrolmen and 8 of the 16 lieutenants were fired.[12]

In the late 1800s, to eliminate politics from the police forces, many cities created police administrative boards, which replaced the control once exercised by the mayors or city councils. The boards were given the responsibility of appointing police administrators and managing police affairs. Generally these boards were unsuccessful in removing politics from police forces. The boards comprised judges, lawyers, and local businessmen who lacked expertise in dealing with police problems. Another reason that the police boards were generally unsuccessful was that they were not directly responsible to the local taxpayers they served.

In some states, the state legislators assumed control over the police forces by requiring that police administrators be appointed by the state. The concept of state control was not uniformly applied and was directed mainly at the larger cities by state legislatures that were dominated by rural legislators. While the state controlled the police forces, they continued to be financed by local taxpayers. When the state-appointed administrator was not in harmony with the views of the majority of the city's citizens, friction more often than not developed. It was not until the 1900s that many cities regained control of their police forces.[13]

During the last part of the 1800s, police forces grew in size and expanded their functions. Sincere attempts at reform included the concepts of merit employment and civil service; by 1900 police training schools were started on a modest basis. In 1895, Theodore Roosevelt (while a member of the New York City Board of Police Commissioners) attempted to raise recruitment standards and discipline corrupt officers. His efforts failed when the corrupt Tammany Hall political machine was returned to power in New York City in 1897.

Police Reform Movement

The police reform era started about 1900 and lasted until the 1960s. As noted earlier, Theodore Roosevelt attempted to reform the New York Police Department in the 1890s. Although he raised police standards and was responsible for the discipline of corrupt and brutal police officers, his efforts failed when the Tammany Hall political machine was returned to power in 1897. The reform era resulted in an increased military ethos of police and the first specialized police units, such as traffic, juvenile, and vice.

From 1900 to 1915, there were several attempts to reform police departments by civic-minded middle-class reformers, but generally the attempts failed. During this period, police salaries continued to lag behind those of other civil service employees. In 1919, the Boston Social Club, a fraternal association of police officers, voted to become a union and to affiliate with the American Federation of Labor (AFL). In September of that year, 70 percent of the Boston police officers went on strike. Governor Calvin Coolidge mobilized the state police to handle the rioting and looting that had broken out. The striking officers were fired and replaced by new recruits. The public turned against the striking officers. By firing them, Coolidge became a hero, which may have helped him later get elected president.

In 1883, the federal civil service was founded by the **Pendleton Act.** Under civil service, covered federal employees were tested, appointed, and promoted based on merit rather than for political reasons. As local governments adopted their own civil service systems, political influence in law enforcement agencies declined. While many individuals were pioneers in promoting professionalism of the police, two individuals stand out: August Vollmer and O. W. Wilson.

PIONEERS IN POLICING

August Vollmer

August Vollmer was born the son of German immigrants in New Orleans. Vollmer is considered by many to be the father of modern American law enforcement. His only formal education (beyond grade school) was a vocational course in bookkeeping, typing, and shorthand that he took at New Orleans Academy. In 1905, at the age of 29, Vollmer was elected to the post of City Marshall in Berkeley, California. This position was changed to Chief of Police in 1909, a post held by Vollmer until 1932. Chief Vollmer's innovations were many: He installed one of the first basic police records systems in the United States and installed the first *modus operandi* (MO) system; he was the first to use scientific investigation; he organized the first motorcycle patrol; he established the first school of criminology at the University of California at Berkeley; he began using intelligence tests in recruiting police officers; he utilized the first lie detector in criminal investigations; and he advocated advanced education for police and established the first known crime prevention division. Vollmer spent the majority of his career improving the state of policing and is known for requiring a high level of ethics, efficiency, and interest among his police officers. Vollmer drafted the section titled "Report on the Police," which was part of the 1931 Wickersham Commission's report.

Source: Corbis / Bettmann

Movement Toward Professionalism

By the 1920s, under the leadership of the newly founded National Police Chiefs Union, police officers were generally under civil service control and entry into the vocation was more restricted. The movement toward **professionalism** of the police began under the leadership of August Vollmer. He contended that the first obligation of police was crime control and public protection. He consulted with other police agencies and wrote extensively about the needs and requirements of a professional police department. Vollmer urged the development of a national records bureau, which eventually became the Federal Bureau of Investigation (FBI). O. W. Wilson, a former student and disciple of Vollmer, pioneered the use of advanced training for police. He also conducted the first systematic study of the effectiveness of one-officer squad cars. He developed workload formulas for police officers based on reported crimes and calls for service. This workload formula remained as the basic formula for police departments for years. Wilson developed management and administrative techniques for policing and was the author of the first two textbooks on police management.

PIONEERS IN POLICING

Orlando Winfield (O. W.) Wilson

O. W. Wilson, born in Veblen, South Dakota, is considered by many to be the greatest police reformer of all times. Wilson graduated in 1924 with a degree in business administration from the University of California at Berkeley. He is credited with being the lead architect of the professional police movement from the 1920s through the 1960s. A protégé of August Vollmer, Wilson studied under Vollmer at the University at Berkeley and worked for Vollmer as a Berkeley police officer. Wilson eventually became Chief of Police in Fullerton, California, and later in Wichita, Kansas, and then Superintendent of Police in Chicago, Illinois. During Wilson's tenure as Chief of Police in Wichita, Kansas (1928–1939), he introduced many innovative approaches to law enforcement. These included techniques for the allocation and distribution of patrol manpower; a new records and communications system; a comprehensive planning program; advances in recruitment, selection, and training; and many other innovations. Also while in Wichita, he led the shift from foot patrol to automobile patrol as well as conducting the first study of the effectiveness of one-officer squad cars. Under Wilson's leadership, the Wichita Police Department became known across the country as the "West Point of law enforcement."

Wilson took over the reins of the Chicago Police Department (1960–1966) at a time when it was considered the toughest police leadership job in America. It was in Chicago where he came up against a system of patronage politics that had become a hegemonic force within the Chicago Police Department. Wilson's accomplishments while in Chicago included hiring a number of African Americans, eliminating the flat feet criteria that had been used to discriminate in hiring decisions, and restructuring the department; he also significantly upgraded the duties of patrol officers, which included requiring them to become more computer literate and giving them the responsibility for preliminary investigation. Wilson authored several influential textbooks including *Police Records* (1942), *Police Administration* (1950), and *Police Planning* (1952). One other noteworthy accomplishment of Wilson was serving as both a professor and the Dean of the School of Criminology at the University of California at Berkeley.

Other pioneers in the movement toward professionalism included Raymond Blaine Fosdick and Bruce Smith, although neither was a police officer. Fosdick is credited with conducting the first scholarly research on policing when he published a book in 1915 on the European police system in which he examined the structures and practices of European police departments. Smith is noted for his efforts in surveying and researching police departments in 18 states and the publication of his book on policing, *Police Systems in the United States.*

The **Volstead Act** (National Prohibition) became law in 1920. Local police departments were unable to stop the alcohol operations of organized crime. Many law enforcement officers became corrupt and aided organized crime in its alcohol operations. As the result of police corruption between 1919 and 1931, 24 states formed crime commissions to study crime and the ability of the police to deal with it.

President Herbert Hoover created the National Commission on Law Observance and Enforcement in 1929. The commission became known as the **Wickersham Commission** after its chair Judge George W. Wickersham. The commission came into being because of the concern that organized criminal gangs and mobs were increasingly using violence to victimize and control major enterprises in the cities. The commission, however, chose to focus its broad mandate on the observance of law as well as its enforcement. Its report concluded that the Volstead Act was one of the roots of what they defined as a national problem and that it should be repealed.

PIONEERS IN POLICING

John Edgar Hoover

John Edgar Hoover led the Federal Bureau of Investigation (FBI) for 48 years. He was born in Washington, D.C. Upon completing high school, he began attending night classes at George Washington University Law School; in 1916, he was awarded his LL.B. and the next year his LL.M.

Source: Getty Images, Inc. / Hulton Archive Photos

Hoover started work for the Department of Justice on July 26, 1917, and rose quickly in government service. He led the department's General Intelligence Division (GID), and in November 1918, he was named Assistant to the Attorney General. When the GID was moved into the Bureau of Investigation (BOI) in 1921, he was named Assistant Director of the BOI. On May 10, 1924, the 29-year-old Hoover was appointed Acting Director of the BOI (later to be called the Federal Bureau of Investigation); by the end of the year, Hoover was named Director.

As Director, Hoover put into effect a number of institutional changes. Director Hoover fired a number of agents whom he considered unqualified to be special agents. He ordered background checks, interviews, and physical testing for new agent applicants, and he revived the earlier bureau policies of requiring legal or accounting training. Under Director Hoover, the bureau grew in responsibility and importance, becoming an integral part of the national government and an icon in American popular culture. In the 1930s, the FBI attacked the violent crime by gangsters and implemented many programs to professionalize law enforcement through training and forensic assistance. For example, the bureau opened its technical laboratory to provide forensic analysis on bureau investigations as well as services to other federal, state, and local law enforcement officials.

Nationalization of the Crime Problem

The Wickersham Commission was the first national commission on crime. It set a precedent by nationalizing the problem of crime in American society and the means of coping with crime. The Wickersham report was issued in 1931. Two volumes of the report, volumes 2 and 14, were concerned primarily with the police. In volume 2, *Lawlessness in Law Enforcement,* the police were described as inept, inefficient, racist, and brutal. According to the commission, the police routinely practiced the use of pain (both physical and mental) to extract confessions or statements from suspects.

In volume 14, *The Police,* methods were presented that the police could use to create a professional police force. This volume, primarily written by August Vollmer, stressed the need to increase pay and benefits for police officers and increase selectivity in the recruitment of officers. While the report upset citizens, police reform became less important as the nation experienced the economic problems of the Depression.

The Depression of the 1930s made employment as a police officer attractive to many individuals who in normal economic times would not have considered careers in policing. The job security aspects of policing encouraged the better-educated middle-class individuals to apply for the police positions.

In 1950, the U.S. Senate appointed a crime committee, chaired by Senator Estes Kefauver. The **Kefauver Committee** held the first nationally televised public hearings on crime; these hearings publicized organized crime and the fact that many law enforcement officers were controlled by organized crime. As a result of the hearings and the public's shock over police corruption, new attempts at police reform began. David R. Johnson described the 1950s as follows:

> The 1950s marked a turning point in the history of [police] professionalism. Following the major scandals, reformers came to power across the nation. Politicians had real choices between the traditional and new models of policing because a number of professional police reformers were available for the first time. With an enraged middle class threatening their livelihoods, the politicians opted for reform.[14]

Social Change of the 1960s and the War on Crime

The 1960s was a period of dramatic social change and involved one of the most unpopular wars in U.S. history. The struggle for racial equality and the antiwar protests were accompanied by marches, demonstrations, and riots. The police were caught in the middle between those who were fighting for civil rights and local government officials who were trying to maintain the status quo.

James Q. Wilson described the decade of the 1960s as follows: "It all began about 1963, that was the year, to over dramatize a bit, that a decade began to fall apart."[15] The civil unrest, the perceived inability of the police to handle the unrest, and the rising crime rates led to the creation of the **President's Commission on Law Enforcement and Administration of Justice** in 1965. The mandate of the commission was to study the nation's response to crime, with a focus on the crime control effect of the administration of criminal justice. The commission differed from earlier crime commissions in that it focused on crime control issues rather than on corruption and law observance, and it was expected to recommend new criminal justice initiatives to address the crime problem.[16] Unlike earlier commissions, this commission was staffed primarily by social scientists rather than lawyers.

The commission published the principal report in a volume titled *The Challenge of Crime in a Free Society* in 1967, and that volume contained a chapter on the police that contained a series of recommendations regarding police functions. The commission also published numerous task force reports, including the *Task Force Report: The Police.* Police issues were also contained in two additional volumes—*Task Force Report: Science and Technology* and *Studies in Crime and Law Enforcement in Major American Cities.*

According to Samuel Walker, the most radical aspect of the commission's work was undermining the traditional approach's assumptions about policing and laying the foundation for a new approach to policing, the community policing approach. Walker stated:

> The President's Crime Commission marks a critical period of transition between an old view of the police and a new one just being born. While the Commission embodied a traditional set of reform assumptions, it also set in motion new thinking that eventually undermined the traditional view. The full significance of the tensions between the old and new is evident only in retrospect.[17]

One of the major goals recommended by the commission was similar to one that had been advocated since the progressive era, that of achieving professional status for police. Recommendations of the commission included the following:

- Diversifying police forces by recruiting racial minorities and more women and by assigning women to routine patrol
- Strengthening staff control
- Requiring supervisors to have higher levels of education
- Achieving social reforms through the intervention of government programs
- Consolidating and coordinating small police departments
- Using state-mandated personnel standards and requiring necessary training
- Improving procedures for handling citizen complaints
- Adopting special community relations programs

Many of the changes in policing since 1967 are attributed to the commission's report; these changes include higher recruitment standards, higher general level of education of police officers, and a more diverse police force. Many of the traditional barriers to women have been eliminated, and women are now assigned to routine patrol duty. The employment of minority police officers has increased significantly. As Walker noted, the commission marked the culmination of a half-century of reform and the birth of a very different view of policing and police reform.[18]

Community Policing Movement

> Community policing is not just a tactic that can be applied to solve a particular problem, one that can be abandoned once the goal is achieved.[19]

Community policing is introduced in this chapter, but it is covered more extensively in other chapters, especially Chapter 3. The authors see community policing as the future of policing. Jeremy Travis, the Director of National Institute of Justice, described community policing as follows:

> Community policing is based on the notion that government and community should work closely together, that the police and the community are co-producers of safety.... In an operational sense, community policing engages the police and community in the art of "problem-solving," where the unit of work is a particular problem of crime and disorder, as identified by the police community partnership.... Within the policing organization itself, emphasis is placed on flexibility and innovation. Discretion is prized; risk-taking is encouraged; accountability is pushed downward within the chain of command.[20]

Most police and sheriff's departments have adopted community policing or are in the process of adopting some forms of it. The problem in this regard is that not everybody has the same definition of what constitutes community policing. In some departments, community policing consists of programs with specialists who work in one or more areas of the community; in others, it is a department-wide philosophy that influences all employees in terms of how they view their role in relation to the community. For purposes of this text, community policing is defined as an approach to policing that is based on meaningful interaction with community members in an attempt to define and solve problems related to crime, fear of crime, and social disorder. Community policing is based on the notion that the government and the community should work closely together and that the police and the community are coproducers of safety. Travis noted that the police have learned three essential lessons from the development of community policing: (1) to view the community as a full partner, (2) to focus on solving the problems that matter to the community, and (3) to pay attention to little things.[21] This definition of community policy requires that police officers and supervisors learn new skills and change the manner in which they assess problems, generate possible solutions, and choose to behave.

To take the community as a full partner, the police must listen to the people they serve, ask them what they feel is important, value their priorities,

Community policing substation in Times Square, New York City.

and explore their capacities to provide solutions. To focus on solving specific problems that are important to the community represents a fundamental and powerful shift. Instead of looking at a crack house and seeing criminals who can be arrested, the police should be closing the place down. By not paying attention to little things, we signal our indifference or tacit acceptance. Our

Community policing substation in a Houston, Texas, shopping center.

acceptance of low levels of disorder creates a hospitable environment for more egregious violations of social norms. As noted by George Kelling, a broken window left unattended invites other windows to be broken.

Kelling compiled a list of 11 principles that should be considered in developing and implementing police guidelines for community policing. While Kelling was examining the role of discretion in community policing, his principles provided insights about the leadership and management aspects of community policing. These are Kelling's 11 principles.[22]

1. Recognize the complexity of police work.
2. Acknowledge police use of discretion.
3. Recognize and confirm how police work is conducted.
4. Advance values.
5. Put police knowledge forward.
6. Undergo development by practicing police officers and citizens.
7. Understand clear and broad public promulgation.
8. Prescribe what officers may not do.
9. Emphasize police adherence to the process.
10. Establish accountability.
11. Receive recognition as an ongoing process.

MYTHS AND REALITIES OF POLICING

In this section, we will examine some of the popular myths regarding policing and compare the realities to the myths. The most popular myth, that the police officer is primarily a crime fighter, will be examined in the next section.

Myth: Traditional police departments are based on the military model of leadership.   The authors were taught that American policing was based on a military model. But according to Thomas J. Cowper, although similarities may be found in structural arrangements (such as in the flow of information and regulatory rules), there are significant differences between traditional police departments and military organizations.[23] As Cowper noted, impersonal rules govern behavior in the military; as a result, historically there has been little encouragement for individual originality and creativity because orders are strictly obeyed and are carried out through a rigid chain of command. Cowper contended that progressive chiefs of police have gone to great lengths to distance themselves and their agencies from the contamination of militarism. The chiefs encourage originality and creativity and the concept of a service agency rather than a military unit.

Cowper stated that the military and police forces should always be completely separate and different organizations in a free society and that the unbridled use of war tactics and highly destructive weaponry of the military must be avoided within our borders and against our citizens. The

The District of Columbia's Approach to Building Community Partnerships Under Community Policing

THREE APPROACHES TO PREVENTION

The District of Columbia's Policing for Prevention applies three approaches to crime and disorder: focused law enforcement, neighborhood partnerships, and systemic prevention. Used together, these approaches address immediate crime problems by focusing law enforcement efforts, building partnerships with community stakeholders to sustain success, and using the resources of government and other organizations to work on the underlying causes of crime in a community.

Focused Law Enforcement.   Focused law enforcement targets high-risk offenders and crime hot spots through the strategic use of both police resources and partnerships with federal law enforcement, regulatory agencies, and criminal justice partners. Police reduce crime while keeping residents informed about planned enforcement efforts.

For example, to reduce underage drinking, police have teamed up with the Alcohol Beverage Control Board (ABC). Together, ABC investigators and police officers conduct undercover operations in bars that serve alcohol to underage youth.

Police make arrests and support the ABC Board's authority to suspend the liquor license of offenders by gathering intelligence, providing documentation, and testifying at hearings. Residents keep police informed about activities that cause fear and harm in the community and about specific crimes and suspects. Police keep residents updated on any planned operations and other focused law enforcement strategies without compromising the security of their operations.

Police programs and safety tips that involve focused law enforcement include:

Automated Traffic Enforcement

Community Prosecution

Cooperative Agreements

Crime Solvers

Drunken Driving Prevention

Hate Crimes: What You Should Know

Non-Emergency Number 3-1-1

Open-Air Mini-Stations

Operation Ceasefire

Smooth Operator

Neighborhood Partnerships.   Neighborhood partnerships bring together police, residents, city agencies, and other community stakeholders. This powerful collaboration effectively tackles crime areas and disorderly conditions that attract crime and degrade quality of life in the community.

For example, a city agency partner that makes and enforces regulations and codes, such as the Department of Consumer and Regulatory Affairs (DCRA), can audit businesses that may be magnets for crime and disorder. By enforcing city codes, laws, and regulations, the DCRA can close businesses that aren't in compliance. In this instance, problem business

(continued)

owners often come around to working with the community instead of against it when faced with the possibility of being closed down.

Once neighborhood partnerships are in place, they can explore systemic prevention approaches that deal with the more chronic, entrenched problems.

Police programs and safety tips that involve neighborhood partnerships include:

Citizens Advisory Councils
Communities on Phone Patrol
Community Prosecution
Non-Emergency Number 3-1-1
Open-Air Mini-Stations
Operation Crackdown
Partnerships for Problem Solving
Police Ride-Along Program

Systemic Prevention. Systemic prevention addresses underlying causes, or risk factors, that are at the root of chronic, long-term problems in a community. Risk factors include drug abuse, lack of quality education and youth programs, family violence, and high unemployment. The organizations that play lead roles in systemic prevention are employment and economic services, schools, and health and human services as well as the private and non-profit sectors. These groups offer intervention strategies that can impact the overall quality of life for people and their communities.

Some examples are job training programs for youth, drug treatment programs, health programs that teach teenage mothers how to care for their infants, and other intervention efforts. These all require long-term involvement from a range of city services and agencies. Police and communities help by involving these groups in neighborhood partnerships and holding them accountable for the commitments they make in the partnership.

Police programs and safety tips that involve systemic prevention include:

Child Passenger Safety Awareness
Hate Crimes: What You Should Know
Metropolitan Police Boys and Girls Clubs
MPDC-CSOSA Partnership

COMPARING THE THREE APPROACHES

Focused law enforcement:

Repeat criminal offenders and regulation violators
Repeat criminal offenses
Communities in distress
Disruption or termination of chronic crime activity, reduction of fear, and building of community confidence in the police
Crime analysis, directed patrol, tactical, follow-up investigations, arrests, and partnership with other regulatory or law enforcement agencies

Neighborhood partnerships:

Physical and social conditions that lead to chronic crime and disorder
Community building

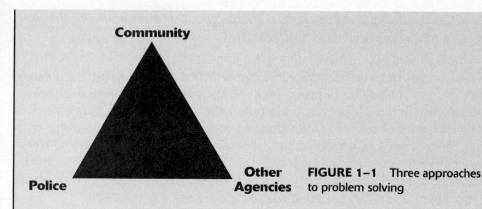

FIGURE 1–1 Three approaches to problem solving

Active involvement of community and other government services, leading to neighborhood stabilization

Problem solving area (PSA) integrity, PSA meetings, problem solving, and partnership with other agencies and the community

Systemic prevention:

Health, social, educational, and economic conditions of individuals, families, and communities

Individuals, families, and communities building a resistance to crime and violence

Methods of sharing information with, working with, and being advocates for the governmental and nongovernmental agencies that effectively serve people and communities

PARTNERSHIPS FOR PROBLEM SOLVING

Partnerships for Problem Solving (PPS) is the Metropolitan Police Department's effort to train police officers, community volunteers, and agency representatives throughout the District of Columbia in the methods and tools for neighborhood problem solving. Training all the partners together—a fundamental aspect of PPS—helps build cooperation and collaboration from the start of the initiative.

The goals of the PPS project are to (1) train police, community, and agency representatives in problem solving citywide; (2) organize at least one active problem-solving group in each PSA that includes community volunteers, police officers, and agency representatives; and (3) develop PSA action plans collaboratively to address neighborhood crime and disorder problems.

The PPS project is developed and coordinated by the Community Partnership section of the Office of Organizational Development of the Metropolitan Police Department. The mission of this section is to advance collaborative problem-solving partnerships among community stakeholders, police officers, and other agency representatives through developing curricula and training materials, delivering training citywide, and replicating community policing successes.

Collaborative problem solving is a process that requires active and engaged participation of all the stakeholders in a neighborhood. Working together in a five-step problem-solving process, the partners target a problem, understand the problem, create a plan, take action and review progress, and celebrate and create a lasting community presence.

police should look at civilians not as enemies but as customers whom they serve and as partners in preventing crime.

Myth: You can be a good police officer without having effective people skills. James O'Keefe pointed out that real police work involves effectively dealing with people.[24] He noted that the reality of police work is that it is a people business, and effective police work is about dealing with people, many times in adverse conditions and negative situations. O'Keefe believed that to meet the responsibilities of police work, the police and the community must dispel the prevailing myths about what police officers do and concentrate on the real business of dealing with people.

Myth: Officer safety and survival are advanced only through defensive skills and the use of force. Experienced police officers soon understand that true officer safety is advanced not only through defensive tactics and the use of force but also through communication skills and cultural competence.[25] Officers need to understand the importance of dealing with people in a respectful manner and integrate that into their professional demeanor. Officers who fail to follow this rule usually have a high number of resisting arrest collars, many uses of force complaints, and a general lack of community support.

Myth: Police officers do not need to be courteous in dealing with citizens. Three words are painted on the doors of New York City's police patrol cars: courtesy, professionalism, and respect. According to Haberfield, citizens expect courtesy and respect from their police officers.[26] A police officer is expected to be "calm, cool, and collected," even in the face of adversity. Police officers are expected to be courteous and respectful to everyone, from the senior citizen to the serial killer.

Myth: Small towns in America have almost none of the crime problems found in major cities. Small towns in America share the same common crime problems, such as violence, domestic crimes, people driving under the influence (DUI), gangs, and drug use, that exist in large cities. The major difference is that they occur less frequently in small towns than in large cities.

CRIME-FIGHTER IMAGE AND ITS CONSEQUENCES

Today's citizens have a romanticized notion of police work, probably because of television, movies, and crime novels.[27] The police officer is not primarily a **crime fighter** but a service provider to the public.[28] Most police officers begin their careers expecting to perform the role of crime fighter in the community. Jerome Skolnick and David Bayley noted that only about 20 percent of an officer's day is devoted to crime fighting per se and that crimes that terrify the public (such as robbery, rape, burglary, and homicide) are rarely encountered by police on patrol.[29] As Kenneth Peak noted, only in the movies does a Dirty Harry have his lunch disturbed by a bank robbery.[30]

The crime-fighter image persists even though it is extremely harmful to the public, individual police officers, and police departments. Many individuals enter police work believing that it will be exciting and glamorous. Only after their training is completed do they realize that much of their time is spent with boring, mundane tasks that are anything but glamorous. This myth is accentuated by the movies, television, and even by recruiting posters. Actual police services include providing the community with traffic management and enforcement, helping disabled motorists, searching for missing children, giving directions to lost individuals, keeping peace in the community, dealing with various local emergency agencies in the community, and preventing crime. Effectively providing those services requires and utilizes different skills and abilities than those required of a crime fighter.

Below is a partial list of New York police officers who died during attempts to rescue victims in the World Trade Center on September 11, 2001.

Date	Status	Name	No.	Unit	Location
Sept 11, 2001	P.O.	Walter Weaver	2784	ESS-3	World Trade Center Attack
Sept 11, 2001	P.O.	Santos Valentin	21630	ESS-7	World Trade Center Attack
Sept 11, 2001	P.O.	Paul Talty	28907	ESS-10	World Trade Center Attack
Sept 11, 2001	P.O.	Ramon Suarez	12671	TD-4	World Trade Center Attack
Sept 11, 2001	P.O.	Moira Smith	10467	13th Precinct	World Trade Center Attack
Sept 11, 2001	P.O.	Glen Pettit	3815	Police Academy	World Trade Center Attack
Sept 11, 2001	P.O.	John Perry	3266	40th Precinct	World Trade Center Attack
Sept 11, 2001	P.O.	Brian McDonnell	6889	ESS-1	World Trade Center Attack
Sept 11, 2001	P.O.	James Leahy	8943	6th Precinct	World Trade Center Attack
Sept 11, 2001	P.O.	Thomas Langone	14356	ESS-10	World Trade Center Attack
Sept 11, 2001	P.O.	Ronald Kloepfer	22403	ESS-7	World Trade Center Attack
Sept 11, 2001	P.O.	Robert Fazio	6667	13th Precinct	World Trade Center Attack
Sept 11, 2001	P.O.	Mark Ellis	11441	TD-4	World Trade Center Attack
Sept 11, 2001	P.O.	Stephen Driscoll	17482	ESS-4	World Trade Center Attack
Sept 11, 2001	P.O.	Jerome Dominguez	10003	ESS-3	World Trade Center Attack
Sept 11, 2001	P.O.	Vincent Danz	2166	ESS-3	World Trade Center Attack
Sept 11, 2001	P.O.	John Dallara	4011	ESS-2	World Trade Center Attack
Sept 11, 2001	Det.	Joseph Vigiano	4511	ESS-2	World Trade Center Attack
Sept 11, 2001	Det.	Claude Richards	244	Bomb Squad	World Trade Center Attack
Sept 11, 2001	Sgt.	Timothy Roy	2926	STED	World Trade Center Attack
Sept 11, 2001	Sgt.	Rodney Gillis	1889	ESS-8	World Trade Center Attack
Sept 11, 2001	Sgt.	Michael Curtin	3256	ESS-2	World Trade Center Attack
Sept 11, 2001	Sgt.	John Coughlin	3751	ESS-4	World Trade Center Attack

ROLES AND FUNCTIONS OF POLICE

Few attempts have been made to accurately describe the **role of police.**[31] The American Bar Association identified 11 elements of the police role.[32]

1. To identify criminals and criminal activity and, where appropriate, to apprehend offenders and participate in court proceedings
2. To reduce the opportunities for the commission of crime through preventive patrol and other measures
3. To aid individuals who are in danger of physical harm
4. To protect constitutional guarantees
5. To facilitate the movement of peoples and vehicles
6. To assist those who cannot care for themselves
7. To resolve conflict
8. To identify situations that are potentially serious law enforcement or government problems
9. To create and maintain a feeling of security in the community
10. To promote and preserve civil order
11. To provide other services on an emergency basis

Police functions can be grouped into one of four basic functions: enforcing the law, performing public service, preventing crime, and protecting individuals. James Q. Wilson chose to divide the activities of police into two larger basic functions: peacekeeping and enforcing the law.[33] He stated that **peacekeeping** (maintaining order) constitutes most of the police's activities and noted that less than 20 percent of the calls answered by police involve enforcing the law and controlling crime. He pointed out that the majority of an officer's time is spent with service activities and that (in many cases) the police deliberately avoid enforcing the law in an attempt to maintain order.

Wilson described the law enforcement function to mean upholding statutes. He contended that the police have traditionally been unsuccessful at performing the law enforcement function and are successful in solving only a fraction of the property and personal crimes that occur.

IMPLICATIONS OF CHANGE

Distinction Between Police and Policing

David Bayley and Clifford D. Shearing foresaw a divergence between "police" and "policing." They argued that the term "police" should be defined as any public law enforcement agency that is authorized by state or federal law to carry out legal police functions; the term **"policing,"**[34] should refer to a method of keeping peace and order. They believed that private police, one of the most rapidly growing resources, also perform policing.

Bayley and Shearing contended that there has been an erosion of social control by public police forces and that in the last 30 years police and policing have become increasingly distinct. They pointed out that there are three times more private security agents than police officers in the United States. These researchers anticipate an increase in civilian employees who do policing work in the years ahead. Part of this increase will be caused by police agencies that hire more civilians to perform crime prevention and technical support functions.

Bayley and Shearing predicted that with the growth of community policing and its openness to the external environment, more police administrators will realize the value of participative management and empowerment of police officers in the workplace. According to them, this development will mark a significant change from the traditional professional model of policing in which chain of command and span of control are highly valued.

These researchers predicted that how public police perform their duties in the future will be related to three important social issues—public safety, equity, and human rights—and that public safety will be the primary issue. They questioned how effective the police will be in the movement to control crime and promote social equity because law enforcement activities are apt to be concentrated in economically disadvantaged neighborhoods where the residents are most vulnerable to both abuse of authority and criminal victimization.

Where Is Community Policing Going?

Jihong Zhao noted that after 20 plus years of community policing, there is no irrefutable evidence that it significantly reduces crime in a community.[35] Zhao predicted that community policing is the future model for American policing and that community policing should progress toward the second stage, the institutionalization of change. This institutionalization has several important aspects. The first is the modification of police structure: Innovative units must become a formal part of patrol operations or criminal investigations rather than isolated units.

Second, community policing, according to Zhao, must go beyond simply measuring citizen satisfaction. The police agencies need to develop technical rationality and clearly defined measures to facilitate institutionalization. Finally, the culture of police departments must be altered in a direction consistent with community policing.

New York Police and 9/11

Robert Wadman and William Allison stated that the terrorist acts of September 11, 2001, completely reversed the downward trend in public acceptance of the police that began in the 1980s.[36] They pointed out that the heroic sacrifices of the police and firefighters and the effective response of police all over the country to safeguard the public placed the police in the most favorable position they have ever experienced. The question remains as to how long this upward ride will last. The authors noted that even with the new successes, old problems remain, which has been the constant American police dilemma. They stated that American police are charged with maintaining law and order in an open society that values personal liberty above all. They also noted that our police history has been influenced by the constant violence between individuals and groups within the rubric of a free, open, and democratic society. According to Wadman and Allison, our police have been placed in the most delicate social balance to protect and serve.[37]

▲ SUMMARY

The majority of police functions in the United States are handled by local independent police departments; there is no national police force. While the police have the highest and most visible role in overcoming the threat and fear of crime, it does not follow that the police alone bear this responsibility. The responsibility is shared with each individual and each level of government.

Policing started as a private matter. Individuals were responsible for protecting themselves and maintaining an orderly community. Organized police departments did not appear until the 14th century in France. The modern police department's origin can be traced to Alfred the Great of England when during the 9th century he structured his kingdom's defenses to prepare for a Danish invasion.

The London Metropolitan Police introduced some new concepts to policing that exist today. Those include the requirement for a stated mission of the police, the military organizational structure of the police, and the need for continual presence of the police. Probably the first modern police forces in the United States were the slave patrols established in the South. The slave patrol was a distinctly American form of law enforcement intended to guard against slave revolts and to capture runaway slaves. Philadelphia was one of the first American cities to develop an organized metropolitan police force.

The Wickersham Commission was the first national commission on crime. It set a precedent by nationalizing the problem of crime in American society and the means of coping with crime.

The 1960s was a period of dramatic social change and involved one of the most unpopular wars in U.S. history. The struggle for racial equality and the antiwar protests were accompanied by marches, demonstrations, and riots. The police were caught in the middle between those who were fighting for civil rights and local government officials who were trying to maintain the status quo. Community policing is based on the notion that the government and the community should work closely together and that the police and the community are coproducers of safety. Most police and sheriff's departments have adopted community policing or are in the process of adopting some form of it. The problem is that not everybody has the same definition of what constitutes community policing.

Effective police work is about dealing with people, many times in adverse conditions and negative situations. Experienced police officers soon understand that true officer safety is advanced not only through defensive tactics and the use of force but also through communication skills and cultural competence. Officers need to understand the importance of dealing with people in a respectful manner and to integrate that into their professional demeanor.

A police officer is expected to be "calm, cool, and collected," even in the face of adversity. Police officers are expected to be courteous and respectful to everyone, from the senior citizen to the serial killer. Today's citizens have a romanticized notion of police work, probably because of television, movies, and crime novels. The police officer is not primarily a crime fighter but is a service provider to the public. The crime-fighter image persists even though it is extremely harmful to the public, individual police officers, and police departments.

Police activities can be grouped into one of four basic functions: enforcing the law, performing public service functions, preventing crime, and protecting individuals.

QUESTIONS IN REVIEW

1. Explain how modern policing developed.
2. What are the various functions of policing?
3. What is the difference between "policing" and the "police"?
4. Who were the Bow Street Runners?
5. Why is a police officer not primarily a crime fighter?
6. Why was the Wickersham Commission important in the development of modern policing?
7. Explain some of the shortcomings of the first modern police departments.
8. Why are police often referred to as "cops"?

◆ POLICE RESOURCES ON THE WEB

Center for Problem-Oriented Policing
http://www.popcenter.org

COPS (Community Oriented Policing Services), U.S. Department of Justice
http://www.cops.usdoj.gov

Denver, Colorado, Police Department
http://www.denvergov.org/police

Fresno, California, Police Department
http://www.fresno.gov/fpd/policing

Kansas City, Kansas, Police Department
http://www.kckpd.org/copps.htm

National Center for Women and Policing
http://www.womenandpolicing.org

New York Regional Community Policing Institute
http://www.jjay.cuny.edu/rcpi

Police Structure and Organization: A State-by-State Guide to Federal Agencies, State/County/Municipal Law Enforcement Agencies
http://faculty.ncwc.edu/toconnor/polstruct.htm

Policing in Canada
http://www.psepc.gc.ca/policing

Tampa, Florida, Police Department
http://www.tampagov.net/dept-police

Vancouver, British Columbia, Police Department
http://www.city.vancouver.bc.ca/police

REFERENCES

1. CARL B. KLOCKARS and STEPHEN D. MASTROFSKI, *Thinking About Police* (New York: McGraw-Hill, 1991).
2. *Webster's New World College Dictionary*, 4th ed. (Foster City, CA: IDG Books, 1997), p. 1114.
3. NATIONAL ADVISORY COMMISSION ON CRIMINAL JUSTICE STANDARDS AND GOALS, POLICE (Washington, DC: GPO, 1973), p. 13.
4. CHARLES R. SWANSON et al., *Police Administration: Structure, Processes, and Behavior,* 4th ed.(Upper Saddle River, NJ: Prentice Hall, 1998), p. 1.
5. CHARLES REITH, *The Blind Eye of History: A Study of the Origins of the Present Police Era* (London: Faber, 1912).
6. T.A. CRITCHLEY, *A History of Police in England and Wales,* 2nd ed. (Montclair, NJ: Patterson Smith, 1972).
7. PRESIDENT'S COMMISSION ON LAW ENFORCEMENT AND THE ADMINISTRATION OF JUSTICE, *The Challenge of Crime in a Free Society* (Washington, DC: GPO, 1967), p. 3.
8. SAMUEL WALKER, *Popular Justice: A History of American Criminal Justice* (Oxford, England: Oxford University Press, 1998), p. 22.

9. ARTHUR CHARLES COLE, "The Irrepressible Conflict, 1859–1865," in *A History of American Life*, vol. VIII. ed. Arthur M. Schlesinger, Sr., and Dixon Ryan Fox, (New York: MacMillan, 1934), pp. 154–155.

10. WALKER, p. 52.

11. ARTHUR M. SCHLESINGER, Sr., "The Rise of the City, 1878–1898," in *A History of American Life*, vol. X. ed. Arthur M. Schlesinger, Sr., and Dixon Ryan Fox, (New York: MacMillan, 1934), p. 115.

12. SAMUEL WALKER, *A Critical History of Police Reform: The Emergence of Professionalism* (Lexington, MA: Lexington Books, 1972), pp. 40–43.

13. It is noted that some states still exercise some control over local police agencies.

14. DAVID R. JOHNSON, *American Law Enforcement: A History* (St. Louis, MO: Forum Press, 1981), p. 121.

15. JAMES Q. WILSON, *Thinking About Crime* (New York: Basic Books, 1983), p. 3.

16. JOHN A. CONLEY, "Introduction," in *The 1967 President's Crime Commission Report: Its Impact 25 Years Later*, ed. John A. Conley (Cincinnati, OH: Anderson, 1994).

17. SAMUEL WALKER, "Between Two Worlds: The President's Crime Commission and the Police, 1967–1992," in *The 1967 President's Crime Commission Report: Its Impact 25 Years Later*, ed. John A. Conley (Cincinnati, OH: Anderson, 1994).

18. WALKER, 1994:33.

19. ROBERT TROJANOWICZ et al., *Community Policing: A Contemporary Perspective*, 2nd ed. (Cincinnati, OH: Anderson, 1998), p. 5.

20. JEREMY TRAVIS, "Lessons for the Criminal Justice System from Twenty Years of Policing Reform." Keynote address to New Beginnings at the First Annual Conference of the New York Campaign for Effective Crime Policy, New York, March 10, 1996.

21. Ibid.

22. GEORGE L. KELLING, " 'Broken Windows' and Police Discretion," *National Institute of Justice Research Report* (NCJ 178259) (October 1999).

23. THOMAS J. COWPER, "The Myth of the 'Military Model' of Leadership in Law Enforcement," in *Contemporary Policing: Controversies, Challenges, and Solutions,* ed. Quint C. Thurman and Jihong Zhao, (Los Angeles: Roxbury, 2004), pp. 113–125.

24. JAMES O'KEEFE, *Protecting the Republic: The Education and Training of American Police Officers* (Upper Saddle River, NJ: Prentice Hall, 2004), pp. 121–123.

25. Ibid., pp. 120–121.

26. M.R. HABERFIELD, *Critical Issues in Police Training* (Upper Saddle River, NJ: Prentice Hall, 2002), pp. 8–9.

27. Ibid., pp. 1–2.

28. O'KEEFE, pp. 124.

29. JEROME H. SKOLNICK and DAVID H. BAYLEY, *The New Blue Line: Police Innovation in Six American Cities* (New York: Free Press, 1986), p. 4.

30. KENNETH PEAK, *Policing in America: Methods, Issues, and Challenges*, 3rd ed. (Upper Saddle River, NJ: Prentice Hall, 2006), p. 61.

31. Ibid., pp. 60–61.

32. AMERICAN BAR ASSOCIATION, *Standards Relating to the Urban Police Function* (Chicago: ABA, 1973), p. 7.

33. JAMES Q. WILSON, *Varieties of Police Behavior* (Cambridge, MA: Harvard University Press, 1968), pp. 140–226.

34. DAVID H. BAYLEY and CLIFFORD D. SHEARING, "The Future of Policing," in Thurman and Zhao, pp. 335–369.

35. JIHONG ZHAO, "The Future of Policing in a Community Era," in Thurman and Zhao, pp. 370–381.

36. ROBERT C. WADMAN and WILLIAM THOMAS ALLISON, *To Protect and to Serve: A History of Police in America* (Upper Saddle River, NJ: Prentice Hall, 2003), p. 123.

37. Ibid., pp. 156–160.

Modern Police Systems

Key Terms

Agencies
Airport police officer
Collective bargaining
Crime clock
Interpol
Jurisdiction
Legats

Multilevel policing
Municipal policing
Officers
Public accountability
Styles of policing
Uniform Crime Reports (UCR)

Outline

Learning Objectives

After reading this chapter, you should be able to:

1. Describe what local law enforcement agencies do and how they differ from state law enforcement agencies.
2. Identify the different federal law enforcement agencies and explain their functions.
3. Discuss the various types of state police agencies and their functions.

4. Explain the duties and functions of municipal law enforcement agencies.
5. List and discuss the functions of Interpol.
6. Distinguish between the various levels of policing.
7. Explain how private security differs from public policing.

INTRODUCTION

Chapter 1 contained a brief introduction to the various modern police systems; in this chapter, the systems will be explored in depth. Characteristics of American policing include its responsiveness to citizen requests, its **public accountability,** and its openness to external evaluation. Policing operations include preventive, investigative, and crime fighting.

JURISDICTION

American law enforcement uses **multilevel policing:** It covers local police departments, urban police agencies, state organizations, and federal departments. Each level covers different aspects of American policing, with a certain degree of overlapping. A law enforcement agency's level of activity is often referred to as the agency's jurisdiction. In this regard, **jurisdiction** refers to the geographical area or crime issue over which an agency has authority. A sheriff's jurisdiction generally includes the unincorporated areas of the county and the county jail as well as small towns that do not have local police departments. An urban police department's jurisdiction generally includes the geographical area of the city or an area within the city limits.

Jurisdiction of an issue refers to the agency's or agencies' responsibility to investigate certain criminal conduct and other law enforcement activities in that area. For example, the U.S. Drug Enforcement Agency (DEA) has jurisdiction over federal drug crimes and federal money-laundering laws within a city. The city police department would also have jurisdiction over the criminal conduct if the conduct constituted a violation of the state criminal laws or city or county ordinances. The FBI has jurisdiction to investigate robberies of federally insured banks as violations of federal criminal law. The local city police department would also have jurisdiction to investigate the same bank robbery within the city as a violation of the state's laws against robbery.

Often agencies will work together and establish joint task forces. Frequently federal, state, and local law enforcement agencies will form a task force to target a particular issue such as a rash of bank robberies or unusual drug activity.

Jurisdiction can become an issue when the same suspect is wanted for crimes by more than one law enforcement agency. Sometimes these jurisdictional issues are resolved by the agency that first apprehends the

Traffic check on an Ohio highway in 1949.

Photo courtesy of Ohio State Highway Patrol

suspect; other times, the jurisdiction with the most resources or investigative expertise assumes control of the suspect. In some cases, the jurisdiction that has the more serious charges against the suspect assumes control.

POLICE ACCOUNTABILITY

Law enforcement agencies in the United States are accountable to the governmental unit and to its citizens through multiple institutions. Most law enforcement agencies are accountable to elected officials, civil and criminal courts, and civilian review boards. Any misdeed by a police officer is subject to oversight by internal discipline procedures, judicial proceedings, and the press. Only in such countries such as France and England are the law enforcement agencies open to the same civilian criticism and pubic pressure as they are in the United States.

STYLES OF POLICING

In Chapter 1, we noted that police functions were normally divided into four basic categories: law enforcement, public service, crime prevention, and citizen protection. James Q. Wilson took a different approach to policing and contended that the police perform two basic functions: peacekeeping and law enforcement. He noted that most police agencies do not determine the problems they address; instead they respond to those problems that the citizens believe are important, and they depend on the goals set by the community.[1] Wilson maintained that there are three distinctive **styles of policing:** the watchman style, the legalistic style, and the service style.

Watchman Style

The organizational form of the watchman style is flat and narrow: flat because there is little opportunity for advancement and narrow because there is limited differentiation in the types of work that each officer does. According to Wilson, this style exists in cities with heavy political patronage and little response to community needs. He also contended that this style tends to experience more police corruption than other styles. Promotion is a function of "who you know," and in-service training is almost nonexistent. The pay is generally low and rewards for good service are limited. According to Wilson, there are few places in which the officer can be transferred in the department and few incentives to seek transfer there. Most of the officers will spend their careers on patrol duty unless they are promoted to detective.

Under the watchman style of policing, the departments are concerned primarily with peacekeeping. Since not much is expected of the officers, they have a wide range of discretion and tend to handle matters informally rather than invoking the official system's regulations. The common practice is to keep drunks off the streets and maintain a general appearance of order. In corrupt departments, discretion is often used as a weapon for shakedowns and bribes.

Legalistic Style

In departments using the legalistic style, a high degree of control is maintained over individual officers. This high degree of control is accomplished by handling every call as a law enforcement matter; accordingly, for every response the officer must make a report. For example, if an officer makes a traffic stop, the officer first calls in and reports the car and its license plate number and the reason for the stop. If the officer does not issue a citation, the officer must explain the reasons for not doing so. In lieu of relying on the officer's assessment of the situation and his or her judgment, there are numerous regulations and controls (often referred to as standards) to guide the officer. In this style of organization, the individual officer has little discretion. The agency is concerned with the strict enforcement of the law and often takes a hands-off approach to otherwise disruptive or problematic forms of behavior that are not violations of criminal law.

New York City police officer lends a helping hand to a young lady in 1893.

Photo courtesy of U.S. Library of Congress

Service Style

The service style, according to Wilson, is an attempt to combine the efficiency of the legalistic style and the broad informal discretion of the watchman style. Under the service style, the police take seriously all requests for assistance or service but are less likely to respond by making an arrest or issuing a citation. The service-style organization is decentralized in order to maintain a sense of local community-oriented police. Community relations are a high priority with service-oriented police departments.

The service-style orientation does not measure an individual officer's performance by the number of arrests or citations issued, but by the way (appropriate or inappropriate) the officer handles various situations. The individual officer has considerable personal discretion in responding to assistance or service requests. Service-oriented agencies are more likely to take advantage of community resources than are other types of police agencies. The service style is marked by a concern with helping individuals rather than by strict enforcement of the law.

PIONEERS IN POLICING

William H. Parker

William H. Parker was born on June 21, 1905, in the Black Hills of South Dakota. Parker joined the Los Angeles Police Department (LAPD) on August 8, 1927. He received his LL.B. in 1930 from the Los Angeles College of Law and was a member of the California State Bar. After serving 15 years with the department, Captain Parker took a leave of absence to serve in the military during World War II; he returned as a highly decorated combat veteran. After military service, Captain Parker returned to the LAPD, where he rapidly ascended through the ranks. He was appointed Chief of Police on August 9, 1950, and served as such until July 16, 1966, when he died as a result of a heart attack.

To date, Chief Parker was the longest serving Chief of Police in LAPD history. He was recognized nationally as one of the leading proponents of professionalism in police work. Chief Parker demanded honesty and discipline from his police officers, and he introduced the motto "To Protect and to Serve" in 1955. During this period, the LAPD set the standards of professionalism echoed in the TV series *Dragnet* and *Adam 12*. Chief Parker is credited with bringing the LAPD to the forefront as a world-renowned police agency and is considered by many to be LAPD's most distinguished Chief of Police.

SCOPE OF THE LAW ENFORCEMENT INDUSTRY

There are 17,784 publicly funded state and local police agencies in the United States that employed at least one full-time sworn officer with general arrest powers or the equivalent in part-time officers.[2] This total includes 12,666 general-purpose local police departments, 3,070 sheriff's offices, 49 primary state law enforcement agencies, 1,376 state and local agencies with special geographical jurisdiction or special enforcement responsibilities, and 623 county constable offices in Texas.

As of June 2000, these state and local law enforcement agencies employed 1,019,496 persons on a full-time basis; approximately 70 percent of them were sworn personnel. About 15 percent of the sworn personnel primarily handled criminal investigations, about 6 percent primarily performed jail-related duties, and 5 percent handled court-related duties such as providing court security or serving civil process. More than 131,000 sworn personnel were designated as community policing officers.

The largest agency is the New York City Police Department, with over 40,000 full-time sworn police officers. The largest sheriff's office is in Los Angeles County, with 8,468 sworn officers, and the largest state law enforcement agency is the California Highway Patrol, with 6,678 sworn officers. About 60 percent of the full-time sworn officers work in an agency

---

Mission Statement of the New York City Police Department

MISSION

The Mission of the New York City Police Department is to enhance the quality of life in our City by working in partnership with the community and in accordance with constitutional rights to enforce the laws, preserve the peace, reduce fear, and provide for a safe environment.

VALUES

In partnership with the community, we pledge to:

- Protect the lives and property of our fellow citizens and impartially enforce the law.
- Fight crime both by preventing it and by aggressively pursuing violators of the law.
- Maintain a higher standard of integrity than is generally expected of others because so much is expected of us.
- Value human life, respect the dignity of each individual and render our services with courtesy and civility.

Source: New York City Police Department.

---

with 100 or more officers; agencies with fewer than 10 full-time officers employ about 6 percent of all full-time local officers.

About 77 agencies employ more than 1,000 sworn officers. This figure includes 47 local police departments, 17 state police or highway patrol agencies, 12 sheriff's offices, and 1 special-jurisdiction police agency (Port Authority of New York-New Jersey Police).

Texas has the most full-time state and local law enforcement **agencies,** and Pennsylvania has the next-highest number of agencies, followed by Illinois and Ohio. California has the most full-time state and local law enforcement **officers;** it is followed by Texas, New York, and Florida.

Nationwide there are 362 full-time state and local law enforcement officers per 100,000 citizens. The District of Columbia has the most officers (859) per 100,000 citizens; Vermont, with 240, has the least. The per capita ratio of uniformed officers whose regular duties include responding to calls for service is the highest in the District of Columbia (357 per 100,000) and the lowest in Oregon (108 per 100,000).

MUNICIPAL POLICING

Municipal policing involves those law enforcement agencies that are city- or town-based and is the primary type of policing in the United States. There are differences between the small urban police departments and the large ones, and these differences call for a variety of organizations and strategies. The small department generally lacks the resources to have special investigators, highly specialized equipment, and crime laboratories. In many cases, when the small department needs such expertise, it is supported by regional crime laboratories or state units.

There are also similarities between the large and small agencies. All police departments, regardless of size, use automobiles to provide patrol services in their jurisdictions, and about 62 percent of them also use foot patrols on a routine basis. More than nine in ten large departments have bicycle patrols, but few departments have routinely scheduled marine or horse patrol units.

Police Departments in Large Cities

There are 62 urban police departments that serve populations of 250,000 or more.[3] The departments in large cities employ about 400 full-time personnel per 100,000 residents; this is an increase of about 20 percent from the 1990s. The New York City Police Department is the largest, with more than 40,000 full-time sworn personnel. The NYPD is three times larger than the next-largest department, the Chicago Police Department with its 13,500 full-time sworn officers.

This driver was stopped by the Washington, D.C., police officer for driving 25 miles per hour in an 18-mile-per-hour zone in July 1922. The officer was required by regulation to inform the driver that it was his duty to look at her operations permit and to give her a card directing her to post collateral at the nearest police station. The officer was forbidden from "bawling out" the driver.

Photo Courtesy of U.S. Library of Congress

Minority representation is about 38 percent of the sworn officers in the large departments. Blacks represent about 20 percent of their personnel and Hispanics about 14 percent. About 13 percent of the sworn personnel are women.

The average agency operating budget for the 62 largest urban police departments is about $212 million, and the cost per resident is about $266. The starting salary for a new officer in the larger urban departments is about $36,000 annually.

Collective Bargaining and Policing

Nationwide about 40 percent of police departments (employing about 72 percent of all sworn officers) have authorized **collective bargaining** (unions) for sworn personnel. Nonsworn personnel in local police departments are less likely to have collective bargaining rights than sworn officers. Overall, only 20 percent of the urban departments (employing about 57 percent of all nonsworn police personnel) authorized collective bargaining for nonsworn employees. The average starting salary for entry-level officers is about $8,000 higher in departments that have collective bargaining agreements.

AIRPORT AND TRANSIT AUTHORITY POLICE AGENCIES

The trend in recent years has been to establish specialized public police agencies, the most common of which are the airport and transit authority police agencies. Generally these agencies have the same authority as municipal police departments, but their jurisdiction (power to act) is limited to their specialized jurisdictions (the airport or the transit authority station).

A Los Angeles advertisement contained the following description: An **airport police officer** is a sworn peace officer authorized to carry a firearm who enforces federal and state regulations, city ordinances, and security, traffic, and safety rules and regulations; engages in law enforcement activities, including uniformed foot, vehicle, motorcycle, and bicycle patrols, plainclothes assignments, arrests, and report writing at airports; provides information to the public regarding locations and operations of the Department; and does related work.

RURAL POLICING

Except in the Northeast, county law enforcement is generally performed by a sheriff's department in most rural areas of the country. In the Northeast, the sheriff's offices perform little active law enforcement, although they sometimes are involved in locating and apprehending suspects who have jumped bail. In the Northeast, the sheriff's offices perform duties involving courtroom security, prisoner transportation, and service of legal notices. Unlike an urban police chief, the sheriff is an elected official, except in Rhode Island and Hawaii where the sheriff is appointed. The present-day powers and duties of the sheriffs in America have not changed much from the frontier days.

Development of the Sheriff's Office

Our present sheriffs originated from the shire-reeves. When the office began, the sheriff exercised considerable powers and was referred to as the king's steward. The office of sheriff was never popular with the citizens in early England. The sheriffs were usually appointed by the king in repayment for money or other favors granted the king. Often the holders of the office were nonresidents and used the offices only to fatten their purses.

By the late 1200s, sheriffs were forbidden to act as justices. During that century, the office of coroner was created, and the coroner acted as a monitor over the sheriff. The office of sheriff still survives in England, but since the 19th century, the English sheriff has had no police powers. The present-day sheriffs in England, much like the sheriffs in our states in the Northeast, act as officers of the court, summon juries, and enforce civil judgments.

Sheriffs first appeared in America in the early colonial period; originally, the sheriffs were appointed by the governors. After the Civil War, sheriffs became popular figures in the legendary Wild West. The frontier sheriff often used citizens to assist in the capture of outlaws: The common citizens were deputized and became the *posse comitatus* to assist the sheriff. The use of the *posse comitatus* declined in the early 1900s because the enlistment of untrained citizens did not meet the necessary requirements as American society became more complex. By the 1880s, sheriffs were elected by the voters within their respective counties.

Modern Sheriff's Offices

Presently, sheriff's offices in the United States employ about 300,000 full-time employees, including about 165,000 sworn officers.[4] Sheriff's offices have a total operating budget of about $18 billion per year, which is up about 50 percent from 1990 after adjustment for inflation. It costs counties about $70 dollars per resident per year to operate a sheriff's office.

Although only one-sixth of sheriff's offices serve a jurisdiction with 100,000 or more residents, such agencies employ about two-thirds of all sworn personnel; about one-fifth of sworn personnel are employed in jurisdictions with 1 million or more residents. About 17 percent of the sworn personnel are members of a racial or ethnic minority, and an estimated 12.5 percent of the sworn personnel are women.

Sheriff's offices typically serve counties and independent cities. Although sheriff's offices may have countywide jail and court-related responsibilities, their law enforcement jurisdiction may exclude county areas served by an urban police department. In certain counties, some municipalities contract with the sheriff's office for law enforcement services. In counties and independent cities with a separate police department, the sheriff's office may not have primary law enforcement jurisdiction.

Sheriff's offices employ a variety of screening methods for hiring new deputies. Nearly all (94 percent) use personal interviews, and a majority (74 percent) use medical exams; 81 percent of prospects are required to take a pre-employment drug test, and 97 percent are subject to a criminal background check before being hired. Only about 18 percent of the offices use pre-employment polygraph exams, and only 4 percent use voice stress analyzers.

State-mandated field and academy training requirements for a new deputy average about 670 hours, and additional training beyond state requirements averages about 380 hours per year. About 13 percent of new deputies have completed at least some college. The average starting pay for new deputies ranges from $22,000 in the smallest jurisdictions to about $33,000 in the largest.

In 2000, 55 percent of the offices had a community policing plan of some type, and about 80 percent of the offices regularly met with community groups. Nearly all the offices used automobiles for routine patrols; about 23 percent routinely used some foot patrols, and 13 percent used bicycle patrols on a regular basis.

Tribal Law Enforcement

There are 171 American Indian tribes that employ at least one full-time sworn officer with general arrest authority.[5] This is in addition to the 37 law enforcement agencies operated by the Bureau of Indian Affairs (BIA). The tribally operated agencies provide a broad range of public safety services and respond to calls for service. A large majority of them engage in crime prevention activities (88 percent), execute arrest warrants (88 percent), and perform traffic enforcement (84 percent). About one-fourth of them operate jails, and over one-half provide court security.

Tribally operated agencies employ about 3,500 full-time personnel, including about 2,300 sworn officers. These numbers average out to 2.3 full-time sworn officers per 1,000 residents.

Constables

The office of constable started in England. The English constable had a variety of duties, including collecting taxes, supervising roads, and serving as magistrate. The constable was elected by the citizens of his parish or township, and it was often an office conferred upon persons of local prominence. With the creation of the justice of the peace offices in the 1200s, the constable was then limited to making arrests with warrants issued by a justice of peace. In 1856, the English Parliament abolished the office of constable.[6]

When first established in the American colonies, the office of constable had similar duties to the early English constable; in addition, the American constable generally had control over the night watch. Since the 1900s, the American constable has declined in popularity and presently functions mostly to support the justices of the peace, although in a few states they have the authority to issue traffic citations and perform other law enforcement functions. Today constables are active in law enforcement in only a few jurisdictions and are probably the most active in Texas.

Justices of the Peace

By 1264, an office of justice of the peace (JP) was created for every county in England. The early JPs were generally wealthy landholders, and they allowed the constables and sheriffs to make arrests by issuing them warrants. With the development of the JPs, the power of sheriffs and constables declined. JP duties eventually included the granting of bail to felons, which led to corruption and criticism as felons who could pay were released. The only qualifications necessary for holding the JP office in England was the ownership of land and the ability to buy the office. By the 1600s, JPs were often referred to as "boobies" and "scum of the earth" because of the caliber of persons holding the office.

By the 1900s, the English abolished the landowning requirement for JPs, and many of their functions were removed. The English JP now possesses only criminal jurisdiction and has no jurisdiction over civil cases.

In the American colonies, the JPs were elected to office and had limited jurisdiction in both civil and criminal cases. Today in many states, the JP is a judicial office rather than a law enforcement office, and JP courts preside over traffic and other minor offenses in rural areas. The federal system replaced its JPs with federal magistrates.

STATE POLICE AGENCIES

In the English tradition, Americans have been wary of a strong state police unit. Traditionally in the United States, policing has been primarily the function of local governments, and state police are seen as an unwanted interference with local authority. Presently all states except Hawaii do have a state police force. In some states, the state police have only limited authority and are restricted to the functions of enforcing traffic and protecting the public on state and federal highways; in other states, the state police have been given general policing authority in criminal matters throughout the state.

The state police agencies were developed to deal with the growing crime in nonurban areas caused by the increasing mobility of Americans and the ease of traveling. The state police agencies were also established by the governors and legislators to lessen reliance on local law enforcement agencies.

State police agencies are generally organized in either centralized or decentralized operational units. The centralized agency performs a wide spectrum of duties in enforcing state penal laws and providing supplemental assistance to local law enforcement agencies. Generally the decentralized units perform only specialized services such as highway patrols and regional crime laboratories.

The state police often carry out many duties, such as managing training academies, crime laboratories, and identification bureaus, for local law enforcement agencies. The most common duties of state agencies include highway patrol, patrol of small towns, and traffic law enforcement.

In some states there are separate state agencies for crime-fighting duties and for other duties such as vehicle code enforcement and regulation, crime laboratories, and drug and alcohol enforcement. The states that use the decentralized model generally have two separate agencies: a highway patrol and a state bureau of investigations.

The Arizona Department of Public Safety is an example of a decentralized agency. It has 4 independent divisions that operate about 30 offices statewide. The divisions are the highway patrol, criminal investigation (with 5 separate offices), agency support, and criminal justice support. The Minnesota State Patrol is an example of a centralized agency, with 11 patrol districts and 61 stations directly under a central headquarters. Each patrol district is under the supervision of the Director of the Minnesota State Patrol.

California is another example of a decentralized agency, with the California Highway Patrol and the California Division of Law Enforcement. The California Highway Patrol is the largest state police agency and has approximately 6,500 sworn personnel. The smallest in the United States is the North Dakota Highway Patrol, with approximately 130 officers.

The Texas Rangers were organized in 1835 to supplement the military forces of the new Texas government. When Texas was admitted into the United States in 1845, the rangers were reorganized as a state police, making them the first state police in America. They were disbanded during the post–Civil War Reconstruction in 1874 and reorganized after

California Highway Patrol

MISSION STATEMENT AND ORGANIZATIONAL VALUES

The mission of the California Highway Patrol (CHP) is to provide the highest level of safety, service, and security to the people of California and to assist governmental agencies during emergencies when requested.

To accomplish our mission, the CHP is committed to the following organizational values as the foundation of our pledge to public safety and service: respect for others, fairness, ethical practices, and equitable treatment for all.

WHAT INFORMATION IS RELEASABLE AND WHAT'S NOT?

Releasable Information of Crime and Arrest Reports.   The following information shall be provided to the media upon request, according to the California Public Records Act. Exceptions include circumstances in which release of information would endanger an investigation or a related investigation or would endanger the safety of a person involved in the investigation: [Government Code Section 6254(f)]

Arrestee's full name (except juveniles)

Arrestee's complete address except as otherwise exempted by statute (including California Vehicle Code Section 1808.4)

Arrestee's occupation, physical description, and date of birth

Victim's name and address (See non-releasable information for exceptions.)

Time, date, location, and circumstances of arrest

Pursuit or use of weapons by officers

Name of arresting/investigating officer and length of investigation unless disclosure would jeopardize personal safety

Limited description of evidence seized (e.g., handgun, not Smith & Wesson .38)

Time, date, and location of booking

All charges, including warrants and probation or parole holds

Amount of bail, court schedule, and time and manner of release

It is CHP policy to release Blood Alcohol Content (BAC) results.

Disclosure of Complaints or Requests for Assistance.   Government Code Section 6254(f) provides for release of:

Time, substance, and location of all complaints or requests for assistance received by the [CHP]

Time and nature of the response

Information regarding crimes alleged or committed or any other incident investigated

Time, date, and location of occurrence

Time and date of report

Name and age of victim (See non-releasable information for exceptions.)

Factual circumstances surrounding the crime or incident

Injuries, property, or weapons involved

Releasable Information for Juveniles. When a juvenile has been in a traffic collision, his or her name, age, and hometown are releasable. If the youth has also been arrested (e.g., driving under the influence), neither arrest information nor collision information is releasable. Name and offense allegedly committed by a juvenile 14 years or older taken into custody for a serious felony—as defined in Penal Code Section 1192.7(c)—may be disclosed. (Welfare and Institutions Code Section 827.5)

Name, description, and alleged violent felony [as defined by Penal Code Section 667.5 (c)] of a minor may be released if an arrest warrant has been issued or if release of information would aid in apprehension or protection of public safety. (Welfare and Institutions Code Section 827.6)

The Following Information Is Not Releasable, According to Government Code Section 6254(F).

Name of a victim of any crime (as defined by Penal Code Section 220, 261, 264, 264.1, 273a, 273d, 273.5, 286, 288, 288a, 289, 422.6, 422.7, 422.75, or 646.9)

Identity of suspect prior to arrest

Investigative reports

Investigations of officer-involved shootings or other personnel actions

Confession or existence of a confession

Officer's opinion of a possible plea bargain

Any photographs or mug shots (except those which aid an arrest or investigation or warn the public of danger)

Identity, credibility, or testimony of prospective witnesses

Officer's personal opinion as to strength of the case or suspect's guilt or innocence

Source: California Highway Patrol.

the Reconstruction period was over. In the early 1900s, the Texas Rangers and their counterparts, the Arizona Rangers (established in 1901) and the New Mexico Mounted Patrol (established in 1905), were primarily responsible for combatting cattle rustlers and thieves along the Rio Grande.

The first modern-day state police organization was formed in 1905 by the state of Pennsylvania. Its original focus was to be on the public dispute between labor and management. Later, the inadequacy of the sheriff-constable system in Pennsylvania and the inability or unwillingness of local police forces to pursue lawbreakers beyond their jurisdictional limits convinced the Pennsylvania legislature of the need for a statewide police force.

Ohio State Highway Patrol

DUTIES AND RESPONSIBILITIES

The Ohio State Highway Patrol is an internationally accredited agency dedicated to professional law enforcement service. The Patrol provides statewide traffic services to keep our roadways safe; statewide emergency response services and support services to the public and the criminal justice community; investigation of criminal activities on state-owned and leased property throughout Ohio; and security for the Governor and other dignitaries.

The Patrol is a division of the Ohio Department of Public Safety, which is administrated by a Director who holds a cabinet-level position in state government. The commander of the Patrol holds the rank of Colonel and is referred to as the Superintendent. The Superintendent is selected from the Patrol ranks upon the retirement or death of a predecessor.

Although personnel strength varies, the Patrol maintains a uniformed complement of about 1,400 officers. In addition, about 1,000 support personnel, including driver examiners, load limit inspectors, motor vehicle inspectors, motor carrier enforcement inspectors, dispatchers, electronics technicians, and civilian specialists, complete the Patrol's personnel strength. An all-volunteer auxiliary force, originally formed during World War II to assist officers after many entered the armed services, continues to donate thousands of hours of service to the citizens of Ohio.

Patrol General Headquarters is located in Columbus. The state is subdivided into 10 districts, with 7 districts containing 6 posts, 2 districts containing 5 posts, and a regional headquarters which is (in 8 of the 9 districts) located at one of the posts. The Ohio Turnpike makes up the 10th district, with 3 posts, administrative offices in Cleveland, and a headquarters in Berea. Each district is commanded by a captain and each post by a lieutenant. Training is conducted at the Patrol Academy, also located in Columbus.

From the ranks of its road troopers, the Patrol trains and maintains a number of officers in specialized law enforcement positions. Among these are plainclothes investigators; traffic and drug interdiction teams and k-9 officers; and commercial enforcement coordinators, inspectors, and crash reconstructionists. The Patrol also maintains a special response team, comprising road troopers who are specially trained in weapons and chemical agent use, extraction techniques, and rapid response methods.

Routine operations are conducted almost exclusively from automobiles; however, the Patrol also utilizes Jeep Cherokees, fixed-wing aircraft, and helicopters in the course of its duties. A fully equipped command vehicle, which can operate as a mobile patrol post, is maintained in a constant state of readiness to respond to natural disasters, civil unrest, and other emergencies requiring extended Patrol presence.

During 2000, troopers assisted almost 600,000 motorists and investigated more than 85,000 crashes. Over 907,000 traffic arrests were made, including 25,320 for DUI, 194,321 for safety belt restraint violations, and more than 3,000 for child safety seat violations; in addition, troopers issued 414,000 warnings.

Source: Ohio State Highway Patrol.

FEDERAL LAW ENFORCEMENT AGENCIES

The U.S. Constitution created three independent arms of government: the judiciary branch, the legislative branch, and the executive branch. It did not establish a national police force. Traditionally law enforcement has been a local activity; in recent years, however, the number of federal criminal statutes has increased, along with the number of federal law enforcement officers. The U.S. Attorney General has always been considered the chief federal law enforcement officer and is appointed by the U.S. President and confirmed by the U.S. Senate. The president also appoints the attorney general's assistants and the U.S. attorneys for each of the judicial districts. The U.S. attorneys in each judicial district supervise all criminal prosecutions within their districts and represent the federal government in most civil legal suits. The U.S. Attorney General also heads the Department of Justice, the official legal branch of the federal government.

As of June 2002, federal agencies employed more than 93,000 full-time personnel authorized to make arrests and carry firearms.[7] The largest number of officers were employed by the Immigration and Naturalization Service (INS), with 19,101 officers; it is followed by the Federal Bureau of Prisons (BOP), with 14,305; the U.S. Customs Service, with 11,634; and the FBI, with 11,248. The latest data were collected before the enactment of legislation that created the Department of Homeland Security (DHS). Women accounted for about 15 percent of the officers, and minority representation was about 32 percent. The BOP, DEA, FBI, and the U.S. Marshals Service are under the Department of Justice. The U.S. Customs Service, the INS, and the Secret Service became part of the DHS in 2003. The Internal Revenue Service (IRS) and the Bureau of Alcohol, Tobacco, and Firearms (ATF) are part of the Treasury Department.

Other federal agencies with at least 500 persons with arrest and firearm authority include the Federal Corrections and Supervision Office of the U.S. Courts, with approximately 4,500 probation officers; the U.S. Postal Inspection Service, with 3,135 officers; the National Park Service, with 2,139 full-time officers; the Veteran's Health Administration, with 1,605 officers; the U.S. Capitol Police, with 1,225 officers; the U.S. Fish and Wildlife Service, with 772 officers; the General Services Administration, with 744 officers; the Forest Service, with 658 officers; and the State Department's Bureau of Diplomatic Security, with 592 officers.[8]

Immigration and Naturalization Service (INS)

The Immigration and Naturalization Service (INS) was created in 1864 by an act designed to encourage immigration into the United States. A commissioner of immigration was created to regulate immigration. Later, the emphasis was changed to prevent the admission of undesirable individuals and to control individuals temporarily in the country for labor purposes.

In June 2002, the Immigration and Naturalization Service was the largest employer of federal officers with arrest and firearm authority. The

INS functions were moved to the DHS in 2003, but the INS organization remained basically the same.

About 50 percent of INS officers worked for the U.S. Border Patrol. Border Patrol duties include the detection and prevention of smuggling and illegal entry of aliens into the United States, with primary responsibility for the areas between the ports of entry. U.S. Border Patrol officers work along, and in the vicinity of, the 8,000 plus miles of U.S. boundaries. INS also employs over 2,000 criminal investigation and immigration agents responsible for investigating crimes under INS jurisdiction as well as over 2,600 agents assigned to detention and deportation duties.

Federal Bureau of Prisons (BOP)

The Federal Bureau of Prisons (BOP) employs over 14,000 officers with arrest and firearm authority. Most are used to maintain the security of BOP institutions and 139,000 federal prisoners. Their duties include supervising prisoners, searching for contraband, and responding to emergencies and disturbances.

Federal Bureau of Investigation (FBI)

The Federal Bureau of Investigation (FBI) has been the most colorful and most glamorous branch of federal law enforcement, and it has also been the subject of many movies and television shows. The FBI was originally created as the Bureau of Investigation in the Department of Justice in 1908; then it had 35 agents and no specific duties other than the investigation of crimes involving federal banks, bankruptcy frauds, antitrust violations, and crimes on tribal reservations. Later, during World War I, its jurisdiction was increased to include espionage and sabotage incidents.

In the 1920s, it was subjected to charges of political corruption. The FBI came of age with the appointment of J. Edgar Hoover as its Director. He demanded that the organization become a career service, with advancements based on personal qualifications and abilities. Special agents were required to be college graduates holding degrees in law or accounting. Under Hoover's controversial leadership, the FBI's jurisdiction expanded, and now it investigates nearly 300 types of crimes.

In 1924, the bureau created its Identification Division; in 1932, with a borrowed microscope and a few other pieces of equipment, its crime laboratory was created. In 1935, the bureau's functions merged with the Bureau of Prohibition and transferred to a Division of Investigation headed by Director Hoover. On March 22, 1935, it was renamed the Federal Bureau of Investigation.

In 1950, the FBI instituted its "Ten Most Wanted Fugitives" list. This list is now published on a Web page and generates over 30 million hits a year. Presently the FBI is divided into 15 divisions. The Identification Division's main purpose now is to help local police agencies in identifying criminal

---

The FBI Today

MOTTO

The FBI motto is "Fidelity, Bravery, and Integrity."

MISSION

The mission of the FBI is to protect and defend the United States against terrorist and foreign intelligence threats, to uphold and enforce the criminal laws of the United States, and to provide leadership and criminal justice services to federal, state, municipal, and international agencies and partners. The organization with these responsibilities has not always been called the FBI.

CORE VALUES

The FBI will strive for excellence in all aspects of its missions. In pursuing these missions and vision, the FBI and its employees will be true to, and exemplify, the following core values:

- Adherence to the rule of law and the rights conferred to all under the United States Constitution
- Integrity through everyday ethical behavior
- Accountability by accepting responsibility for our actions and decisions and the consequences of our actions and decisions
- Fairness in dealing with people
- Leadership through example, both at work and in our communities

FBI

1. Protect the United States from terrorist attack.
2. Protect the United States against foreign intelligence operations and espionage.
3. Protect the United States against cyber-based attacks and high-technology crimes.
4. Combat public corruption at all levels.
5. Protect civil rights.
6. Combat transnational and national criminal organizations and enterprises.
7. Combat major white-collar crime.
8. Combat significant violent crime.
9. Support federal, state, county, municipal, and international partners.
10. Upgrade technology to successfully perform the FBI's mission.

Source: September 2004 FBI press release.

---

suspects, missing persons, and accident victims. The FBI maintains an Instrumental Analysis Unit that stores and analyzes samples of various kinds.

FBI Headquarters is currently located in the J. Edgar Hoover Building on Pennsylvania Avenue in Washington, D.C. The special agents and support personnel who work at Headquarters organize and coordinate

FBI activities around the world. Headquarters personnel determine investigative priorities, oversee major cases, and manage the organization's resources, technology, and personnel.

Headquarters also has a role in gathering and distributing information and plays a key part in fighting terrorism. It is the focal point for intelligence, not only from around the country but from the Central Intelligence Agency (CIA) and various countries overseas. Headquarters takes the intelligence information it collects, analyzes it, and sends it to field offices, state and municipal police departments, and other federal agencies such as the Department of Homeland Security.

As the FBI has grown, some Headquarters functions have been moved to other locations. The Criminal Justice Information Services Division is located in Clarksburg, West Virginia, and the Laboratory and Investigative Technologies Divisions are located in Quantico, Virginia. Other specialized facilities, such as high-tech computer forensics centers, are at various locations across the country.

The nuts-and-bolts work of the FBI is done in its 56 field offices and 400 satellite offices, known as resident agencies. It is the special agent in the field who looks for clues, tracks down leads, and works with local law enforcement to catch and arrest criminals. A Special Agent in Charge oversees each field office, except for the largest field offices (in Los Angeles, New York City, and Washington, D.C.), which are headed by an Assistant Director.

The FBI has 45 offices known as Legal Attachés (or "**Legats**") located around the world. Legats' goals are simple: to stop foreign crime as far from American shores as possible and to help solve international crimes that do occur as quickly as possible. To accomplish these goals, each Legat works with law enforcement and security agencies in its host country to coordinate investigations of interest to both countries. Some Legats are responsible for coordination with law enforcement personnel in several countries. The purpose of these Legats is strictly coordination; they do not conduct foreign intelligence gathering or counterintelligence investigations. The rules for joint activities and information sharing are generally spelled out in formal agreements between the United States and the Legat's host country. The entire worldwide Legat program is overseen by a Special Agent in Charge located at FBI Headquarters.

The FBI publishes crime reports, and the most famous is the **Uniform Crime Reports (UCR),** which combines data received from more than 15,000 law enforcement agencies concerning 29 different types of offenses. The offenses are divided into Part I or index offenses (criminal homicide, forcible rape, robbery, aggravated assault, burglary, larceny, motor vehicle theft, and arson) and Part II or non-index crimes. The UCR is published annually. It has received numerous complaints concerning its accuracy; the major concerns include the uneven reporting of crimes and crimes reported incorrectly or inaccurately. The FBI publishes the annual **crime clock** (see Figure 2–1).

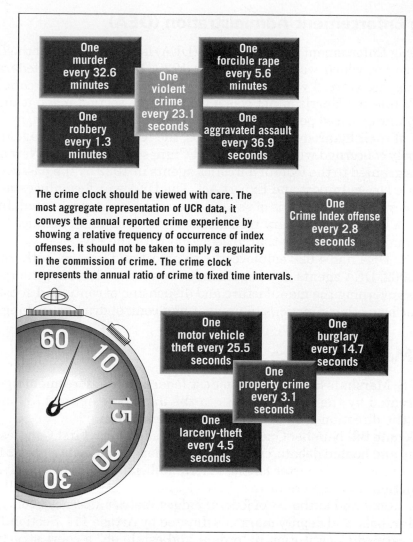

The crime clock should be viewed with care. The most aggregate representation of UCR data, it conveys the annual reported crime experience by showing a relative frequency of occurrence of index offenses. It should not be taken to imply a regularity in the commission of crime. The crime clock represents the annual ratio of crime to fixed time intervals.

FIGURE 2–1 FBI Crime Clock

The National Crime Information Center (NCIC) is under the FBI. This center has millions of records relating to missing persons, fugitives, and stolen property. The records are capable of being transmitted instantaneously to local police agencies upon request.

As of June 2002, the FBI had 11,248 full-time persons with arrest and firearm authority. Nearly all were FBI special agents, responsible for criminal investigation and enforcement. The FBI investigates more than 200 categories of federal crimes including bank fraud, embezzlement, kidnapping, and civil rights violations. The FBI also has concurrent jurisdiction with the Drug Enforcement Administration over drug offenses under the Controlled Substances Act.

Drug Enforcement Administration (DEA)

The Drug Enforcement Administration (DEA) is an outgrowth of the Bureau of Narcotics, which was established in 1930. The creation of federal narcotics agents started with the enactment of the Harrison Narcotic Act in 1914. While the Harrison Act was a tax law, one section made it unlawful for any unregistered personnel to possess heroin, cocaine, opium, morphine, or any of their by-products. In the 1920s, the federal narcotics agents were primarily concerned with the organized Chinese opium gangs. New authority was granted to the federal narcotics agents in 1922 by the passage of the Narcotic Drugs Import and Export Act. The DEA was formally established in 1973 when the functions of several agencies were consolidated. In 1983, the DEA was given primary responsibility for drug and narcotics enforcement, and today it shares that jurisdiction with the FBI.

The DEA had 4,020 employees with arrest and firearm authority as of June 2002. DEA agents investigate major narcotics violators, enforce regulations governing the manufacture and dispensing of controlled substances, and perform other functions to prevent and control drug trafficking.

U.S. Marshals Service

The U.S. Marshals Service is the oldest federal law enforcement agency. It was created by the first Congress in the Judiciary Act of 1789 and was under the direction of President George Washington.

Senate Bill Number One of the First Session of the First Congress, after lengthy and heated debate, created the Judiciary Act of September 24, 1789. The act provided a charter for the federal judicial system by specifying the jurisdiction and powers of the district and circuit courts as well as the qualifications and authority of federal judges, district attorneys, court clerks, U.S. Marshals, and deputy marshals. Invited by Article 111, Section 1, of the newly ratified Constitution to "ordain and establish" a court structure for the new national government, the first Senate moved quickly to the task and mandated that U.S. Marshals provide local law enforcement for the federal government and enforce federal laws and court orders in the colonies.

As of June 2002, the U.S. Marshals Service employed 2,646 officers with arrest and firearm authority. The Marshals Service receives all persons arrested by federal agencies and is responsible for their custody and transportation until sentencing. With BOP assistance, the service transfers sentenced federal prisoners between facilities.

The service also has jurisdiction over federal fugitive matters concerning escaped prisoners, probation and parole violators, persons under DEA warrants, and federal defendants released on bond. The service makes more than half of all federal fugitive arrests.

Other Marshals Service responsibilities include managing the Federal Witness Security and Federal Asset Seizure and Forfeiture Programs and providing security for federal judiciary facilities and personnel.

U.S. Marshals Service News Release

The Marshals Service is the nation's oldest and most versatile federal law enforcement agency. Since 1789, federal marshals have served the nation through a variety of vital law enforcement activities. Ninety-five U.S. marshals, appointed by the president or the U.S. attorney general, direct the activities of 94 district offices and personnel stationed at more than 350 locations throughout the 50 states, Guam, Northern Mariana Islands, Puerto Rico and the Virgin Islands. Each district, and the District of Columbia Superior Court, is headed by a U.S. Marshal. The Marshals Service's headquarters are located in the Washington, D.C., area.

The Marshals Service occupies a uniquely central position in the federal justice system. It is involved in virtually every federal law enforcement initiative. There are approximately 4,200 deputy marshals and career employees nationwide performing the agency's day-to-day operations.

Even after the creation of more than 50 specialized federal law enforcement agencies during the 20th century, the Marshals retained the broadest jurisdiction and authority. For over 200 years now, U.S. Marshals and their deputies have served as the instruments of civil authority used by all three branches of government. Marshals have been involved in most of the major historical episodes in America's past. The history of the Marshals is, quite simply, the story of how the American people govern themselves.

The Marshals Service looks back on a proud heritage—a tradition spanning two centuries of service to the Nation and dedication to the principles of our Constitution and the rule of law.

As our young nation expanded westward, U.S. Marshals embodied the civilian power of the Federal Government to bring law and justice to the frontier. For every new territory, Marshals were appointed to impose the law on the untamed wilderness. And at virtually every significant point over the years where Constitutional principles or the force of law have been challenged, the Marshals were there—and they prevailed.

The challenges faced today by Marshals and their deputies are no less demanding than those of the past. In fact, the skills, devotion, and determination required to carry out our contemporary responsibilities make the modern Marshals Service a unique and elite cadre of law enforcement professionals. And so, in looking back over our history, we would hope you recognize and take pride in the fact that this agency is an intimate part of the continuum of the grand American experiment in self-government.

Source: Excerpts from a U.S. Marshals Service news release in September 2004.

U.S. Customs Service

The Customs Service employed 11,634 officers with arrest and firearm authority as of June 2002. This included 8,167 inspectors and 3,467 criminal investigators. Customs Service officers interdict and seize contraband; process persons, vehicles, and items at more than 300 ports of entry; and administer certain navigational laws. The Customs Service has an extensive air, land, and marine interdiction force as well as an investigations component supported by its own intelligence branch. The service investigates violations of more than 400 laws related to customs, drugs, export control, and revenue fraud.

U.S. Customs Service Press Release

The United States Customs Service was founded in 1789 to save the struggling new Nation from financial collapse. Customs has come to the aid and protection of the Republic for over two centuries. Customs gave America its first source of revenue, became its first Federal law enforcement agency, and has affected and been affected by the Nation's history from the earliest days to the present.

Responding to an urgent need for revenue, the first Congress passed, and President Washington signed, the Tariff Act of July 4, 1789. It established a tariff and a system for collecting duties. The Service was placed, as it is today, under the Treasury Department, headed by 32-year-old Alexander Hamilton.

During the first year of service, U.S. Customs collected two million dollars in duties for the new Nation. Customs Revenue paid the Revolutionary War debt, provided funds for the new Nation's defense, and helped finance public works.

In 1801, Customs revenues paid Barbary pirates a one-million-dollar ransom to free captured American seamen. (Piracy became Customs' province again in 1970, when it was assigned the responsibility of halting an epidemic of skyjacking.)

For nearly 125 years, until the first federal income tax law in 1913, the Customs Service was virtually the only source of income for the U.S. Government. Customs revenues financed a period of awesome growth and acquisition as America moved from 13 states along the East Coast to an interoceanic nation. The opening of the West; the purchase of the Louisiana and Oregon Territories, in addition to Florida and Alaska; the construction of the national road from Cumberland, Maryland, to Wheeling, West Virginia; the Lewis and Clark Expedition and the Transcontinental Railroad—all of these and more were funded by a single agency. Customs collections built the U.S. military and naval academies, not to mention the city of Washington, D.C.

By 1835, Customs revenues had reduced the national debt to zero! By 1860, Customs collections represented 90 percent of all monies raised for government operations. Although passage of the Federal Income Tax Act in 1913 made the Internal Revenue Agency the Nation's number one revenue-producing agency, the Customs Service, even today, contributes more than $20 billion a year to the national treasury.

Beyond revenue, however, it was the Customs Service that taught the fledgling American Government how a federal agency should operate. That task fell to it by default: Customs was not only the first fully formed agency, but for years, it was far and away the largest.

By 1792, the Customs work force totaled nearly 500 people—80 percent of all Treasury employees and more than twice the number of the next largest agency, the Post Office.

Because Customs was, in essence, the nation's civil service in the early years, Congress would turn to it time and again to take charge of the nation's diverse needs.

When America needed lighthouses, for example, to guide ships safely past treacherous shoals, it turned to Customs to build those lighthouses. From 1791 to 1850, Customs supervised the construction of more than 300 lighthouses, from the Great Lakes to the Gulf of Mexico.

When America needed a system to pension agents to honor the debts owed its Revolutionary War heroes, it turned to Customs as the first "Veterans Administration."

When America needed to provide for the relief of sick and disabled seamen, it turned to Customs as the first public health service.

When America needed armed revenue cutters to patrol its shores, it turned to Customs to direct those ships, making Customs the first coast guard. When, in 1930, America needed to devise a system of "uniform authentic weights and measures," to ensure for merchants and consumers alike that a pound was indeed a pound, it turned to Customs, the first "Bureau of Standards."

When masses of immigrants began seeking refuge in America, Congress turned to Customs to manage the influx. It was the first "Immigration and Naturalization Service."

More than 140 years ago, when this country began its first battle against pornography, it was the Customs Service whom Congress first called upon to protect the public. More than 100 years ago, when American-made products started to become the targets of unscrupulous counterfeiters, it was Customs who first entered the fray to protect the rights of American manufacturers.

Nearly 80 years ago, when drug abuse first showed itself as the corruptive force it is, it was Customs who made the first efforts to close ranks in defending our nation in its war on drugs.

The traditional U.S. Customs Service Mission, as outlined in the Tariff Act of 1930, is threefold: to assess and collect customs duties on imported merchandise; to prevent fraud and smuggling; to control carriers, persons, and articles entering and departing the United States.

That was and continues to be the character of Customs: always ready to serve the Nation, to accept any challenges in times of peace and war—to protect, secure, defend. More diversified today than ever, the U.S. Customs Service enforces, in addition to its own statutes, more than 400 provisions of law on behalf of 40 other Federal agencies, all aimed at protecting the quality of American life.

The prevention of smuggling has been a primary Customs Service assignment, and one of its most hazardous, since its inception.

When American pioneers moved West, Customs inspectors accompanied the early settlers, enforcing U.S. laws and territorial statutes relating to revenues, immigration, and smuggling.

In mountain states along the northern border, primitive enforcement conditions prevailed well into the 1920s, easing only with the coming of the automobile and, later, aerial surveillance.

Mounted Customs officers along the southwest border faced difficult terrain and desperate smugglers. Officer Robert Rumsey was one of many killed in the line of duty.

In the Far West, where Customs has had a continuing presence since the territory's acquisition, Customs officers managed to preserve their Customhouse flag during the devastating earthquake of 1906.

With the passage in 1920 of the 18th Amendment—prohibiting the importation, possession, and sale of liquor—smuggling in the U.S. reached a new high. "Bootleggers" worked the borders with boats, trucks, and planes.

Customs countered with seizure after seizure of contraband alcohol. When the rumrunners were caught, Customs officers often confiscated their transport vehicles, along with the liquor they carried. During Prohibition, in fact, the U.S. Customs air interdiction fleet consisted wholly of aircraft seized for liquor smuggling.

Source: Excerpts from an August 2004 press release by the U.S. Customs Service.

Today's Customs Service.   The keyword for the U.S. Customs Service at the dawn of this century is "more." More international travelers, more conveyances, more cargo, and, unfortunately, more opportunities for those who choose to break our laws. Today's Customs Service continues as a vital and integral part of this Nation's security, with a wide array of responsibilities, which include the enforcement of over 400 laws and treaties, often on behalf of other Federal agencies.

In the forefront has been Customs' ability to adapt its responses to the trials of an ever-changing world, modifying its enforcement techniques, technologies, and resources to confront current and future threats to this Nation.

Narcotics Interdiction.   With the repeal of Prohibition in 1933, the market for bootleg liquor was gone, but as the economics of smuggling dictate, a different and deadlier form of contraband began its infiltration onto our shores and into our cities.

Since the 1960s, Customs officials have faced the overwhelming challenge of fighting the influx of illegal narcotics, such as opium, heroin, hashish, marijuana, and amphetamines, into the United States.

The staggering—and ever-increasing—number of conveyances, cargoes, and passengers arriving in the United States each year presents Customs with complex targeting and interdiction challenges requiring a variety of intelligence, investigative, and operational approaches.

Trying to curb the flood of illegal drugs has proven an ambitious task, yet through diligence, close inspection, sophisticated technology, and the sacrifice of lives, Customs has given an excellent account of itself in fighting the flow of illegal drugs into the United States. The U.S. Customs Service, annually, is this Nation's leading drug enforcement agency in terms of the number of illegal narcotics seized and suspects apprehended. In one recent year alone, Customs seized an astonishing 1.4 million pounds of narcotics bound for domestic distribution.

Customs' interdiction efforts, and its unique position at America's frontline, often provide the agency with clear indications of epidemic use of specific drugs. In recent years, sizable seizures of cocaine and new synthetic drugs, such as ecstasy, have tipped law enforcement authorities to the latest "drugs of choice" and the techniques criminals use to smuggle them.

A distinctive, high-profile tool in the Customs drug fight is its force of drug detector dogs, their trainers, and the Customs officers who work with these canine detectors.

First used on a wide scale in 1970, Customs narcotic detector dogs save countless man-hours in locating narcotics in vehicles, in mail, in unaccompanied baggage, on cargo ships, and throughout Customs facilities. A dog and its handler can, incredibly, check 500 packages in only 30 minutes. It would take a Customs mail examiner several days to inspect as many. At border points, a dog can inspect a vehicle in about 2 minutes, while the same search by a Customs inspector would take at least 20 minutes.

With their skill and efficiency, these amazing canines have saved passengers and importers countless delays clearing Customs while concurrently keeping deadly narcotics off our Nation's streets.

Technological advances, such as mobile and fixed truck X-ray systems, assist in Customs' search for illegal substances while providing expedited movement of cargo from our facilities. These devices provide an accurate, detailed look at cargo in a fraction of the time needed for a manual search, allowing for a greater number of conveyances to be searched and moved on.

Customs' narcotics interdiction efforts often extend beyond our Nation's shores. Customs' fleet of aircraft, equipped with sophisticated surveillance and tracking devices, coordinate with their high-speed boats to thwart smuggler aircraft as they drop payloads of narcotics off the American coast. Customs air-wing also coordinates, and participates in, counter-narcotics missions over high-activity areas, such as the Caribbean and certain South American countries.

Money Laundering.   Customs agents are experts in the investigation of international money-laundering schemes devised by sophisticated cartels to hide their criminal proceeds. With the passage of the Bank Secrecy Act, which mandates individuals and corporations must disclose certain assets and transactions, those engaged in illegal activities found it increasingly difficult to channel their riches into legitimate commerce. Customs investigators expertly—and often successfully—negotiate the intricate, calculatedly tangled money trail associated with making illegal proceeds escape scrutiny.

Money laundering, globally, disrupts the legitimate flow of commerce, introducing billions of unregulated dollars into the world's economies while depriving governments of revenue collected in the form of taxes and duties. Customs Money Laundering Coordination Center, one of the government's primary weapons tasked with curbing money-laundering activities, is engaged in continuous undercover financial investigations. This was evidenced during a recent three-year period when Customs conducted 12,000 investigations leading to 3,150 arrests and the seizure of nearly $1.1 billion.

Trade Fraud.   Customs special agents are recognized as being among the finest criminal investigators in the world. Their expertise in border investigative methods and techniques has effectively enabled them to consistently solve many complex types of crimes. Customs has investigated every type of smuggling activity imaginable, from narcotics to exotic and endangered animals, Rembrant paintings, illegal export of munitions of war, international money-laundering schemes, undervaluation schemes, cargo theft and international conspiracies, neutrality violations, and child pornography. Another initiative established by Customs is the Forced Child Labor Command Center, which monitors the importation of prohibited goods manufactured by forced or indentured child labor.

Strategic Investigations. Few crimes are more terrifying, or potentially more devastating, than those involving the importation of arms or explosives intended to do harm to America and its citizens. It is the duty of Customs to halt the trafficking of sensitive and controlled commodities, including weapons of mass destruction (WMD) and related technologies, munitions, and firearms. The threat doesn't end at stopping these items as they enter our country. Customs also is tasked with preventing the export of technical and military-use commodities to other countries, terrorist groups, and criminal organizations. In the recent past, items seized by Customs included military aircraft, missile parts, night-vision systems, bomb-making devices, Phalanx missiles, and stealth and antimissile technology. Customs additionally enforces violations of economic sanctions and embargoes and the import or export of stolen property.

Cybersmuggling. With the arrival and subsequent progression of the Internet, Customs was assigned the lead in enforcing crimes committed over the Internet and through other electronic media. Among the most heinous crimes investigated by Customs Computer Investigation Specialists is child pornography. In addition to developing and implementing the strategies used to track cyber-pornographers, Customs investigators routinely provide training and expertise to prosecutors and law enforcement officials both here and abroad. Despite the relative newness of this type of crime, Customs has already effected hundreds of arrests in child pornography cases. Among the variety of other media-related crimes Customs investigates is telemarketing fraud (e.g., bogus investments, charities, prize offers, travel packages).

Intellectual Property Rights. To secure the rights of creative individuals and those who have a vested interest in their works, Customs protects intellectual property rights (IPR). IPR can be a copyright, which protects original creations of "authorship" such as books, paintings, music, and movies; a trademark, which is a design, slogan, brand name, or configuration used to identify products as originating from a particular source; a patent, which is issued to protect a novel or useful invention; or a trade name, which is used to identify a specific business or occupation. Each year, trade in counterfeit or pirated merchandise in violation of IPR costs industry billions of dollars and nearly 750,000 jobs.

Science and analytical research assist Customs officers in their efforts to stop these illegal and fraudulent activities. The Customs Service maintains eight laboratories in the United States and San Juan, Puerto Rico, where sophisticated equipment analyzes certain imports to determine their appropriate classification. These scientific findings provide key, accurate evidence in the effort to prosecute IPR violators.

Commerce.   With much larger numbers looming, Customs currently processes over $1 trillion (total imports) in trade each year. Along with manpower and policy initiatives designed to assist the effort, technology is also being put in service protecting the public revenue. Technology is as crucial to Customs' commercial role as it is to law enforcement.

A new automated commercial environment (ACE) in the works will rely on account management to streamline the commercial import process, thus lowering the cost of trade compliance and increasing customer service for the trade community. Inspectors will use this system to make paperless cargo clearances as well as targeting noncompliant cargo for examinations.

Customs' current automated system (ACS) helps brokers, Customs agents, the enforcement community, and, ultimately, users perform a variety of functions. Services range from assessing and collecting users' fees to obtaining instant information on new or changing import quotas, monitoring high-risk shipments, and exchanging enforcement information nationwide. Additionally, computer technology has increased and accelerated Customs' role as registrar of statistics vital to U.S. trade, commerce, and security.

Passenger Travel.   International travel and tourism continue to enjoy unparalleled growth and popularity each year. The safe, expedient movement of passengers is made more convenient by the use of Customs' modern technologies and improved equipment. Customs relies on the Treasury Enforcement Communications System (TECS) to perform instant checks on travelers, vessels, aircraft, and importers and to expedite the processing of law-abiding travelers. Customs also maintains a proactive customer service program, which employs initiatives to aid travelers (such as Passenger Service Representatives), outreach activities (meetings with civic organizations, travel clubs, school groups, etc.), helpful brochures, information kiosks, and a dedicated Web site.

Summary.   The job of protecting 96,000 miles of U.S. land, air, and sea borders and more than 300 ports of entry is entrusted each day to the 20,000 dedicated employees of the U.S. Customs Service. U.S. Customs is the principal agency tasked with protecting our Nation's borders, and the only border agency with an extensive air, land, and marine interdiction force to carry out its primary mission: Control all carriers, persons, and articles entering and leaving the United States.

U.S. Secret Service

The U.S. Secret Service employs about 4,200 personnel with arrest and firearm authority. About two-thirds are special agents with investigation and enforcement duties primarily related to counterfeiting, financial crimes,

---

U.S. Secret Service

VISION STATEMENT

"Building on a Tradition of Excellence and Meeting the Challenges of the Future."

MISSION STATEMENT

The U.S. Secret Service is mandated by statute and executive order to carry out two significant missions: protection and criminal investigations. The Secret Service protects the President and Vice President, their families, heads of state, and other designated individuals; investigates threats against these protectees; protects the White House, Vice President's residence, Foreign Missions, and other buildings within Washington, D.C.; and plans and implements security designs for designated National Special Security Events. The Secret Service also investigates violations of laws relating to counterfeiting of obligations and securities of the United States; financial crimes that include, but are not limited to, access device fraud, financial institution fraud, identity theft, computer fraud; and computer-based attacks on our nation's financial, banking, and telecommunications infrastructure.

Source: U.S. Secret Service.

---

computer fraud, and threat against dignitaries. The majority of the other officers are in the Uniformed Division. These officers provide protection for the White House complex and other presidential offices, the Main Treasury Building and Annex, the President and Vice President and their immediate families, and foreign diplomatic missions.

Internal Revenue Service (IRS)

The Internal Revenue Service (IRS) employs about 2,900 special agents with arrest and firearm authority within its Criminal Investigation Division, which is the law enforcement arm of the IRS. They are charged with enforcing the federal tax laws.

Bureau of Alcohol, Tobacco, and Firearms (ATF)

The Bureau of Alcohol, Tobacco, and Firearms (ATF) employs about 2,350 full-time officers with arrest and firearm authority. The ATF enforces federal laws related to alcohol, tobacco, firearms, explosives, and arson. On January 24, 2003, ATF's law enforcement functions were transferred to the Department of Justice (DOJ), and ATF became the Bureau of Alcohol, Tobacco, Firearms and Explosives (ATF). ATF's Mission Statement is listed below.

Bureau of Alcohol, Tobacco, Firearms and Explosives (ATF)

MISSION

The Bureau of Alcohol, Tobacco, Firearms and Explosives (ATF) is a law enforcement organization within the United States Department of Justice with unique responsibilities dedicated to reducing violent crime and protecting the public.

ATF enforces the federal laws and regulations relating to alcohol, tobacco, firearms, explosives and arson by working directly and in cooperation with others to:

- Suppress and prevent crime and violence through enforcement, regulation, and community outreach.
- Ensure fair and proper revenue collection. Provide fair and effective industry regulation.
- Support and assist federal, state, local, and international law enforcement.
- Provide innovative training programs in support of criminal and regulatory enforcement functions.

Vision

ATF...WORKING FOR A SOUND AND SAFER AMERICA...THROUGH INNOVATION AND PARTNERSHIPS

The Bureau of Alcohol, Tobacco, Firearms and Explosives (ATF) must respond to the public outcry against crime, violence, and other threats to public safety. We must also continue to do our part to maintain the economic stability of the country. Our vision will help us chart the course to change the way we serve the public and achieve new levels of effectiveness and teamwork.

VALUES

We value each other and those we serve.
We will:

- Set and uphold the highest standards of excellence and integrity;
- Provide quality service and promote strong external partnerships; and
- Develop a diverse, innovative, and well-trained work force in order to collectively achieve our goals.

Source: Bureau of Alcohol, Tobacco, Firearms and Explosives.

INTERNATIONAL POLICING

Interpol is the world's largest international police organization, with 181 member countries. It was founded in 1923 to enable the world's police to cooperate more effectively in fighting international crime. It facilitates cross-border police cooperation and supports and assists all organizations, authorities, and services whose mission is to prevent or combat international crime.

Since 1989, the General Secretariat has been located in Lyon, France. The organization was previously located in Paris following its re-creation in 1946, after World War II. Interpol operates 24 hours a day, 365 days a year, in four official languages (English, French, Spanish, and Arabic).

Interpol also has five regional bureaus, in Harare, Abidjan, Nairobi, Buenos Aires, and San Salvador, plus a liaison office in Bangkok. These centers provide in-depth experience in regional crime issues and coordinate practical countercrime operations between countries within the region.

Each member country provides a National Central Bureau (NCB) staffed by national law enforcement officers. The NCB is the designated contact point for the General Secretariat, regional bureaus, and other member countries requiring assistance with overseas investigations and the location and apprehension of fugitives.

Interpol

VISION

Interpol exists to help create a safer world. Its aim is to provide a unique range of essential services for the law enforcement community to optimize the international effort to combat crime.

MISSION

To be the world's pre-eminent police organization in support of all organizations, authorities, and services whose mission is preventing, detecting, and suppressing crime.
Interpol will achieve this by:

- Providing both a global perspective and a regional focus;
- Exchanging information that is timely, accurate, relevant, and complete;
- Facilitating international cooperation;
- Coordinating joint operational activities of its member countries;
- Making available know-how, expertise, and good practice.

Interpol will act on the basis of the articulated demands and expectations of these organizations, authorities, and services, while remaining alert to developments so as to be able to anticipate future requirements.

CORE FUNCTIONS

Interpol offers three core services:

1. A unique global police communication system
2. A range of criminal databases and analytical services
3. Proactive support for police operations throughout the world

Source: Interpol.

ASIS International

ASIS International (ASIS) (formerly known as the American Society for Industrial Security) is the preeminent organization for security professionals, with more than 33,000 members worldwide. Founded in 1955, ASIS includes in its functions increasing the effectiveness and productivity of security professionals by developing educational programs and materials that address broad security interests, such as the ASIS Annual Seminar and Exhibits, as well as specific security topics. According to the ASIS International Media Office, ASIS also is an advocate of the role and value of the security management profession to business, the media, governmental entities, and the public by providing members and the security community with access to a full range of programs and services and by publishing the industry's number one magazine—*Security Management.*

Interpol's constitution prohibits "any intervention or activities of a political, military, religious or racial character." The intention is to facilitate international police cooperation even where diplomatic relations do not exist between particular countries. Action is taken within the limits of the laws existing in different countries and in the spirit of the Universal Declaration of Human Rights.

The United States did not become a member until 1938. An officer from the U.S. Department of Treasury serves as the U.S. representative.

PRIVATE SECURITY

In studying policing in America, we tend to overlook private policing, also known as private security. It is estimated that the number of individuals employed in private security are three times more than the number employed in law enforcement agencies.[9] The U.S. Department of Labor's Bureau of Labor Statistics reported in 2003 that the number of security guards and gaming surveillance officers is expected to grow faster than the average for all occupations as the concerns about crime, vandalism, and terrorism continue to increase. The Bureau of Labor Statistics reports that 1.1 million people are employed in private security.[10] Most major companies have either some type of security force or a contract with a security firm for its services.

▲ SUMMARY

American policing is multilevel. It covers local police departments, urban police agencies, state organizations, and federal departments. Each level covers different aspects of American policing, with a certain degree of overlapping. A sheriff's jurisdiction generally includes the unincorporated areas of the county and the county jail as well as small towns that do not have local police departments. An urban police department's jurisdiction generally includes the geographical area of the city or an area within the city limits. Jurisdiction of an issue refers to the agency's or agencies' responsibility to investigate certain criminal conduct and other law enforcement activities in that area.

Law enforcement agencies in the United States are accountable to the governmental unit and to its citizens through multiple institutions. Most law enforcement agencies are accountable to elected officials, civil and criminal courts, and civilian review boards.

James Q. Wilson contended that the police perform two basic functions: peacekeeping and law enforcement. He maintained that there are three distinctive styles of policing: the watchman style, the legalistic style, and the service style. The organizational form of the watchman style is flat and narrow: flat because there is little opportunity for advancement, and narrow because there is limited differentiation in the types of work that each officer does. Under the watchman style of policing, the departments are concerned primarily with peacekeeping. Since not much is expected of the officers, they have a wide range of discretion and tend to handle matters informally rather than invoking the official system's regulations. In departments using the legalistic style, a high degree of control is maintained over individual officers. This high degree of control is accomplished by handling every call as a law enforcement matter; accordingly, for every response the officer must make a report.

The service style is an attempt to combine the efficiency of the legalistic style and the broad informal discretion of the watchman style. Under the service style, the police take seriously all requests for assistance or service but are less likely to respond by making an arrest or issuing a citation. The service-style organization is decentralized in order to maintain a sense of local community-oriented police. Community relations are a high priority with service-oriented police departments.

Municipal policing covers those law enforcement agencies that are city- or town-based and is the primary type of policing in the United States. There are differences between the small urban police departments and the large ones, and these differences call for different organizations and strategies. Except in the Northeast, county law enforcement is generally performed by the sheriff's department in most rural areas of the country. In the Northeast, the sheriff's offices perform little active law enforcement, although they sometimes are involved in locating and apprehending suspects who have jumped bail.

In the English tradition, Americans have been wary of a strong state police unit. Traditionally in the United States, policing has been primarily the function of local governments, and state police are seen as an unwanted interference with local authority. Presently all states except Hawaii have a state police. In some states, the state police have only limited authority and are restricted to the functions of enforcing traffic and protecting the public on state and federal highways; in other states, the state police have been given general policing authority in criminal matters throughout the state.

QUESTIONS IN REVIEW

1. Explain the difference between rural policing and municipal policing.
2. What is the mission of Interpol?
3. What are the differences between the various styles of policing?
4. Why have the states been hesitant to establish strong state police departments?
5. What is the primary type of policing in the United States?
6. Generally what police agency handles crime in the rural areas of a state? In a small unincorporated village?
7. To what persons or agencies are U.S. police agencies accountable?

POLICE RESOURCES ON THE WEB

Federal Bureau of Investigation
http://www.fbi.gov

Metropolitan Washington Airports Authority Police Department
http://www.mwaa.com/authority/police

U.S. Bureau of Alcohol, Tobacco, Firearms and Explosives (ATF)
http://www.atf.gov

U.S. Bureau of Justice Assistance
http://www.ojp.usdoj.gov/bja

U.S. Department of Justice
http://www.usdoj.gov

U.S. Treasury Department
http://www.ustreas.gov

REFERENCES

1. JAMES Q. WILSON, *Varieties of Police Behavior* (Cambridge, MA: Harvard University Press, 1968), pp. 140–226.
2. U.S. DEPARTMENT OF JUSTICE, "Census of State and Local Law Enforcement Agencies, 2000," *Bureau of Justice Statistics Bulletin*, p. 1.
3. U.S. DEPARTMENT OF JUSTICE, "Police Departments in Large Cities, 2000," *Bureau of Justice Statistics Bulletin*.
4. "Sheriffs' Offices, 2000," *Bureau of Justice Statistics Bulletin*.
5. "Tribal Law Enforcement, 2000," *Bureau of Justice Statistics Bulletin*.

6. DAVID R. JOHNSON, *American Law Enforcement History* (St. Louis, MO: Forum Press, 1981); and LEON RADZINOWICZ, *A History of English Criminal Law and Its Administration from 1750,* vol. IV (London: Stevens & Son, 1968).

7. The data on federal law enforcement were taken from "Federal Law Enforcement Officers, 2002," *Bureau of Justice Statistics Bulletin.*

8. BUREAU OF JUSTICE STATISTICS, *Special Report: Federal Law Enforcement Officers, 2002* (Washington, DC: GPO, 2003).

9. PAMELA A. SEXTON-ALYEA, "Police Versus Private Security: Whom Do We Trust?" in *Policing and Crime Prevention,* ed. Deborah Mitchell Robinson (Upper Saddle River, NJ: Prentice Hall, 2002), pp. 31–52.

10. U.S. DEPARTMENT OF LABOR, "Security Guards and Gaming Surveillance Officers," *Bureau of Labor Statistics, Occupational Outlook Handbook.* Retrieved from http://www.bls.gov/oco/ocos159.htm.

Community-Oriented Policing

Key Terms

Community-oriented policing

Evaluation research

Flint, Michigan, Foot Patrol
  experiment

Foot patrol

Futures conference

Kansas City Preventive Patrol
  experiment

Newark Foot Patrol experiment

Organizational change

Problem-oriented policing

Program evaluation

RAND Corporation

SARA

SARA problem-solving model

Team policing

Traditional policing

Value-Based Initiative

Outline

Introduction

Move to Community Policing

Community-Oriented Policing

Problem-Oriented Policing

Evaluations of Community Policing

Future of Community-Oriented
  Policing

Value-Based Initiatives

Learning Objectives

After reading this chapter, you should be able to:

1. Identify factors that led to the evolution of community-oriented policing.
2. List major research studies in policing.
3. Describe community-oriented policing.
4. Explain problem-oriented policing.
5. Discuss the evaluations of community-oriented policing.
6. Describe future themes centering on community-oriented policing.
7. Discuss the objectives of Value-Based Initiatives.

INTRODUCTION

> Police, at all times, should maintain a relationship with the public that gives reality to the historic tradition that the police are the public and the public are the police; the police being only members of the public who are paid to give full-time attention to duties which are incumbent on every citizen in the interests of community welfare and existence.
>
> —*Sir Robert Peel, 1829*

Since 1994, the Office of Community-Oriented Policing Services (COPS) has invested $7.5 billion to add community policing officers to the nation's streets, enhance crime-fighting technology, support crime prevention initiatives, and advance community policing. More than 12,000 of our nation's 18,000 law enforcement agencies have received COPS grants. While COPS has partnered with our largest cities, more than 82 percent of COPS grants have gone to departments serving populations of 50,000 or less. More than 130,000 law enforcement personnel and community members have been trained through the COPS nationwide network of Regional Community Policing Institutes and the Community Policing Consortium. The Office of Community-Oriented Policing Services has provided nearly 4,000 law enforcement agencies with over $1 billion in technology to support community policing efforts.

Currently, about 86 percent of the nation's population is served by law enforcement agencies practicing community policing, compared with 15 percent in 1993.[1] These substantial investments have produced a significant community policing infrastructure across the nation that requires careful ongoing innovative development. COPS continues to provide critical resources, training, and technical assistance to help local law enforcement implement innovative and effective community policing strategies.[2] The COPS Office was created as a result of the Violent Crime Control and Law Enforcement Act of 1994. As a component of the Justice Department, the COPS Office has as its mission to advance community policing in jurisdictions of all sizes across the country.

Community-oriented policing represents a shift from more traditional law enforcement in that it focuses on prevention of crime and the fear of crime on a local basis. Community policing puts law enforcement professionals on the streets and assigns them a beat, so they can build mutually beneficial relationships with the people they serve. By earning the trust of the members of their communities and making those individuals stakeholders in their own safety, community policing makes law enforcement safer and more efficient and makes America safer. As of the end of fiscal year 2003, COPS funded more than 118,500 community police officers and deputies.[3]

In this chapter, we explore why many police agencies have implemented community-oriented policing strategies. We examine what community policing is, what the benefits of the strategy are, and how it can be used as a venue for change. We also discuss **problem-oriented policing** and then examine the evaluations of community policing. This chapter concludes with a discussion on what the future holds for community-oriented policing. When

PIONEERS IN POLICING

Richard Sylvester

Richard Sylvester was Chief of the District of Columbia Police from 1898 to 1915. In 1902, Chief Sylvester became the first President of the newly formed International Association of Chiefs of Police. He was widely regarded as being the first voice to advocate the professionalism of the police. Chief Sylvester advanced a strict paramilitary style of organization and policing, which came to be known as the citizen-soldier model. He is credited with the development of many of the paramilitary aspects of policing. His accomplishments are many, including being an advocate of the scientific crime-fighter model, being responsible for introducing American crime labs, and developing fingerprint repositories.

you have finished reading this chapter, you should have a comprehensive overview of the process of community policing and what it means for the future of American policing.

MOVE TO COMMUNITY POLICING

During the past several decades, community policing has grown from a few small **foot patrol** projects to the preeminent reform agenda of modern policing.[4] In part, community policing evolved from strategies such as police-community relations, team policing, crime prevention, and foot patrol; however, the initial spark of finding better ways to police communities and beginning the movement toward community policing strategies was initiated with the research findings of the 1970s that shattered a few traditional assumptions about police patrol strategies. We begin with a brief review of some research findings that have had an impact on traditional police patrol strategies.

Kansas City Preventive Patrol Experiment

In the **Kansas City Preventive Patrol experiment,** researchers concluded that traditional routine patrol in marked police cars does not appear to affect the level of crime, nor does it affect the public's feeling of security.[5] The experiment demonstrated that urban police departments can successfully test patrol deployment strategies and that they can manipulate patrol resources without jeopardizing public safety.

Patrol is considered the backbone of the police department. Did you know that billions of dollars are spent each year in the United States to maintain and operate uniformed patrol? The traditional assumption underlying such deployment has been that the presence or potential presence of officers patrolling the streets in marked police cars deters people from committing crime, but the validity of this assumption had never been scientifically tested.

A Highway Patrol officer is rendering assistance to a stranded motorist on Interstate 70 in 1965.

Photo courtesy of the Kansas Highway Patrol

In 1972, with funding and technical assistance from the Police Foundation, the Kansas City Police Department launched a comprehensive, scientifically rigorous experiment to test the effects of police patrol on crime. The experiment began on October 1, 1972, and continued through September 30, 1973; it was administered by the Kansas City Police Department and evaluated by the Police Foundation.

Patrols were varied within 15 police beats. Routine preventive patrol was eliminated in 5 beats, labeled "reactive" beats (meaning officers entered these areas only in response to calls from residents). Normal routine patrol was maintained in 5 "control" beats, and in 5 "proactive" beats, patrol was intensified by two to three times the norm. The researchers asked the following questions:

1. Would citizens notice changes in the level of police patrol?
2. Would different levels of visible police patrol affect recorded crime or the outcome of victim surveys?
3. Would citizen fear of crime and attendant behavior change as a result of differing patrol levels?
4. Would their degree of satisfaction with police change?

Information was gathered from victimization surveys, reported crime rates, arrest data, a survey of local businesses, attitudinal surveys, and trained observers who monitored police-citizen interaction. Citizens did not notice the difference when the level of patrol was changed. Further, increasing or decreasing the level of police patrol had no significant effect on resident and commercial burglaries, auto thefts, larcenies involving auto accessories, robberies, or vandalism—crimes traditionally considered to be prevented by random, highly visible police patrol.

The rate at which crimes were reported to the police did not differ in any important or consistent way across the experimental beats. Citizen fear of crime was not affected by different levels of patrol, nor was citizen satisfaction with police altered. Ride-alongs by observers during the experiment also revealed that 60 percent of the time spent by a Kansas City patrol officer typically was noncommitted. For example, officers spent a considerable amount of time waiting to respond to calls for service; furthermore, they spent about as much time on non-police-related activities as they did on police-related mobile patrol.

Can you think of what implications this research had on police patrol strategies? What does this research tell us about traditional patrol strategies? The findings do not necessarily prove that a highly visible police presence has no impact on crime in selected circumstances. What they do suggest, however, is that routine preventive patrol in marked police cars has little value in preventing crime or making citizens feel safe. The overall implication is that resources ordinarily allocated to preventive patrol could safely be devoted to other, perhaps more productive, crime control and prevention strategies. More specifically, the results indicate that police deployment strategies could be based on targeted crime prevention and service goals rather than on routine preventive patrol.

It is important to point out that this experiment was conceived and executed by a local police department, with technical help from outside researchers. The experiment demonstrates that with the right kind of leadership and help, urban police departments can test new approaches to patrol. Thus, they can use their patrol resources to conduct such experiments without jeopardizing public safety. Perhaps more importantly, the Kansas City Preventive Patrol experiment challenged a traditional police practice.

The findings from the Kansas City Preventive Patrol experiment were not without controversy and left many police executives pondering the future of personnel increases within their organizations. Upon learning of the study, some local leaders felt that further increases in police personnel were not warranted and that decreases might even be justified.[6]

RAND Criminal Investigation Study

Consider the following scenario. You are out late one evening celebrating your 21st birthday with your college friends at the local pub. You leave the pub about 11:30 P.M. and begin the drive home to your apartment. After about 10 minutes, you arrive at your apartment and park your car in the parking lot. You walk to the front door of your apartment half asleep and tired from a long evening out. As you approach the door to your apartment,

A driver's license checkpoint near Lawrence, Kansas, in 1948.

you notice that something does not look right—something is definitely wrong! As you walk closer and closer, you see that the lock on the door has been broken and your apartment door is standing wide open. You cautiously peek inside the apartment and turn on the lights. You notice that the drawers in your bedroom have been ransacked and your stereo and other electronic equipment are missing. You then grab your cell phone and call the police and report that you have been the victim of a burglary. The dispatcher on the other end of the phone line tells you an officer will be there shortly.

After about 30 minutes (seems like 3 hours), an officer arrives and apologizes for the delay as she explains that it has been a busy night. The officer begins to write pertinent information down in her field notebook. She asks you many questions, such as what the serial numbers on the stereo unit are, what other items are missing, what time you left for the evening, and what the exact time was that you arrived home to discover the crime. After about 45 minutes, the officer explains to you that she is going to write up a burglary report and that it will be forwarded to the burglary detectives for a follow-up investigation. You ask anxiously about dusting for fingerprints; the officer smiles and relays to you that the suspects probably used gloves and that it was highly unlikely that any usable prints could be obtained. You are somewhat satisfied because the officer indicated to you that the report will be forwarded to the burglary detectives. You are now certain the detectives will take over the case and recover your property. Just hearing the word "detectives" calms you as you think to yourself, "They will get my property back and bring the thief to justice."

Police have relied on follow-up criminal investigation for many years. According to police scholar Joan Petersilia, the detective has developed a certain mystique that is based on the following three assumptions: (1) Most serious criminal cases can be solved, (2) most cases involving unknown criminals are solved through detective investigations that use special training and talents, and (3) all but the most minor criminal cases should be assigned for follow-up investigation.[7]

What do we really know about the effectiveness of criminal investigations? Do detectives solve most of the crimes they investigate? Are criminal investigations really all that effective? For many years, we did not know the answers to these important questions because of the lack of evaluations. In 1975, the **RAND Corporation** undertook a nationwide study of the criminal investigation process.[8] The study's main purpose was to measure the effectiveness of the police criminal investigation process as well as to describe how police investigations were organized and managed. RAND surveyed 150 large police agencies nationwide and conducted interviews and field observations in more than 25 police departments.

The results of the RAND study found that the most important factor that led to the identification of an offender, and thus the solution of a crime, was information that a victim or witness supplied to police officers at the scene of the crime. Furthermore, the cases that were not solved in that manner were solved usually by fingerprint searches or by informants.

Several other consistent conclusions emerged from the RAND study:[9]

1. Many serious crimes are not and often cannot be solved. Patrol officers are responsible, directly or indirectly, for most arrests: Either they arrest the suspect at the scene, or they obtain identification (or usually descriptions) of the criminal from victims or witnesses when the crime is initially reported.
2. Only a small percentage of all index crimes result from detective investigations that require special organization, training, or skill. Special investigations bring very few unknown criminals to justice.
3. Investigators play a critical role in the postarrest process, particularly in collecting evidence that will enable the prosecutor to file formal criminal charges.

The RAND study findings imply that traditional approaches to criminal investigation by police departments do not significantly affect the rate at which cases are solved. The study also suggests that most cases are solved by application of routine administrative procedures and that the effectiveness of criminal investigations would not be unduly lessened if approximately half of the investigative efforts were eliminated or shifted to more productive uses. Significant increases in criminal apprehension rates are more likely to be produced by more alert patrol units and improved citizen partnerships and cooperation than by refinements in investigative work. Among the suggested reforms are reduction of follow-up investigation on all cases except those involving the most serious offenses, establishment of a Major Offenders Unit to investigate serious crimes, employment of police strike forces, and placement of postarrest procedures in investigations under the authority of the prosecutor.[10]

Ohio State Highway Patrol Sgt. Burnet Hughes using an early radar unit in the 1950s.

Photo courtesy of Ohio State Highway Patrol

Foot Patrol Experiments

Over the past two decades, there has been a resurgence of foot patrol. With the advent of the automobile, most police agencies during the 1930s all but abandoned foot patrol strategies. Today one of the reasons that many police departments have returned to foot patrol strategies is to address the growing problem of decreased police-citizen interaction.[11] Foot patrol programs are designed to accomplish the following seven objectives[12]:

1. Decreasing the amount of actual or perceived criminal activity
2. Increasing perception of personal safety
3. Delivering residents a type of law enforcement service constant with community needs
4. Creating community awareness of crime problems and the methods of increasing the ability of law enforcement agencies to deal with actual or potential criminal activity effectively
5. Developing citizen volunteer action in support of the police that is aimed at various target crimes
6. Eliminating citizen apathy about crime reporting to the police
7. Increasing protection for women, children, and the aged

Like patrol deployment and criminal investigations functions discussed above, until relatively recently there were minimal evaluations of the effectiveness of foot patrol activities. One of the more referenced studies on foot patrol is the **Newark Foot Patrol experiment,** which was conducted in 1978. In 1973, New Jersey's state legislature passed the Safe and Clean Neighborhoods Act. Unique in the nation and aptly named, this legislation sought to create safe, clean neighborhoods. Foot patrol was specifically mandated as part of an effort to expand the presence and visibility of police protection.

At the invitation of the Governor of New Jersey, the Police Foundation evaluated foot patrol in 28 New Jersey cities. Newark was selected as the primary evaluation site. The evaluation began in February 1978 and ended in January 1979. The Police Foundation evaluation posed the following questions:[13]

1. Does foot patrol improve police-citizen relationships?
2. Do citizens feel safer when officers patrol on foot?
3. Does foot patrol reduce crime?
4. Will citizens report more crime when they have closer contact with the police?
5. Will more arrests be made in foot-patrolled areas?
6. Will foot patrol officers be more satisfied with their jobs and have more positive attitudes about citizens?
7. Will citizens' fear of victimization be lessened?

Eight foot patrol beats in Newark were matched demographically. Foot patrol was continued in four randomly selected beats and discontinued in four others; foot patrol was also initiated in four beats where it had not previously been used. Researchers then began comparing reported crime, arrest and victimization rates, and citizen fear and satisfaction with police services, as well as the attitude of foot patrol officers and officers on motorized patrol.

The Police Foundation found that introducing foot patrol along with a variety of other police strategies significantly enhances citizens' perception of safety in the neighborhood. This is something no other police strategy had been able to do. Although introducing foot patrol seemed to have little effect on crime rates, it did have the following five positive effects:[14]

1. Residents knew when officers were patrolling their neighborhoods on foot.
2. Residents in areas patrolled by officers on foot thought that crime was less of a problem than did residents in areas with only motorized patrol.
3. Residents in areas with foot patrol felt safer and less likely to be victimized.
4. Residents living in areas with foot patrol took fewer steps to protect themselves against crime.
5. Residents in areas with foot patrol were more satisfied with police services.

Residents in areas where foot patrol was introduced clearly changed their attitudes about how they viewed crime and how they felt about the safety and livability of their neighborhoods. They also were more satisfied with police services.

While foot patrol had no effect on recorded crime rates, it should be remembered that citizens feel threatened by noncriminal (disorderly) behavior as well and that this threat of victimization may dramatically alter their lives. In response to a perceived threat, they may, for instance, nail their windows shut, carry lethal weapons, or avoid walking in their own neighborhood. Thus, fear can undermine the viability of major cities and erode the quality of life for urban dwellers.

We suggest that close contact between police and the citizenry helps the former develop firsthand information about crime and possible criminal behavior. Such information systems are likely to have a positive long-term impact. In short, the results of this experiment suggest that while foot patrol may not reduce crime, it reduces citizens' fear of crime. Residents see their communities as safer and better places to live, and they are more satisfied with police services.

One other noted foot patrol experiment that found similar results as in Newark was the **Flint, Michigan, Foot Patrol experiment.**[15] In the Flint study, the researchers were more interested in examining citizens' perceptions of the police. The foot patrol in Flint greatly reduced the black-and-white perceptual disparity of police performance. The residents not only were satisfied with the program but also felt they had input into the role of the officer and influence on both the priorities of policing and the behavior of the officer. In effect, they felt that they had increased their control over the direction and operation of the police department. The foot patrol officers themselves were responsive to community needs and sensitive to the neighborhood culture. They were able to distinguish between the normative behavioral patterns prevalent in their beat areas and any truly threatening or dangerous acts and/or people. As a consequence, the positive formal interactions between individual foot patrol officers and individual citizens improved significantly. The foot patrol officers, for example, became less prone than motorized officers to conduct pat-downs.

So what does the research of the 1970s and 1980s really tell us? In the case of the Kansas City Preventive Patrol experiment, we discovered that variations of police patrol had little impact on crime or citizens' perceptions of crime or their satisfaction with the police. So placing many police officers into an area of the community has minimal long-term effects on crime and disorder or on citizens' perceptions of the police. The RAND criminal investigation study revealed that follow-up criminal investigation may not be as effective as once thought and that most crimes are solved because someone saw the suspect, someone wrote down a tag number, or someone heard something. Finally, what we know from the evaluations of foot patrol suggests that while foot patrol may not have an impact on reducing crime, it does reduce citizens' fear of crime. Residents see their communities as safer and better places to live and are more satisfied with police services.

Community Relations, Team Policing, and Other Factors

The current community policing movement developed out of the police-community relations programs of the 1950s and 1960s, the team policing strategies of the 1970s, and the increase of citizen fear of crime that began to dominate public policy formation in the 1980s.[16] We point out that **team policing** is a product of a movement called strategic policing, and by this we mean a philosophy of crime fighting emphasizing improving the efficiency and technical capabilities of the police. A remnant of scientific management, it focuses on improving productivity through increased efficiency. While community policing advocates embracing some of these goals, there are significant differences. Team policing is a tactic intended to help the police perform traditional crime fighting more efficiently; it focuses on but fails to specifically assign accountability. Team policing may be effective in certain problem-solving efforts.[17]

The evolution of community policing was sparked by several key elements: First, research studies increasingly challenged police to change their way of thinking as well as their strategies in battling crime and disorder problems; second, a growing fear of crime was present among the general citizenry; third, community-oriented policing strategies are a direct carry-over from past police practices such as team policing and police-community relations programs. While we acknowledge that a change of thinking is not an easy task and that the research findings discussed above created a firestorm at the time, perhaps there are better ways of dealing with crime and disorder. This is exactly what the philosophy of community-oriented policing challenges police executives to think about.

Research on Traditional Policing

The following list presents a review of the research on **traditional policing:**

1. Increasing the numbers of police does not lower the crime rate or increase the proportion of solved crimes.
2. Randomized motor patrol neither lowers crime nor increases the chances of catching suspects.
3. Two-person patrol cars are not more effective in lowering crime rates or catching criminals than one-person cars; they are safer.
4. Saturation patrol does not reduce crime; instead, it displaces crime.
5. The kind of crime that most terrifies Americans (mugging, rape, robbery, burglary, and homicide) is rarely encountered by police on patrol.
6. Improving response time on calls has no effect on the likelihood of arresting criminals or even in satisfying involved citizens.
7. Crimes are not solved through criminal investigations conducted by police; they are solved because suspects are immediately apprehended or someone identifies them (name or license number).

Source: Jerome Skolnick and David H. Bayley, *The New Blue Line* (New York: Free Press, 1986).

COMMUNITY-ORIENTED POLICING

In part, community-oriented policing has evolved through the work of the Police Foundation and the School of Criminal Justice, Michigan State University. Community-oriented policing is presented in the literature as a philosophy as well as a management approach that promotes community, government, and police partnerships and that uses proactive problem solving to address the causes of crime, fear of crime, and other community issues.[18] Community-oriented policing is not a program; it is a philosophy or strategy, a way all department members (from the top to the bottom, sworn to nonsworn) view their job. This philosophy must permeate the entire organization, local government, and the community, not just the community policing officers or the patrol division, for example.[19] Community-oriented policing involves fundamental and strategic change in almost all areas of policing.[20] It requires police officers to identify and respond to a broad array of problems such as crime, disorder, fear of crime, drug use, urban decay, and other neighborhood concerns. Professor Robert Friedmann offers yet another definition of community policing:

> Community policing is a policy and a strategy aimed at achieving more effective and efficient crime control, reduced fear of crime, improved quality of life, improved police services and police legitimacy, through a proactive reliance on community resources that seeks to change crime causing conditions. This assumes a need for greater accountability of police, greater public share in decision making, and greater concern for civil rights and liberties.[21]

Put another way, community-oriented policing is a philosophy of policing based on the concept that the police and citizens working together in creative ways can solve contemporary community problems related to crime, fear of crime, social and physical disorder, and general neighborhood conditions. The philosophy is founded on the belief that achieving these goals requires the police to develop a new relationship with citizens, allowing them the power to set local police priorities and involving them in efforts to improve the overall quality of life in their community. Community-oriented policing shifts the focus of police work from just handling random crime calls to addressing community concerns.

There appears to be some debate as to whether community-oriented policing and problem-oriented policing are two separate strategies. We argue that problem-oriented policing (or problem solving) is an intricate part of community-oriented policing. Most definitions of community policing include problem solving. Thus, community-oriented policing is a strategy that entails crime prevention, problem solving, community partnerships, and organizational transformation.[22] We choose to present problem-oriented policing as a separate section in this chapter, and we argue that problem-oriented policing is an important ingredient in holistic community-oriented policing.

TABLE 3–1

Traditional Versus Community Policing: A Comparison		
Question	Traditional Policing	Community Policing
Who are the police?	Government agency principally responsible for law enforcement	View that the police are the public and the public are the police (but police officers paid to give full-time attention to duties of every citizen)
What is the relation of the police force to other public service departments?	Often conflicting priorities	Police one department among many responsible for improving quality of life
What is the role of the police?	Focus on solving crimes	Broader problem-solving approach
How is police efficiency measured?	Detection and arrest rates	Absence of crime and disorder
What are the highest priorities?	High-value crimes (e.g., bank robberies) and violent crimes	Whatever problems most disturbing to community
What specifically do police deal with?	Incidents	Citizens' problems and concerns
What determines the effectiveness of police?	Response times	Public cooperation
What view do police take of service calls?	Tasks when there is no real police work to do	Vital function and great opportunity
What is police professionalism?	Swift, effective response to serious crime	Closeness to community
What kind of intelligence is most important?	Crime intelligence (study of particular crimes or series of crimes)	Criminal intelligence (information about activities of individuals or groups)
What is the essential nature of police accountability?	Highly centralized; governed by rules, regulations, and policy directives; accountable to the law	Emphasis on local accountability to community needs
What is the role of headquarters?	Provision of necessary rules and policy directives	Dissemination of organizational values
What is the role of the press liaison department?	Act of keeping "heat" off operational officers so they can get on with job	Act of coordinating essential channels of communication with community
How do the police regard prosecutions?	Important goal	One tool among many
Whom do they work for? Who is the boss?	Chief of police, mayor, or city	People of community or city (citizens)
Who is the "enemy"?	Criminals (or anybody who gets in way of doing job)	Things that cause disorder and/or situations that cause people to commit acts destructive to community

TABLE 3–1

Traditional Versus Community Policing: A Comparison (continued)		
Question	Traditional Policing	Community Policing
What is the role of citizens?	Reporting of crimes and cooperation with officers by obeying their requests and otherwise staying out of the way	Reporting of crimes and other information about conditions of community; cooperation with police; obedience to orders in criminal matters; provision of aid and assistance when possible; leadership in determining community standards and actions of priority

Source: William R. Parks II, "Community Policing: A Foundation for Restorative Justice." Web posted at http://www.realjustice.org/pages/t2000/t2000_wparks.html. Accessed April 23, 2004.

The ideas of community policing are relatively simplistic inasmuch as the police take on a role of being more community-oriented and the citizens take on a role of being more involved with assisting the police with information.[23] Some scholars argue that with community policing, police officers will be expected to become partners with the community in maintaining social order.[24]

Community policing differs from traditional law enforcement because it allows police the freedom to expand the scope of their jobs. Police in this sense are challenged to become community problem solvers and encouraged to use their time creatively; likewise, police will be required to use the vast amount of information and available resources to aid them in problem solving.

Many have speculated on the importance of the police working in partnership with citizens, as well as private and public organizations, in order to solve problems and improve the quality of life in neighborhoods. For example, Robert Trojanowicz observed, "Community policing requires a department-wide philosophical commitment to involve average citizens as partners in the process of reducing and controlling the contemporary problems of crime, drugs, fear of crime, and neighborhood decay; and in efforts to improve overall quality of life in the community."[25] There are many police agencies that report receiving federal funding for community policing and that are now working in partnership with community groups and other organizations to identify and solve problems.

What is particularly interesting about community-oriented policing is that it has been implemented across American police agencies in differing ways. In fact, there appears to be some confusion over how community policing is implemented from one agency to the next; despite the benefits claimed for community policing, programmatic implementation has been very uneven. Even though it is universally said to be important, it means different things to different people.[26] For example, evaluations have found that there were stark variations in community policing programs among Florida police agencies.[27] Similarly, evaluations of community policing by the VERA Institute of Justice in eight American cities found that the objectives and uses of community policing grants in these cities were varied in nature.[28]

In spite of the differences in the manner in which community policing is implemented[29] from one agency to the next, there are a number of principles that should be followed regardless of how it is implemented. What follows is a presentation of the 10 well-known principles of community policing proposed by Robert Trojanowicz and Bonnie Bucqueroux.[30]

1. *Philosophy and organizational strategy.* Community policing is a philosophy (a way of thinking) as well as an organizational strategy (a way to carry out the philosophy) that allows the police and the community to work closely together in creative ways to solve the problems of crime, illicit drugs, fear of crime, physical and social disorder (from graffiti to addiction), and neighborhood decay that affect the overall quality of life in the community. The philosophy rests on the belief that people deserve input into the police process in exchange for their participation and support. It also rests on the belief that solutions to today's community problems demand freeing both people and the police to explore creative new ways to address neighborhood concerns beyond a narrow focus on individual crime incidents.

2. *Commitment to community empowerment.* Community policing's organizational strategy first demands that everyone in the police department, including both civilian and sworn personnel, must investigate ways to translate the philosophy of power sharing into practice. This demands making a subtle but sophisticated shift so that everyone in the department understands the need to focus on solving community problems in creative ways that often can include challenging and enlightening people regarding the process of policing themselves. Community policing implies a shift within the department that grants greater autonomy (freedom to make decisions) to line officers, which also implies enhanced respect for their judgment as police professionals. Within the community, citizens (as full-fledged partners with the police) must share in the rights and responsibilities implicit in identifying, prioritizing, and solving problems.

3. *Decentralized and personalized policing.* To implement true community policing, police departments must also create and develop a new breed of line officer who acts as a direct link between the police and the people in the community. As the department's community outreach specialists, community policing officers must be freed from the isolation of the patrol car and the demands of the police radio so that they can maintain daily, direct, face-to-face contact with the people they serve in a clearly defined beat area. Ultimately, all officers should practice the community policing approach.

4. *Immediate and long-term proactive problem solving.* The community policing officer's broad role demands continuous, sustained contact with the law-abiding people in the community so that together they can explore creative new solutions to local concerns, with private citizens serving as supporters and as

volunteers. Regarding law enforcement, community policing officers respond to calls for service and make arrests, but they also go beyond this narrow focus to develop and monitor broad-based, long-term initiatives that can involve all elements of the community in efforts to improve the quality of life. As the community's ombudsman, the community policing officer also acts as a link to other public and private agencies that can help in a given situation.

5. *Ethics, legality, responsibility, and trust.* Community policing implies a new contract between the police and the citizens they serve, one that offers hope of overcoming widespread apathy while restraining any impulse of vigilantism. This new relationship, based on mutual trust and respect, also suggests that the police can serve as a catalyst, challenging people to accept their share of responsibility for the overall quality of life in the community. Community policing means that citizens will be asked to handle more of their minor concerns themselves, but in exchange, this will free police to work with people on developing immediate as well as long-term solutions for community concerns in ways that encourage mutual accountability and respect.

6. *Expansion of the police mandate.* Community policing adds a vital, proactive element to the traditional reactive role of the police, resulting in full-spectrum policing service. As the only agency of social control open 24 hours a day, 7 days a week, the police must maintain the ability to respond immediately to crises and crime incidents, but community policing broadens the police role so that the police can have a greater impact by making changes today that hold the promise of making communities safer and more attractive places to live tomorrow.

7. *Help for those with special needs.* Community policing stresses exploring new ways to protect and enhance the lives of those who are most vulnerable— juveniles, the elderly, minorities, the poor, the disabled, the homeless. It both assimilates and broadens the scope of previous outreach efforts such as crime prevention and police community relations.

8. *Grassroots creativity and support.* Community policing promotes the judicious use of technology, but it also rests on the belief that nothing surpasses what dedicated human beings, talking and working together, can achieve. It invests trust in all those who are on the front lines out on the streets, relying on their combined judgment, wisdom, and experience to fashion creative new approaches to contemporary community concerns.

9. *Internal change.* Community policing must be a fully integrated approach that involves everyone in the department, with community policing officers serving as generalists who bridge the gap between the police and the people they serve. The community policing approach plays a crucial role internally by providing information about and awareness of the community and its problems as well as by enlisting broad-based community support for the department's overall objectives. Once community policing is accepted as the long-term strategy, all officers should practice it (this could take as long as 10 to 15 years).

10. *Focus on the future.* Community policing provides decentralized, personalized police service to the community. It recognizes that the police cannot impose order on the community from the outside but that people must be encouraged to think of the police as a resource they can use in helping to solve contemporary community problems. It is not a tactic to be applied and then abandoned, but a new philosophy and organizational strategy that provides the flexibility to meet local needs and priorities as they change over time.

PROBLEM-ORIENTED POLICING

Every Friday evening, youth from all over the city congregate in the local park, and the police have received many reports of disturbances, profanity, drinking, and vandalism. In fact, it seems that every Friday evening for the past several months, the police respond to the park for disturbances or vandalism. The citizens living in the area are afraid to walk in the park or even to get near it on Friday evenings because of the idle youth. The police officers who work in the area are dumbfounded as to what to do and the citizens are slowly losing faith in the police department.

Police spend an enormous amount of time responding to problems such as the one presented above. The common approach of dispatching the police to the park and making multiple arrests, and directing the idle youth to leave the park, will do very little to solve the problem. With this approach, the problem would be solved only on a short-term basis (most likely for that evening). Problem-oriented policing is an important part of community-oriented policing and is designed to address problems within a community. The goal of problem solving is to eliminate the root causes of problems as well as to eliminate small disorder problems that could very well become serious police-related problems if they are not taken care of early. Thus, problem-oriented policing is designed to identify and remove the causes of recurring crime and disorder problems that harm communities.[31]

Recall that in the late 1970s researchers, police professionals, and policy makers became interested in improving the effectiveness of policing. Research during this period pointed out the limitations of random patrol, rapid response, and follow-up criminal investigation practices that had been the foundation of policing for many years. Much like those for community-oriented policing, these findings laid the groundwork for the emergence of problem-oriented policing. The research yielded some important insights:[32]

1. Police deal with a range of community problems, many of which are not strictly criminal in nature.
2. Arrest and prosecution alone—the traditional functions of the criminal justice system—do not always effectively resolve problems.
3. Giving the officers, who have great insight into community problems, the discretion to design solutions is extremely valuable in solving the problems.
4. Police can use a variety of methods to redress recurrent problems.
5. The community values police involvement in noncriminal problems and recognizes the contribution the police can make to solving these problems.

Professor Herman Goldstein's seminal article, which appeared in *Crime and Delinquency* in 1979, described how police can be more effective by using problem-solving approaches as part of their strategies.[33] Professor Goldstein, considered by many to be the pioneer of problem-oriented policing, started a revolution. As a result, during the 1980s, a number of law enforcement agencies throughout the United States and in other countries began a wide variety of problem-oriented policing initiatives.[34] Herman Goldstein defines problem-oriented policing:

> [It is] an approach to policing in which discrete pieces of police business (each consisting of a cluster of similar incidents, whether crime or acts of disorder, that the police are expected to handle) are subject to *microscopic examination* (drawing on the especially honed skills of crime analysts and the accumulated experience of operating field personnel) in hopes that what is freshly learned about each problem will lead to discovering a *new and more effective strategy* for dealing with it. Problem-oriented policing places a high value on new responses that are *preventive* in nature, that are *not dependent on the use of the criminal justice system,* and that *engage other public agencies, the community and the private sector* when their involvement has the potential for significantly contributing to the reduction of the problem. Problem-oriented policing carries a commitment to *implementing* the new strategy, rigorously *evaluating its effectiveness,* and, subsequently, *reporting the results* in ways that will benefit other police agencies and that will ultimately contribute to building a body of knowledge that supports the further professionalization of the police.[35]

Goldstein's contribution to the idea of problem solving in policing is primarily a response to several concerns. First, police departments tend to overemphasize operational effectiveness outside the department. Second, police departments devote too little time to developing measures for reducing and preventing crime and instead tend to concentrate almost exclusively on reactive policing. Third, police departments largely ignore the wealth of community resources that is available to solve problems that eventually become matters for the police. Similarly, they tend to make poor use of a second important resource: "Within police agencies, police have readily available to them another resource: their rank-and-file police officers, whose time and talent have not been used effectively."[36] Goldstein also argues for organizational change within police agencies and maintains that police agencies have to adapt if they are going be more effective. According to John Eck and William Spelman, there are a number of ways that a problem can be solved in the community: by totally eliminating it, by reducing the number of incidents, by reducing the seriousness of the incidents it creates, by designing methods for better handling of the incidents, or by removing it from police consideration.[37]

Professors Michael Scott and Herman Goldstein, both with the Center for Problem-Oriented Policing, argue that the key elements to problem-oriented policing entail at least 12 important assumptions:[38]

1. A problem is the basic unit of police work rather than a crime, a case, a call, or an incident.
2. A problem is something that concerns or causes harm to citizens, not just the police. Things that concern only police officers are important, but they are not problems in this sense of the term.
3. Addressing problems means more than quick fixes; it means dealing with conditions that create problems.

4. Police officers must routinely and systematically analyze problems before trying to solve them, just as they routinely and systematically investigate crimes before making an arrest. Individual officers and the department as a whole must develop routines and systems for analyzing problems.

5. The analysis of problems must be thorough even though it may not need to be complicated. This principle is as true for problem analysis as it is for criminal investigation.

6. Problems must be described precisely and accurately and broken down into specific aspects of the problem. Problems often aren't what they first appear to be.

7. Problems must be understood in terms of the various interests at stake. Individuals and groups of people are affected in different ways by a problem and have different ideas about what should be done about the problem.

8. The way the problem is currently being handled must be understood and the limits of effectiveness must be openly acknowledged in order to come up with a better response.

9. Initially, any and all possible responses to a problem should be considered so as not to cut short potentially effective responses. Suggested responses should follow from what is learned during the analysis. They should not be limited to, nor rule out, the use of arrest.

10. The police must proactively try to solve problems rather than just react to the harmful consequences of problems.

11. The police department must increase police officers' freedom to make or participate in important decisions. At the same time, officers must be accountable for their decision making.

12. The effectiveness of new responses must be evaluated so that these results can be shared with other police officers and so that the department can systematically learn what does and does not work.

In the early 1980s, experiments in problem-oriented policing occurred in Madison, Wisconsin; Baltimore County, Maryland; and London, England. The first evaluation of an agency-wide implementation of problem-oriented policing took place in the Newport News, Virginia, Police Department by the Police Executive Research Forum in the mid-1980s. Since then, many police agencies in the United States as well as in Australia, Canada, New Zealand, Scandinavia, and the United Kingdom have continued to experiment with problem-oriented policing, to apply it to a wide range of crime and disorder problems, and to change their organizations to better support problem-oriented policing.[39]

There are a number of different problem-solving techniques that exist in problem-solving initiatives; one of the most popular is known by the acronym **SARA,** which stands for scanning, analysis, response, and assessment.[40]

Scanning identifies a problem through a variety of sources of information, such as calls for service and citizen surveys. Citizens must consider the problem as important for this phase to succeed. *Analysis* requires the examination of the nature of the problem. Input from police and residents pertaining to the problem is important, as is the collection of data the

The SARA Model

SCANNING

- Identifying recurring problems of concern to the public and the police
- Identifying the consequences of the problem for the community and the police
- Prioritizing those problems
- Developing broad goals
- Confirming that the problems exist
- Determining how frequently the problem occurs and how long it has been taking place
- Selecting problems for closer examination

ANALYSIS

- Identifying and understanding the events and conditions that precede and accompany the problem
- Identifying relevant data to be collected
- Researching what is known about the problem type
- Taking inventory of how the problem is currently addressed and the strengths and limitations of the current response
- Narrowing the scope of the problem as specifically as possible
- Identifying a variety of resources that may be of assistance in developing a deeper understanding of the problem
- Developing a working hypothesis about why the problem is occurring

RESPONSE

- Brainstorming for new interventions
- Searching for what other communities with similar problems have done
- Choosing among the alternative interventions
- Outlining a response plan and identifying responsible parties
- Stating the specific objectives for the response plan
- Carrying out the planned activities

ASSESSMENT

- Determining whether the plan was implemented (a process evaluation)
- Collecting pre- and post-response qualitative and quantitative data
- Determining whether broad goals and specific objectives were attained
- Identifying any new strategies needed to augment the original plan
- Conducting ongoing assessment to ensure continued effectiveness

Source: Herman Goldstein, *Problem-Oriented Policing,* 1990.

department may have about the frequency, location, and other significant characteristics of the problem. Third, *response* fashions one or more preferred solutions to the problem. This step, as well as the preceding step, benefits from creative deliberation, or "thinking outside the box." Input clearly should come from police personnel, but also from residents, experts, and other individuals who can address the problem thoughtfully. The last part of the **SARA problem-solving model** is *assessment,* which evaluates the effectiveness of the expected solution. Agencies must evaluate the solution as objectively as possible because this step speaks to end products, the key theme in problem-solving initiatives.[41]

EVALUATIONS OF COMMUNITY POLICING

Without some sort of gauge to let us know whether programs actually work, we would be wasting much of our time and energy. **Evaluation research** is typically the last stage of the policy process. For example, once a policy, program, or strategy has been implemented, evaluation usually tells whether the policy or program or strategy has been effective. Thus, evaluation research allows us to gain insight into whether something is effective. Evaluation research asks these types of questions: Do programs work? Do they provide the desired result? Do they provide enough benefits to justify their costs? Are there better ways to attack these problems? Should the programs be maintained, improved, or eliminated?

As discussed previously, community-oriented policing is a strategy whose goals are to make communities and neighborhoods safer, to remove disorder, to solve problems, and to prevent crime. In order to determine the success of community-oriented policing, an evaluation of the strategy must be initiated. An evaluation "is the systematic application of social research procedures for assessing the conceptualization, design, implementation, and utility of social intervention programs."[42] An evaluation is used to judge and improve the ways in which programs have been conducted from the earliest stages of implementation through the program's development. A program should be evaluated so that policy makers, funding sources, program administrators, and stakeholders can obtain feedback as to the effectiveness and efficiency of the program implemented. To obtain answers in a **program evaluation,** the following questions should be answered:[43]

1. What is the nature and scope of the problem requiring new, expanded, or modified social programs? Where is it located, and whom does it affect?
2. What feasible interventions are likely to significantly ameliorate the problem?
3. What are the appropriate target populations for particular interventions?
4. Is the intervention reaching the target population?
5. Is it effective?
6. How much does it cost?
7. What are its costs relative to its effectiveness and benefits?

The answers to these questions are important for local and specialized programs; therefore, they are important to any community policing strategy. The importance of evaluating community policing should not be underestimated. Devising strategies to remove disorder and crime from communities and neighborhoods requires that they be evaluated to determine if they have achieved their intended purpose. Evaluation goes along with the need to initiate purposeful, deliberate, and organized attempts to establish new programs and improve old ones.

Recall that approximately 86 percent of the nation's population is served by law enforcement agencies practicing community policing, compared with 15 percent in 1993. The Bureau of Justice reported that two-thirds of all local police departments and 62 percent of sheriff's offices had full-time sworn law personnel engaged in community policing activities. Community-oriented policing was the recurring theme of the Clinton administration's anticrime policy, and a fair number of police agencies began to use the strategy as a result of federal expenditures to support the implementation of community policing.

Is community policing—with its emphasis on community partnerships, problem solving, and organizational transformation—effective? Some evaluations conducted on community-oriented policing show promising results. Mary Ann Wycoff and Jeffrey Skogan investigated the implementation and impact of community policing in Madison, Wisconsin, and found very positive results. They discovered that it was possible for a traditional police department to change and that the community and officers both benefited from improved attitudes. Attitudes of police toward the organization and their work improved. Accompanying these changes was both a reduction in citizens' perceptions that crime was a problem in their neighborhood and an increase in the belief that police were working on problems of importance to people in the neighborhood.[44]

An evaluation of the Community Patrol Officer Program in New York City found many reasons for satisfaction and optimism for the future. The study evaluated New York City's Community Patrol Officer Program (CPOP), which attempts to put community policing into practice at the beat level. Beginning as a pilot project in 1984 and expanding to all 75 precincts in 1989, the program gives the individual community patrol officer (CPO) responsibility for addressing crime and order-maintenance problems in a 16- to 60-block beat, which is usually patrolled on foot. Data were collected from 1986 to 1988 from interviews with CPOs and their supervisors and from observations and records of 54 CPOP beats.[45] The most important function of the CPO is to carry out problem solving in the beat area. Community patrol officers were most effective in attacking street-level drug problems and least effective in dealing with parking and traffic problems.

There was no evidence of a lasting CPOP effect on reported burglaries or robberies or on the number of calls for service, but community leaders reported that CPOP units contributed significantly to improved relations between the police and the community. The core of CPOP is the application of the problem-solving process in the context of a local community. When done well, it produces significant benefits for the residents, improves police-community relations, and enhances officer job satisfaction. That it can be and has been done well is the most important evaluation finding. Recommendations envision improved training for CPOs and supervisors, disseminating information about successful problem-solving strategies, encouraging the involvement of a representative body of citizens in each beat, and other measures.[46]

Researchers David Weisburd and John Eck found evidence to support continued investment in police innovations that call for greater focus and tailoring of police efforts, combined with an expansion of the toolbox of policing beyond simple law enforcement. The strongest evidence of police effectiveness in reducing crime and disorder is found in the case of geographically focused police practices, such as hot-spots policing. Community policing practices are found to reduce fear of crime, but the researchers did not find consistent evidence that community policing (when it is implemented without models of problem-oriented policing) affects either crime or disorder; a developing body of evidence does point to the effectiveness of problem-oriented policing in reducing crime, disorder, and fear.[47]

The Wichita, Kansas, Police Department initiated community policing by assigning 17 specially trained community police officers to four high-crime target neighborhoods. They were asked to work with the community to accomplish something that many officers felt was impossible.[48] Police held meetings with neighborhood associations. Three goals were identified: (1) Reduce prostitution and crime, (2) improve police-community cooperation through partnerships, and (3) improve the appearance of the neighborhood. The neighborhood created a steering committee to guide the neighborhood initiative. The Wichita Police Department reported most impressive results. During a 20-week evaluation period, prostitution decreased 41 percent and prostitution-related crimes decreased 47 percent; in addition, 911 calls to the neighborhood decreased 16 percent.[49]

In one other evaluation, researchers used the Arrestee Drug Abuse Monitoring (ADAM) program as a research platform for understanding the impact of recent New York City policing initiatives on arrestee behavior.[50] During the second half of 1999, 892 New York City arrestees were interviewed. For this analysis, researchers compiled the responses to the standard ADAM questionnaire, ADAM drug test results, responses to a special New York City Police questionnaire, and official New York State criminal histories.

Initiatives against publicly annoying behaviors, such as loitering, panhandling, beating transit fares, urinating in public, publicly consuming alcohol or using marijuana, and exhibiting disorderly conduct, are called quality-of-life (QOL) policing. The NYPD wanted to know if offenders were aware that police had stepped up efforts to control QOL offenses, and if so, what their response was. As a related issue, the department wanted to know if those arrested for QOL offenses are truthful about their other criminal activities in their postarrest interviews.

The researchers found that the arrestees appeared to be getting the message. Arrestees reported their awareness that police were targeting people for a variety of QOL offenses. On average, about half of the offenders said that in response they had stopped or cut down on those activities in the past 6 months. (The greatest decrease was among fare beaters; almost 70 percent reported that they had stopped or decreased beating their fare after becoming aware of QOL initiatives.)

Offenders primarily cited an increased police presence and a consciousness on the street of a stepped-up police focus on QOL behaviors (rather than their personal contact with the criminal justice system) as the reason for changing their behavior. The researchers concluded that QOL policing initiatives can provide a general deterrent to these types of activities.

FUTURE OF COMMUNITY-ORIENTED POLICING

Community policing represents the next major reform in policing and is a mechanism for fundamental change within policing. This change encompasses not only the manner in which communities are policed but also the way in which organizational change is implemented. **Organizational change** involves changes in management and leadership, organizational structure, purpose and values. We discuss organizational change in detail in Chapter 11. There are several factors that will impact the future of community-oriented policing: federal government support, crime rates, and projected trends.

Federal Government Support

The federal government is the main support behind community policing efforts in the United States. For example, the passage of the Violent Crime Control and Law Enforcement Act in 1994 represents an investment of more than $30 billion over six years; in essence this was the largest federal anti-crime legislation in the nation's history.[51] Subsequent to this legislation, the federal government became directly involved in the implementation of community-oriented policing. Furthermore, the 1994 Crime Act authorized the hiring of 100,000 officers to perform community policing duties within their agencies.

Financial support for community policing has been readily available throughout the 1990s and into the 21st century. For example, recently Deputy Attorney General James Comey and the U.S. Department of Justice Office of Community-Oriented Policing Services (COPS) announced grants totaling $20.7 million to add 194 officers to the nation's schools.[52] The grants are being awarded to 111 law enforcement agencies in 42 states and Puerto

Rico through the COPS in Schools program, which funds the hiring of police officers who are assigned to a school as their community policing beat.

The grants will provide a maximum of $125,000 toward the salary and benefits of each new school resource officer (SRO) over three years. COPS also delivers training on school safety issues for each new SRO and for an administrator from the school to which the officer is assigned. The training includes topics ranging from development of emergency response plans and safety assessments of schools to child development and cultural fluency. Including the $20.7 million grant discussed above, the COPS in Schools program has provided over $700 million to hire and train 6,300 school resource officers.

Similarly, the U.S. Department of Justice Office of Community-Oriented Policing Services (COPS) recently announced $27.1 million in grants to be used by local police and sheriff's departments to hire additional officers. The grants were awarded to 85 law enforcement agencies in 42 states and Puerto Rico and will be used to hire 370 community policing officers. The grants were awarded under the COPS Universal Hiring Program, and they provide 75 percent of the total salary and benefits of each new officer over three years, up to a maximum of $75,000 per officer. In support of making communities safer by helping to increase the number of community policing officers on patrol in local jurisdictions, COPS has funded the addition of over 118,000 officers by more than 13,000 law enforcement agencies since 1994.[53]

Crime Rates

Not only will federal government support of community policing keep its momentum strong in the future, but lowered crime rates will also provide a boost. In the 1960s and 1970s, America saw a burgeoning crime rate, which brought about much fear of crime among the general citizenry; however, since the 1990s the crime rate has been falling. For example, during the first six months of 1993, the nation experienced a 3.1 percent decrease in violent crime and a 0.8 percent decrease in property crime when compared with data submitted for the first six months in 2002.[54] In nearly all major cities, including New York, Los Angeles, and Chicago, the number of murders has dropped significantly.

In light of the downward crime trend since 1994, there is also a belief that American cities are becoming safer.[55] New York City is a prime example. New York's violent crime rate has continued to fall, bringing it down to a level not seen since the 1960s. According to statistics from the New York City Police Department, between January 1 and March 17, 2002, the murder rate in the city was nearly 40 percent (39.7 percent) lower than it was for the same period the previous year; citywide 85 people were murdered, and in Manhattan only 11 homicides were reported, compared with 28 in 2001. Overall violent crime rate was down 7.9 percent.

It is no coincidence that the nation's crime rates began to take a downward turn after the evolution of community policing strategies. We acknowledge the role of community policing in falling crime rates, although we do recognize that there may be other factors that come into play. Community-oriented policing has received much praise. In a 1997 speech, President Bill Clinton stated, "In 1997, crime decreased for the sixth straight year thanks in part to community policing. Our commitment to America's law enforcement officers is working to keep our streets and communities safe."[56]

Projected Trends

In 2000, a **futures conference** was held at the FBI Academy in Quantico, Virginia.[57] The conference, titled "Futuristics and Law Enforcement—The Millennium Conference," was attended by distinguished individuals with diverse backgrounds, including policing, academia, and literature. The purpose of the conference was to take the first steps toward producing a vision for policing in the 21st century in five areas: the future of technology and its effect on law enforcement; the future of leadership and management in policing agencies; future crime/future law; the future of policing practices and philosophies; and the changing face of America (demographics and policing). The attendees examined possible futures for law enforcement and formulated strategies that police leaders will be able to employ to create the "preferred future" for their agencies and communities. There were four trends that we point out here due to their projections for the future of community policing:

TABLE 3–2

Projections for the Future of Community Policing[1]

Trend	Year			
	2005	2010	2015	2020
Agencies will adopt the principles of community policing and problem solving as a daily practice.	38	53	72	88
Formal structures will be adopted to support "combat" policing and community policing specialists.	11	14	19	22
Community policing will foster greater communication within agencies.	31	44	63	73
There will be a continued shift in delivering police services to the local neighborhood level, which allows for more officer empowerment and ownership of neighborhood problems.	32	35	68	81

[1] Expressed in percentages.

The authors anticipate that community policing will continue to be the driving force in American police agencies. We base our projections not only on the plethora of community policing literature but also on many anecdotal accounts from innovative-thinking police practitioners who realize that this is the opportune time to fundamentally change the state of American policing. Specifically we project that community policing will continue to drive needed change in the following four areas of policing:

1. *Organizational change.* There will be a move away from the paramilitary policing model to a more corporate model of policing.
2. *Police partnership with citizens.* There will be increased recognition that the police cannot solve all crime-related problems without the help of the citizenry.
3. *Management and leadership change.* There will be a move toward more modern management and leadership approaches and away from an authoritarian command and control culture.
4. *Policing strategies.* There will be a move toward proactive problem-solving strategies and away from incident-driven policing.

VALUE-BASED INITIATIVES

As you have discovered in this chapter, community policing is a proactive approach to law enforcement that goes beyond the traditional policing model of reacting to crime by arresting and incarcerating criminals. It recognizes that crime does not occur in a vacuum and that the best way to control crime is to address the continuum of human and community issues that lie at the root of most criminal activity. This requires the police to join forces with the community, forming problem-solving partnerships to develop viable strategies for dealing with the constellation of factors associated with crime and disorder. In recent years, the Office of Community-Oriented Policing Services, which created the **Value-Based Initiative** as an effective community policing strategy, has encouraged law enforcement agencies to partner with faith-based organizations through this initiative. Value-Based Initiatives give faith-based organizations a place at the collaboration table, allowing them to share their unique insights about crime and other social problems that plague their communities.[58]

Value-Based Initiatives emphasize problem solving on a community level through community-led initiatives that explore and promote what a community values most, and these initiatives also encourage law enforcement agencies to create or strengthen local projects that build trust between the police and faith-based groups in the community. These initiatives are designed to identify and meet the individual needs of residents, thereby promoting the overall health of a community.

The infrastructure of Value-Based Initiatives builds on past community-based initiatives by leveraging existing resources in the community. A community's capacity to address its own issues is then enhanced.

Goals of Value-Based Initiatives

Value-Based Initiatives have several goals, including strengthening partnerships between law enforcement and the community, furthering the community's role as a partner in crime reduction efforts, identifying and addressing social issues that diminish the quality of life in the community, and linking those in need to services and resources that currently exist in the community.[59]

Summary of Value-Based Initiatives

Following is a list of cities and their Value-Based Initiatives:

- *Boston.* Boston's Value-Based Initiative focuses primarily on prisoner reentry. The Boston Police Department works with four faith-based partners in this collaborative effort: Boston Ten Point Coalition, Nation of Islam, Ella J. Baker House, and Bruce Wall Ministries. Value-Based Initiative mentors meet with inmates while they are still in prison and then continue to work with them upon their release.
- *Fort Wayne, Indiana.* The Fort Wayne, Indiana, Police Department partners with Stop the Madness and the Fort Wayne Ministerial Alliance to focus on helping ex-offenders reenter the community and on stopping youth violence. In addition, almost 200 ministers and community members have graduated from Fort Wayne's Ministerial Police Academy, which is also part of its Value-Based Initiative.
- *Fort Worth, Texas.* Fort Worth, Texas, opened two Value-Based Initiatives Centers in area churches that house its Value-Based Initiatives/Ministers Against Crime program. These ministers are graduates of the Ministers Police Academy training program. Their responsibilities include assisting officers in calming tensions, offering victim assistance, patrolling area hot spots, and working with area youth through their schools and communities.
- *Chicago.* The Chicago Police Department partnered with the Police Executive Research Forum in conducting a series of forums on race relations and improving the Chicago Police Department's relations with minority groups. Among other things, those discussions have resulted in the production of six training videos for police that highlight how to best engage and disengage with the public.
- *Redlands, California.* One of the main goals of the community of Redlands, California, is to reduce juvenile delinquency. The central component of that effort is the collaborative program "Building a Generation." This program is housed at the Value-Based Initiatives Community Training Center, which also houses the new Cyber Café—a safe place for teens to go after school and have access to computers, tutors, and job counselors. In addition, the COPS and Clergy network has resulted in the establishment of new partnerships between the police and faith-based organizations in eight Southern California cities.

▲ SUMMARY

Community policing in part evolved out of research findings throughout the 1970s and 1980s and out of prior innovations such as team policing and foot patrol. Community policing entails fundamental change in policing. Effective community policing has a positive impact on reducing neighborhood crime, helping to reduce citizens' fear of crime, and enhancing the quality of life in the community. It accomplishes these objectives by combining the efforts and resources of the police, local government, and community members.

Community policing is a collaborative effort between the police and the community that identifies problems of crime and disorder and involves all elements of the community in the search for solutions to these problems. It is founded on close, mutually beneficial ties between the police and community members. Community policing differs from traditional law enforcement because it allows police the freedom to expand the scope of their jobs. Police in this sense are challenged to become community problem solvers and encouraged to use their time creatively.

Herman Goldstein is considered by many to be the pioneer of problem-oriented policing, which is a method for improving police effectiveness through examining and acting on the underlying conditions that give rise to community problems. Responses emphasize preventing problems, going beyond the criminal justice system alone, and engaging with other public agencies, the community, and the private sector, where practical.

Without some sort of process to let us know whether community policing is an effective police strategy, we would be wasting much of our time and energy. Program evaluation is the process of assigning worth or determining the value of a program or activity. When we evaluate, we collect information about a program's actual inputs and/or outcomes and then compare that information to some preset standards or expectations; then a judgment is made about the program or activity. Many evaluations that have been conducted on community policing initiatives have shown that community policing has much promise.

The future of community policing is bright. The plummeting crime rates throughout the 1990s and into the early years of the 21st century indicate promise for the future of community policing. Community policing is being advocated by leaders at the highest levels of government. It has even been suggested that community policing can play a primary role in directing the way government services are provided at the community level.

Community policing represents a mechanism for fundamental change within policing. This change not only encompasses the manner in which communities are policed but also organizational change dynamics. Organizational change involves changes in management and leadership, organizational structures, purpose, and values.

Because of the important role that faith-based organizations play in many communities across the country, law enforcement organizations have realized the short- and long-term benefits of partnering with these groups. Although both sides have learned that the partnership is not without its challenges, all have agreed that the end result is well worth the effort. This growing partnership has significantly bolstered the effectiveness of community policing efforts across the country in recent years.

 QUESTIONS IN REVIEW

1. How long do you think it will take for the community-oriented policing strategy to become the normal way of doing business in police organizations?
2. What do you think is the major resistance toward community-oriented policing on the part of the police officers?
3. Why is examining past research on policing important for the future of community policing?
4. How does community policing differ from more traditional policing strategies?

POLICE RESOURCES ON THE WEB

Community Policing Consortium
http://www.communitypolicing.org

Community Policing Pages (dedicated to continuing the work of Dr. Robert C. Trojanowicz)
http://www.concentric.net/~dwoods

Herman Goldstein Award
http://www.ncjrs.ocg/pdffiles1/nij/182731.pdf

List of Community Policing and Problem-Solving Programs
http://faculty.ncwc.edu/toconnor/comlist.htm

National Center for Community Policing, Michigan State University
http://www.cj.msu.edu/-people/cp/webpubs.html

National Crime Prevention Council
http://www.ncpc.org

Office of Community-Oriented Policing Services (COPS)
http://www.cops.usdoj.gov

REFERENCES

1. Office of Community Policing Services. Accessed online April 20, 2004: http://www.communitypolicing.org/about3.html.
2. Ibid.
3. Ibid.
4. GARY W. CORDNER, "Elements of Community Policing," in *Policing Perspectives: An Anthology.* ed. Larry Gaines and Gary Cordners (Los Angeles, CA: Roxberry Publishing, 1999), pp. 137–149.
5. GEORGE KEELING, TONY PATE, DUANE DIECKMAN, and CHARLES E. BROWN, *Kansas City Preventive Patrol Experiment* (Washington, DC: Police Foundation, 1974), pp. 124–127.
6. CHARLES R. SWANSON, LEONARD TERRITO, and ROBERT W. TAYLOR, *Police Administration: Structures, Processes, and Behavior,* 5th ed. (Upper Saddle River, NJ: Prentice Hall, 2001).
7. PETER W. GREENWOOD, JOAN PETERSILIA, and JAN CHAIKEN, *The Criminal Investigation Process* (Lexington, MA: DC Heath, 1977).
8. Ibid.
9. Ibid.
10. Ibid.
11. LARRY K. GAINES, VICTOR E. KAPPELER, and JOSEPH B. VAUGHN, *Police in America* (Cincinnati, OH: Anderson, 1994).
12. ROBERT C. TROJANOWICZ, *An Evaluation of the Neighborhood Foot Patrol Program in Flint, Michigan* (East Lansing, MI: Michigan State University, 1982).
13. THE POLICE FOUNDATION, *The Newark Foot Patrol Experiment* (Washington, DC: Police Foundation, 1981).
14. Ibid.
15. Ibid.
16. JACK R. GREENE, "Foot Patrol and Community Policing: Past Practices and Future Prospects," *American Journal of Police* 6, no. 1 (1987): 1–15.
17. Community Policing Pages: News and Notes, April 22, 2004, [Online] Available at: http://web.indstate.edu/crim/index.html.
18. WILLARD M. OLIVER, "The Third Generation of Community Policing: Moving through Innovation, Diffusion, and Institutionalization," *Police Quarterly* 3, no. 4 (2000): 367–388.
19. STEVEN D. MASTROFSKI and R.R. RITTI, "Making Sense of Community Policing: A Theory Based Analysis," *Police Practice and Research* 1, no. 2 (2000): 183–210.
20. WILLARD M. OLIVER, "The Third Generation of Community Policing: Moving Through Innovation, Diffusion, and Institutionalization," *Police Quarterly* 3, no. 4 (2000): 367–388.
21. ROBERT R. FRIEDMANN, *Community Policing: Comparative Perspectives and Prospects* (New York: St. Martin's Press, 1992).
22. JOHN ECK and WILLIAM W. SPELMAN, "Who Ya Gonna Call? The Police as Problem Busters," *Crime and Delinquency* 1 (1987): 31–52.

23. QUINT C. THURMAN, ZHAO Z. JIHONG, and ANDREW L. GIACOMAZZI, *Community Policing in a Community Era* (Los Angeles, CA: Roxbury, 2001).

24. DAVID L. CARTER and LOUIS A. RADELET, *The Police and the Community,* 6th ed. (Upper Saddle River, NJ: Prentice Hall, 1999).

25. ROBERT C. TROJANOWICZ, "Community Policing Is Not Police-Community Relations," *FBI Law Enforcement Bulletin* 1 (1990): 10–12.

26. DAVID H. BAYLEY, "Community Policing: A Report from the Devil's Advocate," in *Community Policing: Rhetoric or Reality?* ed. J. Green and S. Mastrofski (New York: Praeger, 1988).

27. HELEN H. TAYLOR-GREEN, "Community Policing in Florida," *American Journal of Police* 12, no. 3 (1993): 141–155.

28. SUSAN SADD and RANDOLPH GRINC, "Innovative Neighborhood Oriented Policing: An Evaluation of Community Policing in Eight Cities," in *The Challenge of Community Policing: Testing the Premises*, ed. Dennis P. Rosenbaum (Thousand Oaks, CA: Sage Publishing, 1994).

29. DAVID H. BAYLEY, "Community Policing: A Report from the Devil's Advocate," in *Community Policing: Rhetoric or Reality*? ed. J. Green and S. Mastrofski (New York: Praeger, 1988).

30. ROBERT TROJANOWICZ and BONNIE BUCQUEROUX, *Community Policing: A Contemporary Perspective* (Cincinnati, OH: Anderson Publishing Co., 1990).

31. HERMAN GOLDSTEIN, *Problem-Oriented Policing* (New York: McGraw-Hill, 1990), pp. 50–57.

32. Ibid.

33. HERMAN GOLDSTEIN, "Improving Policing: A Problem-Oriented Approach," *Crime and Delinquency* 25 (1979): 236–258.

34. Ibid.

35. HERMAN GOLDSTEIN, What Is Problem Oriented Policing? Center for Problem Oriented Policing Web site. Accessed April 22, 2004: http//www.popcenter.org.

36. Ibid.

37. JOHN ECK and WILLIAM SPELMAN, *Problem Solving: Problem Oriented Policing in New Port News* (Washington, DC: Police Executive Research Forum, 1987).

38. GOLDSTEIN, 1990.

39. Ibid.

40. Ibid.

41. TERRY EISENBERG and BRUCE GLASSCOOK, "Looking Inward with Problem Oriented Policing," *F.B.I. Law Enforcement Bulletin* (July 2001): 6–11.

42. PETER H. ROSSI and HOWARD E. FREEDMAN, *Evaluation: A Systematic Approach,* 5th ed. (Newbury Park, CA: Sage Publication, 1993), p. 5.

43. Ibid, p. 5.

44. MARY ANN WYCOFF and WESLEY K. SKOGAN, "Community Policing in Madison: Quality from the Inside Out: An Evaluation of Implementation and Impact" (Washington, DC: U.S. National Institute of Justice, 2001).

45. JEROME E. MCELROY, COLLEEN A. COSGROVE, and SUSAN SADD, *CPOP: The Research—An Evaluative Study of the New York City Community Patrol Officer Program* (New York: Vera Institute of Justice, 1998).

46. Ibid.

47. DAVID WEISBURD and JOHN E. ECK, "What Can Police Do to Reduce Crime, Disorder, and Fear?" *The Annuals of the American Academy of Political and Social Science* 593, no. 1 (2004): 42–65.

48. STEVEN COLE, "South Central Prostitution Project," in *Community Policing in a Community Era*, ed. Quint Thurman, Jihong Zhao, and Andrew L. Giacomazzi (Los Angeles, CA.: Roxbury Publishing, 2001), pp. 242–245.

49. Ibid., p. 244.

50. BRUCE D. JOHNSON and ANDREW GOLUB, "Measuring the Impacts of Policing Among Arrestees in New York City: Veracity of Self-Reports, Deterrence Effects of Quality-of-Life Policing, and Net Widening" (Washington, DC: National Institute of Justice). Accessed online April 24, 2004: http://www.ncjrs.org/txtfiles1/jr000250.txt.

51. NATIONAL INSTITUTE OF JUSTICE, *Criminal Justice Research Under the Crime Act 1995–1996* (Washington, DC: U.S. Department of Justice, 1997), p. 2.

52. OFFICE OF COMMUNITY-ORIENTED POLICING SERVICES, "Deputy Attorney General James Comey Awards 20.7 Million in Grants to Hire 194 Police Officers in America's Schools."

53. Ibid.

54. U.S. DEPARTMENT OF JUSTICE, *Uniform Crime Report, 2003*. The data was obtained from the Federal Bureau of Investigation Web site. Accessed online April 24, 2004: http://www.fbi.gov/ ucr/ucr.htm

55. THURMAN, ZHAO, and GIACOMAZZI, 2001.

56. THE OFFICE OF COMMUNITY-ORIENTED POLICING SERVICES, "America's Law Enforcement to Receive Community Policing Boost," Press Release (Wednesday, November 25, 1998).

57. "Futuristics and Law Enforcement: The Millennium Conference." Accessed online April 24, 2004: http://www.fbi.gov/hq/td/fwg/conference.htm

58. MARY BETH GORDON, *Making the Match: Law Enforcement, the Faith Community and the Value Based Initiative* (Washington, DC: U. S. Department of Justice—Office of Community-Oriented Policing Services, 2002).

59. Ibid., p. 2.

Police Culture, Misconduct, and Deviance

Key Terms

Code Blue
Conventionalism
Corruption
Culture
Lautenberg Amendment
Police subculture

Social interactions
Stress
Submissiveness
Syndromes
Unreflectiveness

Outline

Introduction
Police Corruption
Police Brutality
Police Culture
Impact of Police Culture on
Individual Officers

Varieties of Police Misconduct
Case Study: Code of Silence
in the NYPD

Learning Objectives

After reading this chapter, you should be able to:

1. List the reasons for police corruption, and explore the various responses to police corruption (including citizen complaint review boards).
2. Discuss police culture and its effect on individual officers.
3. Identify the varieties of police misconduct.
4. Explain the code of silence of police officers.
5. Discuss the Rampart case study and its findings.

INTRODUCTION

Jerome H. Skolnick noted in an article on **Code Blue** that a police officer's work is unpredictable, is sometimes violent, and is sometimes carried out in a deadly environment.[1] The potential danger of the workplace and the authority to use force to overcome resistance make it not surprising, according to Skolnick, that police actions can have brutal, even fatal, consequences—sometimes for innocent people. He stated that it was also not surprising that to cope with such violence and danger, police have developed a very close-knit **culture**, which has its own set of norms. He contended that an officer understands that his or her fellow officers might, in the heat of the moment, do things that they wouldn't want brought to light later on. Maybe they administered a "tune-up" to teach compliance to a suspect, or maybe they visited a "beat wife" (prostitute) while on duty. A cop also learns to back up the stories colleagues tell to superiors and investigators; in turn, he or she is confident colleagues will back him or her up.[2]

Before we get too involved in the study of police misconduct, it must be remembered that the vast majority of over 800,000 police officers in American law enforcement agencies are ethical and law-abiding citizens who take pride in their jobs and accomplish their duties with the utmost respect for law and order. In this chapter, we are not studying the norm but those few who are not average police officers. Unfortunately, the ethical dilemmas that police officers face will not disappear as our country becomes more sophisticated and technological.[3]

POLICE CORRUPTION

Police **corruption** has been defined in many different ways. For purposes of this chapter, Herman Goldstein's definition is used; he defined police corruption as an "act involving the misuse of authority by a police officer in a manner designed to produce personal gain for himself."[4] Under this definition, a police officer is corrupt when the officer is acting in his or her official capacity and receives a benefit or something of value other than his or her paycheck for doing something or refraining from taking an action. Former New York City Police Commissioner Patrick Murphy once told his officers: "Except for your paycheck there is no such thing as a clean buck."[5] Commissioner Murphy knew what he considered to be corruption and informed his officers that he was going to hold them accountable.

Samuel Walker divided police corruption into four classes: taking gratuities, taking bribes, being involved in theft or burglary, and being involved in internal corruption.[6] Taking gratuities refers to receiving tips or discounts on purchased goods. Many individuals will argue that this is not corruption but merely a method of showing goodwill to the police for the difficult jobs and needed duties they perform. Walker listed

Bribes Versus Gifts

Is it a bribe to accept a free cup of coffee while on duty? Assume you are the Chief of Police in Alexander, Virginia, and a local convenience store advertises that a police officer will receive free coffee if the officer stops at the store while on duty and in uniform. The store had experienced robberies in the past and wants to encourage officers to spend time in the store. What if the benefit was more than a cup of coffee? Would that make a difference? Is it bribery to encourage the officers to be at the store rather than at other locations within their patrol area?

The above situation occurred in Alexander, Virginia, a few years ago. The common-wealth prosecutor considered that the store owner was offering a bribe to officers. Do you agree with this decision? Why?

Law Enforcement Code of Ethics

As a law enforcement officer, my fundamental duty is to serve the community; to safeguard lives and property; to protect the innocent against deception, the weak against oppression or intimidation, and the peaceful against violence or disorder; and to respect the constitutional rights of all to liberty, equality, and justice.

I will keep my private life unsullied as an example to all and will behave in a manner that does not bring discredit to me or to my agency. I will maintain courageous calm in the face of danger, scorn, or ridicule; develop self-restraint; and be constantly mindful of the welfare of others. Honest in thought and deed both in my personal and official life, I will be exemplary in obeying the law and the regulations of my department. Whatever I see or hear of a confidential nature or that is confided to me in my official capacity will be kept ever secret unless revelation is necessary in the performance of my duty.

I will never act officiously or permit personal feelings, prejudices, political beliefs, aspirations, animosities, or friendships to influence my decisions. With no compromise for crime and with relentless prosecution of criminals, I will enforce the law courteously and appropriately without fear or favor, malice or ill will, never employing unnecessary force or violence and never accepting gratuities.

I recognize the badge of my office as a symbol of public faith, and I accept it as a public trust to be held so long as I am true to the ethics of police service. I will never engage in acts of corruption or bribery, nor will I condone such acts by other police officers. I will cooperate with all legally authorized agencies and their representatives in the pursuit of justice.

I know that I alone am responsible for my own standard of professional performance and will take every reasonable opportunity to enhance and improve my level of knowledge and competence.

I will constantly strive to achieve these objectives and ideals, dedicating myself before God to my chosen profession . . . law enforcement.

two forms of taking bribes: formal, regular, periodic payments to overlook a continuing criminal activity (often referred to as "the pad") and a one-time payment to avoid arrest, etc. (often referred to as "the score"). The theft or burglary type of corruption generally occurs while the police are performing their duties; for example, the police are called to a "dead body," and the money found on the body disappears. Walker's internal type of corruption includes situations in which officers pay members of the department in order to obtain special assignments, favorable hours, or promotions.

POLICE BRUTALITY

The term "police brutality" describes a wide variety of police practices, from the use of profanity and abusive language to actual physical violence. To many individuals, the police symbolize brutality. It is difficult to determine the extent of police brutality because most of the time the incidents that constitute the brutality are low-visibility acts, and it is believed that most acts of police brutality are not reported by the victims. An additional problem in measuring the extent of police brutality is defining and classifying what acts constitute brutality. Many researchers concluded that brutality is a racial matter primarily involving white police officers and minority victims.[7] Albert Reiss concluded that approximately one-third of the alleged incidents of brutality occurred in controlled settings such as at the police station or in a patrol car and that in about one-half of those cases in controlled settings, other police officers did not attempt to restrain the officer or stop the brutality; this failure to intervene on the part of other officers indicated to Reiss that the informal police culture did not disapprove of the brutality.[8]

POLICE CULTURE

Culture, as defined in the *Webster's New Collegiate Dictionary,* is "the integrated pattern of human behavior that includes thought, speech, action, and artifacts and depends on a person's capacity for learning and transmitting knowledge to succeeding generations."[9]

Police culture (when we refer to "police culture," we are actually referring to the police subculture) is traditionally studied from the sociological, the psychological, or the anthropological perspective. The sociological perspective is based on the concept of police cynicism, a kind of hardened, institutionalized outlook. The varieties of cynicism range from tragic to comic. Skolnick listed four stages—over-idealism, frustration, disenchantment, full-blown cynicism—and stated that cynicism is highest during the

Racial Profiling

Listed below are the findings that were submitted to HR 2074, which was introduced into the U.S. House of Representatives in 2001:

1. The vast majority of law enforcement agents nationwide discharge their duties professionally, without bias, and protect the safety of their communities.

2. The use by police officers of race, ethnicity, or national origin in deciding which persons should be subject to traffic stops, stops and frisks, questioning, searches, and seizures is a problematic law enforcement tactic. Statistical evidence from across the country demonstrates that such racial profiling is a real and measurable phenomenon.

3. As of November 15, 2000, the Department of Justice had 14 publicly noticed, ongoing patterns and practice investigations involving allegations of racial profiling and had filed five pattern and practice lawsuits involving allegations of racial profiling, with four of those cases resolved through consent decrees.

4. A large majority of individuals subjected to stops and other enforcement activities based on race, ethnicity, or national origin are found to be law-abiding and therefore racial profiling is not an effective means to uncover criminal activity.

5. A 2001 Department of Justice report on citizen-police contacts in 1999 found that although African Americans and Hispanics were more likely to be stopped and searched, they were less likely to be in possession of contraband. On average, searches and seizures of African American drivers yielded evidence only 8 percent of the time, searches and seizures of Hispanic drivers yielded evidence only 10 percent of the time, and searches and seizures of white drivers yielded evidence 17 percent of the time.

6. A 2000 General Accounting Office report on the activities of the U.S. Customs Service during fiscal year 1998 found that black women who were U.S. citizens were 9 times more likely than white women who were U.S. citizens to be X-rayed after being frisked or patted down, and on the basis of X-ray results, black women who were U.S. citizens were less than half as likely as white women who were U.S. citizens to be found carrying contraband. In general, the report found that the patterns used to select passengers for more intrusive searches resulted in women and minorities being selected at rates that were not consistent with the rates of finding contraband.

7. Current local law enforcement practices, such as ticket and arrest quotas and similar management practices, may have the unintended effect of encouraging law enforcement agents to engage in racial profiling.

8. Racial profiling harms individuals subjected to it because they experience fear, anxiety, humiliation, anger, resentment, and cynicism when they are unjustifiably treated as criminal suspects. By discouraging individuals from traveling freely, racial profiling impairs both interstate and intrastate commerce.

9. Racial profiling damages law enforcement and the criminal justice system as a whole by undermining public confidence and trust in the police, the courts, and the criminal law.

(continued)

10. Racial profiling violates the Equal Protection Clause of the Constitution. Using race, ethnicity, or national origin as a proxy for criminal suspicion violates the constitutional requirement that police and other government officials accord to all citizens the equal protection of the law, based on *Arlington Heights* v. *Metropolitan Housing Development Corporation,* 429 U.S. 252 (1977).

11. Racial profiling is not adequately addressed through suppression motions in criminal cases for two reasons. First, the Supreme Court held, in *Whren* v. *United States,* 517 U.S. 806 (1996), that the racially discriminatory motive of a police officer in making an otherwise valid traffic stop does not warrant the suppression of evidence. Second, since most stops do not result in the discovery of contraband, there is no criminal prosecution and no evidence to suppress.

12. Current efforts by state and local governments to eradicate racial profiling and redress the harms it causes, while laudable, have been limited in scope and insufficient to address this national problem.

middle part of a police career.[10] The sociological approach is associated with the cultural characteristics of isolation (often referred to as the "bluewall"), brotherhood (an attack on one officer is an attack on all officers in the department), and action (the ability to recognize danger and symbolic assailants). Skolnick developed the concept of a working police personality and noted that the organization produces the kinds of personalities it needs.[11] Under the sociological perspective, **stress** is a significant factor in police behavior, and this stress (not necessarily unique to police officers) often results in divorce, alcohol abuse, or suicide.

When examining police culture from the psychological perspective, the presence of authoritarianism is considered. Authoritarianism describes a set of attitudes and beliefs that was first observed in people who blindly followed Hitler. It has also been called "fascism" because it's measured by something called the F-scale. There are at least nine basic components to this fascism:

1. **Conventionalism**
2. **Submissiveness**
3. Aggressiveness
4. **Unreflectiveness**
5. Superstition
6. Toughness
7. Destructiveness
8. Projection
9. Sexual exaggeration

Some researchers contend that college students also usually score high on these traits, which are not about dishing out authority but about preferring crystal-clear lines of authority and following that authority to the letter.[12]

The psychological approach considers suspicion as healthy, cynicism as unhealthy, and authoritarianism as a personality trait. Most researchers using the psychological approach contend that an organization, like a police department, attracts certain people with the personalities it needs. This approach is also considered a self-selection point of view. A former U.S. Attorney General once stated that a police officer has to be a "lawyer, scientist, medic, psychologist, athlete, and public servant."[13] The psychological perspective contends that the occupation of policing tends to attract certain types of individuals or "**syndromes.**" Note that the use of the term "syndrome" in this regard does not fit the generally accepted definition of syndrome, but it is frequently used in this context and provides a useful method of explaining certain types of behaviors. Examples of the "syndromes" that are attracted to the law enforcement occupation include the following:

- *Wyatt Earp syndrome*. Being "badge heavy" and macho and feeling like a victim of image.
- *John Wayne syndrome*. Being overserious and cold and having tunnel vision.
- *Doc Holliday syndrome*. Being suspicious, bitter, and quick-tempered.
- *Custer syndrome*. Defending police work and being antiestablishment regarding the rest of the system.
- *Parker syndrome*. Defending the "thin blue line" and having an antisociety attitude.

Studying police culture from an anthropological perspective requires a mentality or cognitive orientation involving how people see themselves and others. Under this perspective, police are said to have a we-they (or us-them) worldview, meaning police versus civilians. This in-group (we-they) solidarity is associated with the idea of **police subculture,** but in practice the more general term "culture" is commonly used to describe everything police share in common.

Police culture is said to have the following elements in its ethos: bravery, autonomy, and secrecy. The ethos is the idea of a spirit or force in the organization that reflects an unwritten (and largely unspoken) value system. It's what makes daily life worth living.

A common theme is the idea of a belief system that regulates or guides the kinds of relationships or **social interactions** (scripts or roles) that people have inside and outside their culture. In the case of policing, for example, the belief that you are never off-duty would be a theme constraining a fully interactive life with the general public.

Postulates are beliefs that integrate (homogenize or make alike) the people in a culture, and they do this by using neat little proverbs that simplify a vast amount of complex information. For example, "Don't talk too much or too little" would be a postulate. Postulates are considered by many as expressing the norms that would be threatened by police deviance.

Many approaches to the study of police culture are devoted to the topic of typologies, or types of police officers. When researchers use this approach, individual police officers are grouped into certain behavioral categories. The most popular typologies are as follows:

Broderick's Typology

1. *Idealist*. Is college-educated and has high ideals and commitment to social order.
2. *Enforcer*. Is ends-oriented and is least likely to choose or recommend a police career.
3. *Optimist*. Is people-oriented and is a management-aspiring "yes" person.
4. *Realist*. Has a "just a job/heck with it" attitude and is "retired in place."

Muir's Typology

1. *Professional*. Has proper integration of coercion and sympathy.
2. *Enforcer*. Is both cynical and coercive.
3. *Reciprocator*. Is wishy-washy and oversympathetic and can't make up mind.
4. *Avoider*. Avoids work, just collects paycheck, and is a shirker/slacker.

White's Typology

1. *Tough cop*. Is outcome-oriented.
2. *Problem solver*. Pays attention to people's needs.
3. *Crime fighter*. Is a zealot on a mission to wipe out a certain kind of crime.
4. *Rule applier*. Goes strictly by the book and would give own mother a ticket.

Coate's Typology

1. *Legalistic-abusive*. Is extremely rigid and has to be right all the time.
2. *Task-oriented*. Is concerned that rules and regulations cover everything.
3. *Community service–oriented*. Is interested in documenting how the community is helped.

Much of the research regarding police culture appears in the literature relating to police deviant behavior, ethics, misuse of force, and discretion. When studying the subculture of policing, it is important to remember that there is not a single organizational culture for all police. Generally research has been focused on large urban police settings, yet most police departments are small or medium-sized; accordingly, many of the cultural generalizations that are made about police do not necessarily apply to all police agencies. The style of policing in any community is affected by the mixture of values and attitudes in the community, the philosophy that the organizational leadership inspires in the agencies, and the relationships with citizens with whom individual police officers find themselves engaged. *Note*: The study of police culture of foreign police agencies is of little assistance in understanding the American subculture of policing because there are significant cultural differences between the American police and foreign police.

Fire a Police Officer for Domestic Violence?
Case of *Gillespie* v. *City of Indianapolis*

In September 1996, Congress passed certain amendments (including the **Lautenberg Amendment**) to the Gun Control Act of 1968, 18 U.S.C. §921 et seq., adding a firearms disability for "any person . . . who has been convicted in any court of a misdemeanor crime of domestic violence." See 18 U.S.C. §922(g)(9). Unlike every other federal firearms disability under §922(g), the Lautenberg Amendment applies to law enforcement officers, for Congress specifically excluded domestic violence misdemeanants from the general exemption for federal and state agencies from §922(g) firearms disabilities. See 18 U.S.C. §925(a)(1).

Plaintiff Jerald Gillespie brought this suit against the city of Indianapolis, the Indianapolis Police Department, and the Chief of Police, challenging the constitutionality of the Lautenberg Amendment.

Gillespie was a police officer employed by the Indianapolis Police Department and had been a full-time law enforcement officer since 1971. In October 1995, Gillespie pleaded guilty to a misdemeanor battery offense involving domestic violence against his ex-wife. The Indianapolis Police Department proposed to terminate Gillespie based on application of the Lautenberg Amendment, which criminalizes possession of a firearm by domestic violence offenders; under Indianapolis Police Department policy, every police officer must be trained and equipped to use and possess a firearm. Gillespie filed suit and moved for preliminary injunctive relief barring his termination of employment, and the defendants, as well as the United States as intervenor, moved to dismiss his complaint.

HOW WOULD YOU RULE?

The U.S. District Court for the Southern District of Indiana denied Gillespie's request for an injunction to prevent the city from firing him and dismissed the case. The court held that there was no Tenth Amendment violation because the act was a proper exercise of the Commerce Clause power and did not compel the states to do anything. The jurisdictional nexus of the act was sufficient to defeat the officer's Commerce Clause challenge. The act was analyzed for equal protection purposes under the rational basis standard, which it satisfied because it did not impinge on a fundamental right. The act's disparate impact on police officers did not violate equal protection because the act was neutral on its face and could not be traced to a discriminatory purpose. The officer received all the procedural due process to which he was entitled because the law affected a general class of persons, and the legislative process satisfied due process. Even giving the most generous construction to the officer's Second Amendment claim, the act survived strict scrutiny (13 F.Supp.2d 811; 1998 U.S. Dist. LEXIS 8691).

IMPACT OF POLICE CULTURE
ON INDIVIDUAL OFFICERS

A police officer's working personality is often described as the personality that an officer demonstrates while in uniform. This working personality is developed within the policing subculture and is a mixture of the officer's personality and the demands of the subculture. The principal variables that influence the personality are the element of danger and the issue of authority. The danger element results in an officer being attentive to signs from individuals that indicate a potential for violence and lawbreaking, and it tends to result in isolation of the police officer.

The officer is expected to enforce the laws of the community; to accomplish this, the officer has a certain degree of authority. The officer may order individuals to stop, direct individuals to take certain actions, or even arrest individuals. This element of authority is not present in other public service occupations. Authority of the officer often makes the officer unpopular with citizens within the community because enforcing laws makes the officer unpopular and tends to further isolate the officer from the community.

VARIETIES OF POLICE MISCONDUCT

The most common cases concerning police misconduct involve the use of excessive force (an officer hurts someone unnecessarily), civil rights violations, false arrest, and malicious prosecution.

Excessive Force

A police officer acts with excessive force when the officer uses more force to accomplish his or her task than is necessary. Police officers are permitted to use force and (in some situations) deadly force; however, the officer may misuse his or her authority and injure someone without a justified reason. For example, an officer stops an elderly person for speeding and directs the driver to get out of the car, and when the driver opens the car door, the officer yanks him from his seat and throws him against the car. Since there was no need to cause injury to the driver of the car, the officer is liable for using excessive force. The concept of liability means that the officer is legally responsible in a civil court of law for the damages that the driver suffers from the officer's abuse. The use of excessive force also constitutes the crime of assault and battery on the driver, and the officer could be punished for that crime.

Civil Rights Violations

A civil rights violation consists of those situations in which constitutional rights of individuals are violated or ignored by the police. Some of the civil rights are created by state and local laws, but most of them are created by the U.S. Constitution.

False Arrest

An arrest is defined for civil liability as any situation that an individual is involved in with an officer where the individual is not free to leave. If the officer does not have a valid reason for arresting an individual, then the

---

Under Color of Law

It is a crime for one or more persons acting under color of law willfully to deprive or conspire to deprive another person of any right protected by the Constitution or laws of the United States (18 U.S.C. §§ 241, 242). The term "color of law" simply means that the person doing the act is using power given to him or her by a governmental agency (local, state, or federal). A law enforcement officer acts under color of law even if he or she is exceeding his or her rightful power. The types of law enforcement misconduct covered by these laws include excessive force, sexual assault, intentional false arrests, or intentional fabrication of evidence resulting in a loss of liberty to another. Enforcement of these provisions does *not* require that any racial, religious, or other discriminatory motive existed.

---

individual may have a false arrest claim. For example, an officer observes a teenager standing on the corner alone, minding his own business. The officer comes up to him and tells him that he must submit to a search (pat-down search). The teenager says no, and the officer tells him that he must submit. The teenager again says no, and the officer forces him into the squad car and takes him down to the station. After searching the teenager at the station and checking his background, the officer releases him. The teenager has a valid false arrest claim. He was arrested without any valid basis and taken to the police station.

Malicious Prosecution

A malicious prosecution claim is similar to a false arrest claim. In this type of case, the officer arrests an individual for no valid reason and then initiates a criminal complaint against the innocent person. Typical cases in this regard are aggravated battery cases in which an officer, for no valid reason, strikes a civilian. The civilian blocks the strike and hits back. The officer then tackles the civilian, arrests him, and charges him with striking the officer—an aggravated battery. The civilian may lodge a civil rights case against the officer for excessive force, false arrest, and malicious prosecution.

CASE STUDY: CODE OF SILENCE IN THE NYPD

Plaintiff Paula White-Ruiz, a police officer in the New York Police Department (NYPD) for eight years, filed a civil action under 42 U.S. Code, Section 1983 (*White-Ruiz* v. *City of New York,* 1996 U.S. Dist. LEXIS 15571), claiming that various officers and officials of the New York City Police Department engaged in a course of harassment against her in retaliation for her having disclosed an instance of corrupt behavior by her fellow officers. She asserted that the defendants, including the city of New York, should be held liable to her for violation of her First Amendment right to speak freely. Apart from the city, the plaintiff named as defendants a captain, two lieutenants, and three sergeants from the 90th Police Precinct, where she was currently assigned, and former New York Police Commissioner Raymond Kelly.

During her first year on the police force and while at a different precinct, Officer White-Ruiz reported to her superior officers that a sum of money had been removed from the body of a deceased person at a crime scene while she and her partner were at the scene (affidavit of Paula White-Ruiz, sworn to February 9, 1995). Her report led to an investigation and the subsequent dismissal of Officer White-Ruiz's partner, Officer John Ward, after he had admitted taking the money.

The plaintiff reported that, contrary to police department policy, details of this incident and her role in the investigation were not kept confidential but were instead reported over police teletype to various commands throughout the city. She further alleged that because of her report, members of the New York Police Department began a deliberate and sustained course of retaliatory activity against her.

She alleged the existence of "long-standing" graffiti on the walls of the 90th Precinct police officer men's room referring both to her and to another officer, Hector Ariza, as "IAD rats" and using offensive language about them, as well as condemning the Civilian Complaint Review Board. She also recited that on several occasions fellow officers left notes on her precinct locker saying "Rat & Black Bitch."

The plaintiff noted that she was soon teamed with Officer Ariza, purportedly because no other officer would work with either one of them. She also alleged that fellow officers refused to provide her with backup in at least one dangerous situation on December 21, 1988, and she reported that during the same incident some of the officers attempted to interfere with her radio transmissions requesting such backup.

According to her, on November 8, 1988, two unidentified men—presumably fellow officers—called her a "rat" and a "cheeseater" during a police radio transmission. On November 23, 1988, someone anonymously sent a copy of the order dismissing Officer Ward to her home. On September 14, 1991, and again on September 18, 1991, she said that her car was deliberately scratched. The plaintiff also alleged that in June 1993 someone tried to tamper with her locker in the precinct.

The plaintiff further alleged that despite her complaints, police supervisors made only perfunctory attempts to identify and track down those who had made retaliatory threats or endangered her. She also reported that supervisory officers at the precinct openly acknowledged that her role in bringing Officer Ward to justice would cause her problems in the precinct.

The plaintiff further alleged that throughout the period from 1989 to 1991, she also suffered retaliatory assignment changes and inappropriate posts, which did not adequately reflect her seniority. She reported that on at least three separate occasions, she requested a specific transfer of duty and was informed that no such posts were available. On all three occasions, the plaintiff discovered that the job had been assigned to someone else shortly after she had made her request.

She offered as evidence the final report (dated July 7, 1994) of the New York City Commission to Investigate Allegations of Police Corruption and the Anti-Corruption Procedures of the Police Department, the so-called Mollen Commission. The Mollen Commission report documented in detail a pattern of extensive police corruption, extending to many city precincts and lasting at least several decades. Accompanying that pattern, and essential to its maintenance, according to the commission, is a so-called code of silence, under which even honest officers are expected to protect corrupt colleagues from detection and punishment. In substance the commission found that this culture "encourage[s] corruption" and "thwart[s] efforts to control corruption."[14]

In explaining the persistence of the code of silence, the commission noted that it was stringently, if informally, enforced in the department[15]:

> Officers who report misconduct are ostracized and harassed; become targets of complaints and even physical threats; and are made to fear that they will be left alone on the streets in a time of crisis. This draconian enforcement of the code of silence fuels corruption because it makes corrupt cops feel protected and invulnerable.

Based on specific instances described in the report, the commission concluded that enforcement of the code of silence is pervasive, extending to virtually all precincts, and that it targets both line officers and higher police officials. Moreover, the code is inculcated at the very start of the new officers' police careers, in the New York Police Academy, where the instructors warn recruits never to become a "rat," and it extends even to the department's Internal Affairs Division, which may disclose the identity of complainants to their colleagues.

The commission also addressed the responsibility of the department itself for this state of affairs. Thus, it noted that the department had neither acknowledged the existence of the code of silence nor taken any steps to end it. Most obviously, it has not ensured confidentiality to officers who report instances of corrupt behavior by fellow officers. More generally, the department's "management practices have often fueled an officer's susceptibility to corruption."[16]

Of particular relevance, the commission found that officers' widespread "cynicism about the Department's commitment to corruption control is justified."[17] The justifications for this view ranged from disinclination by supervisors to enforce anticorruption policies to outright protection or encouragement of such behavior and active thwarting of complaints.

The extent of the problem was underscored in Chapter 4 of the report, titled "The Collapse of the Department's Corruption Controls." In its discussion, the commission documented that the system of oversight installed several decades before, in the wake of the report of the Knapp

Commission, had completely collapsed years ago, with only minimal efforts to trace corrupt activities. Of particular relevance to this case, the commission emphasized that anticorruption efforts had withered because top management in the department not only had lost interest in it but had conveyed the message, especially after one major scandal in 1986, that disclosure of corruption was undesirable and thus to be discouraged.

As the report noted, the enforcement of anticorruption policies and procedures installed in the 1970s turned on the principle of command accountability, and that rule "depended solely on the Police Commissioner's dedication and adherence to that principle. If the Police Commissioner did not enforce a policy of holding commanders accountable when corruption was detected, no other person or unit within the Department accepted responsibility for carrying out that important function. Over time, enforcement of command accountability completely broke down."[18]

In addition, according to the commission, the department failed to exercise continuing supervision over the Internal Affairs Division. This failing was attributed to a lack of interest by the highest-level managers of the department and the "natural reluctance [of the Department] to uncover corruption."[19] As the report observed[20]:

> One of the basic principles of command accountability—that diligence in uncovering corruption will be rewarded—had been completely perverted. In recent years, a message has filtered down from top commanders—including Police Commissioners—that disclosure of corruption, even that resulting from vigilant corruption fighting, would be viewed as a management failure.

As a result, the report noted, "[B]y the time the Commission commenced its inquiries in September 1992, only the skeleton of [the original oversight] system remained. . . . This state of affairs was allowed to continue because it appeared to protect the Department and satisfied its top commanders. No one in the Department had any incentive to fix what had broken, until their feet were held to the fire of public scrutiny."[21] Other failings, including the absence of field supervision and the paralysis of the Internal Affairs Division, were also attributable to a determined lack of interest in corruption controls by top management, including police commissioners.

As recounted by the commission, this documented policy of ignoring police corruption and discouraging efforts to uproot it continued until after the commission itself had begun to investigate the department in late 1992. Thus the report noted the following [22]:

> The Department completely abandoned its responsibility to transform [the police culture that tolerates corruption]. It made little effort to change the attitudes that foster corruption among the rank and file, supervisors or commanders; and it made little effort to convince anyone that its occasional pronouncements on integrity were more than obligatory rhetoric.

The department also has done little to attempt to penetrate the wall of silence, although it is one of the major barriers to identifying and uncovering corruption. The department never aggressively solicited information from its members. It did not reward courageous officers who came forward with valuable information or penalize those who failed to report evidence of widespread or serious corruption about which they had personal knowledge. And it did nothing to try to educate its members as to why reporting and not tolerating corruption are essential to the department and to them.

In addition to the proffer of this report, the plaintiff asserted that in December 1992 she addressed a memorandum to then-Commissioner Kelly recounting the alleged pattern of retaliation against her. She reported delivering the memorandum to a member of Kelly's staff and receiving no response.

Note: This information was taken from the above referenced lawsuit and does not presently reflect on the status of the New York City Police Department and its present commissioner.

▲ SUMMARY

The potential danger of the workplace and the authority to use force to overcome resistance make it not surprising, according to Skolnick, that police actions can have brutal, even fatal, consequences—sometimes for innocent people. A police officer also learns to back up the stories colleagues tell to superiors and investigators; in turn, he or she is confident colleagues will back him or her up.

Police corruption has been defined in many different ways. A commonly used definition defines "police corruption" as an act involving the misuse of authority by a police officer in a manner designed to produce personal gain for him or herself. Under this definition, a police officer is corrupt when the officer is acting in his or her official capacity and receives a benefit or something of value other than his or her paycheck for doing something or refraining from taking an action. Samuel Walker divided police corruption into four classes: taking gratuities, taking bribes, being involved in theft or burglary, and being involved in internal corruption.

The term "police brutality" describes a wide variety of police practices, from the use of profanity and abusive language to actual physical violence. To many individuals, the police symbolize brutality. It is difficult to determine the extent of police brutality because most of the time the incidents that constitute brutality are low-visibility acts, and it is believed that most acts of police brutality are not reported by the victims. An additional problem in measuring the extent of police brutality is defining and classifying what acts constitute brutality. Many researchers conclude that brutality is a racial matter primarily involving white police officers and minority victims.

Rampart Report and Police Corruption

In 1991, during the aftermath of the Rodney King beating, but before the Los Angeles riots, an independent commission headed by future U.S. Secretary of State William Christopher released the results of its investigation of the Los Angles Police Department (LAPD) (known as the Christopher Commission). Among the commission's significant findings were the following:

- A significant number of LAPD officers repeatedly use excessive force, especially in minority and poor communities.
- Instead of restraining or punishing these officers, based on ample evidence of their misdeeds, the department's managers and supervisors have rewarded and promoted them.
- These problems are caused by a professional organizational culture that has been actively promoted by the LAPD, including a "war on crime" and "us versus them" mentality that often fails to distinguish between "good" and "bad" members of particular minority groups.

The Rampart area, west of downtown Los Angeles, had the highest population density in the city and one of the highest crime rates. To counter the drug problem in the area, the LAPD started the Community Resources Against Street Hoodlums (CRASH) program. It was a high-prestige paramilitary-style unit, and the officers assigned to the program had wide latitude to aggressively fight gangs.

The LAPD by the Numbers

Almost half the members of the Los Angeles Police Department have been hired since the Rodney King beating in 1991. The ethnic makeup of the force has changed dramatically in recent years. It now more closely resembles that of the city.

Rank	White	Latino	Black	Asian	Native American
Command Staff	22	3	5	0	0
Captains/Lieutenants	207	38	38	9	1
Sergeants/Detectives	1,408	611	389	121	15
Patrol Officers	2,647	2,399	839	478	33
Total	4,284	3,051	1,271	608	49

It was considered a success by the LAPD. Free of departmental oversight, the CRASH unit developed its own close-knit culture and its own rules. Members of the unit aggressively confronted gang members through tactics such as physical beatings, shootings, planted evidence, framed crimes, and false police reports as well as false evidence and testimony about their actions in court.

CRASH members dispensed their own brand of vigilante justice. For example, Samuel Bailey, a gang member, encountered Rampart officers outside a gang party one night. The

(continued)

officers arrested him without apparent cause and framed him for possession of an illegal weapon. After hearing the officers testify that he had pulled a gun and realizing that his denials would not be worth much in the face of the officers' testimony, Bailey pleaded guilty. The pattern held for several other falsely accused gang members, many of whom were falsely accused of possessing a weapon and pleaded guilty because it was clear that no one would believe them.

Two CRASH officers shot two gang members in an apartment complex, killing one and seriously wounding the other. Contrary to the statements of several eyewitnesses, the officers testified that the gang members had pointed guns at them. The guns that the officers alleged had been used were fully loaded and had not been fired.

These misdeeds and others crimes committed by CRASH officers were eventually discovered when a former CRASH officer Rafael Perez confessed. These incidents and other related incidents tied to current or former Rampart officers eventually caused the LAPD to become suspicious: a bank robbery by former Rampart officer David Mack in November 1997, the false imprisonment and beating of a suspect by Rampart officers Brian Hewitt and Daniel Lujan in February 1998, and the theft of three kilograms of cocaine from an evidence locker by Rafael Perez in March 1998. The department appointed a task force to investigate these events. Prosecutors charged Perez with possession of cocaine for sale, grand theft, and forgery. Faced with prison time, Perez decided to plead guilty and cooperate with investigators. He eventually revealed a long list of beatings, shootings, framings, and perjury by CRASH officers. Although some in the department have denied these allegations, most of Perez's confessions were independently corroborated.

Approximately 70 LAPD officers are under suspicion for illegal activity associated with CRASH. Financially, the cost to the city is staggering. The city's legislative analyst estimated that it would cost $125 million just to settle the nearly 200 lawsuits and other claims against the city. A state legislative analyst estimated that it would take an initial outlay of $20 million to $40 million for the year 2001 and cost an additional $30 million to $50 million each year after that to mitigate the effects of the scandal.

On March 1, 2000, the LAPD's Board of Inquiry, composed of two deputy police chiefs, a police administrator, and a police commander, released its report. On September 11, USC law professor Erwin Chemerinsky released his independent analysis of the Board of Inquiry's report. On November 16, the Rampart Independent Review Panel, composed of over 200 volunteer judges, lawyers, law enforcement officials, business executives, and educators, released its report. Each of these manuscripts contains different reform proposals aimed at solving the problems that led to the Rampart scandal. The Los Angeles City Council has reluctantly agreed to settle a pending civil rights lawsuit with the U.S. Department of Justice by entering into a wide-ranging federal consent decree designed to radically alter the structure and practices of the LAPD.

Professor Chemerinsky concluded: "The Rampart scandal reveals serious problems with the entire criminal justice system in Los Angeles. The conviction, by guilty plea or verdict, of innocent people is a failure of the entire system. Judges, prosecutors, and defense attorneys all must share the responsibility. There must be scrutiny of the court, the District Attorney, the City Attorney, and the Public Defender to determine how all can better serve to check police abuse and improve the criminal justice system."[23] His proposed reforms included all of the following[24]:

- Requiring officers to present prosecutors with all reports concerning an incident
- Requiring judges to inform prosecutors and the police department if they have discovered an officer to have made false statements or committed perjury
- Limiting the ability of the district attorney's office to exclude judges from criminal cases
- Requiring judges to take seriously their responsibility to make sure there is a true factual basis for a guilty plea
- Encouraging diversity and balance in the selection of judges, and promoting increased sensitivity to the issues of police perjury and misconduct
- Creating an independent commission to investigate the district attorney's office's handling of Rampart cases
- Developing policies and procedures within the district attorney's office to identify and prevent police misconduct during trials, including a policy to enforce prosecutors' responsibility to disclose exculpatory evidence to defendants and procedures to report and track police perjury
- Requiring prosecutors to inform the Inspector General and the police chief whenever they have probable cause that an officer has lied or committed misconduct
- Creating an effective mechanism for Special Investigations Division (SID) prosecutors to notify other prosecutors of problems with specific officers
- Requiring officer lies to other court-related officials to be investigated and disclosed to defense counsel
- Creating an independent commission to investigate the city attorney's office's role in the Rampart scandal
- Requiring attorneys in the city attorney's office to discover and report police perjury or misconduct
- Requiring the public defender's office to release its report on its own responsibility for the Rampart scandal

Professor Chemerinsky noted that additional reforms might be necessary in order to force judges not just to report but also to impose stiffer penalties for police perjury and to change their interpretive rules in search-and-seizure cases.[25]

Sources: Jason E. Whitehead, "BEYOND SCANDAL: The Rampart Corruption Incident as 'Business-as-Usual' in LA," *LA Times*, online edition, Sunday, June 11, 2000. Professor Erwin Chemerinsky, University of Southern California, "Executive Summary of an Independent Analysis of the Los Angeles Police Department's Board of Inquiry Report on the Rampart Scandal." Consent decree in *United States of America* v. *City of Los Angeles, et al.* (U.S. District Court for the Central District of Los Angeles). *United States* v. *City of Los Angeles*, No. 01-55182, No. 01-55453, U.S. Court of Appeals for the Ninth Circuit, 288 F.3d 391; 2002 U.S. App. LEXIS 7348; 52 Fed. R. Serv. 3d (Callaghan) 538; 2002 Cal. Daily Op. Service 3440, March 6, 2002, Pasadena, California; argued and submitted April 22, 2002. *Fitzpatrick* v. *Gates*, No. CV 00-04191 GAF (AJWx), U.S. District Court for the Central District of California, 2001 U.S. Dist. LEXIS 13774; decided April 17, 2001; filed April 18, 2001; entered April 19, 2001. *Ovando* v. *City of Los Angeles*, No. CV 99-11835 GAF (AJWx), U.S. District Court for the Central District of California, 92 F.Supp.2d 1011; 2000 U.S. Dist. LEXIS 4537, March 28, 2000; decided March 28, 2000.

Studies of police culture are traditionally studied from the sociological, the psychological, or the anthropological perspective. The sociological perspective is based on the concept of police cynicism, a hardened, institutionalized kind of outlook. The varieties of cynicism range from tragic to comic. Skolnick listed four stages: over-idealism, frustration, disenchantment, and full-blown cynicism.

Studying police culture from an anthropological perspective requires a mentality or cognitive orientation involving how people see themselves and others. Under this perspective, police are said to have a we-they (or us-them) worldview, meaning police versus civilians. This in-group (we-they) solidarity is associated with the idea of police subculture, but in practice the more general term "culture" is commonly used to describe everything police share in common.

Much of the research regarding police culture appears in the literature relating to police deviant behavior, ethics, misuse of force, and discretion. When studying the subculture of policing, it is important to remember that there is not a single organizational culture for all police. Generally research has been focused on large urban police settings, yet most police departments are small or medium-sized; accordingly, many of the cultural generalizations that are made about police do not necessarily apply to all police agencies.

A police officer's working personality is often described as the personality that an officer demonstrates while in uniform. This working personality is developed with the policing subculture and is a mixture of the officer's personality and the demands of the subculture. The principal variables that influence the personality are the element of danger and the issue of authority. The danger element results in an officer being attentive to signs from individuals that indicate a potential for violence and lawbreaking, and it tends to result in isolation of the police officer.

The most common cases concerning police misconduct involve the use of excessive force (an officer hurts someone unnecessarily), civil rights violations, false arrest, and malicious prosecution.

QUESTIONS IN REVIEW

1. What constitutes police misconduct?
2. Should police officers be allowed to accept free food while on duty?
3. Explain the meaning of Code Blue.
4. What was the purpose of the Lautenberg Amendment?
5. Explain the various types of police corruption.
6. Is there a subculture of policing? Explain.
7. What lessons should we learn from the Rampart case study?

POLICE RESOURCES ON THE WEB

Drug Enforcement Administration
www.usdoj.gov/dea

FBI National Center for the Analysis of Violent Crime (NCAVC)
www.fbi.gov/hq/isd/cirg/ncavc.htm

International Association of Chiefs of Police
www.theiacp.org

Latest Crime and Justice News
www.crimenews.info

Links to law enforcement agencies nationwide
http://police.sas.ab.ca

National White Collar Crime Center (NW3C)
www.nw3c.org

REFERENCES

1. JEROME SKOLNICK, "Code Blue," *American Prospect* 11, no. 10 (March 27, 2000–April 10, 2000), pp. 10–27.
2. Ibid.
3. JAMES N. GILBERT, "Investigative Ethics," in *Critical Issues in Criminal Investigations*, 2nd ed., ed. Michael Palmiotto (Cincinnati, OH: Anderson, 1988), pp. 7–14.
4. HERMAN GOLDSTEIN, *Police Corruption: A Perspective on Its Nature and Control* (Washington, DC: Police Foundation, 1975), p. 3.
5. Ibid., p. 29.
6. SAMUEL WALKER, *Policing in America: An Introduction*, 2nd ed. (New York: McGraw-Hill, 1992), pp. 175–177.
7. ALBERT J. REISS Jr., "Police Brutality: Answers to Key Questions," *Transaction* (July–August 1968): 10–19.
8. Ibid.
9. *Webster's New Lexicon Collegiate Dictionary* (New York: Lexicon Publishers, 1988), p. 258
10. J. SKOLNICK, *Justice Without Trial* (New York: Wiley, 1966).
11. Ibid.
12. A. NEIDERHOFFER, *Behind the Shield* (New York: Anchor, 1967).
13. *New York Times*, July 11, 1973, p. A8.
14. *White-Ruiz* v. *City of New York*, 1996 U.S. Dist. LEXIS 15571, 15583.
15. Ibid.

16. Ibid.
17. Ibid.
18. Ibid., p.15585.
19. Ibid., p.15588.
20. Ibid., p.15589.
21. Ibid., p.15589.
22. Ibid., p.15591.
23. Professor Erwin Chemerinsky, University of Southern California, "Executive Summary of an Independent Analysis of the Los Angeles Police Department's Board of Inquiry Report on the Rampart Scandal," *Los Angeles Times,* online edition, Sunday, June 11, 2000.
24. Ibid.
25. Ibid.

Legal Issues in Policing

Key Terms

Arrest

Color of law

Custody

Due process

Exclusionary rule

False arrest

False imprisonment

Good-faith exception

Negligence torts

Nullum crimin sine leg

Private person arrest

Probable cause

Search

Standing to object rule

Terry stop

Writ of *habeas
    corpus*

Wrongful death

Outline

Introduction

Legal Authority: Federal and State
    Constitutions and Statutes

Due Process

Role of the Courts

Fourth Amendment

Fifth Amendment

Handling of Evidence

Police Officer as Witness

Police Liability

Learning Objectives

After reading this chapter, you should be able to:

1. Identify and describe the authority of and limitations on police officers
   regarding searches and seizures.
2. Discuss due process concepts.
3. Explain the role of the courts in the criminal justice process.

4. Describe the limitations placed on law enforcement officers by the Fourth and Fifth Amendments.
5. List the significant factors involved in handling physical evidence.
6. Describe the rules that a police officer should follow when called as a witness in a criminal case.
7. Explain the bases for police liability and when individual officers may be liable in civil actions.
8. Distinguish between state tort causes of action against law enforcement agencies and the causes based on 42 U.S. Code, Section 1983.

INTRODUCTION

The U.S. Supreme Court in *Hiibel* v. *Sixth Judicial District Court of Nevada* held that a Nevada statute that required an individual to provide identification when requested by a law enforcement officer was constitutional.[1] Consider this scenario. You are a police officer and approach a woman who is standing on a corner in a high-crime area for no apparent reason, and you ask her for identification. She remains silent; you then arrest her. You break out your *Miranda* card and begin to advise her of her rights. The first warning states: You have a right to remain silent. The scenario sounds like a comedy skit; however, it illustrates a statement by the great Supreme Court Justice Felix Frankfurter that "due process is more a reflection of experience than reason."[2]

 POLICING IN ACTION

Hiibel v. *Sixth Judicial District Court of Nevada*

The following scenario is based on a case (No. 03-5554) argued before the U.S. Supreme Court on March 22, 2004, and decided on June 21, 2004. A police officer responded to a call reporting that a man had assaulted a woman. The officer found defendant standing outside a parked truck with a woman inside the truck. The officer asked for defendant's identification 11 times and was refused each time. The officer arrested defendant. Defendant was convicted for obstructing the officer in carrying out his duties under Nev. Rev. Stat. 171.12, a "stop and identify" statute, that required defendant to disclose only his name. The U.S. Supreme Court determined that the *Terry* stop (a temporary stop based on a reasonable suspicion), the request for identification, and the state's requirement of a response did not contravene the guarantees of the Fourth Amendment because the request for identity had an immediate relation to the purpose, rationale, and practical demands of the *Terry* stop. Also, the request for identification was reasonably related in scope to the circumstances that justified the *Terry* stop. The Court also determined that defendant's conviction did not violate the Fifth Amendment's prohibition on compelled self-incrimination because disclosure of his name presented no reasonable danger of incrimination.

In this chapter we will explore the legal aspects of policing, including due process issues, search and seizure, abuse of police authority, individual rights of suspects, handling of evidence, testifying in court, and police liability.

LEGAL AUTHORITY: FEDERAL AND STATE CONSTITUTIONS AND STATUTES

The first requirement of a sound body of law is that it should correspond with the actual feelings and demands of the community, whether right or wrong.

—Justice Oliver Wendell Holmes, The Common Law, 1881

What authority does a police officer have to stop a person on the street, and what are the limitations on this authority? Together the police, the courts, and the correctional agencies determine the nature and quality of American justice. Each agency is governed by constitutions, statutory legislation, judicial rulings, and other governmental regulations. Police officers derive their authority and are subject to the restrictions encompassed in the U.S. Constitution, the applicable state constitution, federal and state statutes, federal and state judicial decisions, federal and state administrative regulations, local ordinances, and departmental rules and regulations.

While the common law is often used to interpret the meaning of a legal provision, it does not provide or limit the activities of a police officer in the United States. Common law was the earliest source of our criminal laws,

Squad of mounted police in New York City, 1905.

Photo courtesy of U.S. Library of Congress

and most of our criminal law principles are traceable to the common law of England. This is especially true of the underlying philosophy of criminal law.

The supreme law of the land is the U.S. Constitution. If there is a conflict between any statute, regulation, etc., and the U.S. Constitution, the federal constitution controls. The U.S. Constitution and the state constitutions generally do not list crimes, except for treason, and they operate as primarily a restriction on the powers of the government, including the local police officer. In general, the local police officer enforces state statutes and local ordinances, and his or her conduct is restrained by the federal and state constitutions.

DUE PROCESS

> Bad men, like good men, are entitled to be tried and sentenced in accordance with the law.
>
> —*Justice Hugo Black, Green v. United States, 1961*

Due process is a basic constitutional principle based on the concept of privacy of the individual and limitations on governmental power, and it is a safeguard against arbitrary and unfair government actions. Due process includes, but is not limited to, the basic rights of a defendant in a criminal investigation and subsequent criminal trial.

There are two due process clauses in the U.S. Constitution: One in the Fifth Amendment protects an individual from actions by the federal government, and one in the Fourteenth Amendment protects an individual from actions by state and local governments.

A key concept of due process is that crimes are required to be described such that an individual is reasonably aware of what conduct is prohibited by a criminal statute. A second key concept is that the investigation and prosecution of an individual in a criminal case must be conducted in a manner that does not violate the person's individual rights that are protected by constitutions and statutes.

One problem a police officer faces is that the concept of due process is not a concrete concept; it is flexible and changing. This changing process

---

U.S. Constitution: Fourteenth Amendment

Section 1. All persons born or naturalized in the United States, and subject to the jurisdiction thereof, are citizens of the United States and of the State wherein they reside. No State shall make or enforce any law which shall abridge the privileges or immunities of citizens of the United States; nor shall any State deprive any person of life, liberty, or property, without due process; nor deny to any person within its jurisdiction the equal protection of the laws.

requires that the officer keep updated regarding recent court decisions and changes in statutes and regulations.

Kenneth Culp Davis has identified 12 principal elements of a due process hearing[3]:

1. Timely and adequate notice
2. Chance to make oral statement or argument
3. Chance to present witnesses and evidence
4. Confrontation of adverse witnesses
5. Cross-examination of adverse witnesses
6. Disclosure of all evidence relied on
7. Decision based on record of evidence
8. Right to retain attorney
9. Publicly compensated attorney for indigent
10. Statement of findings of fact
11. Statement of reasons or reasoned opinion
12. Impartial deciding officer

The principle of legality is included in the concept of due process. The first part of this principle promotes the concept of *nullum crimin sine leg* (no crime without law). The second part is that government must give prior notice of what conduct it considers a crime. The third part of the principle is the prohibition against bills of attainder; a bill of attainder is a special law that declares a specific person to be guilty of a crime and thus subject to punishment without a trial or conviction. The principle of legality was developed to move the operation of law further from the historical barbarism toward the rule of law.

ROLE OF THE COURTS

The criminal courts in the United States have three primary missions: to administer justice in a fair and impartial manner, to protect the individual rights of persons accused of crimes, and to provide an authority for controlling crime. Our courts are established either by the federal or state constitution (constitutional courts) or by statutes (legislative or statutory courts). There is a dual court system in the United States (state and federal), and most criminal trials occur in state courts.

Under the principle of separation of power, it is the duty of the police, as part of the executive branch of the government, to investigate and arrest suspected criminals. The prosecutor, also a part of the executive branch, has the duty to determine which cases to prosecute and then to prosecute them. The courts, as part of the judicial branch, conduct the trials and make findings of guilty or not guilty based on the evidence collected by the police and presented by the prosecution. Under our system, until the prosecution brings a charge before the court, the court has no authority to act in a case.

The courts cannot force a prosecutor to present a case before the court, nor can the courts order the police to conduct an investigation of suspected criminal activity.

Federal Courts

The general trial courts in the federal system are the U.S. District Courts. These courts have criminal jurisdiction over cases involving violations of federal law, including civil rights abuse, interstate transportation of stolen vehicles, and kidnapping. While there are only 94 U.S. District Courts, there are almost 600 U.S. District Court judges. Each district court has at least 2 judges assigned to it, with each judge sitting as the judge of the district court. For example, the U.S. District Court for the Southern District of New York has 27 judges assigned to it.

 The federal district courts handle thousands of criminal cases each year, and some of the courts are busier than others. For example, in recent years the U.S. District Court for the Southern District of California has been the busiest federal district court in the judicial system. There is at least 1 federal district court in every state; Alaska has only 1 district court and California and New York both have 4 district courts. There are about 45,000 criminal cases filed in federal district courts each year. Federal courts are involved in state criminal prosecutions only when there is a federal question involved.

Writ of *Habeas Corpus*

The most common federal issue involved in state criminal prosecutions is found in cases in which defendants go to the federal court and claim that their federal constitutional rights were violated by the state or local courts or the police. Generally these issues are brought before a federal court by a writ of *habeas corpus*. In a **writ of *habeas corpus,*** the person filing the writ (normally a prisoner) claims that he or she is being illegally detained in **custody** in a jail or prison and requests the federal court to issue a writ to the custodian to appear before the court and justify the legality of the custody.

 Many legal scholars consider the writ of *habeas corpus* the most important human right in the U.S. Constitution. In 1769, Samuel Johnson wrote about the greatness of the British form of government, stating, "The Habeas Corpus is the single advantage our government has over other countries."[4]

Article I, Section 9, United States Constitution

The privilege of the Writ of Habeas Corpus shall not be suspended, unless when in Cases of Rebellion or Invasion the public safety may require it.

Folklore of Habeas Corpus Act of 1679

At the time the Habeas Corpus Act of 1679 was being debated in the English House of Lords, the act received strong support from an exceedingly portly member of the house. When the Lords lined up to be counted, the parliamentary monitor (the person who recorded the vote), as folklore had it, jokingly counted the portly lord's vote as ten votes. The monitor allowed the vote to stand when no one noticed his joke. The act passed by only two votes.[5]

Scholars have traced the origins of the writ as a protection against illegal imprisonment back to at least New Testament times when Festus the Roman sought justice for Paul's imprisonment in Palestine. The writ was adopted in England by the Habeas Corpus Act of 1679.

State Courts

While no two state systems are exactly alike, most states have a three-tiered system with courts of limited jurisdiction (county, municipal, or city courts), courts with general jurisdiction (district or superior courts), and appellate courts.

There are over 13,000 state courts in the United States. It is estimated that over 90 million civil, traffic, and criminal cases are filed in state courts each year. The overloaded court dockets have resulted in charges of assembly-line justice. Many researchers conclude that the only reason the state criminal courts function is because of the high percentage of guilty pleas (about 90 percent). If every defendant pleaded not guilty and demanded a jury trial, the state criminal courts would be deadlocked.

The state systems have lower trial courts of limited jurisdiction designated as county, municipal, or city courts. These courts try misdemeanor cases and hold preliminary hearings in felony cases that are then referred to the appropriate district or superior court. The general trial courts in the state systems are the district courts or superior courts; for the most part, state trial courts handle most of the criminal cases tried each year. Several states, including California, are consolidating their trial courts into a single trial court that tries both felony and misdemeanor cases.

The major problem facing our courts is the sharply increasing caseloads and the diminishing resources to handle the cases. Because of the heavy caseloads, not all violations of criminal law are prosecuted. Often there are issues between the police and the prosecution because of the failure to prosecute certain cases. Frequently, the police will present a case to the prosecutor, who will decline prosecution because of the lack of resources or because of evidentiary problems.

Amendment IV, United States Constitution

The right of the people to be secure in their persons, houses, papers, and effects, against unreasonable searches and seizures, shall not be violated, and no Warrants shall issue, but upon probable cause, supported by Oath or affirmation, and particularly describing the place to be searched, and the persons or things to be seized.

FOURTH AMENDMENT

All police officers are affected by the Fourth Amendment to the U.S. Constitution. The amendment regulates governmental searches and the arrest of suspects (seizures). Not all searches or arrests are prohibited by the amendment, just those that the courts consider unreasonable. The issues surrounding searches and seizures are complex, and even experienced police officers lose sight of the rationale and the reasons for some of the restrictions imposed by the courts based on the Fourth Amendment.

The Supreme Court has defined a **search** as a government intrusion into an area where a person has a reasonable expectation of privacy.[6] Accordingly, if a person abandons property, there is no continuing expectation of

POLICING IN ACTION

Fourth Amendment Diagrammed

1. The right of the people to be secure in their
   a. Persons
   b. Houses
   c. Papers
   d. Effects
2. No warrants shall issue, but
   a. Upon probable cause
   b. Supported by oath or affirmation
3. Particularly describing the
   a. Place to be searched
   b. Persons or things to be seized

Source: U.S. Constitution, Fourth Amendment (designations added).

privacy in that property. In *California* v. *Greenwood*[7] the Court held that it was not a search for the police to examine the contents of garbage bags left on the sidewalk for pickup by a trash collector, so if your property is in plain view, there is no reasonable expectation of privacy.

The Fourth Amendment deals with the "seizures" of both persons and property. To properly understand its scope and ramifications within the justice system, an examination of the exclusionary rule is necessary.

Exclusionary Rule

The U.S. Supreme Court imposed the **exclusionary rule** on local law enforcement officers in order to prevent police misconduct in the conduct of searches and seizures. In 1949, the Court in the case of *Wolf* v. *Colorado* refused to apply the exclusionary rule to local law enforcement officers.[8] In 1961, the Court overruled the *Wolf* case and noted that in the intervening years (since its decision in that case), a number of states had accepted the validity of the exclusionary rule, and experience had demonstrated that other options and remedies had failed to prevent illegal searches and seizures by law enforcement officers.

In *Mapp* v. *Ohio,* three Cleveland police officers arrived at Dolree Mapp's home to search for a person who was wanted for questioning in connection with a recent bombing.[9] Mapp and her daughter lived on the second floor of a two-family dwelling. Upon arrival at the home, the officers knocked on her door and demanded entry, but Mapp, after telephoning her attorney, refused to admit them without a search warrant. Three hours later, after additional officers were on the scene, the officers forced a door in the house and searched her home. The officers found obscene pictures of Mapp's daughter in a trunk in the home.

In overturning Mapp's conviction for possession of obscene material, the Supreme Court imposed the exclusionary rule on state prosecutions. Under the rule, if a person's constitutional rights are violated and (as a result of the violation) evidence is obtained, the evidence may not be used to prosecute that person. Note there are several recognized exceptions to the exclusionary rule. In addition, before an individual may successfully invoke the rule, his or her rights must have been violated. This latter rule is referred to as **"standing to object"** and means that an individual whose rights have not been violated has no "standing to object" to the introduction of the illegally obtained evidence. For example, the police may conduct an illegal search of Jim Brown and use the evidence obtained in the search to prosecute another criminal whose rights were not violated by the search.

Restrictions on Arrests

The term **"arrest"** is included in the seizure clause of the Fourth Amendment. The word "arrest" is derived from the French word *arrêter,*

POLICING IN ACTION

Honest Mistake Made in Search Warrant

How would you rule in this situation if you were the judge? A city police detective was investigating a homicide and needed a search warrant, but because it was Sunday, his clerical staff was not available. The detective could only find the form that was used to obtain permission for searches of controlled substances. He pointed this out to the magistrate; the magistrate instructed him to strike out the language in the form that pertained to controlled substances. The detective, however, neglected to make some changes, and when the magistrate signed the form authorizing the search, the warrant authorized the search for controlled substances even though there was no probable cause contained in the affidavit attached to the warrant to look for those substances. The search discovered evidence that was offered in court to convict the defendant of murder. Since the warrant was clearly defective, should the evidence be excluded?

The Court upheld the admission of the evidence in *Massachusetts* v. *Sheppard*.[10] The Court, relying on the **good-faith exception** set forth in *United States* v. *Leon* (decided the same week as the *Sheppard* case), stated that the rule should be modified so as not to bar the evidence obtained by officers acting in good faith and relying on a search warrant issued by a magistrate that was later found to be unsupported by probable cause.[11] The Court reasoned that the rule was designed to safeguard Fourth Amendment rights through its deterrence effect on police and that it should not apply to mistakes made by magistrates.

which means to stop or stay and signifies a restraint of a person, thereby depriving the person of his or her own will and liberty and binding him or her to become obedient to the will of the law. It is considered as the beginning of imprisonment.[12] The validity of an arrest is determined by the law of the jurisdiction within which the arrest occurred.[13] Generally there are four elements to an arrest: intention to arrest, authority to arrest, seizure and detention, and understanding by the arrestee that he or she is being arrested.

In cases in which the individual being arrested is under the influence of drugs or other substances or for some reason lacks the mental ability to understand that he or she is being arrested, the courts generally hold that if a reasonable person in that situation would have understood that he or she was being arrested, then the arrest is complete.

In most cases, the only requirement for an arrest is **probable cause** to believe that the individual being arrested committed a criminal offense; in cases of misdemeanors, many state statutes require that the offense must be committed within the presence of the officer. If an individual is illegally arrested, but after the arrest there is sufficient evidence to hold that person for suspected criminal activity, the individual may still be retained in custody. The critical issue involving an illegal arrest claim is whether any evidence discovered during the arrest is admissible in court. For the most part, fruits (evidence) of an illegal arrest are not admissible in court against the arrested individual.

Arrests by Private Persons

A **private person arrest** is an arrest by an individual who is not a law enforcement officer. Every state recognizes the authority of private individuals to make arrests, and this authority is commonly referred to as "citizen's arrest authority." That is a misnomer because there is no requirement that the individual making the arrest be a citizen of any state in the United States. Second, when police officers make arrests, they are citizens even though they are acting in an official capacity.

An arrest by a private person generally requires that the crime for which the arrest is made has been committed or attempted in the presence of the arresting person. The statutes in some states provide for the private arrest of a felon even though the crime occurred in the absence of the private party.

 POLICING IN ACTION

Should Police Arrest Person for Offense Punishable by Fine?
ATWATER v. *CITY OF LAGO VISTA,* 149 L.ED.2D 549 (2001)

The *Atwater* case was one of the most controversial cases decided by the U.S. Supreme Court regarding the arrest without the warrant authority of a local police officer. Gail Atwater was driving her pickup in Lago Vista, Texas, with her three-year-old daughter when she was stopped by a local policeman for not wearing a seatbelt. Apparently the officer and Atwater knew each other. According to her civil complaint, as the officer approached her vehicle, he yelled something to the effect of "We have met before" and "You are going to jail." The officer called for backup and asked to see her driver's license and insurance papers. She stated that she did not have her driver's license because her purse was stolen the day prior to the incident. She was then arrested and released on a $310 bond; later she pleaded guilty to the seatbelt violation and paid the maximum $50 fine. She then sued the city and the officer for violation of her civil rights under 42 U.S. Code Section 1983.

The Court, in a 5-4 decision, held that a police officer could arrest without a warrant under the Fourth Amendment for a misdemeanor not amounting to or involving a breach of peace. The majority opinion stated that there was no dispute that she had committed an offense in the presence of the officer and that the officer was authorized to make a custodial arrest without balancing the costs and benefits or determining whether or not her arrest was in some sense necessary. The Court also stated that the standard of probable cause applied to all arrests, without the need to balance the interests and circumstances involved in particular situations. *Note:* The seatbelt offense for which she was arrested was punishable only by a fine of $50.

The idea that citizens are responsible for policing their communities dates back to before the Norman conquest of England in 1066, when the shire-reeve (similar to a present-day sheriff) could call on any free male subject to serve on a posse. The free males were expected to constrain felons and in some cases to administer justice. As noted in Chapter 1, the concept of an organized police force is a relatively recent development.

Frequently, private arrests turn into a "he said, she said" confrontation. For example, in November 2002, an angry motorist in Sacramento, California, tried to make a private arrest of Jason Meggs, who was a member of an organization called Critical Mass and who was demonstrating to promote the rights of cyclists. Meggs and his cohorts, in turn, retaliated by trying to arrest the original arresting party.[14]

The number of private arrests differs wildly from state to state and even from city to city. In 2003, the Washington, D.C., Police Department reported no private arrests, while the Los Angeles Police Department reported 6,441 arrests—all for misdemeanor offenses. For the most part, private arrests are made by security guards employed by private industries to curb shoplifting and employee thefts. The records of one national drugstore chain reflect that the security guards of that chain average more than 12,000 private person arrests annually.

Arrest and Search Warrants

The general rule for searches is that you must get a search warrant unless you are unable to, but this rule does not apply to arrests. Other differences between a search warrant and an arrest warrant include the fact that search warrants are effective for a limited time whereas an arrest warrant is valid until recalled by the court. Generally search warrants must be executed during daylight hours unless the warrant authorizes a nighttime search; arrest warrants may be executed at any time.

Terry Stops

As noted earlier, to make an arrest without a warrant the officer needs probable cause. There are situations, however, in which a police officer needs to stop an individual based only on a suspicion. This situation was addressed in the U.S. Supreme Court case *Terry* v. *Ohio*.[15] The *Terry* case developed the concept of stop and frisk. The ***Terry* stop** must be a temporary stop and not an arrest, and it must be based on reasonable suspicion that criminal activity is involved. After the stop, if the officer has reason to fear that there is danger involved, the officer may pat the clothes of the person being stopped. The pat-down is only for purposes of detecting any weapons.

> **Fifth Amendment**
>
> No person shall be held to answer for a capital, or otherwise infamous crime, unless on a presentation or indictment of a Grand Jury, except in cases arising in the land or naval forces, or in the Militia, when in actual service in the time of war or public danger; nor shall any person be subject for the same offense to be twice put in jeopardy of life or limb; nor shall be compelled in any criminal case to be a witness against himself, not be deprived of life, liberty, or property, without due process of law; nor shall private property be taken for public use, without just compensation.

FIFTH AMENDMENT

Self-Incrimination

As you will note from the above, the Fifth Amendment is the longest and most diverse of the amendments in the Bill of Rights. The most well-known right is the right against self-incrimination, commonly known as "taking the Fifth": A defendant cannot be compelled to testify against himself or herself. This right has been controversial because many Americans see it as an admission of guilt. This was especially true during the "Communists in the Government" investigations led by Senator Joseph McCarthy in the 1950s. Senator McCarthy applied the term "Fifth Amendment Communists" to individuals such as Howard Hughes who "took the Fifth" when testifying before Congress about Communists in the U.S. Government.

During the religious persecutions in England in the 1500s, Church officials and ministers were called before the Court of Star Chamber and questioned about their religious beliefs. The Court of Star Chamber was a series of courts that convened without juries and was used to enforce political policies and mete out severe punishments for individuals whose beliefs did not conform to those of the government. If the Church leaders lied about their beliefs, then their souls were in jeopardy. If they told the truth, they would lose their freedom or their lives.[16]

In 1637, John Lilburne, a Puritan printer, was accused of distributing treasonous pamphlets. He refused to take the oath required by the Court of Star Chamber. He accused the court of trying to "ensnare" and stated that the court was trying to get new charges against him. His assertion of the right against self-incrimination led the English Parliament to abolish the Court of Star Chamber and to forbid any oath forcing a person to confess or to accuse himself of any crime.[17] In colonial America, many of the colonial courts used tactics similar to those of the Star Chamber. By the start of the 18th century, however, the right against self-incrimination was recognized in most of the colonies; in 1776, the Commonwealth of Virginia guaranteed the right in the Virginia Declaration of Rights.

POLICING IN ACTION

Handwriting Exemplars

Timothy McVeigh was arrested for bombing the Oklahoma City federal building, which caused many deaths. A federal grand jury issued a subpoena ordering him to furnish exemplars of his handwriting. He refused, contending that the subpoena was a violation of his Fifth Amendment privilege against self-incrimination. If you were the judge in this case, how would you rule? See *United States* v. *McVeigh*, 896 F.Supp. 1549 (W.D. Okla., 1995).

The privilege against self-incrimination applies only to evidence that is testimonial in nature, and McVeigh was forced to provide the court with a sample of his handwriting. A defendant may be forced to provide fingerprints, voice exemplars, and blood tests because physical evidence is not included in the self-incrimination privilege. In *Pennsylvania* v. *Muniz*, the police arrested the defendant for drunk driving.[18] At the time of his arrest, he was not warned of his rights under *Miranda* and stated that he had had several drinks. The Court held that the statement that he had had several drinks was not admissible because it was the result of an in-custody interrogation; however, the officer was allowed to testify that the defendant exhibited slurred speech.

A frequent test used by the courts to determine if the statement being offered into evidence is testimonial is whether or not it is capable of being true or false. If it is not capable of being true or false, then generally it is considered nontestimonial. Requiring a person to sign a form authorizing release of foreign bank records was considered by one court as nontestimonial. If the form had stated "I authorize the bank to release my records," it would have been testimonial evidence because it contains an admission that the defendant has bank records in that bank.[19]

An individual can be ordered to produce preexisting private records. In *Fisher* v. *United States*, the Supreme Court held that the contents of an existing document are not protected by the Fifth Amendment since the preparation of that document was not compelled by the government.[20] If the existence of the document is obvious and not incriminating, the act of producing it is not incriminating; if, however, the existence of the document is not known and the act of producing it incriminates the defendant, then he or she cannot be ordered to produce it. For example, if the court orders the defendant to produce all records he may have regarding his involvement in illegal drug trafficking, the fact that he has the records helps establish the fact that he is involved in the illegal trafficking, so the order violates the privilege. Fifth Amendment protection does not apply to business entities, however, and an order to a corporate officer to produce certain corporate records is not a violation of the privilege.

The privilege against self-incrimination protects individuals from answering any questions in any proceedings if the answers might incriminate them in future criminal proceedings. Accordingly, the privilege applies to both civil cases and administrative hearings.

Does a police officer have the right to invoke the privilege in an investigation? In *Gardner* v. *Broderick*, a police officer was discharged from duty as a New York police officer after he refused to waive his privilege against self-incrimination and to sign a waiver of immunity from prosecution in a grand jury investigation of police corruption.[21] On appeal, the U.S. Supreme Court noted that the officer was discharged not for failure to answer relevant questions about his official duties but for refusal to waive a constitutional right and that he was dismissed solely for his refusal to waive the immunity to which he would be entitled if he was ever required to testify despite his constitutional privilege. The Court ruled that his dismissal was contrary to the Fifth Amendment. It is proper, however, to terminate a police officer who refuses to answer questions that are directly related to the official performance of his or her duties, provided that the officer has been informed that any answers that are provided may not be used later in criminal proceedings.[22]

Miranda Rights and Exceptions

On the night of March 2, 1963, 18-year-old Barbara J., while walking to a bus stop in Phoenix, Arizona, was accosted by a man who shoved her into his car, tied her hands and ankles, drove her to a dark street, and raped her. He then drove her to a street near her home and released her. Ernesto Miranda was arrested by the police for investigation of her rape. Miranda was placed in a lineup and was identified by several women as the man who had raped them. Miranda, while in custody, was then questioned by the police and made a statement in writing that described the rape of Barbara J. Miranda's court-appointed attorney objected to the admission of the statement on the grounds that he was not advised of his rights against self-incrimination. *Note*: Miranda was a 23-year-old eighth-grade dropout with a police record, and he had received an dishonorable discharge by the U.S. Army.

In reversing his conviction, the Court announced that it would no longer uphold confessions as voluntary unless the accused had been advised of the following by the police[23]:

- You have a right to remain silent.
- Anything you say can be used against you in court.
- You have the right to an attorney and to have the attorney present while you are being questioned.
- If you cannot afford an attorney, one will be appointed for you before any questioning begins.

Miranda was retried and served prison time for the rape. Years later he was killed in a barroom fight. Found on his body were autographed *Miranda* warning cards, which he had been trading for drinks.

The *Miranda* warnings are required only for in-custody interrogation. The courts have broadened the meaning of interrogation to include the "functional equivalent" of interrogation; for example, interrogation includes any words or actions by the police that the police should know are reasonably likely to elicit an incriminating response from the suspect. The Court in *Rhode Island* v. *Innis* held that the focus in determining if interrogation has occurred is on the suspect.[24]

Under the *Miranda* definition, a person is in **custody** when the individual is otherwise deprived of his or her freedom of action in any significant way. In *Berkemer* v. *McCarty*, the Court established an objective test to determine whether the suspect is in custody.[25] The Court stated that an officer's unarticulated plan to arrest the suspect has no bearing on the question of custody; the only relevant inquiry, according to the Court, is how a reasonable person in the suspect's position would have understood his or her situation.

Exceptions to the *Miranda* warning requirement include covert investigations and public safety issues. When the accused was talking to an undercover police officer who was in the same prison cell with the accused, the Court held that no advisement was necessary because the accused did not realize that he was talking to a police officer and the coercive nature of the interrogation was missing. In addition, the warning is not needed when it is necessary to question the accused for reasons of public safety such as the location of a gun that was apparently hidden in a store open to the public.[26]

The defendant does not have a right to commit perjury on the witness stand. In *Harris* v. *New York*, the defendant had made a statement regarding his involvement in drugs to the police that was tainted because he was not properly warned.[27] He then took the stand and testified that he had never been involved with drugs. The Court held that if the defendant had given a voluntary statement that was inadmissible because of a *Miranda* rights violation, the prosecution could use that statement to impeach his testimony in court. The Court held that a defendant's right to testify in his or her own defense does not include the right to commit perjury.

HANDLING OF EVIDENCE

Many defendants have escaped punishment because the police or the prosecutor has mishandled the evidence. Two major principles apply in the control of evidence: continuity and security.[28] Continuity of evidence means that there is a clearly documented record of where a piece of evidence has been (a record of who handled it and why) from the time the evidence was taken from the crime scene until it appears in court. This is generally accomplished by the collection of the evidence in sealed containers (to prevent contamination) that are marked for identification; in addition, a chain of custody of the evidence is maintained. Any break in continuity may provide the defense with grounds to have the evidence excluded.

The security of the evidence is also paramount. Special background checks are normally made on individuals who are assigned responsibility for the security of evidence. Even small quantities of drugs offer a temptation of quick money for any individual with access to the evidence.

POLICE OFFICER AS WITNESS

Police officers are often called as witnesses in criminal cases. In many situations, the testimony of the officer will determine whether the defendant is convicted or acquitted. According to Harvey Wallace and Cliff Roberson, good police officers do not simply arrive in court the day of the trial, do battle with the defense attorney, and convince the jury that they are telling the truth and the defendant is lying. They prepare for court.[29]

Prior to going to court, the officer should review the written reports in detail. Juries fail to understand that officers have made numerous other arrests in addition to the one connected with their case. The officer should contact the prosecutor prior to trial to discuss the case. In many jurisdictions, the arresting officer is permitted to sit next to the prosecutor during the trial; in others, the "rule" is invoked and the officer is not permitted in the courtroom until he or she is called to testify. The "rule" refers to the practice of keeping witnesses out of the courtroom so that they will not be influenced by the testimony of other witnesses.

Law enforcement officers are frequently uncomfortable standing or sitting in front of a group and talking, but this skill is exactly what every police officer must master. Occasionally, the officer will testify in a closed hearing or an empty courtroom. The majority of an officer's testimony, however, will be in open court in front of the jury and the public, and the officer will be subjected to cross-examination by the defense attorney, who may attempt to destroy the officer's credibility.

Goals of Direct Examination

To testify more effectively in court, the officer should understand the goals of direct examination when he or she is called by the prosecutor in a criminal case. Most prosecutors attempt to satisfy two generally accepted objectives during all direct examinations: to present all legally sufficient evidence to support the charges filed against the defendant, and to convince the fact finder (the jury or the judge in a trial by judge alone) of the integrity of the evidence and (ultimately) the truth of the charge.

At a seminar for police officers, the San Diego, California, District Attorney's Office published the Ten Commandments for Witnesses:

1. Tell the truth. In a trial, as in all other matters, honesty comes first.
2. Do not guess. If you do not know, say so.
3. Be sure you understand the question. You cannot possibly give a truthful and accurate answer unless you understand the question.

POLICING IN ACTION

Courthouse Conduct

Devallis Rutledge, former Senior Deputy District Attorney for Los Angeles County, California, warns that a police officer's conduct in the courthouse can cause a mistrial or make prosecution more difficult for the state. Rutledge, the author of ten books on police issues and a frequent lecturer to police departments, cautions police officers that their conduct in the courthouse may have an unwanted effect on the conduct of a trial. For example, the officer who carries evidence to the courtroom in plain view of spectators in the hallway may be exposing it to a potential juror and therefore create a fairness issue. Rutledge has compiled a list of nine do's and don'ts for police officers in the courthouse[30]:

1. Be punctual. Judges and jurors do not like to be kept waiting.
2. Practice courtesy. The person you hold the door open for may be a jury member.
3. Avoid controversy. Do not engage in discussions around the courthouse about such things as religion, politics, or other volatile issues.
4. Gag yourself. Do not talk about the case to the press or others except when in the line of duty.
5. Keep physical evidence concealed when you are asked to bring it with you.
6. Do not argue with a prosecutor or defense counsel.
7. Dress appropriately. Dress like a professional police officer.
8. Use plain English that is understandable and eliminate "cop-speak" when testifying.
9. Be disciplined and exercise thoughtful behavior. Above all, be a professional.

4. Take your time and answer the question asked. Give the question as much thought as is required to understand it, formulate your answer, and then give your answer.
5. Give a clearly audible answer. Everything you say is being recorded. Do not nod your head yes or no.
6. Do not look for assistance when you are on the witness stand. If you think you need help, request it from the judge.
7. Beware of questions involving distance and time. If you make an estimate, make sure everyone understands that you are making an estimate.
8. Be courteous. Answer yes or no, and address the judge as Your Honor.
9. Admit it freely if you are asked whether you have talked to the prosecutor regarding your testimony and you have done so.
10. Avoid joking and making wisecracks. A lawsuit is a serious matter.

POLICE LIABILITY

There are three general theories under which a police officer, a department, or a city may be the subject of civil litigation: as the result of an action based on an intentional tort (such as battery, false arrest, infliction

---

42 U.S. Code Section 1983

Every person who, under the color of any statute, ordinance, regulation, custom, or usage of any State…subjects or causes to be subjected any citizen…to the deprivation of any rights, privileges, or immunities secured by the Constitution and laws shall be liable to the party injured in an action at law.

---

of mental distress, and conversion of property); as the result of an action based on negligence (such as negligent driving, negligent discharge of a firearm, and negligence in the use of lawful force to effect an arrest); and as the result of an action based on an infringement of a constitutional right (such as illegal search, denial of right to counsel, and illegally preventing a person from exercising a constitutional right).[31]

42 U.S. Code Section 1983

The majority of civil litigation against police agencies and individual officers is based on violations of constitutional rights, which are filed pursuant to Title 42, U.S. Code, Section 1983. Many states have similar statutes.

Section 1983 became law on April 20, 1871. For the first 90 years of its existence, there was relatively little action under Section 1983. Historical research by the authors via the Lexis database indicated that only six cases were filed against law enforcement officers or agencies during its first 90 years. In 1961, the U.S. Supreme Court, in *Monroe* v. *Pape*, held that when a police officer is alleged to have acted improperly in conducting an illegal search, the officer can be sued in federal court by alleging that the officer deprived the injured party of his or her constitutional rights.[32] After the *Pape* case was published, the number of court filings increased significantly. It is estimated that in the calendar year 2003, over 7,000 court actions were filed alleging Section 1983 damages.

Under 42 U.S. Code Section 1983, any person whose constitutional rights have been violated by a police officer may file a civil action against the officer and his or her employer for both compensatory damages (actual damages) and punitive damages. The most popular types of actions filed under Section 1983 include the following:

- False arrest
- Illegal search and seizure
- Verbal harassment
- Denial of the right to counsel
- Denial of the right of association under the First Amendment
- Excessive use of force in effecting an otherwise legal arrest
- Retaliatory prosecution

POLICING IN ACTION

Monroe v. Pape, 365 U.S. 167 (1961)

The Monroes (petitioners) filed a complaint alleging that 13 Chicago police officers broke into petitioners' home in the early morning, routed them from bed, made them stand naked in the living room, and ransacked every room, emptying drawers and ripping mattress covers. It further alleged that James Monroe was then taken to the police station and detained on "open" charges for 10 hours while he was interrogated about a two-day-old murder, that he was not taken before a magistrate although one was accessible, that he was not permitted to call his family or his attorney, and that he was subsequently released without criminal charges being filed against him. It is alleged that the officers had no search warrant and no arrest warrant and that they acted "under color of the statutes, ordinances, regulations, customs and usages" of Illinois and of the city of Chicago.

The Supreme Court held that the guarantee against unreasonable searches and seizures contained in the Fourth Amendment of the U.S. Constitution was applicable to the states by reason of the due process clause of the Fourteenth Amendment of the U.S. Constitution. The Court further held that 42 U.S.C.S. Section 1983 meant to give a remedy to parties deprived of constitutional rights, privileges, and immunities by an official's abuse of his position, as the federal remedy was supplementary to any state remedy, and the latter need not have been first sought and refused before the federal one was invoked.

- Denial of medical treatment of a person in custody
- Denial of mail rights of a person in custody
- Illegal interrogation
- Failure to provide police protection
- Wrongful use of deadly force

Section 1983 may be used to bring civil actions against state and local law enforcement officers, but federal law enforcement officers generally cannot be sued under that section because it requires that the officer be acting under "color of state law." Federal officers may, however, be sued for violations of individual constitutional rights under the rule in the *Bivens* case.[33] The *Bivens* case is a judicially created counterpart to Section 1983 for federal law enforcement officers.

There are several general principles involving litigation under Section 1983:

- Section 1983 does not create any substantive rights but merely provides remedies for violations of substantive rights created by the federal constitution or federal statutes.
- Section 1983 is available even if the conduct in question violates a state law.
- A person bringing an action under Section 1983 need not bring separate state and federal actions in cases in which the conduct also violated state law. The causes of action may be combined in one single action.

POLICING IN ACTION

County of Sacramento v. *Lewis*, 523 U.S. 833 (1998)

The police officer was involved in a high-speed automobile chase aimed at apprehending a suspected offender. The individual bringing the action (plaintiff) was a passenger on a motorcycle driven by the offender. The driver of the motorcycle tipped over, and the officer's vehicle struck the plaintiff. The plaintiff filed suit under 42 U.S. Code Section 1983 alleging a deprivation of his due process right to life under the Fourteenth Amendment of the U.S. Constitution.

The Supreme Court held that high-speed chases with no intent to harm the suspects physically or to worsen their legal plight did not give rise to liability under the Fourteenth Amendment of the U.S. Constitution. The motorcycle driver's outrageous behavior prompted the officer's response as a law enforcement officer. The officer was not liable because there was no improper or malicious motive in following the motorcycle in a high-speed chase.

The Court noted that California Vehicle Code Section 17004 provided that a public employee was not liable for civil damages on account of personal injury to or death of any person or damage to property resulting from the operation, in the line of duty, of an authorized emergency vehicle when in the immediate pursuit of an actual or suspected violator of the law.

The Court also stated that high-speed police chases with no intent to harm suspects physically or to worsen their legal plight do not give rise to liability under the substantive due process guarantee of the federal Constitution's Fourteenth Amendment, redressable by an action under 42 U.S. Code Section 1983 for violation of a federal right, as (1) a police officer deciding whether to give chase must balance the need to stop a suspect and show that flight from the law is no way to freedom against the high-speed threat to everyone within stopping range, be they suspects, their passengers, other drivers, or bystanders; (2) when unforeseen circumstances demand an officer's instant judgment, even precipitate recklessness fails to inch close enough to harmful purpose to spark the shock that implicates the large concerns of the governors and the governed; and (3) just as a purpose to cause harm is needed for liability under the Constitution's Eighth Amendment in a prison riot case, so it ought to be needed for due process liability in a pursuit case.

- Unlike the Federal Tort Claims Act and most state tort claims acts, there is no requirement that the plaintiff first submit an administrative claim; also, there is no requirement for the individual to exhaust his or her state remedies prior to filling an action under Section 1983.
- The conduct complained of must have been taken under color of law or use of authority. An officer is acting under **color of law** if the officer uses his or her office to carry out the conduct in question.
- The conduct complained of must have been the legal cause of the harm alleged by the plaintiff.
- Unless there was direct participation by police supervisory personnel, they are not generally liable for Section 1983 damages even if there are broad allegations of failure to properly train and supervise officers who are liable under the section.

The *Lewis* case does not hold that police officers and their employers are not liable for injuries caused by high-speed chases. The case stands for the concept that the chases are not actionable under Section 1983 unless there has been a violation of an individual right. In most cases involving high-speed chases, the injured person seeks redress under state statutes.

State Tort Liability

At common law, the government could not be sued based on the concept "The king can do no wrong." Because of this concept, before a state, county, or city can be sued, there must be a statutory provision that permits the action. All states have some form of state tort claims act, and most of these acts require that the aggrieved party first file an administrative claim with an appropriate agency before filing suit against the state or political subdivision. In most cases, the individual officer may be sued without the filing of the individual claim.

State tort liability is normally based on one of three torts: strict liability tort, intentional tort, and negligence tort. In general, state tort actions against law enforcement officers provide a greater scope of liability than do Section 1983 actions. Accordingly, tort actions under state laws cover a greater range of behaviors than Section 1983 and *Bivens* actions.

Strict liability torts are usually associated with behaviors that are extremely dangerous, and any person engaging in such behaviors can be substantially certain that his or her conduct will result in injury or damage. Rarely do these torts apply to law enforcement officers, with the possible exception of when certain law enforcement policies allow for the use of chemical agents to control illegal drug crops.

To recover under the theory of an intentional tort, the injured party must establish that an officer's behavior was intentional and that this intentional conduct led to damage or injury. The intentional requirement does not mean that the officer must have intended to do injury or damage, only that he or she intended to do the act that caused the injury or damage. An intentional tort assumes the elements of knowledge and foreseeability of the danger associated with the particular behavior. The most common intentional torts include the following:

- *Wrongful death*. Generally, actions for wrongful death are filed by the family of the decedent and contend that the decedent was wrongly killed by the police. For example, in *Tennessee* v. *Garner*, two Memphis police officers answered a "prowler inside call."[34] The officers saw Edward Garner fleeing the scene, and one of the officers shot and killed him as he was running away. *Note:* While the officer may not have intended to kill Edward, this was found to be an intentional tort because the officer's act of shooting at the fleeing individual was intentional. The Supreme Court held that the use of deadly force to prevent the escape of all felony suspects, whatever the circumstances, was constitutionally unreasonable. The Court reasoned that it was not better that all felony suspects die than that they escape. The Court held that deadly force could be used to prevent the escape of a felon only when the escaping felon posed an immediate danger to the officer or the public.

- *Assault and battery.* A law enforcement officer may use reasonable force to complete an arrest; if, however, the officer uses unreasonable or excessive force, he or she is guilty of assault and battery on the suspect.
- ***False arrest.*** To establish a false arrest, a plaintiff must show that the police willfully detained him or her, the detention was against his or her will, and the detention was made without legal authority.
- ***False imprisonment.*** False imprisonment is similar to a false arrest but is different in that it is the *continued detention* that is the tort, whereas in a false arrest it is the *act of detention* that constitutes the tort. To establish the tort of false imprisonment, the plaintiff must establish the police intention to confine him or her, the acts resulting in the confinement, and the knowledge of the confinement. It is an affirmative defense for the police that the detention was authorized by law. Being an affirmative defense, the government or the officer being sued must prove the legality of the detention.

Negligence torts refer to inadvertent behaviors that cause damages or injuries. Negligence requires a lower level of foreseeability of danger than does an intentional tort. The standard applied is whether an officer's act or failure to act created an unreasonable risk of harm to another member of society. In most cases, four elements are required to be established before an aggrieved party can recover damages under a negligence cause of action:

1. *Legal duty.* The officer or individual complained about must have had a legal duty to either take action or refrain from taking action.
2. *Breach of duty.* The aggrieved party must establish that the officer or individual complained about breached the legal duty.
3. *Proximate cause.* The plaintiff must establish that the conduct at issue was the proximate cause of the injury or damage.
4. *Damage or injury.* The plaintiff must prove that there was actual damage or harm and that the damage or harm was such that it substantially interfered with an interest of a person or his or her property.

Research of the Lexis legal database indicates that the most frequent forms of negligence torts brought against police officers and law enforcement agencies include negligent operation of emergency vehicles, negligent failure to protect, negligent failure to arrest, and negligent failure to render assistance.

Who Can Be Sued?

Generally, the individual officers involved in the questioned action may be sued. This general rule applies even though the individual officer may not have known the boundaries established by law. The more difficult question arises when the supervisors, the department, the city, or the county can be sued. To an injured party, this issue is critical because it is the city or county that has the financial resources to pay a judgment; in legal slang, they have the "deep pockets."

State and federal courts in recent years have expanded the extent in which private employers can be sued for torts of their employees but have been reluctant to extend this to public agencies. There are two often-quoted reasons for this failure to extend liability to public agencies: First, public agency supervisors and administrators have limited discretion in making hiring decisions; second, official duties of public employees (like those of police officers) are established by governmental authority rather than by their supervisors.

These are the four general areas in which law enforcement agencies and cities or counties have been held liable for civil torts:

1. *Negligent hiring.* The departments have a duty to weed out those individuals obviously unsuited for law enforcement employment.
2. *Negligent assignment, retention, or entrustment.* Supervisors have a duty to supervise errant officers, and they must take reasonable action against officers who are unfit for the duty assigned or for continued entrustment as an officer.
3. *Negligent direction or supervision.* Supervisors have the duty to develop and implement appropriate policies and procedures.
4. *Negligent training.* Supervisors have a duty to properly train officers before assigning them to law enforcement duties. *Note:* In the *City of Canton* v. *Harris* case, the Supreme Court limited the use of inadequate police training as a basis for Section 1983 actions.[35] The Court ruled that inadequate police training may form the basis for a Section 1983 claim "where the failure to train amounts to deliberate indifference to the rights of the persons with whom the police come in contact" and such official indifference amounted to "policy or custom."

▲ SUMMARY

Police officers derive their authority and are subject to the restrictions encompassed in the U.S. Constitution, the applicable state constitution, federal and state statutes, federal and state judicial decisions, federal and state administrative regulations, local ordinances, and departmental rules and regulations.

The supreme law of the land is the U.S. Constitution. If there is a conflict between any statute, regulation, etc., and the U.S. Constitution, the federal constitution controls. The U.S. Constitution and the state constitutions generally do not list crimes, except for treason, and they operate primarily as a restriction on the powers of the government, including the local police officer.

Due process is a basic constitutional principle based on the concepts of privacy of the individual, limitations on governmental power, and a safeguard against arbitrary and unfair government actions. Due process includes, but is not limited to, the basic rights of a defendant in a criminal investigation and subsequent criminal trial.

There are two due process clauses in the U.S. Constitution: The one in the Fifth Amendment protects an individual from actions by the federal government, and the one in the Fourteenth Amendment protects an individual from actions by state and local governments. One problem that faces a police officer is that the concept of due process is not a concrete concept; it is flexible and changing.

The criminal courts in the United States have three primary missions: to administer justice in a fair and impartial manner, to protect the individual rights of persons accused of crimes, and to provide for an authority for controlling crime. Our courts are established either by the federal or state constitution (constitutional courts) or by statutes (legislative or statutory courts). There is a dual court system in the United States (state and federal), and most criminal trials occur in state courts.

The most common federal issue involved in state criminal prosecutions arises in cases in which defendants go to federal court and claim that their federal constitutional rights were violated by the state or local courts or by the police.

The general trial courts in the state systems are the district courts or superior courts; for the most part, state trial courts handle most of the criminal cases tried each year. The major problems facing our courts are the sharply increasing caseloads and the diminishing resources to handle the cases.

All police officers are affected by the Fourth Amendment to the U.S. Constitution. The amendment regulates governmental searches and arrests of suspects (seizures). Not all searches or arrests are prohibited by the amendment, just those that the courts consider unreasonable.

The validity of an arrest is determined by the law of the jurisdiction within which the arrest occurred. Generally there are four elements to an arrest: intention to arrest, authority to arrest, seizure and detention, and understanding by the arrestee that he or she is being arrested. Every state recognizes the authority of private individuals to make arrests; this authority is commonly referred to as "citizen's arrest authority." The general rule for searches is that you must get a search warrant unless you are unable to, but this rule does not apply to arrests.

The privilege against self-incrimination applies only to evidence that is testimonial in nature. The *Miranda* warnings are required only for in-custody interrogation. The courts have broadened the meaning of interrogation to include the "functional equivalent" of interrogation. Under the *Miranda* definition, a person is in custody when the individual is otherwise deprived of his or her freedom of action in any significant way.

The majority of civil litigation against police agencies and individual officers is based on violations of constitutional rights, which are filed pursuant to Title 42, U.S. Code, Section 1983. Many states have similar statutes.

QUESTIONS IN REVIEW

1. What is a Section 1983 action?
2. Explain the "standing to object" concept.
3. What constitutes a *Terry* stop?
4. Explain the meaning of *nullum crimin sine leg*.
5. What is the purpose of the writ of *habeas corpus*?
6. When may a private person make an arrest?
7. Explain the good-faith exception.
8. What constitutes false imprisonment?
9. Explain the concept of due process.

 ## POLICE RESOURCES ON THE WEB

Administrative Offices of the U.S. Courts
www.uscourts.gov

American Academy of Forensic Sciences
www.aafs.org

American Bar Association
www.abanet.org

Federal Judicial Center
www.fjc.gov

Justice Information Center
www.ncjrs.org

U.S. Department of Justice
www.usdoj.gov

REFERENCES

1. *Hiibel* v. *Sixth Judicial District Court of Nevada*, 124 S.Ct. 2451 (decided June 2004).
2. SUPREME COURT JUSTICE in *Graves* v. *New York,* 360 U.S. 466 (1939).
3. KENNETH CULP DAVIS, *Administrative Law of the Seventies* (Rochester, NY: Lawyers Cooperative, 1976), p. 242.
4. SAMUEL JOHNSON, *A Journey to the Western Islands of Scotland* (London, Strahan, 1796), p. 122.
5. CLIFF ROBERSON, *Criminal Procedure Today: Issues and Cases*, 2nd ed. (Upper Saddle River, NJ: Prentice Hall, 2003), p. 39.

6. *Katz* v. *United States*, 389 U.S. 347 (1967).

7. 486 U.S. 35 (1988).

8. 338 U.S. 25 (1949).

9. 367 U.S. 643 (1961).

10. 468 U.S. 981 (1984).

11. 468 U.S. 897 (1984).

12. Taken from the court opinion in *Legrand* v. *Bedinger*, 20 Ky. 539 (1827).

13. 267 U.S. 132 (1925).

14. KATHERINE MARSH, "Playing Police," *Legal Affairs* (July/August 2004): 16–20.

15. 392 U.S. 1 (1968).

16. LINDA R. MONK, *The Bill of Rights: A User's Guide*, 3rd ed. (Alexandria, VA: Close-up Publications, 2000), pp. 127–128.

17. Ibid., p. 130.

18. 496 U.S. 582 (1990).

19. *Doe* v. *United States*, 487 U.S. 201 (1988).

20. 425 U.S. 391 (1976).

21. 392 U.S. 273 (1968).

22. *Gibrilowitz* v. *Newman*, 582 F.2nd 100 (1st Cir. 1978).

23. *Miranda* v. *Arizona*, 384 U.S. 436 (1966).

24. Ibid.

25. 446 U.S. 291 (1980).

26. 468 U.S. 420 (1984).

27. 401 U.S. 222 (1971).

28. EDWARD T. THIBAULT, LAWRENCE M. LYNCHAND, and BRUCE R. MCBRIDE, *Proactive Police Management*, 6th ed. (Upper Saddle River, NJ: Prentice Hall, 2004), p. 281.

29. HARVEY WALLACE and CLIFF ROBERSON, *Written and Interpersonal Communication Methods for Law Enforcement*, 3rd ed. (Upper Saddle River, NJ: Prentice Hall, 2004), pp. 114–117.

30. DEVALLIS RUTLEDGE, "Courthouse Conduct," *Police Magazine*, vol. 28, no. 6 (June 2004): 70–74.

31. INTERNATIONAL ASSOCIATION OF CHIEFS OF POLICE, *Police Supervision: A Manual for Police Supervisors* (Arlington, VA: IACP, 1985), pp. 44–47.

32. 365 U.S. 167 (1961).

33. *Bivens* v. *Six Unknown Named Federal Agents*, 403 U.S. 388 (1971). The case name has been the subject of considerable discussion. How can an unknown federal agent be "named"?

34. 471 U.S. 1 (1985)

35. 389 U.S. 378 (1989).

Police and the Community: Policing a Diverse Society

Key Terms

Citizen Police Academy

Community Relations Service (CRS)

Discrimination

Kerner Report

Labeling theory

Melting pot model

Multiculturalism

Police-community relations

Police crackdown

Self-fulfilling prophecy

Sir Robert Peel

Slave catchers

Thin blue line

Outline

Introduction

Changing Demographics of Communities

Nature of Police-Community Relations

Policing of Diverse Populations

Contemporary Problems

Improvement in Police-Community Relations

Learning Objectives

After reading this chapter, you should be able to:

1. Discuss the importance of effective police-community relations.
2. List historical factors that impact contemporary police-community relations in minority communities.
3. Explain the impact that changing demographics have on police relations with the community.
4. Define multiculturalism.
5. Describe police-community relations.

6. Discuss the recommendations of various reports (such as the President's Commission Report and the Kerner Report) for effective police-community relations.
7. Identify and discuss methods to improve police-community relations in minority communities.

INTRODUCTION

The communities of the United States in which the police operate have been constructed by people from many different shores.

—Ronald Takaki, A Different Mirror: A History of Multicultural America, 1993

It was Friday, August 13, 1965, on a hot and sultry California evening, when Watts (a Los Angeles neighborhood) erupted in chaos and anarchy. The Watts riots started with a routine arrest of a drunk driver. A Los Angeles police officer flagged down motorist Marquette Frye, whom the officer suspected of being intoxicated. When a crowd of primarily African-American onlookers began to taunt the police officer, a second officer was called in. According to eyewitness accounts, the second officer struck crowd members with his baton, and news of the act of police brutality soon spread throughout the neighborhood. The incident—combined with escalating racial tensions, overcrowding in the neighborhood, and a summer heat wave—sparked violence on a massive scale. Despite attempts the following day aimed at quelling antipolice sentiment, residents began looting and burning local stores.

The rioting lasted five days: More than 34 people died, at least 1,000 people were wounded, and an estimated $200 million in property was destroyed. An estimated 35,000 African Americans took part in the riot, which required 16,000 National Guardsmen, county sheriff's deputies, and police to put down. Although city officials initially blamed outside persons for the insurrection, subsequent studies showed that the majority of participants had lived in Watts all their lives. These studies also found that the protesters' anger was directed primarily at white shopkeepers in the neighborhood and at members of the nearly all-white Los Angeles police department.[1] The rioters left black churches, libraries, businesses, and private homes virtually untouched.[2]

Some 26 years after Watts, on March 3, 1991, in Los Angeles, Rodney King (an African American) was pulled over for a traffic violation. According to the officers, King emerged from his automobile in an aggressive manner that suggested he might have been high on drugs. Before handcuffing King, the police delivered some 56 blows and kicks and a number of shocks from a Taser stun gun to the fallen body of the suspect while almost 20 other officers stood by and watched. A man named George Holliday, standing on the balcony of a nearby building, videotaped the incident. The next day, he gave his 81-second tape to Los Angeles TV Channel 5. By the end of the day, the video was being broadcast by TV stations around the world. Four days later, all the charges against King were dropped, and 4 officers were charged with felony assault and other beating-related charges.

The Independent Commission on the Los Angeles Police Department (also called the Christopher Commission) came out three months later documenting the "systematic use of excessive force and racial harassment in the LAPD"; it also noted management problems and condemned the department's emphasis on crime control rather than crime prevention, which served to isolate the police from the public.[3]

On April 29, 1992, the 4 police officers were found not guilty of committing any crimes against Rodney King. After the announcement of the verdict, the local police were caught fleeing the area where large-scale riots had erupted; the National Guard was then called in. The riots ended six days after they began and resulted in the deaths of 42 people, the burning of 700 structures, the arrest of nearly 5,000 people, and almost $1 billion in property damage. Because of the riots, the Justice Department resumed the investigations that had begun due to the King beating.

Almost a year after the riots, Sergeant Stacey Koon and Officer Laurence Powell were convicted by a federal jury for violating the civil rights of Rodney King. The other two officers involved, Timothy Wind and Theodore Briseno, were acquitted.

Violent social disruptions such as these give rise to a plethora of important questions regarding the state of police-community relations. What caused these riots to erupt? What caused the horrendous resentment on the part of some citizens toward the police? Why are there strained relationships between police and minority communities? What can be done to improve police-minority relations? These are a few of the questions we will take up in the pages that follow.

Our purpose in this chapter is to explore the nature of police-community relationships, with particular emphasis on the minority community. Likewise, we examine the changing demographics of communities and the role of the police in policing diverse communities. We conclude the chapter with a discussion on ways the police can improve their response to and their relations with minority communities.

CHANGING DEMOGRAPHICS OF COMMUNITIES

Throughout history the ethnic and cultural diversity of the U.S. population has grown constantly. During much of that time, established American groups assumed that newcomers would be assimilated into existing cultural patterns; this is referred to as the **melting pot model.** In the 21st century, the melting pot model has been recognized as neither a good description of what has happened nor a plausible prediction of what can happen as our population continues to rapidly diversify. The religious and cultural patterns of American society are now more varied than ever, and police must continually strive to develop appropriate methods to police a pluralistic society.

Police officers entering the policing profession in the 21st century face both a citizen population and a set of professional values that require skills for negotiating cultural difference. **Multiculturalism** is a definition that

Helicopter pilot and Kansas Highway Patrol Officer Jerry Daniels talks to a group of students regarding his duties as a helicopter pilot with the State Highway Patrol.

Photo courtesy of Kansas Highway Patrol

has taken on different meanings over the years, and we now define it as a society that is made up of many different ethnic and racial groups.[4]

Growth and Change

The population of the United States continues to grow increasingly diverse. For example, in recent years Hispanics have grown faster than the population as a whole. Farai Chideya in her most informative book *The Color of Our Future,* revealed that America's racial composition is changing more rapidly than ever and that the number of immigrants in America is the largest of any post–World War II period.[5] The proportion of African Americans has been rising gradually; by 2020, they are predicted to make up about 12.9 percent of our total population.[6] Similarly, by 2020 Asian Americans will represent about 6.5 percent of the American population, and Hispanics will be responsible for more than 37 percent of our total population.[7] Some scholars have suggested that by the year 2030 one out of four U.S. residents will be Hispanic or Asian in ethnic makeup.[8] According to the U.S. Census Bureau, the current total U.S. population is estimated at 281,421,906, based on current growth rates applied to the 2000 Census figures (see Table 6–1).

Racial and ethnic diversity has always been a hallmark of American society. Immigration from different parts of the world, and the different fertility and mortality rates among recent migrants, has kept the racial and ethnic composition in flux. In 1999, African Americans were the largest minority in the United States, accounting for 12.1 percent of the population; however, according to the 2000 U.S. Census Report, the Hispanic popula-

TABLE 6–1

U.S. Population		
	Total Population	Percent of Population
Total population	**281,421,906**	**100.0**
Whites	211,460,626	75.1
Blacks or African Americans	34,658,190	12.3
American Indians and Alaska Natives	2,475,956	0.9
Asians	10,242,998	3.6
Native Hawaiians and other Pacific Islanders	398,835	0.1
Some other races	15,359,073	5.5
Two or more races	6,826,228	2.0
Hispanics or Latinos	35,305,818	12.5

Note: Percentages add up to more than 100 because Hispanics may be of any race and are therefore counted under more than one category.
Source: U.S. Census Bureau, *U.S. Census Report, 2000.*

tion grew at nearly four times the rate of the U.S. population overall during the last two years, cementing the Latinos' position as the country's largest minority group.[9] By 2025, Hispanics will account for 18 percent of the U.S. population, while only 13 percent of the population will be African-American. Over the same period, the percentage of whites will decline by 10 percentage points, to 62 percent. If current trends continue, almost half of the U.S. population will be nonwhite by 2050.[10]

The Population Reference Bureau[11] recently reported that over the next 25 years, minority concentrations are projected to increase in all parts of the country, but especially in the South, Southwest, and West. By 2025, minority groups are expected to account for over 50 percent of the population in four states (Hawaii, California, New Mexico, Texas) and the District of Columbia.[12] To illustrate this point, demographic data on five major U.S. cities (taken from the 2000 Census Report) have been provided in Table 6–2.

TABLE 6–2

Demographics of Selected American Cities						
	Total Population	Asian	Black/ African-American	Hispanic/ Latino	White	Other
Boston	589,141	7.5%	25.3%	13.1%	54.5%	0.06%
Detroit	951,270	1.0%	81.6%	5.0%	12.3%	0.3%
Houston	1,953,631	5.3%	25.3%	37.4%	49.3%	0.5%
New York City	8,008,278	9.8%	26.6%	27.0%	44.7%	0.6%
Los Angeles	3,694,820	10.0%	11.2%	46.5%	46.9%	1.0%

Source: U.S. Census Bureau, *U.S. Census Report, 2000.*

NATURE OF POLICE-COMMUNITY RELATIONS

Police-community relations can best be defined as the process of interaction between the police and the vast public entities they serve, including governmental agencies, community groups, schools, neighborhoods, and private individuals (representing a wide array of interests). When effective, police-community relations can minimize misunderstandings between citizens and the police.[13] Police-community relations should not be confused with police relations, for they are different in scope and context. Police relations (or public relations, as it is sometimes called) entail a number of activities that have the express intent of creating a favorable image for the police. Police-community relations include the combined efforts of the police and the community working in partnership to minimize misunderstandings and resolve mutual concerns.[14]

As American communities become more racially and ethnically diverse, the nature of police-community relations increasingly becomes challenging. It is in the context of healthy police-community relations that citizens feel more connected with their police and more secure within their communities. In 1829, **Sir Robert Peel,** the founder of modern policing in London, noted that the police needed to be part of, not apart from, the people served, which is readily seen in Peel's nine principles of policing[15]:

1. The basic mission for which the police exist is to prevent crime and disorder.
2. The ability of the police to perform their duties is dependent on public approval of police actions.
3. Police must secure the willing cooperation of the public in voluntary observance of the law to be able to secure and maintain the respect of the public.
4. The degree of cooperation of the public that can be secured diminishes proportionately to the necessity of the use of physical force.
5. Police seek and preserve public favor not by catering to public opinion but by constantly demonstrating absolute impartial service to the law.
6. Police use physical force to the extent necessary to secure observance of the law or to restore order only when the exercise of persuasion, advice, and warning is found to be insufficient.
7. Police, at all times, should maintain a relationship with the public that gives reality to the historic tradition that the police are the public and the public are the police, the police being only members of the public who are paid to give full-time attention to duties which are incumbent on every citizen in the interests of community welfare and existence.
8. Police should always direct their action strictly toward their functions and never appear to usurp the powers of the judiciary.
9. The test of police efficiency is the absence of crime and disorder, not the visible evidence of police action of dealing with it.

The father of the London Metropolitan Police, Sir Robert Peel argued that the police should protect the rights, serve the needs, and earn the trust

Inspecting school buses for a local school district is a common activity for law enforcement agencies.

Photo courtesy of Kansas Highway Patrol

of the population they police. Over time these principles were incorporated into American police departments.

In our democratic form of government, it is sometimes overlooked that the power and authority of our policing agencies come from, and with the consent of, the people served. Some argue that the historical secrecy and institutional separation of the police and the public they serve have been disastrous for effective police-community relations.[16] Some police agencies recognize the need for effective police-community relations. For example, in an attempt to improve police-community relations during the early part of the 20th century, the New York City Police Department engaged in such activities as massive Christmas parties for poverty-stricken children and their families, job hunts for released prisoners from Sing-Sing prison, and other non-crime-fighting endeavors.[17]

Reform and the Thin Blue Line

American police reformers during the early and middle 20th century felt that it was necessary both to overcome the contempt that middle-class citizens felt for the police and to "sell" the police to the people.[18] According to professors Ronald Hunter, Thomas Barker, and Pamela Mayhall, during the reforms of the 1950s the police put forth the notion that they are the **"thin blue line,"** the last bulwark of defense against the forces of crime and disorder, and they go on to assert that there were three key elements that were notable in these efforts[19]:

1. At their best, the police employed highly sophisticated techniques of advertising, selling, and, of course, public relations.

2. To police the public (in a public relations sense) essentially meant policing middle-class adults and youth ("solid citizens" and their offspring).

3. No attempt was made to improve the "product"; the programs were designed solely to improve the police "image." There was little or no provision made to recommend or effect needed changes in departmental policy or procedure.

Even O. W. Wilson, who was one of the leading police reformers of the 20th century, recognized later in his writings that the emphasis in the police field shifted from a concentration on building public image to the achievement of a comprehensive set of objectives and policies. Wilson and Roy McLaren noted these key points[20]:

- Public support is essential to effective police administration.
- The motivation for increasing public support should be not so much to receive praise and support per se as to secure the benefit of the support in terms of increased finances and backing to do a better job.
- The only long-term way to improve the image of the police is to provide effective, enthusiastic, fair, and just service in as professional a manner as possible. Communicating the news of progress in this direction, however, should be deliberate and immediate.
- The police must realize that improvement in police services and the police image can be neither achieved overnight nor enhanced by adoption of superficial community relations programs. If the public senses that community relations programs are insincere, the efforts will probably fail.
- Improvement of police services can be facilitated through dialogue with the community.
- The community relations effort should emphasize crime resistance and public education programs.
- Fair and just treatment of all citizens should be a fundamental policy of the department.

The thin blue line mentality advanced by police reformers was counterproductive to effective police-community relations, and over time the idea caused strained relations with those citizens in the lower economic classes. Likewise, delinquents (primarily from the lower classes) on the verge of criminal behavior were not counseled or prevented from criminal activity, which might have happened if the police had had rapport with this population.

The police should attempt to prevent crimes as opposed to merely reacting as a thin blue line when crimes are committed. The thin blue line mentality is fundamentally flawed and perpetuates a we-they attitude on the part of the police. This is not conducive to police-community relationship building.

Volatile Times

The 1960s were a time of change in America. Many young people participated in activism while attempting to make America a better place for all people.[21] It was an era marked by the Vietnam War, the civil rights movement, young persons' mistrust of those in authority, and the assassinations of John F. Kennedy, Martin Luther King, Robert Kennedy, and Malcolm X. These events brought the police into increasing contact with the citizenry, and police-community relations during this time became increasingly strained. The police were seen by many to be a force whose purpose was to uphold status quo practices, which were viewed as unfair and unjust.

In the summer of 1964, African Americans rioted in Harlem, Philadelphia, and Rochester (New York), attacking both police and property. The following summer, the violence and disorder were more widespread as outbursts occurred in the Watts section of Los Angeles and then in Chicago, Springfield (Massachusetts), and Philadelphia.

During the summer of 1967, racial confrontations escalated into full-scale urban riots in Newark, New Jersey; New York City; Cleveland, Ohio; Washington, D.C.; Chicago; Atlanta; and Detroit, Michigan. On the morning of July 23, 1967, Detroit police raided an illegal black drinking establishment, handcuffed its patrons, and forced them outside. A crowd of black observers gathered at the scene, and the police retreated, fearing for their safety. Initially, the crowd looted and burned white-owned stores, but as the riot moved into its second day, African-American stores were destroyed as well. Before the National Guard ended the rioting, 43 African Americans were killed, 1,189 were injured, and 7,231 were arrested.[22]

The number and intensity of riots in 1967 prompted an in-depth study of 75 of the disorders, including riots that had occurred in Newark and Detroit, by the National Advisory Commission on Civil Disorders. The commission found that although specific grievances varied somewhat from city to city, there were consistent patterns in who the rioters were, how the riots originated, and what the rioters wanted. The most-cited causal factors were police practices, unemployment and underemployment, and inadequate housing.[23]

Kerner Report

The **Kerner Report** was released after seven months of investigation by the National Advisory Commission on Civil Disorders and took its name from the commission's chairman, Illinois Governor Otto Kerner.[24] President Lyndon B. Johnson appointed the commission on July 28, 1967, while rioting was still underway in Detroit. President Johnson charged the commission with analyzing specific triggers for the riots, deeper causes of the worsening racial climate of the time, and potential remedies.

The commission presented its findings in 1968, concluding that urban violence reflected the profound frustration of inner-city blacks and that racism was deeply embedded in American society. The report's most famous passage warned that the United States was "moving toward two societies, one black, and one white, separate and unequal."[25] The commission marshaled evidence on an array of problems that impacted African Americans with particular severity; these including not only overt **discrimination** but also chronic poverty, high unemployment, poor schools, inadequate housing, lack of access to health care, and systematic police bias and brutality. The report recommended sweeping federal initiatives that were directed at improving educational and employment opportunities, public services, and housing in black urban neighborhoods and that called for a national system of income supplementation.

President's Commission Report

Further impetus was provided by the President's Commission on Law Enforcement and Administration of Justice in its report, *The Challenge of Crime in a Free Society*.[26] The President's Commission recognized the significance of effective police-community relations in preventing riots and disorder in communities. The commission considered police indifference, police mistreatment of citizens, and citizen hostility toward the police to be disruptive influences in the community. Police officers who work in communities that are hostile toward them will have difficulty providing police protection to that community; conversely, citizens who are hostile toward the police will often not report crimes to the police or provide them with the information necessary to solve crimes.[27] The President's Commission outlined five principles of police-community relations[28]:

1. A community relations program is not a public relations program to "sell the police image" to the people. It is not a set of expedients whose purpose is to tranquilize for a time an angry neighborhood by, for example, suddenly promoting a few black officers in the wake of a racial disturbance.
2. Community relations are not the exclusive business of specialized units but of an entire department, from the chief down. Community relations are not exclusively a matter of special programs but are a matter that touches on all aspects of police work.
3. The needs of good community relations and of effective law enforcement will not necessarily be identical at all times.
4. Improving community relations involves not only instituting programs and changing procedures and practices but also reexamining fundamental attitudes. The police will have to learn to listen patiently and understandingly to people who are openly critical of them or hostile to them, since those people are precisely the ones with whom relations need to be improved.
5. The police must adapt themselves to the rapid changes in patterns of behavior that are taking place in America. This is a time when traditional ideas and institutions are being challenged with increasing insistence.

The ideas of the President's Commission are just as relevant today as they were in the 1960s when they were written.

POLICING OF DIVERSE POPULATIONS

As you have undoubtedly discovered thus far in this chapter, police-community relations have at times been less than congenial, especially in minority communities; likewise, relationships between minority communities and the police have been slow to develop. Not only do minorities distrust the police, but research points out that they possess more negative attitudes toward the police, compared with attitudes of white Americans.[29] Professor Elijah Anderson argued that because the young African-American male is aware of many cases when an "innocent" African-American person was wrongly accused and detained, he develops an "attitude" toward the police.[30] The mistrust and negative attitudes toward the police may in part be explained if we carefully examine the history of police-minority relations.

Much of the policing literature overlooks the evolution of police-minority relations, so the discussion that follows is important in the context of fully understanding the nature of contemporary police-minority relations. The historical significance of the relations between the police and minorities must be examined, starting with the dark days of slavery.

Police-Minority Relations: A Gloomy History

The police role in society is to enforce the law impartially and not to question it. From the inception of the police in this country, they were charged with upholding the status quo, a status quo that legally mandated inequality.[31] The following is an excellent description of this legacy:

> The fact that the legal order not only countenanced but sustained slavery, segregation, and discrimination for most of our nation's history–and the fact the police were bound to uphold that order–set a pattern for police behavior and attitudes toward minority communities that has persisted until the present day. That pattern includes the idea that minorities have fewer civil rights, that the police have little responsibility for protecting them from crime within their communities.[32]

During slavery, **slave catchers,** acting with police authority in some Southern states, were charged with the duty of returning runaway slaves to their masters. It is an uncomfortable fact that American police in the South actively pursued slaves and that slave patrols proved to be an integral step in the development of Southern police organizations.[33] Police historian Samuel Walker referred to slave patrols as a "distinctly American form of law enforcement" and as the "first modern forces in this country."[34] Every slave-owning state had active, established slave patrols; although they had many functions within the community, they had one basic job–to act as the first line of defense against a slave rebellion. They caught runaway slaves, enforced slave codes, discouraged any large gathering of blacks, and generally perpetuated the atmosphere of fear that kept the slaves in line.[35] Slaves faced a very hostile and vigilant nation armed with laws that sanctioned chasing, catching, punishing, and returning runaway slaves.[36] Slave patrols were made up of mostly poor whites who frequently whipped and terrorized slaves caught without passes after curfew.[37] The influence of slave patrols on police departments in the South is a cornerstone of the institutional racism that continues to plague American police departments.[38]

At the conclusion of the radical Reconstruction era in the South, the criminal justice system was one of the major instruments of white supremacy.[39] Some scholars argue that the police maintained white supremacy through the brutal and discriminatory practices toward African Americans.[40] African Americans have faced a long and engrained history of discrimination and racism in U.S. society.[41] Slavery was officially abolished in 1865; however, its dark shadow would continue to haunt African Americans for many years to come. Southern whites found ways to defy Reconstruction, preserve their social order, and thus continue to unwittingly limit economic growth.[42] The "humiliation and subjugation" of African Americans continued through enforcement of Jim Crow laws, economic and educational segregation, and acceptance of lynching as a means of social control.[43]

One example of the subjugation of African Americans occurred in September 1962 when a federal court ordered the University of Mississippi to accept James Meredith, a 28-year-old African American, much to the vehement opposition of segregationists. Mississippi Governor Ross Barnett said he would never allow the school to be integrated. After days of violence and rioting by whites in Oxford, Mississippi (home to the University of Mississippi), Meredith, accompanied by federal law enforcement officials, enrolled on October 1, 1962. This was all done with minimal or no protection by the state and local police authorities in Mississippi.[44]

It was common throughout the 1960s, especially in the Southern states, for the police to refuse to protect African Americans.[45] Mildred Pitts Walter described police practices in Mississippi during the 1960s in her book *Mississippi Challenge*[46]:

> Good citizens averted their eyes. Law-Enforcement officers, if not actually involved, did nothing to prevent the seizure of jailed suspects, and no mob leader is known to have been punished. Police officials refused to launch investigations when ordered to do so. Some victims were seized in daylight hours and blowtorched immediately after their trials for murder. Yet no one was able to identify the mob leaders.

Law enforcement's refusal to protect citizens can be further exemplified by the many civil rights leaders who, during peaceful protests, were routinely pelted with rocks and bottles from all-white crowds while the police offered no protection.[47] In Canton, Mississippi, the police were the actual aggressors when they used tear gas to disrupt a peaceful civil rights march.[48]

Images such as Birmingham, Alabama, Police Chief Eugene "Bull" Connor further demonstrate how law enforcement was used by the white power structure to maintain segregationist practices. In 1963, Birmingham was the center of the storm of the civil rights movement. Birmingham's Police Chief Bull Connor had become the symbol of white supremacist police power. Connor was most famous for his staunch defending of racial segregation and for ordering the brutal use of police dogs and fire hoses to disperse civil rights demonstrators in Birmingham during the spring of 1963.[49]

One may also recall Neshoba County (Mississippi) Sheriff Lawrence Rainy and Deputy Sheriff Cecil Ray Price, who were two of eighteen Mississippians convicted in 1967 of conspiring to violate the civil rights of three civil rights workers who were murdered in 1964. The murders were carried out old-fashioned lynching style, with the help of the Neshoba County Sheriff's officials and the Ku Klux Klan.[50] The three civil rights workers Michael Schwerner, Andrew Goodman, and James Chaney were all savagely beaten and shot on a lonely, dark road in Neshoba County.[51]

More recently, four Detroit police officers beat to death black motorist Malice Green in 1992. Also, there was the 1997 beating of Haitian immigrant Abner Louima at the hands of New York City police officers. Louima suffered a torn bladder and intestine (which required several surgeries to repair) after New York police officers beat him and rammed the handle of a toilet plunger into his rectum and mouth at a Brooklyn police station. Subsequently, a federal grand jury handed down a twelve-count indictment against five New York police officers accused of assaulting Louima.

The case of Tyisha Miller, who was shot and killed by police in Riverside, California, also was shocking. Police fired twenty seven shots at Miller after she was startled awake while sleeping in a disabled car. The African-American teenager allegedly had a gun, and according to the police, she reached for it when one of the officers broke the car window. The police claimed Miller fired at them first, but they later recanted that story.

In yet another case that gained national attention, nearly 10 percent of the African-American residents of the small town of Tulia, Texas, were arrested and indicted on bogus drug charges.[52] In the Tulia case, an eighteen-month drug sting led to the arrest of fourty six of the town's 4,699 residents. Coordinated by the Panhandle Regional Narcotics Trafficking Task Force, the operation netted thirty eight narcotics-trafficking convictions, with defendants receiving sentences as long as ninety years in prison.[53]

The sting operation earned undercover officer Tom Coleman the coveted Outstanding Lawman of the Year award, presented by the Texas Narcotic Control Program. Subsequently, a state district court judge ruled that all thirty eight convictions should be overturned due to revelations that Coleman, the sole undercover officer in the sting, fabricated evidence and perjured himself while testifying against the defendants. Of those convicted, twelve were immediately released; the remaining defendants have already been paroled or released since the judge's ruling.

On February 6, 2005, thirteen-year-old Devin Brown decided to go out for a joyride shortly before 4:00 A.M. Los Angeles police officers noticed the car when it ran a red light and suspected the driver of being drunk. When the officers attempted to stop the car, Brown refused to stop and took the officers on a three-minute chase through South Los Angeles. The thirteen-year-old African-American youth skidded 102 feet to a halt on a sidewalk and then backed up, striking a police car. An officer fired ten shots at the car, killing the thirteen-year-old driver.[54] As a result, the Los Angeles Police Department quickly contacted leaders of the African-American community in an attempt to thwart a community uprising due to public anger over the shooting.

These events are germane to our discussion of policing diverse communities and police-community relations. It is a constellation of both the past and present that leaves minority citizens with haunting suspicions of the police. There is even a perception by many minority citizens that race continues to play a central role in police brutality in the United States.[55] Some have alleged that the police subject minorities to discriminatory treatment and have physically abused minorities while using racial epithets.[56]

Past incidents of real or perceived police abuse have sparked civil unrest, including costly and violent uprisings, and a lingering distrust between racial minority communities and the police. The same conclusions that were reported by the Kerner Commission and the President's Commission of the 1960s relating to police-community tensions are echoed in the 1991 *Report of the Independent Commission on the Los Angeles Police Department (Christopher Commission Report)*, published in the aftermath of the notorious beating of Rodney King.[57] The report stated:

> Within minority communities of Los Angeles, there is a widely-held view that police misconduct is commonplace. The King beating refocused public attention to long-standing complaints by African-Americans, Latinos and Asians that Los Angeles Police Department officers frequently treat minorities differently from whites, more often using disrespectful and abusive language, employing unnecessarily intrusive practices such as the "prone-out" ["prone-out" refers to the police practice of placing individuals who are being questioned on the street facedown on the pavement], and engaging in use of excessive force when dealing with minorities.[58]

Professor Egon Bittner argued that the modern police officer emerged as the thin blue line, not against crime but between blacks and whites.[59] Professor Bittner contended that though the police did not create racism, their activities contribute to the magnitude of the gulf between the groups.[60] To many African Americans, the white urban police officer has come to symbolize racial oppression; many of their personal experiences include seeing African Americans beaten or even killed with impunity.[61] On the other hand, white people see the police as protectors of their communities.[62]

It would be naïve to ignore past injustices directed toward minority groups when examining contemporary police-community relations. By critically examining these injustices, the police can move toward reconciliation and a more harmonious relationship with the community. However, this is a two-way street: In order to make police-minority relations work, the minority community must be willing to engage in productive dialogue with the police, as opposed to just verbalizing concerns. Minority community members can get involved by doing the following[63]:

- Engage in dialogue about solutions rather than emphasize blame.
- Encourage one another to apply for employment with the police department, and support those who do.
- Develop a broad understanding of professional police practices (perhaps through contacts with national and state police organizations) in order to form an objective standard by which to judge police actions.
- Acknowledge police officers who promote positive police-community relationships with awards or other commendations.

The past injustices inflicted on minorities have had a profound effect on the nature of police-minority relations. The unfortunate reality is that it was within a socially and racially stratified system that over the course of two centuries police organization evolved in the South. Although the Northern experience with immigrants in large urban cities is similar, it is only remotely so, for the Southern experience with race is a much more intense, deep, and embedded phenomenon.[64] We urge students of the police not to shy away from critically examining the effects of race and racial injustices of the past on contemporary police-minority relations. By examining these effects, perhaps we can better understand the nature of contemporary police-community relations.

CONTEMPORARY PROBLEMS

The state of police-minority relations is far from congenial. Many in the minority community view the police with considerable suspicion.[65] For example, there is a fair amount of scholarship that has revealed that minority neighborhoods offer the greatest hostility toward the police.[66] The accusation about the police engaging in the practice of racial profiling has further exacerbated the already-strained relationship between the police and members of the minority community.

Racial Profiling

There is some evidence suggesting that the police disproportionately target and stop African Americans for traffic-related stops.[67] A 1999 Gallup poll of citizens found that about 60 percent of Americans believe that race-based profiling is widespread. In Maryland from January 1995 through December 1997, 70 percent of the drivers stopped on Interstate 95 were African Americans while only 17.5 percent of the traffic and speeders on that road were black, according to an American Civil Liberties Union (ACLU) survey.[68]

Data showed that the New Jersey State Police routinely stop a disproportionate number of African-American drivers. For example, in

State v. *Pedro Soto*, it was determined by a windshield survey that out of 40,000 New Jersey Turnpike drivers, 13.5 percent were black motorists. Defense attorneys in this case then conducted a "violator survey" in which defense attorneys drove on the I-95 turnpike at sixty miles an hour in a fifty five-mile-per-hour zone and noted the race of the drivers who passed them (hence they would be speeding), and 15 percent of the violators were black. The paradox here is that black drivers made up more than 46 percent of the drivers stopped by the New Jersey State Police; thus a disparity of more than three to one existed.[69]

Police-Community Tensions

The contemporary twenty-first-century police assume that they provide police service to all communities in a fair and equitable manner, regardless of the racial, ethnic, or class makeup of the community; however, many minority citizens simply do not believe that they are treated fairly by the police. Minority communities still remain suspicious of the police.[70]

Professor Samuel Walker argued that police-community relations problems in a particular department are probably not the result of the actions of all officers and all units, but of those of particular units.[71] Enforcement patterns often vary according to the characteristics of the neighborhood. Police practices in low-income areas are not necessarily the same as those in middle-class neighborhoods. For example, the Los Angeles Police Department's CRASH unit, a specialized enforcement unit that concentrates on drugs and gangs primarily in minority neighborhoods, has been accused of straining relations in some neighborhoods. The CRASH unit was disbanded after members of the Rampart Division allegedly committed unjustified shootings, stole drugs, planted evidence, and perjured themselves to frame innocent people.

Police Crackdowns

A **police crackdown** is any sudden and dramatic increase in police officer presence, sanctions, and/or threats of apprehension either for specific offenses or for all offenses in a specific place.[72] Crackdowns usually involve high-risk visibility and numerous arrests. They may use undercover or plainclothes officers working with uniformed police and may involve other official actions in addition to arrests.

Police should be cautious about conducting crackdowns because improperly conducted crackdowns can worsen police-community relations and thereby undermine police legitimacy. Many of the urban riots of the 1960s were at least partly due to widespread crackdowns in minority communities. When crackdowns are aimed at street activity, they can be criticized for their disparate impact on the poor, who typically spend more time on the street than do the affluent.[73] Also, when police use highly aggressive tactics (such as military strategies, weapons, and attire) for relatively routine enforcement and patrol activities, they risk heightening fear among offenders and casual observers.[74]

Police should use careful planning when conducting crackdowns and engage in dialogue with the affected neighborhoods about the reasons for a crackdown. Studies have shown that when police explain the purpose and scope of crackdowns to the public (as well as to the people they stop during crackdowns) ahead of time, they can gain public support that continues while the crackdown is in effect.[75]

Minorities' Experiences with the Police

Minorities often have different experiences with the police compared to those of whites. For example, Hispanic Americans call the police less frequently than either whites or African Americans.[76] Likewise the literature points out that African Americans, especially the youngest age group (sixteen to twenty years old), are much more likely than their white counterparts to feel aggrieved by the police.[77]

Data obtained from a national survey by the Bureau of Justice Statistics found that 21 percent of U.S. residents had contact with the police in 1999; 52 percent of these contacts were in traffic stops, and 19 percent were to report a crime. Of the drivers stopped, 10 percent were white, 12 percent were black, and 9 percent were Hispanic. Overall, 84 percent of the drivers stopped regardless of race considered the stop legitimate.[78] In light of these data, it appears that blacks (12.3 percent) were more likely than whites (10.4 percent) to be stopped at least once, and blacks (3.0 percent) were more likely than whites (2.1 percent) to be stopped more than once. During the traffic stops, police were more likely to carry out some type of search on black drivers (11.0 percent) or Hispanic drivers (11.3 percent) compared to white drivers (5.4 percent).[79]

Self-Fulfilling Prophecy

There is another problem that impacts police-minority relations: the attitudes of some of the police officers who work in minority neighborhoods. It is important for police management to curtail the belief among some officers who patrol primarily in minority neighborhoods that minorities commit all the crimes. This is a dangerous stereotype for police officers to possess.

In certain situations, police officers may respond to negative stereotypes and act on them, with the result that false definitions become accurate to the officers, which is known as a **self-fulfilling prophecy.** The self-fulfilling prophecy was conceptualized by sociologist Robert Merton. According to Merton, the phenomenon occurs when a false definition of the situation evokes a new behavior that makes the original false conception come true.[80] A self-fulfilling prophecy can be devastating for minority groups, particularly when police patrolling a minority neighborhood develop the false notion, for example, that African Americans or Hispanics commit all the crimes.

Labeling Theory

Police officers may also be guilty of labeling a person based on one or several characteristics. For example, a police officer labels a young African-American male from the inner city as a gang member based solely on his sagging jeans, a Raiders football jacket, and a stocking cap. **Labeling theory,** a concept introduced by sociologist Howard Becker, is an attempt to explain why certain people are viewed as different from or less worthy than others; it views deviance as a label assigned to behaviors and to individuals by particular figures of authority.[81] That means that no one is actually a deviant and no action is deviant unless so specified by society. The acts that are considered deviant in the United States today may be acceptable or even normal in some other part of the world or at some future time.

Students of crime and delinquency have relied heavily on the use of the labeling theory, and it is germane to our current discussion. Consider the African-American youth from the inner city who misbehaves and thus (according to labeling theory) may be considered and treated as a delinquent by the police. On the other hand, another youth from a white middle-class family who exhibits the same misbehavior might be given another chance before being arrested by the police. The labeling theory directs police management to recognize and deal with officers who exhibit negative stereotypes regarding certain racial and ethnic groups. It is these very stereotypes that can be disastrous to police-minority relations.

Here are some actions to avoid if a police agency is to maintain successful relationships with minority groups: lecturing (educating without a willingness to be educated); withholding information rather than being candid about, and taking responsibility for, incidents that cause harm; and becoming defensive (for example, immediately justifying a deadly use-of-force incident that draws community ire by explaining police policies and procedures without acknowledging the unfortunate loss of life).[82]

IMPROVEMENT IN POLICE-COMMUNITY RELATIONS

The remainder of this chapter will address two important questions: What can be done to improve police-community relations? What can the police do to minimize the mistrust on the part of many minority neighborhoods that have historically felt the brunt of police aggression?

Diversity

In an effort to improve police-community relations, California Police Departments are concentrating on including diverse members of their community in decision making and in programs. Some of these programs include citizen participation, multicultural training programs for police employees and members of the community, and community outreach programs.[83] The Long

Beach Police Department, in collaboration with the National Conference on Christians and Jews, developed a forty-hour course on cultural awareness for all department employees.[84]

One other innovative approach was implemented in the San Jose and Garden Grove, California, Police Departments. These agencies placed substations in distinct neighborhoods, and citizen volunteers who were capable of speaking the residents' language were stationed at these substations.[85]

Elimination of Perceived Discrimination

A recent report by the Police Executive Research Forum provided a three-pronged guide both to eliminate forms of discrimination and perceived discrimination that exist and to improve the quality of police services and relations in minority communities.[86] First, each law enforcement agency should undertake a critical self-assessment to determine which aspects of its current operations may be the source of tensions in racial and ethnic minority neighborhoods. Where problems are identified, appropriately focused remedies should be developed. Second, leaders of the law enforcement profession should begin to develop a specific package of best practices related to the particular problem areas that have been identified. These best practices might include early warning systems, model use of force policies, model citizen complaint procedures, and appropriate procedures for the collection and use of data on traffic stops. Third, research on policing needs to focus on two issues. Research should determine how police practices in particular units affect general relations with racial and ethnic minority communities. At the same time, the various best practices need to be subject to independent evaluation to determine whether they achieve their intended goals and/or whether certain practices are more effective than others.

Goals for Improvement

Police Captain Robert Shusta and his colleagues suggested to police officers that they perform the following activities in order to improve their relationships with multicultural communities:[87]

- Make positive contact with community group members from diverse backgrounds. Don't let them see you only when something negative has happened.
- Allow the public to see you as much as possible in a nonenforcement role.
- Make a conscious effort in your mind, en route to every situation, to treat all segments of society objectively and fairly.
- Remember that all groups have some bad, some average, and some good people in them.
- Go out of your way to be personable and friendly with minority-group members. Remember, many don't expect it.
- Don't appear uncomfortable with or avoid discussing racial and ethnic issues with other officers and citizens.

- Take responsibility for patiently educating citizens and the public about the role of the officer and about standard operating procedures in law enforcement. Remember that citizens often do not understand police culture.
- Don't be afraid to be a change agent in your organization when it comes to improving cross-cultural relations within your department and between police and the community. It may not be a popular thing to do, but it is the right thing to do.

Community Policing

Improving the state of police-community relations is a perplexing dilemma for the police. How to best go about this awesome task is the crux of the matter. Professor Robin D.G. Kelly argued that she would go as far as to propose the complete dismantling of police departments: "Perhaps we might return to the long-standing radical proposal for community-based policing. Imagine institutions for public safety structured along nonmilitary lines and run by elected community boards."[88]

Recall from our discussion in Chapter 3 that community policing is a viable strategy to improve police-community relations. Both community policing and problem-solving efforts have the potential to serve as powerful conduits for such community access. By actively embracing community input regarding crime and disorder reduction, police can demonstrate the benefits of mutual respect and open communication.[89] With community policing, citizens are viewed by the police as partners who share responsibility for identifying priorities as well as developing and implementing responses to neighborhood problems.[90] Accurate surveying of citizen needs and priorities is required under community policing to determine the problems that drive police services and to give the public ownership of the problem-solving process.

Community policing encourages the use of non–law enforcement resources within a law enforcement agency. Volunteerism results in citizens' participation with their law enforcement agency. The law enforcement organization educates the public about ways they can partner with the organization and its members to further community policing, and it provides an effective means for citizen input. Volunteer efforts can help to free up officer time and allow sworn personnel to be more proactive and prevention-oriented. Examples of such resources might include police reserves, volunteers, Explorer Scouts, service organizations, and citizen or youth police academies.

With the use of the community policing philosophy, it is anticipated that police-community relations will improve as the police and citizens have more contact with each other. This is crucial in those areas of the community such as minority neighborhoods where police-community relations have been strained. In Wichita, Kansas, police recruits are volunteering their time to assist several neighborhood associations in collecting valuable information on neighborhood issues and needed improvements. In one neighborhood, recruits contacted approximately 540 households and solicited their input.[91]

These contacts have the potential to nurture good police-community relations, and the process instills in police recruits that citizen input and interaction are important.

Community policing is said to improve police-community relations in the following six areas[92]:

1. Closer relations with underprivileged and minority groups, where the need is greatest for police understanding and involvement
2. More effective and more open communication between the police and the community
3. Increased citizen involvement in crime prevention and in solutions to social problems as a means of reducing crime
4. Improved understanding between the police and the community, with both gaining recognition of each other's problems
5. Heightened awareness of problems in police-community relations and encouragement of officers to help solve them
6. Direction of all department efforts toward improving relations with the total community in areas such as crime prevention, public relations, and neighborhood problem solving

Citizen Police Academy

The Citizen Police Academy has become increasingly popular among police departments as a means to foster and improve police-community relations.[93] The **Citizen Police Academy** is a program designed to provide a working knowledge and background of the law enforcement agency and to foster a closer relationship between the agency and the community. It provides an avenue for community involvement and firsthand experience in policing. Interested citizens apply for the Citizen Police Academy; if accepted, they complete a specified amount of time in the academy, usually ranging from a few weeks to several weeks for one or two evenings each week.

The Sedgwick County Sheriff's Department in Wichita, Kansas, is one of many law enforcement agencies across the nation that conduct a Citizen Police Academy. Here are some of the topics and activities academy attendees are exposed to[94]:

- Patrol operations (including riding assignments with a Sedgwick County sheriff's deputy or a Wichita police officer)
- Overview of investigations
- Presentations by the Gang Unit
- Tour of the Wichita/Sedgwick County Law Enforcement Firearms Training Facility
- Polygraph operations
- Presentations by the Exploited and Missing Children's Unit
- Presentations by the Homicide and Robbery Investigations Unit
- Tours of the Sheriff's Crime Lab, Wichita Police Department Crime Lab, Records Bureau, and 911 Emergency Communications Center

- Tour of the Sedgwick County Adult Detention Facility (including an opportunity to sample jail food)
- Overview of community affairs and community policing
- Air Section helicopter fly-in and presentation
- Traffic radar demonstration
- SWAT demonstration
- Bomb squad demonstration

Citizen Police Academies are intended to develop a harmonious working relationship between members of the community and law enforcement while at the same time opening a mutually supportive avenue for communication. Citizen Police Academies offer an opportunity for citizens to learn more about their local law enforcement, ask questions, and gain a more thorough understanding of the inner workings of their police department. The academy is also a means for participants and police personnel to share information and ideas about the police profession. The Citizen Police Academy provides for improved police-community relationships, enhanced cooperation, and reduced stereotyping.[95]

Multicultural Training

Knowledge of cultural diversity is important for police officers in the 21st century. It has only been in the recent past that police agencies have begun to include diversity training as part of the preservice and post-service training requirements.[96] Education that helps familiarize officers with ethnic and cultural groups in their community is invaluable. No police officer can effectively address a community's needs if he or she does not understand the cultural traditions, mores, and values of that community.[97]

Multicultural training can reduce the number of lawsuits (as well as the possibility of civil disorder), but it can succeed only with the acceptance and management of cultural diversity. Historically, strategies employed by police in dealing with minorities and minority issues have differed from those of other groups. While improvements in those strategies have occurred in the last decade, further progress is needed. Although these improvements often have focused on African Americans, many cultural diversity issues have similar implications for other racial and ethnic groups.[98] Chief of Police Gary Coderoni, who serves with the Muscatine, Iowa, Police Department, wrote:

> Cultural diversity training helps police break free from their traditional stance of being "apart from" the community to a more inclusive philosophy of being "a part of" the community. Realizing the difficulty of becoming a part of something that they do not understand causes a desperate need for an intense and ongoing educational process for developing an understanding of cultural differences and how those differences affect policing a free and culturally diverse society.[99]

There are four primary factors associated with achieving a more culturally aware police organization. First, police officers need to understand how their own cultural background molds their values and behavioral patterns. Second, officers must understand that cultural assimilation no longer is the norm in the United States, and they must learn about the different cultural, ethnic, and racial groups in the neighborhoods they patrol. Third, it is critical that officers understand the effective use of cross-cultural communication. Police officers who have a deeper insight into the beliefs, behaviors, and value orientations of various ethnic groups will rely less often on authority and force to resolve problematic situations. Finally, law enforcement officers must develop cross-cultural communication, analytical, and interpretive skills.[100]

Police officers can make their jobs easier by taking the time to learn about various cultures that they will come in contact with. Knowledge of and sensitivity to minority concerns, diversity, and historical backgrounds of various races and groups in a community will enhance and facilitate the crime-fighting and peacekeeping functions of the police.[101] For example, consider the case of an officer called to the home of an Asian-American family regarding a miscellaneous complaint. In most Asian-American families, the relationship and communication patterns tend to be quite hierarchical, with the father as the identified head of the household. While many of the decisions and activities may appear to be decided by the father, other people may come into the picture. Generally, if there are grandparents, the father would still act as the spokesperson of the family; however, chances are that he would consult with the grandparents prior to making a decision.[102]

It is equally important and justifiable for the police to possess a contextual understanding of those racial and ethnic groups represented in the United States. For example, consider the following information pertaining to African Americans that may be useful to law enforcement[103]:

- The experiences of slavery and racism as well as cultural differences have shaped African-American culture.
- For many African Americans, particularly those on the lower socioeconomic rungs of society, the history of slavery and later discrimination continues to leave psychological scars.
- There is tremendous diversity among African Americans—varying socioeconomic levels, a number of religions, different regions of the country (as well as rural and urban settings), and various countries of origin.
- The changing terms that African Americans have used to refer to themselves reflect stages of racial and cultural growth as well as empowerment.
- African Americans react as negatively to stereotypes that they hear about themselves as officers do when they hear such statements as "Police officers are biased against blacks" or "All police officers are capable of brutality."
- The predominance of households headed by women (particularly in the inner city), coupled with the myth of African-American women being the head of the household, has created situations in which officers have dismissed the importance of the father.

- Young African-American males in particular, as well as their parents (at all socioeconomic levels), feel a sense of outrage and injustice when officers stop them for no apparent reason.
- The use of African-American varieties of English does not represent any pathology of deficiency and is not a combination of random errors, but rather it reflects patterns of grammar from some West African languages.
- People in positions of authority have often misunderstood aspects of black non-verbal communication, including what has been termed the "cool pose."
- Cultural differences in verbal communication can result in complete misinterpretation.
- The existence of excessive force and brutality is still a reality in policing in the United States, even if it is only a small minority of officers who commit these acts. When there is police brutality, everyone suffers, including officers and entire police departments.
- A dynamic exists between some officers and African Americans, particularly in poor urban areas, whereby both the officers and the citizens are on the alert for the slightest sign of disrespect.

Recruitment of Minority Police Officers

Increasing the representation of minorities in police departments will foster good police-community relations.[104] Better representation of minorities in policing sends the right message that the police service is open. Increasing diversity within police agencies is important in light of the projection that by the year 2010 more than one-third of all American children will be black, Hispanic, or Asian.[105]

Community Contacts

It is good practice for police to establish rapport with local minority groups such as the National Association for the Advancement of Colored People (NAACP), Urban League, Boy's and Girl's Clubs, minority faith communities, Hispanic coalitions, and Asian or Indo-Chinese community centers and coalitions. Developing contacts in organizations such as these will keep management informed about the minority community's issues and concerns. Police organizations that are striving to meet the challenges of promoting and managing a diverse workforce successfully can achieve this goal more effectively by following these nine strategies.[106]

1. Develop training programs that promote awareness of cultural differences.
2. Promote positive attitudes toward racial and cultural differences among ethnic groups.
3. Recognize common links between different ethnic groups.
4. Use alternative channels of communication to maximize understanding between ethnic and cultural groups.
5. Express organizational concerns.

6. Identify the concerns and needs of ethnic groups in decision-making processes.
7. Recognize that no "one size fits all" solutions exist.
8. Challenge all stereotypes and assumptions about ethnic groups.
9. Include members of all ethnic groups in all after-work organization-sponsored events.

Racial Tensions

Where there are good police-community relations and high confidence within the minority community in the integrity and accountability of the police department, a use-of-force incident may result in little turmoil. In communities where there is a lack of confidence between police and minority residents and a perception that complaints about police misconduct will not be addressed fairly, no issue can be more racially explosive or more easily lead to violent disturbances.

The **Community Relations Service (CRS),** an agency of the U.S. Department of Justice, is the federal government's "peacemaker" for community conflicts and tensions arising from differences of race, color, and national origin and has been effective at assisting police agencies and local governments with preventing and resolving racial and ethnic tensions. Created by the Civil Rights Act of 1964, CRS is the only federal agency whose purpose is to assist state and local units of government, private and public organizations, and community groups with preventing and resolving racial and ethnic tensions, conflicts, and civil disorders and in restoring racial stability and harmony.

Through its mediation process, CRS channels community tensions and anger into a constructive discussion of other issues that often surface after a use-of-force incident. Police may review community concerns regarding its use-of-force policy, workforce diversification, minority officer recruitment, hiring and selection criteria, training programs on race relations and diversity, promotion of minority officers, and creation of permanent mechanisms for improved police and community dialogue.[107]

While issues regarding the specific incident must be addressed, attention should also be given to broader underlying concerns that often are at the root of community frustration and conflict. Departmental policies on the use of force and the use of deadly force, including firearm policy and use of restraints, may be reviewed by a community coalition. A coalition of leaders can be formed to address how to achieve better police-community relations. Community input, including requests for public comment and discussion, should be solicited during this review. Communities should know the various options that are available at the federal, state, and local levels to address concerns about police use of force, use of deadly force, and allegations of excessive use of force. The following examines four communities where CRS has been successful at mediating what could have been costly social eruptions.

Coatesville, Pennsylvania. When there was a threat of widespread disruption following a fatal police shooting involving an African-American man by a Caucasian police officer, CRS (at the request of the district attorney and city manager) helped convene a community meeting with law enforcement officials, clergy, and city officials immediately after the shooting. The meeting helped dispel rumors and explain the status of the investigation. CRS mediated discussions among law enforcement, the city, and community groups. During the investigation, CRS conducted an assessment of potential community tensions in the event that the district attorney determined there would be no criminal prosecution.[108]

Santa Maria, California. The shooting death of a Hispanic-American youth by a police officer was followed by a series of angry protests, demonstrations, and heightened racial tensions. At a community meeting convened by the Latino Chamber of Commerce, CRS arranged for a clear explanation of the investigative and legal processes and the options available to the victim's family and community. The meeting helped to defuse anger and afforded an opportunity for the media to report the proceedings to the public at large.[109]

New Brunswick, New Jersey. Following the shooting of a young African-American woman by a Caucasian police officer, the local prosecutor, the U.S. Attorney, and the Civil Rights Division engaged in a joint grand jury investigation. After the county prosecutor determined that the police officer had acted in self-defense and the Civil Rights Division concluded that the case could not be successfully prosecuted under civil rights laws, CRS convened a meeting with the victim's family, community leaders, ministers, police department officials, the mayor, a representative from the local U.S. Congressman's office, and Civil Rights Division and U.S. Attorney representatives to brief the partners prior to the public announcement of the decision. As a result of this meeting, the announcement was received by the community without incident.[110]

Kansas City, Missouri. A shooting of a young African-American man by a police officer led to a mass gathering of youth who taunted and hurled rocks, bottles, and other missiles at police arriving at the scene following the shooting; adult residents were unable to curtail the violent response. Tensions were still volatile upon the arrival of CRS mediators, who began communicating with the youth in a series of street meetings. CRS arranged constructive discussions of their issues with the police, city officials, and other community members. The tension levels were lowered, and further violence and property destruction were averted.[111]

▲ SUMMARY

The population of the United States continues to grow racially and ethnically diverse, which is referred to as multiculturalism. Multiculturalism is an approach to cultural diversity that emphasizes understanding, respecting, and adapting to other cultures and cultural differences. In recent years, minority racial groups have grown faster than the population as a whole. Today members of different cultures are coming in contact with each other more frequently; likewise, the police are frequently coming in contact with persons from diverse racial and ethnic backgrounds.

The new racial and ethnic demographics of America are becoming more evident and will have a direct impact on police relations with the community. The police should become increasingly knowledgeable about culture and the changing demographics in communities in order to maintain healthy relations with the communities.

Police-community relations continue to be a perplexing issue for contemporary American police. Effective police-community relations are important because without the support of the public, the police would be less effective. Much of the literature that addresses police-community relations with minority communities overlooks past injustices such as slavery, Jim Crow laws in the South, and the long history of police oppression of minorities. These events are merely a few of many that shape contemporary police-minority relations. The state of police-minority relations in many communities is not terribly good. Many citizens in minority communities view the police with considerable suspicion, and there is a sizable amount of scholarship that has revealed that minority neighborhoods exhibit the greatest hostility toward the police.

In 1929, Sir Robert Peel, founder of the modern London Metropolitan Police, considered that the police should at all times maintain a relationship with the public that gives reality to the historic tradition that the police are the public and the public are the police, the police being only members of the public who are paid to give full-time attention to duties which are incumbent on every citizen in the interests of community welfare and existence. In essence, Sir Robert Peel was advocating that the police and the public must work together.

There have been many recommendations as to how best to improve the state of police-community relations. These recommendations have included implementing community policing and Citizen Police Academies, providing cultural diversity training to police, and increasing the minority representation in the police department. It is also good practice for the police leadership to maintain contact with minority groups such as the NAACP, minority faith communities, Urban League, Hispanic organizations, and many other minority organizations. Developing contacts in organizations such as these will keep police informed about the minority community's issues and concerns.

■ QUESTIONS IN REVIEW

1. What implications do the changing demographics of communities have on police-community relations?
2. How does history influence the current state of police-minority relations?
3. Discuss the major points from the Kerner Report and the President's Commission Report regarding police-community relations.

4. What are some contemporary problems that impact police-minority relations?
5. Identify and discuss strategies for improving police-community relations.

 ## POLICE RESOURCES ON THE WEB

Alexandra, Virginia, Police-Community Relations Programs
http://ci.alexandria.va.us/police/pd_csp.html

Civil Rights and Police Reform in Los Angeles
http://www.cali.org/riots/time_line.html

Commission on Race and Police-Community Relations
http://www.crpcr.ri.gov/index.htm

Community Relations–Philadelphia Police Department
http://www.ppdonline.org/cmty

Constitutional Rights Coalition–Cops and Kids
http://www.crf-usa.org/copskids/copskids_home.html

REFERENCES

1. ERIC BENNETT, "Los Angeles Watts Riots of 1965." Web posted at http://www.africana.com/research/encarta. Accessed April 28, 2004.
2. Ibid.
3. INDEPENDENT COMMISSION ON THE LOS ANGELES POLICE DEPARTMENT, *Report of the Independent Commission on the Los Angeles Police Department* (Los Angeles, 1991), p. ii (hereafter cited as *Christopher Commission Report*).
4. ROBERT M. SHUSTA, DEENA R. LEVINE, PHILLIP R. HARRIS, and HERBERT Z. WONG, *Multicultural Law Enforcement: Strategies for Peace Keeping in a Diverse Society* (Upper Saddle River, NJ: Prentice Hall, 1995), pp. 123–124.
5. FARAI CHIDEYA, *The Color of Our Future* (New York: William Morrow and Company, 1999).
6. R.W. JUDY and C. D'AMICO, *Workforce 2020: Work and Workers in the 21st Century* (Indianapolis, IN: Hudson Institute, 1997).
7. Ibid.
8. W.H. FREY, "The United States Population: Where the New Immigrants Are," *U.S. Society and Values* (June 1999). Web posted at http:// usinfo.state.gov/journals/itsv/0699/ijse/clin.htm. Accessed May 3, 2004.
9. U.S. CENSUS BUREAU, "2002 Data Profiles." Web posted at http:// www.census.gov/. Accessed May 3, 2004.
10. SOCIAL SCIENCE DATA ANALYSIS NETWORK, "The Changing American Pie, 1999 and 2005." Web posted at http://www.prb.org/AmeristatTemplate.cfm?Section=Social_Science_Data_Analysis_Network. Accessed April 28, 2004.

11. Ibid.

12. Ibid.

13. RONALD D. HUNTER, THOMAS BARKER, and PAMELA D. MAYHALL, *Police Community Relations and the Administration of Justice*, 6th ed. (Upper Saddle River, NJ: Prentice Hall, 2004), p. 213.

14. GEORGE E. RUSH, *The Dictionary of Criminal Justice*, 6th ed. (Dubuque, Iowa: Dushkin-McGraw-Hill, 2003), p. 137.

15. C. REITH, *The Blind Eye of History* (London: Faber and Faber, Ltd., 1952), p. 154.

16. Ibid.

17. HUNTER, BARKER, and MAYHALL, 2004, p. 215.

18. Ibid p. 214.

19. Ibid p. 217.

20. ORLANDO W. WILISON and ROY C. MCLAREN, *Police Administration*, 4th ed. (New York: McGraw-Hill, 1977), pp. 221–222.

21. EDWARD K. SPANN, *Democracy's Children: The Young Rebels of the 1960s and the Power of Ideals* (Wilmington, DE: SR Books, 2003), p. 5.

22. DAVID BOESEL, *Cities Under Siege: An Anatomy of the Ghetto Riots, 1964–1968* (New York: Basic Books, 1971), pp. 45–47.

23. VINCENT N. PARRILLO, *Strangers to these Shores: Race and Ethnic Relations in the United States* (Boston: Simon & Schuster Co., 1994), pp. 23–24.

24. NATIONAL ADVISORY COMMISSION ON CIVIL DISORDERS, *The Kerner Report* (Washington, DC: GPO, 1968).

25. Ibid.

26. THE PRESIDENT'S COMMISSION ON LAW ENFORCEMENT AND ADMINISTRATION OF JUSTICE, *The Challenge of Crime in a Free Society* (Washington, DC: GPO, 1967), pp. 31–34.

27. MICHAEL J. PALMIOTTO, *Policing: Concepts, Strategies, and Current Issues in American Police Forces* (Durham, NC.: Carolina Academic Press, 1997), p. 198.

28. THE PRESIDENT'S COMMISSION ON LAW ENFORCEMENT AND ADMINISTRATION OF JUSTICE, 1967), p. 3.

29. THOMAS B. PRIEST and DEBORAH BROWN CARTER, "Evaluations of Police Performance in an African American Sample," *Journal of Criminal Justice* 27, no. 5 (1999): 457–465.

30. ELIJAH ANDERSON, *Street Wise: Race, Class, and Change in an Urban Community* (Chicago: The University of Chicago Press, 1990).

31. DAVID E. BARLOW and MELISSA HICKMAN BARLOW, *Police in a Multi Cultural Society: An American Story* (Prospect Heights, IL: Waveland Press, 2000), p. 121.

32. HUBERT WILLIAMS and PATRICK V. MURPHY, *The Evolving Strategies of Police: A Minority Perspective* (Washington, DC: National Institute of Justice, 1990), p. 13.

33. ROBERT C. WADMAN and WILLIAM T. ALLISON, *To Protect and to Serve: A History of Police in America* (Upper Saddle River, NJ: Prentice Hall, 2004).

34. SAMUEL WALKER, *The Police in America: An Introduction*, 3rd ed. (New York: McGraw Hill, 1999), p. 105.

35. SALLY E. HADDEN, *Slave Patrols: Law and Violence in Virginia and the Carolinas* (Cambridge, MA: Harvard University Press, 2001).

36. EUGENE D. GENOVESE, *Roll Jordon Roll: The World the Slaves Made* (New York: Vintage Books, 1976).

37. Ibid.

38. WADMAN and ALLISON, 2004.

39. SAMUEL WALKER, *Popular Justice: A History of American Criminal Justice* (New York: Oxford University Press, 1980).

40. BARLOW and BARLOW, 2000.

41. ORLANDO PATTERSON, *Rituals of Blood: The Consequences of Slavery in Two American Centuries* (New York: Basic Civitas, 1998).

42. JOHN R. LYNCH, *Facts of Reconstruction* (New York: Arno Press, 1968).

43. WADMAN and ALLISON, 2004.

44. PAUL HENDRICKSON, *Sons of Mississippi: A Story of race and Its Legacy* (New York: Alfred A. Knopf, 2003).

45. Ibid.

46. MILDRED PITTS WALTER, *Mississippi Challenge* (New York: Bradbury Press, 1992), p. 79.

47. Ibid.

48. WILLIAM LOREN KATZ, *Eyewitness: A Living Documentary of the African-American Contribution to American History* (New York: Touchstone, 1995).

49. WILLIAM A. NUNNELLY, *Bull Connor* (Tuscaloosa: University of Alabama Press, 1991).

50. WILLIAM BRADFORD Huie, *Three Lives for Mississippi* (Jackson: University Press of Mississippi, 2000).

51. Ibid.

52. LAURA PARKER, "Texas Scandal Throws Doubt on Anti-Drug Task Forces," *USA Today*, March 31, 2004, p. 3A.

53. LEONARD POST, "Trouble in Tulia Still Resounds; As Trial Looms, Role of Solos Emerges," *National Law Journal* 26, no. 31 (April 4, 2004): 1.

54. RICHARD FAUSSET and RICHARD WINTON, "Police Kill Driver, 13, at End of Chase," *Los Angeles Times*, February 7, 2005, Part B, p. 1.

55. HOWARD SWINDLE, *Deliberate Indifference: A Story of Murder and Racial Injustice* (New York: Viking Penguin, 1993).

56. DONALD BLACK, *The Manners and Customs of the Police* (New York: Academic Press, 1980).

57. CHRISTOPHER COMMISSION, *Final Report of the Independent Commission on the Los Angeles Police Department*, (Los Angeles, 1991).

58. Ibid., p. 70.

59. EGON BITTNER, *Aspects of Police Work* (Boston, MA: Northeastern University Press, 1996).

60. Ibid.

61. ROBERT M. FOGLESON, "From Resentment to Confrontation: The Police, the Negroes, and the Outbreaks of the Nineteen-Sixties Riots," *Political Science Quarterly* 83, no. 2 (June 1968): 217–247.

62. HOMER HAWKINS and RICHARD THOMAS, "White Policing Black Populations: A History of Race and Social Control in America," in *Out of Order: Policing Black People*, ed. Ellis Cashmore and Eugene McLaughlin (New York: Routledge, 1991), pp. 65–86.

63. POLICE EXECUTIVE RESEARCH FORUM, Community Oriented Policing Services, *"Racially Biased Policing"* (Washington, DC: Police Executive Research Forum, 2001), p. 101.

64. WADMAN and ALLISON, 2004.

65. CHARLES W. PEEK, JON P. ALSTON, and GEORGE D. LOWE, "Comparative Evaluation of the Local Police," *The Public Opinion Quarterly* 42, no. 3 (autumn 1978): 370–379.

66. DAVID L. CARTER and LOUIS A. RADELET, *The Police and the Community*, 6th ed. (Upper Saddle River, NJ: Prentice Hall, 1999).

67. DAVID HARRIS, "Driving While Black and all Other Traffic Offences: The Supreme Court and Pretextual Traffic Stops," *Journal of Criminal Law and Criminology* 87, no. 2 (1997): 544–582.

68. DAVID COLE, *No Equal Justice: Race and Class in the American Criminal Justice System* (New York: New Press, 1999).

69. Ibid.

70. KEITH D. PARKER, ANNE B. OKYEAWULUJE, and KOMANDURI S. MURTI, "African American's Attitudes Toward the Local Police: A Multivariate Analysis," *Journal of Black Studies* 25, no. 3 (1995): 396–409.

71. SAMUEL WALKER, *Police Interactions with Racial and Ethnic Minorities: Assessing the Evidence and Allegations, 2000* (Washington, DC: Police Executive Report Forum).

72. MICHAEL S. SCOTT, *The Benefits and Consequences of Police Crackdowns* (Washington, DC: Office of Community Oriented Policing Services, 2002), p. 1.

73. Ibid.

74. PETER KRASKA and VICTOR KAPPELER, "Militarizing the American Police: The Rise and Normalization of Paramilitary Units," *Social Problems* 44, no. 1: 1–18.

75. JOHN ECK and E. MAGUIRE, "Have Changes in Policing Reduced Violent Crime?: An Assessment of the Evidence," in *The Crime Drop in America,* ed. A. Blumstein and J. Wallman (Cambridge, England: Cambridge University Press, 2000).

76. BUREAU OF JUSTICE STATISTICS, *Criminal Victimization in the United States* (Washington, DC: GPO, 1997).

77. PARKER, OKYEAWULUJE, and MURTI, 1995.

78. PATRICK A. LANGRAM, et al., *Contacts Between Police and the Public: Findings from the 1999 National Survey* (Washington, DC: Bureau of Justice Statistics, 2001).

79. Ibid, p. 3.

80. ROBERT K. MERTON, *Social Theory and Social Structure* (New York: Free Press, 1968).

81. HOWARD S. BECKER, *Outsiders: Studies in the Sociology of Deviance* (New York: Free Press, 1973).

82. POLICE EXECUTIVE RESEARCH FORUM, 2001, pp. 101–102.

83. PALMIOTTO, 1997.

84. Ibid.

85. Ibid.
86. WALKER, 1999, p. 11.
87. SHUSTA, LEVINE, HARRIS, and WONG, 1995, p. 36.
88. ROBIN D.G. KELLEY, "Slangin' Rocks Palestinian Style," in *Police Brutality, Annotated*, ed. Jill Smith (New York: W.W. Norton and Company, 2000), p. 51.
89. HENRY I. DeGENESTE and JOHN P. SULLIVAN, *Fresh Perspectives: Policing a Multicultural Community* (Washington, DC: PERF Publications, 1997).
90. THOMAS BARKER, JEFF RUSH, and RON HUNTER, *Police Systems and Practices: An Introduction* (Upper Saddle River, NJ: Prentice Hall, 1994).
91. JANET JOHNSON, "Recruit Officers Survey Neighborhood." Web posted at http://www.wichitagov.org/news/city/events. Accessed on May 23, 2004.
92. ARTHUR A. NIEDERHOFFER and ALEXANDER B. SMITH, *New Directions in Police Community Relations* (San Francisco, CA: Holt, Rinehart, and Winston, 1974).
93. ELLEN G. COHN, "The Citizen Police Academy: A Recipe for Improving Police-Community Relations," *Journal of Criminal Justice* 22, no. 3 (1996): 265–271.
94. SEDGWICK COUNTY SHERIFF'S DEPARTMENT, Citizen Police Academy. Web posted at http://www.sedgwickcounty.org/sheriff/CPA. Accessed May 19, 2004.
95. SYLVIA WHITMAN, "Police Academies for Citizens," *Law and Order* (June 1993): 66–71.
96. MICHAEL L. BIRZER, "Police Training in the 21st Century," *FBI Law Enforcement Bulletin* (July 1999): 16–19.
97. DeGENESTE and SULLIVAN, 1997.
98. GARY R. CODERONI, "The Relationship Between Multicultural Training for Police and Effective Law Enforcement." *FBI Law Enforcement Bulletin* (November 2002): 12–14.
99. Ibid. p. 14.
100. GARY WEAVER, "Law Enforcement in a Culturally Diverse Society," *FBI Law Enforcement Bulletin* (September 1992): 1–7.
101. MICHAEL L. BIRZER and RONALD L. TANNEHILL, "A More Effective Training Approach for Contemporary Policing," *Police Quarterly* 4, no. 2 (2001): 233–252.
102. SHUSTA, LEVINE, HARRIS, and WONG, 1995, p. 157.
103. Ibid., pp. 188–190.
104. RONALD WEITZER, "White, Black, or Blue Cops? Race and Citizen Assessments of Police Officers," *Journal of Criminal Justice* 28, no. 4 (2000): 313–324.
105. RALPH OSBORN, Police Recruitment: "Today's Standard, Tomorrow's Challenge," *FBI Law Enforcement Bulletin* (June 2002): 21–26.
106. A. HILL and J. SCOTT. "Ten Strategies for Managers in a Multicultural Workplace." *Resource Focus Magazine,* July 1992, pp. 21–35.
107. COMMUNITY RELATIONS SERVICE U.S. DEPARTMENT OF JUSTICE, "Police Use of Force: Addressing Community Racial Tensions," *Community Relations Bulletin,* (Washington, DC: United States Department of Justice, 2004).
108. Ibid., p. 2.
109. Ibid., p. 3.
110. Ibid., p. 3.
111. Ibid., p. 3.

Human Resources: Recruitment and Selection

Key Terms

Active recruiting

Adverse impact

Affirmative action

Americans with Disabilities Act (ADA)

Bona fide occupational qualification (BFOQ)

Civil Rights Act

Conditional offer of employment

Equal Employment Opportunity Commission (EEOC)

Griggs v. *Duke Power Company*

Human resources

Job-related selection device

Learning strategies

Recruitment

Selection

Test reliability

Title VII

Outline

Introduction

Recruitment Process

Selection Process

Selection Devices

Innovative Approaches

Changes in Police Officer Selection

Learning Objectives

After reading this chapter, you should be able to:

1. Define recruitment and selection.
2. Discuss the legal environment, centering on recruitment and selection.
3. Explain the various approaches to police recruiting.
4. List the stages of the police selection process.
5. Identify and discuss specific selection devices used in police officer selection.

6. Describe ways to increase recruitment of minorities and women.
7. Identify and discuss innovative approaches to police officer selection.

INTRODUCTION

If we lowered our standards in terms of hiring or graduating rookie police officers, we would only end up shooting ourselves in the foot. Pinning a badge on less qualified individuals would come back to haunt us.

—*Willie L. Williams, 1996 Former Chief of Police, Los Angeles Police Department*

Simply put, the purpose of **recruitment** and **selection** is to find and retain qualified men and women to serve in the police profession. Most police administrators and human resources specialists would probably agree that this can be a difficult task. It is through recruitment and selection that the future of the agency is determined. Of those recruited and selected into the police service, some will gravitate to investigation positions, some will lead others as supervisors, still others will make it to command and administrative positions, while a few may go on to become agency heads.

The 20th-century police reformer O. W. Wilson once asserted that the appointment of unqualified or poorly qualified persons who are unable to become good police officers constitutes an economic loss that is usually many times the cost of the entire selection process for all the newly appointed recruits.[1] We find this to be just as relevant today as it was when reformer Wilson was masterminding the professional model of policing. Recruitment and selection cannot be carried out haphazardly if policing is to attract and retain the best police officers to work in an ever-changing society and an ever-changing police profession.

There are a number of factors that affect police recruitment and selection. First, it is predicted that the 21st-century labor market will increasingly demand highly educated workers who can create and apply sophisticated new technologies; these workers will be rewarded handsomely.[2] If these predictions are true, it may shrink the available labor pool for police organizations as they compete for highly educated applicants who may be lured to the private sector. The applicant pool may not be there in large numbers as it once was. Furthermore, less than 4 percent of those who apply to become police officers are actually hired. The predicted reduction in the entry-level pool requires that measures be taken to counter the inadequacies of traditional hiring practices.[3]

A second factor that will affect recruitment and selection is the changing police profession. In the past, the police mission was to enforce the law; in recent years that mission has changed its focus to community relations and to community-oriented policing. Under the axiom of community-oriented policing, a different type of police officer will be desired. For community-oriented policing strategies to be successful, police agencies will increasingly move away from recruiting the Rambo-type personality. The recruiting process will change its focus, and people who have good social skills, possess critical thinking skills, are effective problem solvers, and have excellent communication skills (and understand that a large part of the police job is communicating with people) will become the targets for recruitment into the police service.

The stakes are high when recruiting police officers. As a rule of thumb, the wrong person costs an organization three times his or her annual salary; for example, a $50,000 employee with poor job performance actually costs $150,000.[4] Additionally, there is lost opportunity as well as negative public perception if the public becomes aware of an officer's poor performance (or even worse, a lawsuit could result if the officer violates a citizen's constitutional rights or engages in some other form of gross police misconduct). The sacrifices in quality made today may be felt for many years into the future.

The private sector goes to great lengths to ensure employee quality when hiring; consider the following hiring approach. Bob, the owner of a San Diego-based company, narrows his search down to several candidates and invites each one to dinner. The candidate is unaware that the restaurant belongs to Bob's friend, and the waiter is instructed to screw up his order. If he orders a steak well-done, he gets it rare, and Bob watches his reaction. If he complains to the waiter, Bob knows he is an assertive person (has a lot of drive and may prove to be too pushy). If he says nothing, Bob asks, "How is your food?" If he replies, "Fine," it reveals that he may be eager to get along and may be too accommodating and a pushover. To be certain, Bob says, "I thought you ordered the steak well-done." If he answers, "I did, and normally I would mention it to the waiter, but I am here because of the job, not because of the food," he reveals that he is good at setting priorities, is quick at sorting the important from the superfluous, and knows how to act appropriately in each situation.[5]

Obviously, it would be unrealistic (not to mention costly) to take each police applicant out to dinner. We offer this example to merely get you thinking "outside the box" about new and innovative possibilities for recruiting and selecting future police officers.

RECRUITMENT PROCESS

In order for police departments to have excellent personnel, an excellent recruitment program is essential. Recruitment and selection, while sometimes used interchangeably, are actually different in scope and purpose. Recruitment is the process of locating, identifying, and attracting capable applicants who have the minimum qualifications to be eligible for the selection process.[6] On the other hand, the selection process (as discussed later in this chapter) involves subjecting police applicants to what amounts to a rigorous testing protocol. Selection is an exercise that seeks to predict which applicants will be successful if hired and to weed out the unqualified candidates.[7] An outstanding recruitment program usually results in better-quality applicants from which to select.

The scope of the recruitment program and the amount of effort devoted to it will be largely influenced by the size of the organization. In general, the larger the police organization, the easier it is to recruit police applicants. Larger police organizations are more visible to potential applicants and may be perceived as offering more opportunities as well as higher starting wages. Recruitment should be an ongoing year-round process. If continuous recruiting is not conducted, the organization risks losing qualified candidates.

Recall that the purpose of recruitment is to attract qualified individuals to apply for police positions. The term "qualified" denotes those individuals who possess—or who can acquire through entry-level training—the required skills, knowledge, abilities, and job behaviors to successfully perform the tasks and duties of a police officer.[8] The organization should consider providing travel funds for recruiters and for other recruiting activities such as advertising, and imaginative techniques are necessary for effective recruiting. In essence, the organization must be willing to go anywhere to seek out applicants with high potential.

The recruitment process involves a number of activities:

- Advertisements in professional publications, with college and university placement services, and in local, state, and regional newspapers
- Interviews with students enrolled in criminal justice internship programs
- Internal and external searches
- Inquiries and referrals

Missouri State Highway Patrol recruiting booth at a university job fair.

Photo by Cliff Roberson

- Professional contacts with community organizations promoting interests of minority groups
- Publications and pamphlets
- Special activities and events for prospective applicants
- Audiovisual packages
- Internet advertising

Vacancy Announcements

There are a number of important factors involved in announcing the vacancy for a police officer position. The goal of vacancy announcements is to reach as many men and women as possible in order to attract the best candidates for the job, but there are some legal precautions to consider when announcing police officer vacancies. Any recruitment activity that intentionally restricts or impacts a protected classification under Title VII of the Civil Rights Act of 1964 may unnecessarily subject the agency to scrutiny by the U.S. Department of Justice or (in more extreme cases) to costly civil litigation brought by prospective applicants. In order to avoid potential litigation when announcing police officer vacancies, the following suggestions should be considered[9]:

- The agency should employ an array of recruiting approaches to target the broadest range of eligible candidates. In addition to posting job notices and referrals from current employees, efforts should extend to newspapers and radio stations, churches, recreational programs, and criminal justice programs.
- It is also beneficial to use certain publications and organizations, such as minority newspapers and radio stations, churches, national and state minority organizations, community action groups, and minority higher education institutions, to reach minority and/or female applicants.
- Success in this area can be benchmarked through the use of a marketing survey completed by the applicant during the orientation program. Such a device verifies which mechanisms are effective for communicating the department's recruiting efforts. These data could also assist the police department in defending claims that it relied solely on word-of-mouth advertising methods.
- A demographic analysis should be made of the relevant labor market or the geographical area from which the department can expect to draw potential applicants.

Advertisements

Effective advertising is about reaching and influencing police candidates regardless of where they are and what they read, hear, or see. Advertising is about delivering the right message to the right audience in the right media (newspapers, trade publications, radio, or the Internet). A well-written job advertisement consists of (1) specific job qualifications; (2) specific job experience expected; (3) specific job skills needed; (4) specific job description; and (5) specific salary range and benefits package.[10]

The benefit of widespread effective advertising is that a large population or specific groups can be targeted; however, this can be a double-edged sword inasmuch as a wide advertising distribution can also generate many unqualified applicants. Nevertheless, proper advertising can be an invaluable tool for attracting large numbers of potential applicants.

Traditionally, police organizations have relied on advertisements to recruit men and women into the police service. In the age of technology, the Internet has become increasingly popular as a recruiting device; likewise, the greatest geographical reach for recruitment is, of course, the Internet. Some departments have their own Internet Web page with links to recruitment information that potential applicants can log on to and have many of their questions answered. Police organizations should increasingly explore the Internet as a mechanism to allow applicants to submit their employment applications online.

While the latest and furthest-reaching job search medium is the Internet, the long-standing tradition of placing employment advertising in the metropolitan Sunday newspaper continues be a viable recruitment source, and the local newspaper should be used to place recruiting ads whenever possible. Publishing job openings in a newspaper of good size (especially the metropolitan Sunday paper) ensures reaching a large and diverse audience. In a world of high-tech information, newspapers are trying innovative approaches to remain competitive. As costly and unwieldy as the print medium may sometimes seem, there is no getting around the fact that when people hunt for a job, most of them look in the local newspaper.

Brochures are another effective medium for recruiting. An attractive brochure should be colorful and include photographs and information about salary, benefits, working conditions, promotional and career opportunities, contact information for questions, and basic minimum qualification information as well as where to apply. If the recruiting brochure is complete with photographs (which is always best), it should reflect diversity. A brochure that depicts both female and minority police officers has the propensity to attract underrepresented groups to the policing occupation and gives the impression that the police organization is open to these groups. Where ethnic minorities normally speak languages other than English, a brochure translated into those languages spoken locally has been found useful; for example, in areas where there is a large population of Spanish speakers, a brochure printed in Spanish can help in getting the word out.

In an effort to diversify their sources of applicants, the Los Angeles Police Department (LAPD) ended its tradition of concentrating on military bases, which is a traditional recruiting technique used by many police organizations. Recruiters in the LAPD began using more television and newspaper advertisements and holding more recruitment expos in various parts of the city as well as making visits to colleges in an effort to recruit minorities and women.[11]

Following are two suggestions that police personnel in **human resources** should take into consideration when developing advertising programs. First, advertising must be cost-effective. Most police departments have a limited marketing and advertising budget, so the organization can't afford to waste its entire budget on expensive advertisements that fail to bring in applicants. Second, the organization must be able to measure the effectiveness of the marketing and advertising program. For example, when the organization spends money on an advertisement they need to know how many applicants they get from the advertisement and how many of these applicants ultimately receive employment offers. It is ill-advised to carry out marketing and advertising initiatives if the results cannot be tracked. The marketing and advertising program has only one aim: to attract a large number of qualified applicants for the police organization.

Employee Referrals

Employee referrals result when police officers recruit by word of mouth. For example, the police organization may offer recruitment incentive plans for employees: If an employee successfully refers a qualified police applicant who is hired, the employee would receive time off with pay or some other monetary reward. Research has found that word-of-mouth recruitment by friends, associates, and relatives of police officers is one of the most effective sources of police recruitment.[12]

College and University Campuses

College and university campuses continue to be ideal recruiting locations. Many colleges and universities conduct job fairs, which attract a large number of potential employers to the campuses. Police recruiters have an ideal venue at college job fairs. Not only are job fairs excellent sources for recruiting, but many universities offer police internship programs for students. Each college intern should be viewed as a potential recruit.

The importance of setting educational standards for police officers has been recognized for several decades. In the early 1970s, the National Advisory Commission on Criminal Justice Standards and Goals recommended that in order for police officers to perform their police duties properly, every police department should establish guidelines for entry-level educational requirements.[13] What better way to accomplish this than by focusing recruiting efforts on college campuses.

Minorities and Women

A top priority for many police executives is recruiting and retaining a workforce that reflects their community's diverse culture. The recruitment of minorities and women is essential for the police organization. In recent years there has been significant progress in increasing the numbers of minorities and women in the ranks of sworn officers. From 1987 to 2000, the minority representation in local law enforcement agencies increased from 14.5 percent to 22.7 percent while minorities in sheriff's departments accounted for 17.4 percent of sworn deputies, up from 13.4 percent in 1987.[14] Likewise, women now represent 10.6 percent of all sworn officers, up from 8.1 percent in 1990.[15] While these data are grounds for optimism in many respects, the fact remains that many police departments have yet to meet the affirmative action composition of the communities they serve.[16] In some cases recruitment efforts of minority candidates have failed for three primary reasons: (1) Police departments failed to make their searches extensive enough to attract the best-qualified candidates for the job, (2) many blacks don't possess the minimum education qualifications for employment consideration, and (3) many blacks have a negative impression of police work.[17]

Muncie, Indiana, policewoman in uniform with badge, January 26, 1914.

Photo courtesy of U.S. Library of Congress

The National Advisory Commission on Criminal Justice Standards and Goals recommended that every agency seeking to employ qualified ethnic minority members should research, develop, and implement a variety of specialized minority recruitment methods[18]:

1. Assignment of minority police officers to the specialized recruitment effort
2. Liaison with local minority community leaders to emphasize police sincerity and to encourage referral of minority applicants to the police agency
3. Recruitment advertising and other materials that depict minority group police personnel performing the police function
4. Active cooperation of the minority media as well as the general media in minority recruitment efforts
5. Emphasis on the community service aspect of police work
6. Regular personal contact with minority applicants from initial application to final determination of employability

Police recruiters should not take a passive approach in recruiting minorities and women, in other words, just wait for them to come to the police department to apply. Recruiting should not be a passive activity; **active recruiting** is an aggressive endeavor to seek out those who ideally want a career in the police service, not just a job. Posting a notice on the bulletin board outside city hall is not nearly enough. Recruiters should take active approaches and seek out qualified minorities and women in large numbers for potential police employment. Just because minorities and women don't apply for police service doesn't mean they are not interested. It very well could be the perception that police service is an occupation for white males and is closed to minorities and women.

Like minority police officers, women police officers have historically faced discrimination. There is a growing amount of evidence that suggests that women possess many traits that are ideal for police work. For example, after the 1991 Rodney King police brutality incident involving Los Angeles Police Department officers, the Christopher Commission, which investigated LAPD practices, reported that women officers did not employ excessive force as often as their male counterparts. Male and female officers interviewed for the report said they thought women were better skilled at defusing confrontations with suspects through verbal communication.[19]

It is best, whenever possible, that police recruiters themselves reflect diversity. An all-white and all-male team of recruiters does not send the right message. A recent study suggested that the race of organizational recruiters may be important for minority recruiting efforts.[20] Specifically, the study showed that African-American and Hispanic applicants were more interested when minority recruiters were depicted (white applicants' reactions were unaffected by representative race). Moreover, the extent to which potential applicants believed themselves to be similar to the recruiter fully mediated the effect for the minority applicants.[21]

Programs to make the police organization more representative of the diversity in the community are best adapted to the particular characteristics of the department and the community itself. The following steps are recommended[22]:

1. All job announcements should state that the department is an equal opportunity employer.
2. Responsibility for affirmative action efforts should be assigned to a particular individual with management authority.
3. Specially trained recruitment task forces should be developed and put into operation.
4. Referral sources (educational institutions, military services, and minority organizations) should be identified and continual liaison with them maintained.
5. The department should provide recruitment counseling at neighborhood centers and to walk-ins, if possible.
6. The time period from recruitment to selection should be kept to a minimum.
7. All tests should be validated and based on job-related skills and abilities, as determined by periodic job analyses.
8. All police personnel should participate in in-service training programs that develop their understanding of the need for diverse representation and that elicit their involvement in it.

Many local government jurisdictions have successfully implemented strategies to tap into diverse applicant pools. The City of Santa Ana, California, improved its ability to hire a diverse workforce by strengthening linkages to the local university and targeting some jobs specifically to ethnic groups that were underrepresented in its workforce.[23] To recruit females for nontraditional jobs, the city of Pasadena, California, posts job announcements at health spas, gyms, and fitness centers.[24]

High School Recruiting

Because many young persons decide to enter the police profession during high school, recruitment efforts should naturally begin there. Some high school youth start their involvement with law enforcement through Explorer Scouts programs. The Explorer Scouts is a law enforcement program for young men and women who have completed the eighth grade and are between the ages of 14 and 20. Law enforcement Explorer Scouts programs help youth gain invaluable insight into the police occupation; for young men and women who are interested in a career in policing, these programs offer experiential learning that promotes growth and development.[25] In an effort to keep high school students' interest in a law enforcement career, the New York City Police Department (NYPD) allows them to take the written exam when they are 16 years old, and those who pass the test and stay out of trouble are guaranteed a job when they reach the appropriate age.[26]

Affirmative Action

Affirmative action employment programs cover a wide spectrum of activities involving **affirmative action**—the recruitment, hiring, placement, training, and advancement of historically underrepresented and/or underutilized groups within the workforce. Put another way, "Affirmative Action is any action that is taken specifically to overcome the results of past discriminatory employment practices."[27] These activities focus on enhancing the representation of American Indians/Alaskan Natives, Hispanic Americans, Asian Americans/Pacific Islanders, African Americans, females, and persons with disabilities. Institutions with affirmative action policies generally set goals and timetables for increased diversity, and they use recruitment as a way of achieving those goals.

Affirmative action remains controversial. Some (in the majority group) blame affirmative action for robbing them of promotions and other opportunities, which has led them to call for "color-blind" policies. The problem is that color-blind policies imply a very limited role on the part of the state in addressing social inequality in hiring practices. While many minorities and women support affirmative action, a growing number say its benefits are no longer worth its side effect (the perception that their success is unearned). The reality is that the playing field is still tilted very much in favor of the white male majority.[28] Research shows that minorities and women are vastly overrepresented in lower-paying jobs and still face discrimination in some sectors.[29]

It is in the best interest of the police agency as well as the community that affirmative action programs are in place to ensure a diverse representation. Despite its controversial nature, until absolute equity is achieved in employment, affirmative action constitutes a viable program to even the playing field.

SELECTION PROCESS

After applicants have been recruited, the selection process begins. Selection is the screening of job applicants to ensure that the most qualified candidates are hired. As previously discussed, selection is an exercise in prediction; in other words, the selection process seeks to predict who will be successful if hired for police work. It is an absolute necessity that the most qualified men and women are selected for the police service.

Legal Environment and Selection

There are a number of legal considerations in the selection process. In 1964 the U.S. Congress established the **Equal Employment Opportunity Commission (EEOC).** The EEOC is charged with the responsibility of administering the provisions of the **Civil Rights Act.** In 1972 the jurisdiction of the EEOC was expanded to include public-sector employees. **Title VII** of the Civil Rights Act makes it illegal for public employers to discriminate against persons on the basis of race, sex, color, religion, or national origin. All criteria for hiring must be based on a ***bona fide* occupational qualification (BFOQ).** A BFOQ is any physical attribute and/or skill that an employer has proven is necessary for satisfactory performance of a particular job. According to the EEOC guidelines, the use of any selection procedure that has an adverse impact on the hiring, promotion, or other employment or membership opportunities of members of any race, sex, or ethnic group is considered to be discriminatory.[30] Under EEOC guidelines, **adverse impact** is a substantially different rate of selection in hiring, promotion, or other employment decision that works to the disadvantage of members of a specific race, sex, or ethnic group.

The following suggestions may assist police organizations in ensuring that their selection process is in compliance with EEOC guidelines[31]:

1. Selection criteria should be related to the job they presume to measure, which means they should be good, reliable, accurate predictors of job success.
2. Selection criteria and procedures should be validated to ensure they are job-related and reliable predictors of job success. Selection criteria should not remain static but should be regularly reviewed.
3. Selection criteria should be applied equally to all applicants considered. (There may be exceptions when, for example, affirmative action programs apply.)
4. Selection criteria should not result in disparate impact on a protected group. If more than one procedure is available, the one with the least impact should be used.
5. Selection criteria should be flexible, not arbitrary. For example, one might substitute experience for a college degree in certain situations.
6. Departments should be wary of basing decisions on subjective factors when the tasks involved are of a low level and need objective evaluation or measurement.

Police departments use pre-employment tests as a way to screen out applicants who are not suitable for the job. These tests typically include skills tests, aptitude tests, psychological tests, personality tests, honesty tests, medical tests, and drug tests. Although police organizations have an obligation to conduct testing of applicants, both state law and federal law impose numerous restrictions on what testing is acceptable and not acceptable. These restrictions are often vague and open to contradictory interpretations; as a result, only tests that are an absolute business necessity should be administered. Police administrators and human resources specialists should consult with their legal department or attorney before administering tests to make sure the tests will pass legal muster.

Any **job-related selection device** used by a police organization, such as application forms, written tests, physical tests, interviews, and background investigations, must be valid. If a test is valid, there is a proven relationship between the selection device and some relevant criterion.[32]

For example, the law prohibits managers from using a test score as a selection tool unless there is evidence that, once on the job, individuals with high scores on this test outperform individuals with low test scores.[33] Likewise, police applicants cannot be tested on their knowledge of the law or police procedures because they have not been trained in these areas; instead, they must be evaluated on the basis of their potential to accept training and to apply the often-difficult abstractions presented by laws and regulations.[34]

A testing device must also be reliable. **Test reliability** indicates whether the device measures the same thing consistently; for example, if a test is reliable, any single individual's score should remain consistent over time, assuming that the characteristics the test is measuring are also stable.[35]

Americans with Disabilities Act

The **Americans with Disabilities Act (ADA)** was signed into law in 1990 and became effective on July 26, 1992. The ADA impacts many areas of police personnel selection. Congress enacted the ADA to help ensure that individuals with physical and/or mental disabilities receive equal employment opportunities.[36] Title II of the ADA covers all activities of state and local governments regardless of the government entity's size or receipt of federal funding; it requires that state and local governments give people with disabilities an equal opportunity to benefit from all of their programs, services, and activities (including public education, employment, transportation, recreation, health care, social services, courts, voting, and town meetings). Title II of the ADA applies to all areas of police employment, such as testing, hiring, assignments, evaluations, disciplinary actions, training, promotions, sick leaves, and terminations.[37]

Police departments are not required to take actions that would result in undue financial and administrative burdens; however, they are required to make reasonable modifications to policies, practices, and procedures when necessary to avoid discrimination, unless they can demonstrate that doing so would fundamentally alter the nature of the service, program, or activity being provided. The following factors should be considered: nature and cost of the accommodation, overall financial resources of the employer and the particular facility where the accommodation is needed, number of persons employed at such facilities (and by the employer in general), and impact of the accommodation on the operation of the facility.[38]

The Americans with Disabilities Act provides protections similar to those provided by Title VII of the Civil Rights Act of 1964 as well as Section 504 of the Rehabilitation Act of 1973, which is the foundation for the Americans with Disabilities Act. The ADA utilizes a three-pronged definition of the term "disability." An individual with a disability is any person who (1) has a physical or mental impairment that substantially limits one or more major life activities, (2) has a record of such an impairment, or (3) is regarded as having such an impairment.[39]

Commonly Asked Questions and Answers: Police Selection and ADA

Q: Recently a job applicant for a police officer's job came into the police department with fingers that were visibly impaired. The police department required that he demonstrate that he could pull the trigger on the police-issued firearm and reload it before a conditional job offer was made. Did this violate ADA guidelines?

A: No. If an individual has a known disability that would reasonably appear to interfere with or prevent performance of job functions, that person may be asked to demonstrate how these functions will be performed, even if other applicants are not asked to do so.

Q: Can I refuse to consider an applicant because of his current use of illegal drugs?

A: Yes. Individuals who currently engage in the illegal use of drugs are specifically excluded from the definition of "an individual with a disability" when an employer takes action on the basis of their current use.

Q: What about applicants with a history of illegal drug use? Do they have rights under the ADA?

A: It depends. Casual drug use is not a disability under the ADA, only individuals who are addicted to drugs, who have a history of addiction, or who are regarded as being addicted or have an impairment under the law. In order for an individual's drug addiction to be considered a disability under the ADA, it would have to pose a substantial limitation on one or more major life activities; in addition, the individual could not currently be using illegal drugs. Denying employment to job applicants solely because of a history of casual drug use would not raise ADA concerns. On the other hand, policies that screen out applicants because of a history of addiction or treatment must be carefully scrutinized to ensure that the policies are job-related and consistent with business necessity. If safety is asserted as a justification for such a policy, then the employer must be able to show that individuals excluded because of a history of drug addiction or treatment would pose a direct threat (a significant risk of substantial harm) to the health and safety of the individual or others that cannot be eliminated or reduced by reasonable accommodation.

Q: May an applicant be asked prior to a conditional job offer whether he or she has ever used illegal drugs or been arrested for any reason?

A: Yes. It does not violate ADA guidelines to ask whether the applicant has ever used illegal drugs or been arrested for such use; however, a law enforcement agency may not ask at the preoffer stage about frequency of past illegal drug use or whether the applicant has ever been addicted to drugs or undergone treatment for addiction.

Q: Can I disqualify all applicants with felony convictions?

A: Yes. This type of disqualification is allowed as long as you can show that the exclusion is job-related and consistent with business necessity.

Q: Does the ADA have any impact on the use of drug testing?

A: No. Police departments may subject current employees to testing for illegal use of drugs and may require job applicants to undergo such testing at any stage of the application process.

(continued)

Q: I know I can't give a job applicant a medical exam before a conditional job offer is made, but what about physical agility and physical fitness tests?

A: You can give job applicants tests measuring the ability to perform job-related tasks or physical fitness tests (tests measuring performance of running, lifting, etc.) before any job offer is made. Tests that simply measure an applicant's ability to perform a task are not considered to be medical examinations. But remember, job requirements that screen out or tend to screen out persons with disabilities are legitimate only if the targeted areas are job-related and consistent with business necessity.

Q: Are alcoholics covered by the ADA?

A: Yes. While a current illegal user of drugs is not protected by the ADA if an employer acts on the basis of such use, a person who currently uses alcohol is not automatically denied protection. An alcoholic is a person with a disability and is protected by the ADA if he or she is qualified to perform the essential functions of the job. An employer may be required to provide an accommodation to an alcoholic; however, an employer can discipline, discharge, or deny employment to an alcoholic whose use of alcohol adversely affects job performance or conduct. An employer also may prohibit the use of alcohol in the workplace and can require that employees not be under the influence of alcohol.

An individual must satisfy at least one of the three items above in order to be considered an individual with a disability under the ADA. Qualified employees or prospective employees with disabilities may request accommodations in order to perform essential functions of their job or to gain access to the hiring process. Employers must reasonably accommodate the known physical or mental limitation of an otherwise qualified applicant unless the accommodation would impose an undue hardship on their business operation.

A disabled person must be qualified for the job, program, or activity to which he or she seeks access. To be qualified under the ADA, a disabled person must be able to perform the essential functions of a job or meet the essential eligibility requirements of the program or benefit, with or without an accommodation to his or her condition. Police departments should use screening devices that follow established ADA guidelines.

Police applicants currently using illegal drug substances are not protected by the ADA, and testing for illegal drug use does not violate ADA guidelines. Alcoholics and illegal substance abusers can be held to the same standard as other applicants.

Police agencies are not required to employ a disabled person, but they must be able to justify their decision not to. For example, police officers can be called on to perform various physical activities in the performance of their duties, and some disabilities may prevent an individual from performing them. Thus, the police agency would be justified in not employing a disabled person who could not perform those physical activities.

SELECTION DEVICES

Selection is best described as a multiple-hurdle process because applicants have to successfully pass one test (or hurdle) in order to go to the next phase (or next hurdle). There are a number of selection devices that are used to screen out unqualified candidates while at the same time identifying qualified candidates. The more accepted selection devices include a review of each candidate's written or electronically submitted application form, written examination, physical agility test, polygraph testing, oral interview, psychological testing, background investigation, and medical and drug screening.

Application Form

The employment application form offers an often-overlooked device to determine an applicant's qualifications. The application form can be reviewed relatively quickly to determine that the applicant meets the minimum qualifications for the job. Job requirements usually include such criteria as minimum age, minimum education (such as high school diploma or its equivalent), no felony convictions, weight proportional to height, vision no less than 20/100 uncorrected and correctable to 20/20, valid driver's license, and U.S. citizenship. Applicants who do not meet the minimum

---

New York City Police Department Minimum Qualifications

- Candidates must be at least 21 years of age on or before the day of hire.
- Candidates must be a U.S. citizen on or before the day of hire.
- On or before the day of hire, candidates must have successfully completed either:

  Sixty (60) college credits with a 2.0 G.P.A. from an accredited college or university, or two (2) years of full-time, active military service in the United States Armed Forces with an honorable discharge and have a high school diploma or its equivalent.

- Candidates must reside either within one of the five boroughs of New York City or in one of the surrounding counties (Suffolk, Westchester, Orange, Rockland, Nassau, or Putman) on the day of hire.
- Candidates must possess a valid, unrestricted New York State driver's license on the day of hire.
- Candidates must pay a $75 fee for fingerprinting as part of the investigation process.
- Candidates must pass a drug/alcohol screening.
- Candidates must pass a character and background investigation.

Source: New York City Police Department, 2005. Web posted at http://www.nypd2.org/html/recruit/requirements.html.

requirements are disqualified early in the process, thus saving the applicant and the police organization valuable time. For example, if a police applicant is only 19 years of age and the minimum age requirement is 21, the applicant is directed out of the selection process and encouraged to apply once he or she reaches the age of 21.

Written Examination

The written examination is usually administered early in the selection process and after the initial application form has been completed and checked to ensure minimum qualifications. The written examination is an effective and cost-effective method of screening large numbers of police applicants.

There have been a few legal challenges to some written examinations on the basis that they are not job-related. For example, many reform police chiefs of the past (most notably O. W. Wilson) advocated the use of intelligence tests, with an intelligent quotient of 112 as a minimum qualification for police employment.[40] Police managers should be cautious about using intelligence tests with a minimum quotient cutoff score because the 1971 *Griggs* v. *Duke Power Company* decision prohibits such tests when adverse impact occurs.[41] In the *Griggs* decision, the Court makes clear that the employer has the burden of showing that any job requirement has a manifest relationship to the job in question when the requirement tends to reduce job opportunities because of race. A key element of the Court's holding in *Griggs* is that good intent or the absence of discriminatory intent does not redeem testing procedures that have adverse impact on protected classes but that are unrelated to measuring job capability.

Written examinations for entry-level police positions are most likely to test areas such as basic arithmetic ability, reading comprehension, grammar, spelling, and writing skills. These areas have been shown to be job-related for police work.

There are two approaches to using the written examination as a selection device. First, applicants take the examination and their score is factored into a constellation of all tests administered during the selection process; in other words, the test itself is not used as a disqualifying device. The benefit to this approach is that it allows the candidate to continue in the selection process regardless of test score. The disadvantage would obviously be the large number of applicants proceeding through the selection process.

In the second approach, there may be a minimum passing score set on the examination; if an applicant fails to reach the minimum score, he or she is disqualified from further consideration. For example, suppose a police organization sets 70 percent as the minimum passing test score and the applicant scores 60 percent. The applicant in this case is disqualified from the remaining selection process. The advantage to this approach is that it narrows a large pool of candidates down quickly and early in the selection process.

Some have argued that one of the major disadvantages of written examinations is that they may be culturally biased, which has an impact on some minority groups. Professor Richard Holden pointed out that examinations are usually written by white middle-class personnel and that these examinations may contain cultural bias.[42] Individuals who create tests use language and examples with which they are most familiar, often resulting in the examinations being written from a white middle-class perspective.[43] Police management should not interpret a high failure rate on the written examination among minority groups as an indicator of intelligence because the latent factor may very well be the cultural bias of the test.

Research has not determined that those applicants who score higher on a written examination necessarily make better police officers or perform better on the job.[44] However, a written examination that is both job-related and valid is an effective way to eliminate a large number of candidates who may have problems comprehending and analyzing written material.

Physical Agility Test

The physical agility portion of the selection process tests applicants on specific physical activities routinely expected of a police officer. Physical tests measure minimum levels of endurance, strength, agility, and coordination. Police agencies employ variants of two basic forms of physical ability testing: job simulation exercises and physical agility and/or stamina tests.

The purpose of physical agility testing is to simulate any number of job-related activities such as jumping down from porches, climbing stairs, and walking along walls, rafters, pipes, or beams while in being in foot pursuit or while checking buildings for suspects. A period of running may be incorporated into each of the events to simulate the apprehension and control of a fleeing suspect. While these physical skills may appear to be those that police use, there is a lack of agreement regarding the physical capabilities that should be tested and the standards that should be used to evaluate effective physical performance.[45]

There are a few police selection devices that have been the subject of debate and scrutiny, as has physical agility testing. Some physical agility tests have been the subject of legal challenges on the grounds that they are not job-related. In some jurisdictions physical agility tests have been shown to have an adverse impact on female police applicants, which is in violation of Title VII of the 1964 Civil Rights Act.[46] Despite the controversy centering on physical agility testing, surveys of police departments reveal that agility testing of applicants is still a widely used selection device.[47]

If legally challenged, departments can be required to defend the validity of their physical testing procedures. The greatest problem with physical agility tests is that unless the test is based on a comprehensive job analysis of the jurisdiction in which it is used, the test may be open to legal scrutiny.[48] What has further complicated the use of physical agility testing is ensuring that testing does not violate the Americans with Disabilities Act. The Equal

Employment Opportunity Commission has ruled that if a physical agility test is proven to screen out disabled persons, the agency must demonstrate that the test is job-related and that it is consistent with the necessity of the business.

Due to the controversy and legal scrutiny of physical agility testing, some police organizations have done away with their tests, without negative consequences.[49] Health-based screening may be a viable substitute for physical agility testing to assess general physical fitness. As an alternative, testing can be postponed until after the training academy so that recruits can prepare with a regimen of physical conditioning, and performance standards can better reflect actual job tasks.[50]

Polygraph Testing

Although prohibited from use in the private sector by the Employee Polygraph Protection Act of 1988, government organizations can use polygraph testing. A polygraph test (also known as the lie detector test) records the body's involuntary responses to an examiner's questions in order to ascertain deceptive behavior. The test measures physiological data from three or more systems of the human body, generally the respiratory, cardiovascular, and sweat gland systems. The underlying theory of the polygraph is that when people lie, they also get measurably nervous about lying: the heartbeat increases, blood pressure goes up, breathing rhythms change, perspiration increases, etc. A baseline for these physiological characteristics is established by asking the subject questions whose answers the investigator knows. Pre-employment polygraph screening of police applicants has become increasingly popular, and the number of police organizations that use the polygraph test as a selection tool has increased.[51]

Pre-employment polygraph screening is used to verify information contained on a job application and to learn if some relevant information has been omitted. Of particular concern is the applicant's past criminal activity, drug usage, morals, and job history. Two specific advantages to using the polygraph test as a pre-employment screening device are (1) that some potential candidates will decide not to apply because they feel the polygraph examination will reveal prior acts that will disqualify them from further consideration, and (2) that it sends a message to the community that the department is expending every effort to hire only the most qualified people as officers.[52]

The pre-employment polygraph examination should be considered a separate phase from the background investigation; however, these two stages are mutually reinforcing when used correctly. The polygraph test is designed to query areas that normally cannot be examined during the background investigation (a background investigation cannot yield information that only the applicant would know), and it enables the examiner to solicit and gain relevant information regarding an applicant's behavior and character.

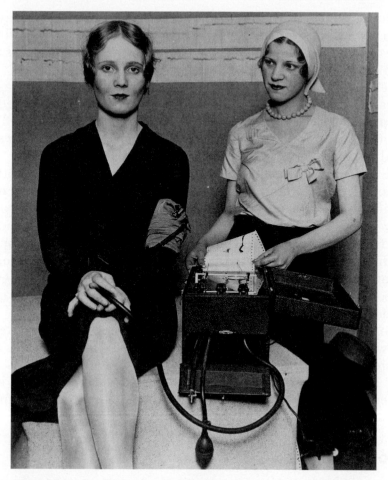

Administration of a lie detector examination in Chicago, Illinois, on May 17, 1930.

Photo courtesy of U.S. Library of Congress

Despite the widespread use of the polygraph test as a police pre-employment selection device, there is increasing criticism of its use by both the scientific and legal communities. The polygraph test is criticized for providing inaccurate and misleading information. The polygraph is also controversial, and at the center of the controversy is the question of its validity: Does a polygraph examination actually identify truthful and nontruthful individuals? This question will continue to be the topic of much debate among both proponents and opponents of polygraph testing.

Oral Interview

The oral interview gives the interview board an opportunity to meet the candidate and observe the communication skills of the candidate. During the interview, the candidate is usually asked about background information he or she provided on the application form. The candidate may also be asked to respond to several hypothetical scenarios, which are used to assess how the candidate would respond to stressful situations as well as to assess problem-solving skills.

There are generally two types of oral interviews: the nonstressful and the stressful. In the nonstressful interview, the candidate is asked general questions about his or her background and perhaps asked several hypothetical questions. There is no attempt to place pressure or stress on the candidate.

On the other hand, the interview board may place a great amount of stress on the candidate and may try to force the candidate into making a disqualifying mistake. In a stressful interview, the interview board may actually take a hostile or adversarial position against the candidate. The focus in this kind of interview is emotional: The interviewers attempt to push the candidate verbally into an emotional outburst of some kind.[53] Some police organizations have discontinued use of the stressful interview, believing that it is a poor way to measure problem-solving skills on the part of the candidate and that it is difficult to find any justification for its use.[54]

There are a few considerations to keep in mind when planning candidate interviews. First, women and minority officers should be included as members of the interview board. Second, the interview board should be diverse in terms of rank; in other words, those officers at the bottom of the rank structure should be given the opportunity to be involved in the selection process by serving on the interview board.

Psychological Testing

Psychological testing is usually conducted after a conditional offer of employment is made to the applicant, but this may vary from department to department. A **conditional offer of employment** occurs when the applicant is offered police employment contingent on passing the remaining selection tests. The liability is much too great for a police agency to not use psychological testing of candidates. For example, in *Hild* v. *Bruner*, the court found the police department negligent for not using psychological screening.[55]

Psychological tests are written, visual, or verbal evaluations administered to assess the cognitive and emotional functioning of police applicants. More specifically, psychological tests are used to assess a variety of mental abilities and attributes, including achievement and ability, personality, and neurological functioning. Psychological tests used in police officer selection may include the Minnesota Multiphasic Personality Inventory (MMPI), California Personality Inventory (CPI), Rorschach inkblots, figure drawings, and sentence completion tests.

All psychological tests should be administered, scored, and interpreted by a trained professional, preferably a psychologist or psychiatrist with expertise in the appropriate area. Psychological tests are only one element of a psychological assessment. They should never be used alone but should be one of several devices in the selection process.

Pre-employment psychological testing is an effective way of screening out police applicants who present high risks of personality traits related to psychological distress. Psychological factors have been found to have an effect on many factors including workplace stress, judgment, illnesses, and injuries.

There is always concern about employing an individual who has the potential to break down in a stressful situation or who has a psychological disorder that may prevent him or her from functioning effectively as a police officer. Pre-employment psychological testing can weed out those applicants with serious psychological disorders. One problem with pre-employment psychological screening, however, is that it only depicts what the applicant is like at the time of hire. Current research is inconclusive regarding the usefulness of psychological tests in predicting future police performance. Nevertheless, psychological screening remains an important selection device in weeding out persons with dangerous personality disorders.

Background Investigation

The background investigation is literally the investigation into an applicant's background. It provides a wealth of insight into the candidate's personal and professional life and may provide some of the most important indicators of job success.[56] Established past bad behavior has a tendency to repeat itself, and the background investigation assists in identifying patterns of bad behavior. Performing background checks on applicants is one of the most effective tools available to assist in making correct hiring decisions. A properly conducted background investigation may take several months to complete and should naturally be carried out toward the end of the selection process. In some organizations, the background investigation is conducted after a conditional offer of employment is made.

The background investigation usually concentrates on the following areas: information from employers, neighbors, acquaintances, and former teachers; references provided by the applicant; credit checks; military records and civil court records; information about drug use or abuse and habitual use of intoxicants; and investigation into past criminal behavior. The background investigation concentrates on obvious and not-so-obvious character qualities.

As part of the background investigation, reference checks are generally conducted; however, the information they provide is sometimes questionable. Generally, references furnished by the applicant provide little valid information for the selection decision.[57] Most references furnished by the applicant will provide biased information about the applicant. Imagine yourself applying for a police position; you will most likely list only references that will provide glowing information about your character, work habits, and attitude.

The more useful information will be gleaned from references not listed by the applicant but developed from listed references. For example, the investigator asks the listed references for the names of other persons who know the applicant. The extent to which the investigator develops references from references, the more likelihood of finding out revealing information about the character of the applicant.

Former employers are also contacted during the background investigation. Like personal references, the accuracy or usefulness of information from past and present employers is questionable. Past and present employers are reluctant to give candid evaluations of the applicant's job performance for fear of legal repercussions.[58] A recent survey found that only 55 percent of human resources executives would "always" provide accurate references to potential employers.[59] What is more surprising is that 7 percent reported that they would never give an accurate reference.[60]

Laws in some states permit employers to sue other employers if during employment background checks they omit or lie about serious employee acts, especially if the employee again commits the same or similar acts on the job. Police organizations face a tremendous liability if they do not screen employees through thorough background checks and someone suffers injury because of it.

Table 7–1 shows background checks used in the selection of new police recruits in local police departments, by size of population served.

TABLE 7–1

Background Checks Used in Selection of New Officer Recruits in Local Police Departments, by Size of Population Served, 2000

Population Served	Background Investigation (percent)	Criminal Record Check (percent)	Driving Record Check (percent)	Credit History Check (percent)	Volunteer Service Check (percent)
All sizes	96	96	93	48	6
1,000,000 or more	100	100	100	87	20
500,000–999,999	94	97	94	85	12
250,000–499,999	98	100	100	93	13
100,000–249,999	99	99	98	79	7
50,000–99,999	99	100	100	80	9
25,000–49,999	99	99	99	76	7
10,000–24,999	98	99	96	73	10
2,500–9,999	97	98	96	52	5
Under 2,500	95	93	89	28	5

Source: Bureau of Justice Statistics, Local Police Departments, 2000.

Medical and Drug Screening

Medical and drug screening is one of the last tests in the selection process and is usually administered after a conditional offer of employment is made to the applicant. During the medical screening, a designated physician performs a physical examination of the applicant to ensure that the applicant has no underlying medical condition that would prevent or limit him or her from performing the essential functions of the job.

Drug testing is usually conducted as part of the medical screening. Pre-employment drug testing has become a very common selection device for police employment. The Bureau of Justice Statistics shows that about 88 percent of local police departments use drug testing as a pre-employment selection requirement.[61] Courts have consistently upheld the legality of requiring a pre-employment drug test as a condition of employment. It is a best practice to obtain consent and to clearly indicate drug testing is a requirement for employment. Most drug testing is done by sending an applicant to a collection site where a urine sample is obtained, which is sent to a certified laboratory for analysis. Negative results are normally available within 24 hours.

Table 7–2 details interviews, tests, and examinations used in the selection of new officer recruits in local police departments, by size of population served.

TABLE 7–2

Interviews, Tests, and Examinations Used in Selection of New Officer Recruits in Local Police Departments, by Size of Population Served, 2000

Population Served	Personal Interview (percent)	Medical Exam (percent)	Drug Test (percent)	Psycho-logical Evaluation (percent)	Physical Agility Test (percent)	Written Aptitude Test (percent)	Personality Inventory (percent)	Polygraph Exam (percent)
All sizes	96	81	67	61	44	43	31	21
1,000,000 or more	100	100	100	93	87	73	47	73
500,000–999,999	94	94	85	94	88	91	71	61
250,000–499,999	95	100	90	93	90	80	60	80
100,000–249,000	95	96	89	94	83	84	62	72
50,000–99,999	99	98	87	97	81	78	60	53
25,000–49,999	98	99	87	95	81	79	54	50
10,000–24,999	98	98	78	86	69	68	45	32
2,500–9,999	96	87	74	65	48	48	29	23
Under 2,500	94	65	52	41	24	21	20	7

Note: List of selection methods is not intended to be exhaustive.

Source: Bureau of Justice Statistics, Local Police Departments, 2000.

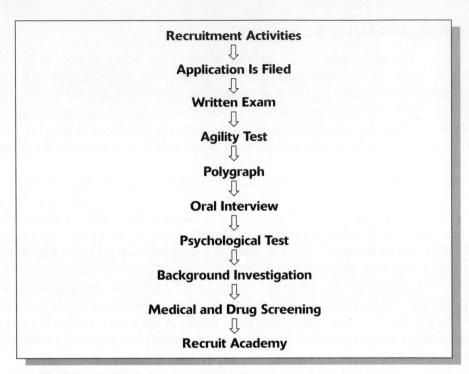

FIGURE 7–1   Major Steps in Police Hiring Process

INNOVATIVE APPROACHES

As noted previously in this chapter, the private sector goes to great lengths in recruitment and selection. Police organizations also will have to go to great lengths to attract a new breed of officer that best works in a community-oriented policing environment. In what follows, we present an overview of some innovative approaches that are currently being used in recruitment and selection.

Fulton, New York, Police Department Experience

In an effort to substantially increase the qualified applicant pool, the Fulton, New York, Police Department recently engaged in some innovative techniques to increase their applicants as well as to assist applicants with the physical agility portion of selection testing. Fulton Police Chief Mark A. Spawn described their innovative process in a case study that appeared in the *FBI Law Enforcement Bulletin*.[62]

The Fulton Police Department historically maintains an active police candidate list for at least two years and often up to four years. But because of an insufficient number of candidates several years ago, the agency offered the civil service test (the first phase of the testing process) for police officers for the second time in two years. In 1996, 144 applicants took the written examination for the police officer position, and of those, 100 individuals passed. When the department offered the police test again in 1999, 47 applicants took the test and 36 (76 percent) passed.

The next stage in the testing process consists of the physical agility test. The department tests candidates for flexibility, number of push-ups and sit-ups performed in a certain time frame, and completion of a 1.5-mile run. In 1999, more than 58 percent of the applicants could not pass the agility test, which left a short list of candidates. After the remaining group completed background investigations and psychological and polygraph testing, 7 more applicants were excluded from the list, leaving only 12 percent of those who had taken the written test eligible for appointment. The shortage of eligible candidates seriously concerned the department.

For the written test in 2000, the department embarked on a serious recruitment campaign; it sent posters to area colleges and press releases to local newspapers and radio and television stations as well as highlighted the recruitment drive (and the physical standards) on a special page on its Web site. The department's officers and their families, as well as the department staff, assisted with the production of a television commercial that aired in the region and drew the most attention. It showcased Fulton and its police department by starting with a community theme and then showing a police officer talking with a citizen, investigating an accident, and examining crime scene evidence.

To help candidates meet the required physical fitness standards, each applicant received a summary of the requirements. Even though the standards constitute a part of the basic application package, the department added emphasis by attaching a simplified chart that showed applicants what the department would require if they passed the written examination. Candidates received the fitness standards once again several weeks prior to the physical agility testing. By providing this information to the candidates well in advance, the department hoped that the elimination rate would decrease significantly.

The results of candidate testing showed that the department's efforts paid off. A record 160 candidates took the written examination and 111 (69 percent) passed. A segment of those applicants with a passing score underwent the physical agility testing. Of that group, 71 percent passed, a 29 percent increase from the previous year. Even though a 7 percent greater failure rate existed for the written examination compared to the previous year's exam, the significant increase of those who successfully completed the physical agility test gave the department a much larger candidate pool; it also validated the recruitment campaign and, particularly, the emphasis on the physical agility component.

Assessment Centers

The use of assessment centers in police departments has increased over the years. While the trend in most agencies is to use the assessment centers for upper-level positions, they offer an invaluable way to assess police at all levels. The problem with subjecting entry-level police applicants to an assessment center is the cost and time to administer such tests, especially to larger applicant pools. Because of the costs and time commitment, assessment centers may lend themselves to departments that have low rates of hiring, for example, 10 to 20 recruits per year.

The assessment center administers multiple standardized evaluations of behavior including job-related simulations, interviews, and/or psychological tests. Job simulations are used to evaluate candidates on behaviors relevant to the most critical aspects (or competencies) of the job.

Several trained observers and techniques are used. Judgments about behaviors are made and recorded, and these judgments are pooled in a meeting among the assessors or by an averaging process. In discussions among assessors, comprehensive accounts of behaviors, often including ratings, are pooled. These discussions result in evaluations of the performance of the candidates on the behavioral dimensions or other variables.

While assessment centers vary in the number and type of exercises included, two of the most common exercises are the in-basket and the oral exercise. In a traditional in-basket exercise, candidates are given time to review the material and initiate in writing whatever actions they believe to be most appropriate in relation to each in-basket item. When time is called for the exercise, the in-basket materials and any notes, letters, memos, or other correspondence written by the candidate are collected for review by one or more assessors.

Often the candidates are then interviewed to ensure that the assessors understand actions taken by the candidate and the rationale for the actions. If an interview is not possible, it is also common to have the candidate complete a summary sheet (a questionnaire). A more recent trend has been the development of selection procedures that are based on the assessment center model, which can be turned into low-fidelity simulations.[63]

Low-fidelity simulations involve having an applicant read about a work situation and then respond to the situation by choosing one of five alternative answers. Some procedures have the applicant choose the response he or she would most likely make in a situation and the response that he or she would least likely make. These samples of hypothetical work behaviors have been found to be valid predictors of job performance.[64]

Today the assessment center method is utilized in a variety of settings—including industry and business, government, armed forces, educational institutions, and police departments—to select individuals for supervisory, technical, or management positions. Assessment centers vary in length, time, and selection of exercises. The current trend is in the development of assessment centers that have the capability of testing a large pool of applicants.[65] This holds much promise for those police departments that test large groups of entry-level candidates.

While assessment center testing for police is increasingly popular, we point out that very little research about the validity of assessment center testing exists. However, some recent research shows assessment center testing of police applicants to be a good predictor of future work success; thus it holds much promise.[66]

Situational Tests

Situational tests are very similar in scope and purpose to those administered at assessment centers. The situational tests may be more conducive to entry-level positions when compared to the assessment center. About 58 percent of police departments use some type of real-life simulated testing.[67] These tests typically include mock crime scenes, simulated traffic stops, shoot/don't shoot decisions, leaderless group discussions, or role-playing scenarios. As discussed previously, assessment centers also use these types of exercises that incorporate many of the traditional techniques of selection; the difference is that situational tests emphasize simulations and decision-making exercises. Some individuals view this approach as an increasingly promising method of selection.[68]

Appleton, Wisconsin, Police Department Experience

The Appleton, Wisconsin, Police Department uses various innovative assessment exercises to assess their police officer candidates[69]:

- *Group discussion.* A leaderless interaction is held regarding a law enforcement topic that an entry-level candidate can understand that will elicit information on a candidate's interpersonal and communication skills.
- *Situational response.* Observation of a department-prepared videotape requiring a written response regarding the situations presented is used to obtain information to help gauge a candidate's problem-solving and written communication skills.
- *Oral presentation.* A candidate is assigned a topic to present, with limited preparation time, to stimulate stress. Topics should elicit information on how well a candidate can adapt and react to adverse situations.
- *Background/achievement report.* Responses to questions convey information about each candidate's life history and preparation for a law enforcement career.
- *Observational response.* A candidate is asked to analyze a crime scene or a prepared room, with instructions to document observations or find clues, which illustrates a candidate's information-gathering and problem-solving skills.

CHANGES IN POLICE OFFICER SELECTION

Previously in this chapter, we suggested that a different type of police officer is now desired to work in a community and in a problem-oriented policing environment. In the past, police were chosen on the basis of a military hiring philosophy more geared toward recruiting soldiers or selecting ace crime fighters involved daily in violence. The present-day police officer is characterized by the capacity to communicate with people, establish partnerships, solve problems, and make independent decisions on the basis of maturity and intellect. A recent report suggested that now police officers will be skillful mediators who are not arrogant, aloof, or abrasive and who will not use unnecessary force; they will be given higher status (by supervisors shifting responsibility, initiative, and decision making down the organization), will experience a role change, will need enhanced communication and leadership skills, and will develop initiative, creativity, problem solving, and team-building skills.[70]

Professor Herman Goldstein wrote, "Of all the changes required, redefining the role of rank-and-file police officers is the most important and has the greatest implications for the future of policing."[71] The role redefinition would, in Professor Goldstein's view, make a college education and police work more compatible. Moreover, minority recruitment would enhance problem-oriented policing by better reflecting the community in the agency's composition, and it would be necessary to attempt to hire those whose abilities and skills make them best suited to functioning in a problem-oriented milieu.[72] These are the skills he considered most appropriate to the new role[73]:

- Creativity
- Flexibility
- Imagination
- Intelligence
- Ability to function independently
- Problem solving
- Critical reasoning
- Conflict mediation
- Capacity to relate to others
- Sensitivity to problems of urban life and community organization
- Ability to relate to people

The rationale, then, for improving recruitment and selection procedures is the change of role required by police officers as a result of community-oriented policing and the different skills and demands of a more service-oriented organization, which is keen to improve dialogue and interaction between police and the community. Some have emphasized that necessary qualifications are the ability both to communicate effectively (especially with diverse groups) and to empathize with those holding different values and goals, a good understanding of self and others, an understanding of technology, intellect, a good education, and maturity.[74] Others have compiled a different list of attributes: human relations skills, interpersonal skills, leadership, motivation, initiative, integrity, and less authoritarianism.[75]

The challenge for police agencies is to explore the best selection techniques that will identify the traits desired for the new police officer. In part, we suggest the aggressive recruiting of college graduates and of female and minority candidates. Some research has found that African-American police officers demonstrate better attitudes toward community policing and are more likely to practice community policing skills compared to white police officers.[76]

Learning Strategies and Police Selection

Learning strategies are the techniques and skills individuals use in order to accomplish a learning task.[77] In other words, learning strategies deal with the ways that people approach specific learning situations. For example, police officers who are required to learn a new conflict resolution skill may use different individual approaches to acquire this new skill: One officer may read about the conflict resolution skill, while another may simply learn it hands-on by practicing the new skill.

One of the authors of this textbook recently completed research on the learning strategies that police officers utilize in the field and found that those officers assigned to community policing duties predominately use a similar learning strategy.[78] The instrument Assessing the Learning Strategies of Adults (ATLAS) was used to determine learning strategies used by a group of police officers serving in a medium-sized Midwestern city. The ATLAS instrument is designed to place people in one of three categories based on their learning strategies: Navigator, Problem Solver, and Engager. Each of these strategies constitutes a different approach to learning. After completing ATLAS, those officers assigned to community policing duties were predominately identified as using the Problem Solver learning strategy.

The Problem Solver learning strategy utilizes skills very similar to those required in community policing. Table 7–3 compares the similarities between community policing strategies and the traits used in the Problem Solver learning strategy.

As Table 7–3 shows, the Problem Solver learning strategy and the skills and traits desired for community-oriented policing closely parallel each other. Furthermore, many of the names of the Problem Solver learning process and the community-policing philosophy are the same.

What are the possibilities of using the ATLAS instrument as a police selection device? As pointed out in this chapter, police agencies use many selection tests to assist in making personnel decisions. Gleaning additional information about the applicant's psyche would assuredly assist police managers in making a more informed selection; having knowledge of the learning strategies may also assist in the training of police officers. Additional research and validation studies are needed to see if the ATLAS instrument is a viable test.

TABLE 7–3

Comparisons Between Skills/Traits in the Problem Solver Learning Strategy and Community-Oriented Policing	
Problem Solver Learning Strategy	**Community-Oriented Policing**
Critical thinking	Critical thinking
Generate alternatives	Generate alternatives to solve problems
Identify resources	Identify resources to solve problems within the community
Test assumptions	Test assumptions as they pertain to traditional police responses in dealing with community problems
Adjusting learning processes	Adjusting learning processes to respond to different community problems
Use many external aids	Use many external aids to solve problems within the community
Provide environment of practical experimentation	Experiment with different approaches to solve community problems
Give examples from personal experience	Use personal experience to solve problems
Assess learning by asking open-ended questions	Assess problem solving by open discussion with citizens
Problem-solving activities	Problem solving central to community policing
Hands-on activities	Hands-on activities working with the community
Spontaneity and creativity	Encouragement of innovation and creative problem solving. Encourage creativity and risk taking

Sources: Community-oriented policing traits adapted from Michael J. Palmiotto, *Community Policing: A New Strategy for the 21st Century* (Gaithersburg, MD: Aspen Publishing, 2000). Problem Solver Learning Strategy adapted from Gary J. Conti and Richard A. Fellenz, "Assessing Adult Learning Strategies." Proceedings of the 32nd annual adult education research conference (pp. 64–73). University of Oklahoma, Norman (1991).

 SUMMARY

The recruitment and selection of police officers is one of the most important areas of police management. It is through recruitment and selection that the future of the agency is determined. Those hired today for police service become tomorrow's leaders. The selection of one unqualified person can be costly to the police agency both monetarily and in terms of the loss of public support.

Recruitment and selection are separate but mutually reinforcing processes. Recruitment involves attracting candidates to apply for police employment and may entail advertisements through both the print and electronic media, brochures, and the Internet. Recruitment may also consist of visits to college campuses, job fairs, and high schools, as well as by word of mouth. The goal of recruitment is to attract the largest number of applicants possible to apply to the agency.

Selection is the process of weeding out unqualified candidates and identifying qualified candidates. The selection process may involve a number of devices including a written and physical examination, psychological examination, polygraph examination, records check, credit check, background investigation, and medical and drug screening. It is important that all tests administered to applicants be job-related and a *bona fide* occupational qualification because a selection test that is not job-related is unlawful. Police management must be prepared to defend the job relatedness of their tests.

The Americans with Disabilities Act (ADA) recognizes and protects the civil rights of people with disabilities and is modeled after earlier landmark laws prohibiting discrimination on the basis of race and gender. The ADA covers a wide range of disabilities, from physical conditions affecting mobility, stamina, sight, hearing, and speech to conditions such as emotional illness and learning disorders. The ADA addresses access to the workplace (Title I), state and local government services (Title II), and places of public accommodation and commercial facilities. The ADA impacts many areas of police personnel selection, and police managers and human resources specialists are cautioned to ensure that all selection devices are within ADA guidelines.

Police human resources specialists should continually identify the most innovative tests and approaches to recruit and select police officers. Likewise, recruitment and selection strategies should increasingly attract and retain those officers who have the attributes to work in a community-oriented policing environment.

QUESTIONS IN REVIEW

1. Distinguish between police recruitment and police selection.
2. What are some factors that will impact the ability of the police to effectively recruit?
3. List and describe various police recruitment techniques.
4. Identify and discuss various police selection techniques.
5. Explain how the police officer now desired differs from the police officer of the past.
6. Discuss how recruitment material can be enhanced to attract minorities and women.

POLICE RESOURCES ON THE WEB

Law Enforcement Jobs on the Web
http://www.smarthunt.com/smart-jobs.cfm?catid=33

Los Angeles Police Department Recruiting
http://www.joinlapd.com/index3.html

NCJRS Recruiting and Selection Articles and Research
http://virlib.ncjrs.org/lawe.asp?category=48&subcategory=93

New York City Police Department Recruiting
http://www.nypd2.org/html/recruit/policeofficer.html

Public Safety Recruitment Information
http://www.publicsafetyrecruitment.com

San Diego Police Department Recruitment and Selection
http://www.sandiego.gov/police/join/selection.shtml

United Capital Police Recruiting
http://www.uscapitolpolice.gov

Wichita, Kansas, Police Department Recruiting
http://www.wichita.gov/cityoffices/police/training/recruiting.htm

---

REFERENCES

1. ORLANDO W. WILSON and ROY C. MCLAREN, *Police Administration*, 4th ed. (New York: McGraw–Hill, 1977), pp. 321–322.
2. RICHARD W. JUDY and CAROL D'MICO, *Workforce 2020* (Indianapolis, IN: Hudson Institute, 1997), p. 43.
3. MICHAEL HUAMS, "Recruitment, Selection and Retention: A Matter of Commitment," *The Police Chief* (September 1991): 17–24.
4. Hiring Breakthrough, Hiring the Wrong Person Costs You Three Times Their Annual Salary," *Executive Focus* (June 2004): 33–34.
5. Ibid., p. 33.
6. T.J. BERGMANN and M.S. TAYLOR, "College Recruitment: What Attracts Students to Organizations?" *Personnel* (May–June 1984): 34–46.
7. STEPHEN P. ROBBINS and ANN COULTER, *Management* (Upper Saddle River, NJ: Prentice Hall, 1999), pp. 124–128.
8. ANTHONY R. MORIARTY and MARK R. FIELD, *Police Officer Selection* (Springfield, IL: Charles C. Thomas Publisher, 1994), pp. 47–51.
9. Ibid.
10. Ibid., p. 66.
11. WILLIE L. WILLIAMS and BRUCE B. HENDERSON, *Taking Back Our Streets: Fighting Crime in America* (New York: Scribner Publishing Co., 1996), pp. 188–191.
12. H.R. SLATER and M. REISER, "A Comparative Study of Factors Influencing Police Recruitment," *Journal of Police Science and Administration* 16 (1988): 168.
13. NATIONAL ADVISORY COMMISSION ON CRIMINAL JUSTICE STANDARDS AND GOALS, *The Police* (Washington, DC: GPO, 1973) p. 17.

14. BUREAU OF JUSTICE STATISTICS, *State and Local Law Enforcement Statistics, 2002,* U.S. Department of Justice. Accessed online June 10, 2004 at www.oip.usdoj.gov.

15. Ibid.

16. ROBERT J. KAMINSKI, "Police Minority Recruitment: Predicting Who Will Say Yes to an Offer for a Job as a Cop," *Journal of Criminal Justice* 21 (2002): 395–409.

17. MICHAEL D. LYMAN, *The Police: An Introduction* (Upper Saddle River, NJ: Prentice Hall, 1999), p. 315.

18. National Advisory Commission on Criminal Justice Standards and Goals, 1973), p. 329.

19. HILDA MUNOZ, "On the Law," *Los Angeles Times*, May 30, 2003, part 2, p. 2.

20. DEREK R. AVERY, MORELA HERNANDEZ, and MICHELLE R. HEBL, "Who's Watching the Race? Racial Salience in Recruitment Advertising," *Journal of Applied Social Psychology* 34, no. 1 (January 2004): 146–162.

21. Ibid.

22. WILLIAM GELLER, *Local Government Police Management*, 3rd ed. (Washington, DC: International City Managers Association, 1991), p. 275.

23. CHERYL FARR, "Cultural Diversity in the 1990s," *Public Management* (February 1992): 18–21.

24. Ibid.

25. Law Enforcement Exploring Homepage. Accessed online June 10, 2004 at www.learningforlife.org/exploring/lawenforcement.

26. RALPH S. OSBORN, "Police Recruitment: Today's Standard, Tomorrow's Challenge," *FBI Law Enforcement Bulletin* (June 1992): 27–31.

27. FRANCINE S. HALL and MARYANN H. ALBRECHT, *The Management of Affirmative Action* (Santa Monica, CA: Goodyear, 1979), p. 26.

28. MICHAEL L. BIRZER and RICK ELLIS, "A Descriptive Study of Discrimination in Topeka, Kansas," *Free Inquiry in Creative Sociology* 31 (2003): 133–141.

29. Ibid.

30. Equal Employment Opportunity Commission Guidelines. Accessed June 21, 2004 at http://www. ecoc.gov.

31. GERALD P. PANARO, *Employment Law Manual* (Boston, MA: Warren Gorham & Lamont, Inc., 1990), pp. 211–216.

32. ROBBINS and COULTER, 1999, p. 119.

33. Ibid.

34. RICHARD N. HOLDEN, *Modern Police Management*, 2nd ed. (Englewood Cliffs, NJ: Prentice Hall, 1994), pp. 111–121.

35. ROBBINS and COULTER, 1999, p. 121.

36. Americans with Disabilities Act of 1990, 42 U.S.C. § 12101 et seq.

37. EDWARD T. THIBAULT, LAWRENCE M. LYNCHAND, and BRUCE R. MCBRIDE, *Proactive Police Management*, 6th ed. (Upper Saddle River, NJ: Prentice Hall, 2004), p. 211.

38. JEFFREY HIGGINBOTHAM, "The Americans with Disabilities Act," *FBI Law Enforcement Bulletin* 60, no. 8 (March 1992): 30.

39. Americans with Disabilities Act, 1990.

40. ORLANDO W. WILSON and ROY C. MCLAREN, *Police Administration*, (New York: McGraw–Hill, 1950), p. 132.

41. *Griggs* v. *Duke Power Co.*, 401 U.S. 424 (1971)

42. HOLDEN, 1994, p. 120–121.

43. Ibid.

44. Ibid.

45. KIMBERLY A. LONSWAY, "Tearing Down the Wall: Problems with Consistency, Validity, and Adverse Impact of Physical Agility Testing in Police Selection," *Police Quarterly* 6 (2003): 237–277.

46. MICHAEL L. BIRZER and DELORES E. CRAIG, "Gender Differences in Police Physical Ability Test Performance," *American Journal of Police* 15 (1996): 93–108.

47. LONSWAY, 2003, pp. 109–111.

48. W.S. BOOTH and C.W. HORNICK, "Physical Ability Testing for Police Officers in the 80s," *The Police Chief* (January 1984): 13–17.

49. LONSWAY, 2003 p. 109.

50. Ibid.

51. MICHAEL L. BIRZER, "Pre–Employment Polygraph Screening: A Brief Overview," *American Association of Police Polygraphists Quarterly Journal* (January 1995): 12–17.

52. CHARLES R. SWANSON, LEONARD TERRITO, and ROBERT W. TAYLOR, *Police Administration*, 5th ed. (Upper Saddle River, NJ: Prentice Hall, 2001), pp. 83–84.

53. HOLDEN, 1994, p. 121.

54. Ibid.

55. *Hild* v. *Bruner*, 496 F. Supp. 93 (1980).

56. MORIARTY and FIELD, 1994, p. 49.

57. P.M. MUCHINSKY, "The Use of Reference Testing in Personnel Testing: A Review and Evaluation," *Journal of Occupational Psychology* (April 1979): 187–197.

58. ROBBINS and COULTER, 1999, pp. 120–121.

59. Ibid.

60. Ibid.

61. BUREAU OF JUSTICE STATISTICS, *State and Local Law Enforcement Statistics, 2002,* p. 7.

62. MARK A. SPAWN, "A Case Study in Police Recruitment," *FBI Law Enforcement Bulletin* 72, no. 3 (March 2003): 14–19.

63. STEPAHN J. MOTOWIDLO, MARVIN D. DUNNETTE, and Gary W. CARTER, "An Alternative Selection Procedure: The Low Fidelity Simulation," *Journal of Applied Psychology* 75, no. 6 (December 1990): 640–652.

64. Ibid.

65. Information accessed from the *HR–Guide.com Website.* Accessed June 20, 2004 at http://www.hr-guide.com.

66. KOBI DAYAN, RONEN KASTEN, and SHAUL FOX, "Entry–Level Police Candidate Assessment Center: An Efficient Tool or a Hammer to Kill a Fly? *Personnel Psychology* 55, no. 4 (winter 2002): 23.

67. P. ASH, K.B. SLORA, and C.F. BRITTON, "Police Agency Officer Selection Practices," *Journal of Police Science and Administration* 17, no. 4 (1990): 258–269.

68. DAVID A. DECICCO, "Police Officer Candidate Assessment and Selection," *FBI Law Enforcement Bulletin* 69, no. 12 (December 2000): 1.

69. BRYCE D. KOLPACK, "The Assessment Center Approach to Police Officer Selection," *The Police Chief* (September 1991): 44–46.

70. STEPHEN J. GAFFIGAN, *Understanding Community Policing: A Framework for Action–Monograph* (Washington, DC: Bureau of Justice Assistance, 1994).

71. HERMAN GOLDSTEIN, *Problem–Oriented Policing* (New York: McGraw–Hill, 1990), p. 148.

72. Ibid.

73. Ibid., pp. 265–266.

74. HOLDEN, 1994, p. 124.

75. P.A. ALPERT and ROGER G. DUNHAM, *Policing Urban America*, 3rd ed. (Prospect Heights, IL: Waveland Press, 1997), p. 44.

76. DONALD L. YATES and VIJAYAN K. PILLAI, "Attitudes Toward Community Policing: A Causal Analysis," *Social Science Journal*, 33, no. 2 (1996): 193–209.

77. GARY J. CONTI and RICHARD A. FELLENZ, "Assessing Adult Learning Strategies," *Proceedings of the 32nd Annual Adult Education Research Conference* (Norman: University of Oklahoma, 1991), pp. 64–73.

78. MICHAEL L. BIRZER and ROBERT E. NOLAN, "Learning Strategies of Selected Urban Police Related to Community Policing," *Policing: An International Journal of Police Strategies and Management* 25, no. 2 (2002): 242–255.

Police Training, Development, and Education

Key Terms

42 USC 1983 liability
Andragogy
Case study method
Community-oriented policing
Curriculum
Deliberate indifference
Direct liability
Education

Field training program
Indirect liability
In-service training
Military training model
Problem-based learning
Student-centered approach
Training

Outline

Introduction
Training Environment
Changes in Training
    Curriculum
Innovative Approaches to
    Training Delivery

Postacademy Training and
    Development
Training and the Legal
    Environment
College Education for
    Police Officers

Learning Objectives

After reading this chapter, you should be able to:

1. List the differences between education and training.
2. Identify current and future issues in police training.
3. Discuss why training is an important police function.
4. Explain the potential legal liability that police executives face for failing to train recruits.

5. Describe the adult learning theory of andragogy.
6. Discuss the changing nature of police training curriculum.
7. List the issues that center on requiring college education for police officers.
8. Distinguish between the various learner-centered approaches that can be utilized in the training classroom.
9. Explain the purpose of postacademy training programs.

INTRODUCTION

Next to the recruitment and selection of police officers, **training** is one of the most important functions of the police organization: It is through training that neophyte police officers learn the skills of policing; likewise, it is through training that veteran police officers learn new techniques while at the same time honing existing skills. In 1931 the Wickersham Commission's report on the police showed that only 20 percent of the municipalities provided police academy training, and these were for the most part police departments located in large cities.[1] In many cities, the police were simply issued a badge and a gun and told to go out and police the city. Can you imagine police today being given a badge and a gun and told to go police the city without any formal training? This would assuredly result in much chaos and potential legal liability. Things have changed considerably since the Wickersham report of 1931. Today's police are required to receive formal academy training prior to performing police duties.

   The need for police officers to continually stay abreast of the latest legal decisions, technology, and advancements in the field and the need to stay proficient in job-related skills and to learn new ones are many of the reasons that police find themselves in the classroom. In this chapter, we discuss some of the more pressing issues that impact police training today. Furthermore, we take a look at the future of police training as well as innovative approaches to training delivery. We conclude the chapter with a discussion of college education for police.

TRAINING ENVIRONMENT

We have many anecdotal accounts as well as field observations that tell us that many police academies operate in a very militaristic manner. This means doing military drills, saluting superiors, standing at attention, close drill marching—all carried out in a drill sergeant atmosphere. Likewise, a large majority of police training is carried out via the lecture method, with very little input on the part of the trainee.[2] The philosophy of most police training programs is based on three precepts: (1) It should closely follow the **military training model,** (2) it should be a punishment-centered experience in which trainees must prove themselves, and (3) it should help screen out those who aren't up to par.[3] The problem with a police academy ingrained in a military culture is that many recruits have a difficult time adapting to a paramilitary training structure because one day recruits find themselves living a normal life and the next day they find themselves thrown into an academy environment whose structure is based on a semimilitary system.[4]

The militaristic police academy may not be the best environment for effective teaching-learning transactions to occur. In fact, some have argued that the paramilitary model of policing has created a myriad of problems not only in the training environment but also in the general culture of the organization.[5] Some experts have pointed out that the behavioral and paramilitary training environment has created a warrior-like mentality on the part of the police. Scholar William McNeill stated:

> The police constitute a quasi-military warrior class. In common with warriors generally, they exhibit bonds of solidarity [that] are fierce and strong indeed, [their] human propensities find fullest expression in having an enemy to hate, fear, and destroy and fellow fighters with whom to share the risks and triumphs of violent action.[6]

This traditional high-stress military training model is no longer recommended, and academies are encouraged to move toward an environment that promotes adult learning.[7]

Some contemporary scholarship has reported a disturbing growth of military tactics and ideology within U.S. law enforcement agencies.[8] When police organizations look and act like soldiers, a military mind-set is created that declares war on an enemy. In civilian policing, that enemy may very well be interpreted as criminals who are part of the American public. In this mentality, the American streets may become the "front," and American citizens exist as "enemy combatants."[9] Once an organization with a militaristic orientation becomes institutionalized, the members exist in a culture that fosters the belief that they are literally engaged in combat.

When police organizations train officers to act and think like soldiers, these organizations alienate them from the communities of which they are supposed to be a part. Soldiers at war operate under a code of domination, not service. Thus, all actions (or perceived offenses) by civilians must be handled by domination, by force, and by control. With this mentality, laws may be applied arbitrarily without the validation of civilian voices and the courts. In part, the job of the police is to investigate violence inflicted on others, to apprehend criminal suspects, and to deliver them over to a court of law. A soldier, on the other hand, does not think; he or she initiates violence on command and doesn't worry about the Bill of Rights.[10]

Police trainers should move toward the adult education model of police training and put less emphasis on the militaristic environment. We offer several observations in our assessment of the militaristic police training culture. First, it is debatable whether effective learning really takes place in this type of training environment, which does very little to promote the acquisition of many nontechnical competencies such as problem solving, judgment, and leadership.[11] Second, we argue that the militaristic training environment perpetuates a warrior-like mentality on the part of the

Final inspection for the first class of the Kansas Highway Patrol in 1938.

Photo courtesy of Kansas Highway Patrol

police: There is an enemy, and that enemy is any citizens who have violated the law. Third, we submit that many recruits who enter police service in the 21st century do not have formal military training and may leave the police academy when exposed to this rigid environment; thus, many qualified men and women may opt out of the police service prematurely. It has also been proposed in the literature that the military boot-camp approach of using stress in academy training may make officers question their self-worth and willingness to follow orders blindly.[12] Finally, the military model of police training may actually train the officer to act in a robotic fashion. The paradox here is that training for a robotic response is in direct conflict with what is now desired in today's police officer under community-oriented policing strategies.

CHANGES IN TRAINING CURRICULUM

One of the more exciting changes taking place in policing today is **community-oriented policing.** As discussed in Chapter 3, community-oriented policing is a strategy that entails crime prevention, problem solving, community partnerships, and organizational transformation.[13] The ideas of community policing are relatively simplistic: The police take on a role of being more community-oriented, and the citizens take on a role of being more involved with assisting the police with information.[14] With community policing, police officers will be expected to become partners with the community in maintaining social order.[15]

Community policing differs from traditional law enforcement because it allows police the freedom to expand the scope of their jobs. Police in this sense are challenged to become community problem solvers and encouraged to use their time creatively; likewise, police will be required to discern vast amounts of information and to recognize available resources that apply to problem solving.[16]

Community policing is a departure from the way the police, with their reactive strategies, have done business in the past. In order for community-oriented policing to be successful, training must play a pivotal role. The police **curriculum** (what is taught in the police academy) is beginning to make room for newer and more innovative training and methods that will support the move toward community-oriented policing.

Recall that police academy training in America is not uniform in either content or number of hours required for certifying a police officer. The time required for police recruit training can vary from as little as 8 or 10 weeks up to 1 year. For example, the state of Georgia requires 8 weeks of recruit training for police recruits; the Wichita, Kansas, Police Department requires 22 weeks (or 840 hours); and the Los Angeles, California, Sheriff's Department requires 1 year of training.[17] The Bureau of Justice Statistics survey of more than 12,000 law enforcement agencies found that, on the average, departments required 640 training hours for new police recruits.[18]

The method in which police training is facilitated has for the most part been delivered in the same manner. This hegemonic form of police training is primarily mechanistic in nature and usually performed in a militaristic environment.[19] It is well documented that police training has been a field dominated by a rigid militaristic approach.[20] Much of the literature aiming a spotlight on police training indicates that the militaristic environment in policing may be effective when teaching technical and procedural skills but that this type of environment does little to promote the acquisition of essential nontechnical competencies such as problem solving, judgment, and leadership.[21] As we discussed in the previous section, the militaristic environment of police training may also run counter to many of the ideas inherent in community policing.

Police academies place an enormous emphasis on enforcement methods and mechanical techniques of the job. The paradox is that police perform crime-fighting functions during a relatively small percentage of their on-duty time. The Bureau of Justice Statistics found that about 10 percent of actual patrol activity is spent on criminal-related matters; the other 90 percent is spent dealing with a vast diversity of service-related calls.[22] The problem is that the majority of police subjects in the training curriculum deal with what the police do during 10 percent of their on-duty time (crime-related tasks) and tend to place less emphasis on what the police do 90 percent of the time (service-related activities).

Police training should reflect both the changes in operating strategy and the changes in society. Certainly those police departments that have implemented community policing will be required to examine their training curriculum and make the needed changes to ensure that the community policing strategy is supported. We suggest that even in those police agencies that have not implemented community-oriented policing, they should still undertake an evaluation of the training curriculum to ensure that it represents the demands placed on their police officers. Also there are certain subjects that have historically been absent from the police training curriculum that should probably be included for contemporary policing.

One such subject that has been absent from the police training curriculum is police history. You may ask if it is really necessary to teach police history in the police academy. We submit that if American policing is to effectively transition to community-oriented policing strategies, police history should be taught in the police academy.

Police recruits should have knowledge of the history of the profession they have chosen and know the contributions that police reformers such as August Vollmer and O. W. Wilson have made to the policing profession. It is important that recruits have some idea of American policing's early roots in the English police system and the contributions of English reformers such as Sir Robert Peel. Police officers should be trained in their history; more importantly, in order to effectively understand the evolving community-oriented policing strategy, police must understand past strategies. Simply stated, the police have to know where they have been to know where they are going. Other subjects that have historically been absent from the police training curriculum are cultural diversity, interpersonal communication skills, problem solving, conflict resolution skills, sexual harassment issues, ethics, information on blood-borne pathogens, stress training, American with Disabilities Act (ADA), domestic terrorism, public speaking, community resources, community organizing, values, professional orientation, victims' issues, and community demographics.

We offer a comprehensive training model developed by Professors Michael J. Palmiotto, Michael L. Birzer and N. Prabha Unnithan.[23] This training model is designed to provide a foundation for building on community policing. In this model, subjects such as organizational structure and police history are placed up front in the curriculum. Next the recruit becomes familiar with the community; this section includes the socioeconomic makeup of the community. It is extremely important that police recruits become familiar with the community they will be serving. Police misconduct and police culture are important topics for the recruit to become familiar with. Crime prevention and community policing/problem-oriented policing concepts are then covered to provide the framework to help recruits incorporate community-oriented values early on in the training process.

Suggested First Four Weeks of Police Training Program

FIRST WEEK

Philosophy of Police Department.
1. Activities with community
2. Building of trust in community
3. Democratic values respected
4. Customer-based policing

Training hours: 4

Organizational Structure of Police Department.
1. Description of organizational structure
2. Internal communication channels
3. Evolving organizational change to community-oriented policing (COP)
4. Importance of organizational communication with community

Training hours: 8

Socioeconomic Makeup of Community.
1. Demographic makeup of community
2. Social strata of community
3. Quality-of-life issues
4. Victim characteristics in neighborhoods
5. Political makeup of community

Training hours: 8

Cultural Diversity of Community.
1. Definition of cultural diversity
2. Value of understanding cultural diversity
3. Identification of cultural organizations and leaders
4. Hate/bias crimes

Training hours: 16

Police History.
1. Historical development of policing
2. Police development in America
3. Modern law enforcement
4. Major law enforcement research findings (e.g., Kansas City Study)

Training hours: 4

SECOND WEEK

Police Operations.

1. Patrol
2. Investigation
3. Records and communication
4. Police-community relations

Training hours: 8

Police Mission.

1. Values of policing
2. Mission of policing
3. Long-range goals/objectives of policing
4. Professional orientation

Training hours: 8

Police Culture.

1. Definition of police culture
2. Police cynicism
3. Police myths
4. Evolving police culture

Training hours: 8

Police Discretion.

1. Definition of police discretion
2. Complexity of police role in relation to discretion
3. Recent approaches (legal and departmental) to police discretion
4. Value and importance of police discretion

Training hours: 8

Police Misconduct.

1. Police misconduct:
   a. Perjury
   b. Sex on duty
   c. Sleeping on duty
   d. Drinking/drugs
   e. Corruption
   f. Excessive force
   g. Crimes committed by police
2. Internal Affairs

Training hours: 8

(continued)

THIRD WEEK

Police Ethics.

1. Definition of terms
2. Morality and the law
3. Morality and behavior
4. Analysis of ethical dilemmas

Training hours: 20

Problem-Oriented Policing (POP).

1. Broken windows theory
2. Definition of problem-oriented policing
3. SARA model (Scan, Analyze, Respond, and Assess)
4. Identification of resources

Training hours: 20

FOURTH WEEK

Crime Prevention.

1. Definition of crime prevention
2. Environmental design and defensible space
3. Crime prevention programs
4. Situational crime prevention

Training hours: 20

Community-Oriented Policing.

1. Philosophy of community-oriented policing
2. Description of COP fundamentals
3. Examination of various COP strategies
4. Future and long-range implementation of COP

Training hours: 20

INNOVATIVE APPROACHES TO TRAINING DELIVERY

Recall from our earlier discussion that the majority of police training has traditionally been conducted in a very rigid and militaristic manner. In fact, many police academies use military drills and inspections, which result in a fair amount of stress being placed on trainees. Likewise, much of the content of police subjects in the academy is delivered in the lecture format or a teacher-centered format, with little or no interaction on the part of trainees. In other words, the academy instructor stands in front of the class and lectures for a specified period of time; the trainees are expected to sit straight at their desks and keep their mouths shut. At some point in the future, the trainees regurgitate on an examination what they heard during the lectures. It is questionable whether effective learning takes place in this type of environment.

Today's police officer works in an ever-changing environment. In light of this, there is a myriad of choices in adult education literature that may serve as guides for police trainers. These choices become increasingly important as policing methods evolve into community-oriented strategies.

Learning is a process central to human behavior that has been of interest to philosophers, psychologists, and educators for centuries. Systematic investigations of learning phenomena have resulted in many different explanations. Although these investigations may not allow us to construct a fully comprehensive theory of learning, the insights are important for two reasons. First, on a practical level they provide police trainers with information when they are fostering and teaching new skills and competencies.[24] Second, the adult education theory of andragogy, which we discuss below, may actually enhance learning at the same time.[25]

The training conducted in the police academies should highlight, whenever possible, self-directed learning on the trainee's part; this can go hand in hand with community policing. For community policing to be successful, police officers will have to be self-starters. When they discover a problem, they will be expected to solve it by working with members of the community. Thus, this self-directed culture should be initiated within the context of training. The theory of andragogy may in part be one mechanism to assist police trainers in accomplishing this perplexing task.

Adult education scholar Malcolm Knowles argued that adults must be taught differently than children and that the learning process of adults is drastically distinct when compared to that of children or the traditional pedagogical approach.[26] Knowles, a strong proponent of self-directed learning and the teacher's role as a facilitator in the process of adult education, is well known for his theory of andragogy. According to Knowles, **andragogy** is a theory that is vastly different from the traditional pedagogical or lecture model; instead, it advocates both the self-directed learning concept and the teacher as the facilitator of learning.[27] Knowles contended:

> Adults are motivated to devote energy to learn something to the extent that they perceive that it will help them perform tasks or deal with problems they confront in their life situations. Furthermore, they learn new knowledge, understandings, skills, values, and attitudes most effectively when they are presented in the context of application to real life situations.[28]

Knowles pointed out several key concepts of andragogy[29]:

1. Adults need to know why they need to learn something before undertaking to learn it.
2. Adults have a self-concept of being responsible for their own lives.
3. Adults come into an educational activity with both a greater volume and a different quality of experience from those of youths.

4. Adults become ready to learn those things they need to know to cope effectively with their real-life situations.

5. In contrast to children's and youths' subject-centered orientation to learning (at least in school), adults are life-centered (or task-centered or problem-centered) in their orientation to learning.

6. While adults are responsive to some extrinsic motivators (better jobs, promotions, salary increases, and the like), the more potent motivators are intrinsic motivators (desire for increased self-esteem, quality of life, responsibility, job satisfaction, and the like).

Andragogy represents a well-known theory of how adults learn in both formal and informal training and education.

The training of police officers should be made experiential, interactive, and participatory. For example, every aspect of law enforcement training could include simulation exercises and problem-solving activities that help develop communication and language skills.[30] Police trainers and police officers could be used as actors to construct, for example, a domestic violence or a bias crime situation. Learners would then be required to bring to bear their experience, powers of observation, and communication skills to solve the problem. Situations should be designed so that learners can use previous knowledge and can connect theory and practice. Obviously, role plays and improvisations are not new adult learning techniques, but they are often relegated to one or two hastily conceived practical skills sessions that are poorly performed, monitored, and evaluated. Properly prepared activities lead to increased retention.[31] Thus, police officers are more likely to understand legal concepts and may be able to better empathize with citizens they encounter on the street because of their classroom experience.[32]

We now turn our discussion to an example of how police trainers can use a **student-centered approach** when teaching subjects in the academy. For this example, we take up legal training that police recruits receive while in the academy. After being given general lectures on specific legal subjects, trainees should participate in group case study methods pertaining to what they have learned. This approach is an active learner-centered approach and can be used when teaching most legal subjects. For example, trainees can be instructed on search and seizure, laws of arrest, admissions, and confessions utilizing a case study method.

A **case study method** approach is an instructional technique based on real-life examples. Case studies stimulate the real world, and they can be used to orient trainees to ethical dilemmas of the law enforcement profession. The case study method was developed by Christopher Langdell of Harvard University School of Law in the 1880s and later introduced into Harvard Business School.

Case studies have been used in a wide variety of professional training programs; for example, in law schools cases are frequently the backbone of a course, with separate cases used throughout the course. Case studies help future lawyers organize complex bodies of facts and information on their own and to inductively arrive at principles and apply them to new situations.[33] The central aims of the case study are to stimulate self-development in a blend of understanding that combines intellectual ability (the power to think clearly, incisively, and reasonably about specific facts and about abstractions) and to develop practical judgment and social awareness.[34]

The case study technique can be used when teaching many subjects in the police academy; it has a long history of use in technical and professional schools. Cases typically include three interrelated components: case study or report, case analysis, and case discussion.

In law enforcement training, trainees could be required to read a fact case situation and then identify the key issues of the case; present a rationale of whether, for example, a warrantless search could be made; and support the rationale with the appropriate search and exception to the search warrant requirement. The following box presents a simple real-life case.

The first step is to engage the trainees in a discussion of the facts of the case. The trainer should start by asking the trainees about their understanding of the case. The trainees should then be asked to analyze the facts and key issues of the cases and to provide a rationale (a basis) for the seizure. Each group of trainees should then report on the problems and issues involved in the case. Minority and conflicting viewpoints should always be elicited; however, it is important that the trainer bring the discussion back to the facts of the case. In the present case example, the trainer should ensure that the recruits can discern that the officer had a legal right to be in the location (the living room) based on both the call

---

Case Example

A police officer is called to a residence to take a burglary report; while at the residence, he is standing in the living room taking the report from the victim/complainant and owner of the residence John C. Doe. The officer looks down the hallway and observes several of what he believes to marijuana plants (approximately two feet high) growing in flowerpots. The only portion of the residence that was burglarized was the living room area, where a television and VCR were taken. The victim notices that the officer has spotted the plants and relates to the officer that he has changed his mind about reporting the burglary and asks the officer to leave the residence at once. The officer does not leave but instead proceeds down the hallway (despite the protests of the victim) and seizes the suspected marijuana plants. While standing in the hallway, the officer can see into a bedroom through an open door and spots two more suspected marijuana plants growing in flowerpots. The officer enters the bedroom and seizes the suspected marijuana plants. John Doe relates to the officer that he has no right to be back in the bedroom area and demands that the officer leave at once and threatens to sue the police department.

to take the burglary report and the subsequent invitation by the complainant into the residence, specifically the living room, and that while in the living room the officer could clearly see several plants at the end of the hallway that he believed to be marijuana.

The trainer should ensure that the trainees base the rationale for the seizure on the plain view exception to the Fourth Amendment requirement for a search warrant. In concluding the case, the trainer should have the trainees sum up the points from the case. When the discussion winds down, it is important that the trainees' learning is connected to concepts covered in the subject objectives, to other similar problems and challenges in the area covered by the case, and to the learners' personal development.

Case method techniques can be utilized when teaching other exceptions to the Fourth Amendment's requirement for a search warrant, laws of arrest, admissions and confessions, and even traffic laws. The objective here is to encourage the recruits to think critically about and analyze a fact situation. The case method technique makes training more realistic and active; designing case studies will also serve to break the monotony of the lecture. The technique should include essential lectures and then use of the case study method.

The case method instructional technique should be well planned and thought out by the trainer, with the assistance of content area experts; for example, it may be beneficial to involve a person who has received legal training in the area of search and seizure laws. The case should be written with the mode of delivery in mind. Case study methods require that the facilitator allow enough time for trainees to fully understand the nature of the problem or case scenario; using a video or other relevant audiovisual will cut down on the time needed for understanding but will increase the design time. Once again, case study methods work best when trainees are allowed to work in groups.

One other example of how instruction in a subject can be enhanced regards firearms training. Much firearms training is done at the firearms range, where police shoot their firearms and ultimately are required to qualify on the firearms course. Firearms training can be made more relevant and realistic for the police trainee; for example, trainers could include discussions on controversial police shootings around the United States. The well-publicized shooting that occurred in New York City would be an excellent case for trainers in the academy to discuss with trainees. This is the case in which Amadou Diallo was shot at 41 times by New York City police officers, and of those 41 shots, 19 hit and subsequently killed Diallo. A case such as this illustrates the realities of the job, and trainers should use the classroom as a vehicle to discuss controversial shootings. Critical discussions regarding controversial police shootings are currently not done that often in police academy training; however, there is a growing body of literature that suggests that critical discussions, even of imperfections of police actions or of the criminal justice system, should be made part of the academy training experience.[35]

Trainers should allow recruits to discuss, for example, the Diallo shooting in the classroom and solicit what the trainees think the officers did right or wrong, how well the situation was handled, what the officers should have done differently, and how this situation could have been avoided in the first place. These questions lay at the heart of a critical discussion and case study and will allow the trainer to glean important information about trainees' thinking. The trainer will be in a position to see how effectively trainees are bringing their specific training into the shooting case study.

One of the major aims in allowing these case critiques in firearms training is that (because they are thought-provoking in nature) they open the mind of the trainees to major problems that may occur in shootings related to the police occupation. There is no expectation that the students will acquire a new skill from a case exercise but rather that they discover they may have to look at a situation in a new light.

Veteran police officers and neophyte police officers alike can benefit from an environment that incorporates many of the principles from the andragogy model of learning. Police training academies should increasingly deviate from the mechanical, militaristic, and behavioral aspects of training to programs that inform police recruits how to identify, respond to, and solve problems such as crime, drugs, fear of crime, and urban decay in the neighborhoods they serve.[36] It is essential that training be conducted in such a way as to be as meaningful as possible to adult participants.[37] Training should become mission-oriented and should respond to what police recruits have to know to perform their jobs effectively; for example, if the mission of the organization is written from the standpoint of community-oriented policing, then training should reflect this. So often there is a disconnect between the mission, the organization, and training, as when a police organization is striving to implement community-oriented policing in their operations but fails to change training in both the curriculum and the learning environment. (The term "learning environment" means the context in which trainees are allowed to discuss and critique issues or case studies and allowed to initiate debate and dialogue on current policing philosophy.)

POSTACADEMY TRAINING AND DEVELOPMENT

Field Training Program

Once recruits have graduated from the police training academy, they enter what is called the **field training officer program (FTO).** Demands placed on today's police are complex: Police officers are expected to utilize good judgment; have confidence; be creative, independent thinkers; and be problem solvers and risk takers. A department's FTO program is critical to successfully meeting these complicated demands. The field training of new police officers is a vital supplement to the classroom training received in the police academy. The initial exposure to law enforcement provided through the field training program plays a significant role in shaping the future careers of new police officers and in many cases provides the recruits with their first opportunity to practice what has been learned in the academy. The FTO program has different phases in which the recruits demonstrate different skills and competencies.

The field training officer program is a concept that originated in 1972 in the San Jose, California, Police Department, and since 1972 FTO programs have become fairly widespread. An FTO program attempts to bridge the gap between the academic experiences of the classroom and the actual practices of policing; the number of hours required for the FTO program varies from agency to agency. During the FTO program, a recruit who has recently graduated from the academy is assigned to ride with a field training officer, who has been trained to direct, evaluate, and correct the performance of recruits, for a specified period of time. Field training officers are carefully selected and regard their selection as a tribute to the trust and confidence the police agency has in them. They are usually selected from patrol officers who have several years of patrol experience, have a level of experience above the norm, and possess superior skills and abilities in written and verbal communications. Successful experience as a field training officer is considered a positive career step.

Problem-Based Learning

Problem-based learning is an instructional method that challenges students to "learn to learn," working cooperatively in groups to seek solutions to real-world problems.[38] These problems are used to engage students' curiosity and to initiate their learning of the subject matter. Problem-based learning prepares students both to think critically and analytically and to find and use appropriate learning resources; it is ideal for field training of new officers.

Problem-based learning is a curriculum development and delivery system that recognizes the need to help students develop problem-solving skills as well as acquire necessary knowledge and skills. The first application of problem-based learning was in medical schools, which rigorously tested the knowledge base of graduates. Problem-based learning utilizes real-world problems, not hypothetical case studies with neat, convergent outcomes. It is in the process of struggling with actual problems that students learn both content and critical thinking skills.

Recently the U.S. Department of Justice's Office of Community-Oriented Policing Services announced the first new postacademy field training program for law enforcement agencies in more than 30 years.[39] The police training officer (PTO) program incorporates community policing and problem-solving principles and produces officers who have the necessary knowledge, skills, and attitudes for today's law enforcement environment.

A variety of community policing skills is needed in contemporary law enforcement. The new training model presents trainees with real-life problems that have no easy solution and encourages them to view the problems in a broad community-focused context and to hypothesize, research, and then solve the problems. The Reno, Nevada, Police Department was the first to use the PTO program.

Reno, Nevada, Problem-Based Learning

The Reno, Nevada, Police Department is utilizing an innovative adult education approach that more appropriately reflects community-oriented and problem-oriented policing in their training. The Reno Police Department calls it "problem-based learning," which requires that trainees learn to analyze complex problems as they occur in real life. The program structure allows the trainees and trainer to proceed using daily policing activities. The trainees receive problem-based learning exercises from the police training officer (PTO) that they must complete within the training phase. Throughout training, the trainees and PTO respond to calls for service and perform normal police activities, and these activities provide the necessary background information to complete the training phase and weekly assignments.[40]

The Reno Police Department defines this problem-based learning as a trainee-centered teaching model that incorporates problem solving as the vehicle for learning. Traditionally, learning involved a teacher or instructor delivering information as content to the learner. Problem-based learning, however, begins with presentation of a real-life problem that the trainee must attempt to solve, so the trainee follows a pattern of discovery whereby he or she expresses ideas about resolving the problem, lists known facts, decides what information to use (including naming sources for that learning), and develops action plans to solve the problem. Several evaluation methods follow the process to determine success or failure of the trainee's action plan.[41]

There are six objectives of Reno's problem-based learning model[42]:

1. To provide learning opportunities for new officers that meet or exceed the needs of both the community and the policing agency
2. To develop and enhance the trainees' learning from the academy within the community environment through a series of real-life problem-solving activities
3. To foster a growing independence from the police training officer over the course of the program to a stage where the trainees are able to work effectively while alone on patrol
4. To produce graduates of the training program who are capable of providing customer-centered, responsible, community-focused police services

5. To teach transferable learning skills using a problem-based learning model that trainees can apply to problems throughout their careers

6. To provide consistent, fair evaluations that not only address trainees' skills, knowledge acquisition, and application but also evaluate their ability to problem-solve effectively

After Reno implemented, evaluated, and enhanced the program as needed, it was then pilot-tested by the Savannah (Georgia), Lowell (Massachusetts), Colorado Springs, Richmond (California), and Charlotte-Mecklenburg (North Carolina) Police Departments. The results of the pilot testing indicated that the program produces highly trained officers who are well prepared to serve their community and that the program is flexible and allows agencies to tailor it to their unique training needs.

In-Service Training

Many states require that police receive a certain number of training hours each year to maintain their law enforcement license in that particular state, and this is sometimes referred to as **in-service training** or post-academy training. The purpose of in-service training is to enhance lifelong learning and career development for police officers.[43] Furthermore, changes in departmental policies and procedures, court decisions, and operational strategies and techniques demand that training be done on an ongoing basis throughout a police officer's career.[44] There is some evidence that suggests that in-service training may reduce the likelihood of citizen complaints and future litigation.[45]

The number of hours of in-service training is set by each individual state's Peace Officers Standards and Training (POST) requirements: In the state of Kansas, all commissioned law enforcement officers are required to complete 40 hours of in-service training each year to maintain their law enforcement license; in Massachusetts, municipal police officers are required to attend specified days of annual in-service training. For example, the Massachusetts Veteran Officer Annual Professional Development Training includes the following programs[46]:

1. *Veteran Patrol Officer Annual Professional Development.* A 3- to 5-day training program for patrol personnel that includes updates on motor vehicle laws and criminal laws, domestic violence, cardiopulmonary resuscitation (CPR) and automatic external defibrillator (AED) training, first responder (first aid), sexual harassment, community policing, use of force, firearms qualification, and other courses as necessary.

2. *Supervisor Annual Professional Development.* A 3- to 5-day program that includes updated information on motor vehicle laws and criminal laws, community policing, CPR, criminal offender record information, domestic violence, evaluation and motivation of subordinates, and firearms qualification.

3. *Detective Annual Professional Development.* A 3- to 5-day program for investigative personnel that includes legal updates, narcotics investigations,

searches and seizures, sex crimes, collection of physical evidence, CPR, and firearms qualification.

4. *Chief/Command Annual Professional Development.* A 3- to 5-day program for command-level personnel that includes legal updates, updates on motor vehicle laws, community policing, domestic violence, use of force, motivation of subordinates, and total quality management (TQM).

5. *Reserve/Intermittent Officer Annual Professional Development.* A 20- to 30-hour training program, usually delivered during evening hours or on weekends, for part-time officers that includes legal updates, updates on motor vehicle laws, community policing, sexual harassment, tactical communications, and infectious diseases.

With the advent of technology (especially the computer), it may very well be that police will be allowed to do their in-service training by completing specified blocks of courses online via computer. Online classes have become a very popular means of instruction on many college campuses and tend to cater to the working or nontraditional student who lives a great distance from campus. This method is advantageous for police officers who need to complete required in-service training because it allows them to take online in-service courses at their own convenience. Police officers can log on to the computer, work for a while, and then log off while the computer keeps track of the time and the amount of material completed. Of course, online training would have to be approved by each individual state's board in charge of requirements for Peace Officers Standards and Training.

TRAINING AND THE LEGAL ENVIRONMENT

Training is the lifeblood of a police organization. There are a number of critical factors involved in why police organizations place so much emphasis on training. We know that one such reason is because police officer recruits have to learn the skills of policing and veteran police officers need to continually hone their skills and learn new techniques and developments in the field. Another important factor is the legal environment that police operate in; simply put, police management can be sued for failing to provide adequate training for their personnel.

Imagine, for example, that Officer Jones has just been issued a new PR-24 baton. Officer Jones begins to wear his new shiny baton on patrol but has not received any formal training in how to use the baton. Two weeks after being issued the baton, Officer Jones is on patrol and receives a call to report to a barroom disturbance. Upon Officer Jones's arrival at the bar, he sees several persons fighting in the parking lot. He orders the persons to stop fighting and they all do—except for one. Officer Jones retrieves his PR-24 baton and begins to strike the one unruly person who would not comply with his order. Officer Jones strikes the unruly person five times; two of the blows are delivered to the head and result in a deep laceration.

That person falls to the ground unconscious and bleeding and has to be transported to the hospital for medical attention, which ends up being a five-day hospital stay. In this scenario, did Officer Jones do anything wrong? Can Officer Jones or the police organization be held liable?

The short answer is yes! Both federal and state laws hold police officers and police management accountable for negligence on the part of police officers. This awesome accountability underscores the importance of effective training. The failure of police management to provide police officers with the proper training has resulted in lawsuits that ultimately cost the police organization and the general citizenry their tax dollars. Each year in the United States, thousands of plaintiffs file civil suits claiming injury at the hands of law enforcement.[47] Thus, police management is hauled into court to defend against these litigations due to their positions within the organization.

There are two distinct forms of liability that police management face: The first is direct liability, and the second is indirect liability. **Direct liability** is liability incurred for the actions of supervisors or managers themselves. For direct liability to exist, managers usually have to engage directly in the activity. There are a number of ways that police management can incur direct liability[48]:

1. Supervisors authorize the act. They give officers permission to do something that ultimately results in liability.
2. They participate in the act. They engage in activities with other officers that ultimately result in liability.
3. They direct others to perform the act. They order officers to do something that ultimately results in liability.
4. They ratify the act. Once the act is completed, they fail to admonish or take corrective action when the act comes to their attention.
5. They are present when an act for which liability results occurs. They stand by and watch an act occur that results in liability and fail to take corrective action.

On the other hand, **indirect liability** (or vicarious liability, as it is sometimes called) is the liability that supervisors and managers face for the actions of their employees. For example, let's apply indirect liability to the previous hypothetical case of Officer Jones, who was issued the PR-24 baton and not provided any formal training in how to use the baton and who seriously injured a suspect with the baton. In this case, police management can be held vicariously liable under indirect liability. Likewise, the police chief or manager who fails to properly train his or her officers can be held vicariously liable.

Today police officers receive formal training in the recruit academy and then additional training or in-service training throughout their careers. Training across police organizations is in no way uniform and varies in length and content. Because of these factors and the criticism levied at the adequacy of training procedures, failure to train has been a favored bias of **42 USC 1983 liability.**[49] This liability is also referred to as a 1983 action and is the most common legal vehicle by which the federal courts can acquire jurisdiction of these lawsuits. Thus, these lawsuits are brought under the provision of Section 1983 of Title 42 of the U.S. Code. This law, passed by Congress in the aftermath of the Civil War and commonly referred to as the Civil Rights Act of 1871, was designed to secure the civil rights of the recently emancipated slaves. In a nutshell, it prohibits depriving any person of life, liberty, or property without due process of the law.[50]

In cases pursued under 43 USC 1983, **deliberate indifference** must be alleged connecting the particular violation to inadequate training. For example, in one landmark case in this area, Justice White, in a rare unanimous opinion, spoke for the Court in *City of Canton* v. *Harris:*

> [W]e are asked to determine if a municipality can ever be liable under
> 42 U.S.C. 1983 for constitutional violations resulting from its failure to
> train municipal employees. We hold that under certain circumstances,
> such liability is permitted by the statute.[51]

The *Harris* case brings to light the reality regarding management liability and failure to train. In this case, Harris was arrested for charges not disclosed by Canton, Ohio, police officers. She was carried to the police station in a patrol wagon; upon her arrival, police officers at the station noticed she was sitting on the wagon floor. When police officers asked her if she needed medical attention, she answered incoherently. While in the police station, she slumped to the floor on two occasions, and the police left her lying there to prevent her from falling again; no medical treatment was provided by the police. After an hour she was released from custody to her family, who took her by ambulance to a hospital where she was diagnosed to be suffering from emotional ailments.

Subsequently Harris sued the city of Canton claiming a violation of her due process rights to receive appropriate medical treatment while in custody. During the jury trial, evidence was presented that showed there was a municipal ordinance authorizing shift commanders to use their discretion to determine whether a detainee required medical treatment. It was revealed in trial that the Canton Police Department had not provided special training for police commanders in how to determine who was entitled to medical care.

The Court rejected the city's argument that only unconstitutional policies can be a basis for an action under U.S. Code for civil rights violations (42 USC 1983). Next in the *Harris* case, the Court set forth the degree of fault that must be evidenced by the municipality's inaction before liability can be permitted:

> We hold today that inadequacy of police training may serve as the basis
> for 1983 liability only where the failure to train amounts to deliberate
> indifference to the rights of persons with whom the police come into
> contact. Thus in the case at hand, respondent must still prove that the
> deficiency in training actually caused the police officers' indifference to
> her medical needs. Would the injury have been avoided had the employee
> been trained under a program that was not deficient in the identified
> respect?[52]

The courts have constructed a three-pronged approach to determine if police management can be held liable for inadequate training:

> [The courts need to determine] (1) whether, in failing adequately to train and supervise subordinates, he was deliberately indifferent to the [plaintiff's constitutional rights]; (2) whether a reasonable person in the supervisor's position would know that his failure to train and supervise reflected deliberate indifference; and (3) whether his conduct was casually related to this constitutional infringement by his subordinates.[53]

In the case of *Cooper* v. *Merrill*, the police pursued Cooper, a robbery suspect who was believed to be armed and dangerous. After a car chase, Cooper jumped out of his car and then ran and hid behind some bushes in an attempt to flee the police officers. They subsequently fired a number of shots at Cooper, three of which struck him. Cooper sued the police department's trainer for, among other claims, the lack of any policy on the use of deadly force, which incidentally the department did not have.

The court found that in order to show such a claim, Cooper would have to show (1) that the police had inadequate training, (2) that the inadequate training represents a policy reflecting a deliberate indifference to plaintiff's constitutional rights, and (3) that the police caused the alleged violation of constitutional rights.[54] Other than the use-of-force statutes of the state, the borough had no use-of-force policy; likewise, there was no evidence that the borough provided any training either in the field or in the form of a manual or procedure to guide its officers, so the requested summary judgment for the borough was denied.[55] In this case, the decision was based in part on the fact that the borough did not have any such training or standard operating procedure that governed the use of deadly force. Therefore, the plaintiff failed to prove what the court suggested he must prove. Nevertheless, it should be clear: Potential liability problems can be created for any police organization that fails to adequately train its personnel.

Not only can police management face potential legal liability for failing to adequately train and instruct their personnel, police management can also be held vicariously liable for acts of their employees. The majority of lawsuits are filed by citizens who claim they were injured by the police.[56] Thus, the chief or the employee's immediate command is usually named in the lawsuit because of personal involvement or because of vicarious culpability (meaning that he or she was involved because of a policy-making role). Police management should be aware of the potential liability they face in this area of failing to adequately train their employees and should seek to stay informed about civil liability and its parameters as well as keep up-to-date with current litigation in this area. This is a burdensome task but an important one. The following points should help agencies and supervisors guard against liability: Do not allow untrained officers to perform any field duties; official departmental policies should be reflected in training (critical issues such as deadly force, pursuit driving, arrest procedures, and weaponless defense should be carefully outlined in

POLICING IN ACTION

The city of Dallas had a policy that required that police officer applicants not have more than three moving traffic violations in the preceding year and at least 45 college credits with at least a C average. Was this requirement legal?

The U.S. Court of Appeals, Fifth Circuit, approved the policy. The court stated that unlike other work positions this court or the Supreme Court has considered, the position of officer on the Dallas police force combines aspects of both professionalism and significant public risk and responsibility. The court also concluded that a law enforcement employer would enjoy greater latitude when hiring police officers than when hiring clerical employees because police officers have a more direct role in preserving public safety.

Source: *Davis* v. *City of Dallas,* 777 F.2d 205, 211 (5th Cir. 1985), cert. denied, 476 U.S. 1116 (1985).

the context of the academy and updated in in-service training courses); and all lesson plans, policies, training bulletins, and instructional techniques should be reviewed periodically and updated.[57]

COLLEGE EDUCATION FOR POLICE OFFICERS

Training and **education** differ in terms of scope and objectives; also, the purpose of education is broader and more general compared to that of training.[58] Education is concerned with the development of the mind (of the intellect), while training deals with learning specific skills. Education is a more personal activity in that its main purpose is the enhancement of an individual's ability to use his or her mind for personal pleasure or gain; training means developing skills that will be used more for social and economic reasons than for personal purposes. Education should come first, and then training should follow. Police scholars Stan Shernock and Gail Dantzker offered what is perhaps one of the more comprehensive views to differentiate training from education:

> When educated people are faced with a novel situation, they should be able to analyze, interpret, and make judgments about the situation themselves rather than rely on others to tell them what to do. . . . A person [who] has been merely trained, on the other hand, is more likely to rely on others to tell him or her what to do in a particular situation and is less likely to understand the reasons for doing what he or she is directed to do.[59]

It would seem that higher education would better prepare men and women to enter the police academy and the field of policing. In this light, training and education complement each other; however, the issue of college education for police continues to be a perplexing issue and the topic of much debate and scrutiny. National police commissions, police scholars, and police executives have consistently echoed the theme that many of the problems faced in policing could in part be solved if more qualified people, particularly college-educated people, were sought out for police work. The idea of the college-educated police officer is not new and can be dated back to 1916 when the University of California at Berkeley established a law enforcement program for police officers. The initial push for the development of crime-related studies came primarily from August Vollmer, who was Chief of the Berkeley Police Department and a faculty member at the University of California at Berkeley. Vollmer devised a program in criminology.[60] It was between 1930 and 1945 that the expansion in criminal justice education was significant. In 1931 the National Commission of Law Observance and Enforcement proposed the application of science to police work, with the goal of more effectively dealing with crime.

Not only was education for police thought to be one way to reduce crime (that is, if practitioners had education in scientific methods), but education also became the cornerstone of the movement to professionalize the police. As a reaction both to the social disruption and violence in the 1960s (when the police increasingly confronted anti–Vietnam War protesters) and to the inability of the police to cope with ghetto riots, it was increasingly believed that higher education for police officers was desirable. In 1968 the National Advisory Commission on Civil Disorders discovered that in many cities aggressive police patrol tactics and harassment were a result of society's fear of crime and that these practices only created hostility and conflict between the police and minorities.[61] President Lyndon Johnson's Commission on Campus Unrest advocated higher education for police:

> Law enforcement agencies desperately need better educated and better trained policeman. . . . There should be special monetary incentive for all who enter the police service with college degrees or who obtain degrees while in police service.[62]

The consensus of the commissions formed to study the police in the 1960s overwhelmingly was that in order to improve law enforcement, the quality of police personnel had to be upgraded through education. The importance of setting educational standards for the selection of police officers has been debated for many years. In the early 1970s, the National Advisory Commission on Criminal Justice Standards and Goals recommended that in order for police officers to perform their police duties properly, every police department should establish guidelines for entry-level educational requirements. Here are four of the commission's recommendations[63]:

1. Every police agency should require immediately, as a condition of immediate employment, the completion of at least one year of education (30 semester units) at an accredited college or university. Otherwise qualified police applicants who do not satisfy the condition, but who have earned a high school diploma or its equivalent, should be employed under a contract requiring completion of the educational requirement within three years of initial employment.

2. Every police agency should, no later than 1975, require as a condition of initial employment the completion of at least two years of education (60 semester units) at an accredited college or university.
3. Every police agency should, no later than 1978, require as a condition of initial employment the completion of at least three years of education (90 semester units) at an accredited college or university.
4. Every police agency should, no later than 1982, require as a condition of initial employment the completion of at least four years of education (120 semester units or a baccalaureate degree) at an accredited college or university.

Despite the recommendations of various commissions of the 1960s and 1970s for better-educated police officers, as of 1993, 86 percent of all police agencies still require only a high school diploma for employment.[64] Police officers today must continue to seek college education, and police selection strategies should target individuals who possess a college education. Police management should increasingly move toward college education requirements for police applicants prior to their being admitted to the training academy. The evidence is clear that the benefits of college education for police officers are insurmountable. For example, a 1988 Police Executive Research Forum study found several advantages of college education for police officers[65]:

1. It develops a broader range of information for decision making.
2. Course requirements and achievements inculcate responsibility in the individual and a greater appreciation for constitutional rights, values, and the democratic form of government.
3. College education engenders the ability to flexibly handle difficult or ambiguous situations with greater creativity or innovation.
4. Higher education develops a greater empathy for diverse populations and their unique life experiences.
5. The college-educated officer is assumed to be less rigid in decision making and more readily accepts and adapts to organizational change.
6. The college experience will help officers to better communicate and to respond to crime and service needs of a diverse public in a competent manner with civility and humanity.
7. The college experience tends to make the officer less authoritarian and less cynical with respect to the milieu of policing.

Some research has found a positive relationship between policing and a college education. For example, as a result of a comparative study of Los Angeles Police Department officers, several key correlations were found to exist between college education and policing: In the academy, college-experienced individuals scored higher; individuals with a four-year degree were found to have the fewest number of complaints lodged against them, compared to those officers with two years of college and those with no college; and individuals with a four-year college degree used less sick time and fewer injury days.[66] It was also found that during the 10-year time frame in which the comparison was made, only 3 percent of the individuals with a four-year college degree had been terminated, compared to 90 percent of those without college education.[67]

Education and Minorities

Despite research that indicates the value of college-educated police officers, there are some fundamental concerns about requiring a degree as a prerequisite for employment. The push for increased education for police came at the same time that concern for civil rights and equal opportunity for all Americans became a national priority, so it has been argued that requiring a college degree for police employment may be discriminatory.[68]

The logic of this argument has been framed around four primary concerns.[69] First, there have been past practices of discrimination in the admissions process of colleges and universities; second, many minorities are unable to attend college because of severely limited financial resources to pay for educational expenses. Third, there has been a history of inadequate academic preparation of minority students in the elementary and secondary schools to facilitate their college admission, and if admitted, they are inadequately prepared to perform at the college level. Finally, during their youth minorities have been taught to believe that college is mostly for whites and that they should not expect to continue their education past high school. These four concerns are real and should be taken seriously by police executives who are pondering requiring college education for their police officers. Police executives must take a proactive approach in ensuring that minority candidates have equal access to a policing career, and these executives must remain cognizant of the past discriminatory practices that have prevented minorities from attending colleges and universities.

Education and Future Police Officers

The police officer who will be desired in the future will be one who has been educated in liberal arts and sciences and one who can think and make decisions on his or her own and solve problems with the community's interest as a priority. The new police officer will also be more interested in providing community service than in simply being a crime fighter.

Will college curriculum in its present state prepare this police officer of the future? Professors Michael Birzer and Michael Palmiotto argued that college curriculums should increasingly align with the Academy of Criminal Justice Sciences (ACJS) recommendations.[70] The ACJS recommendations suggest that a criminal justice curriculum should focus on five areas: (1) criminal justice and juvenile justice processes, (2) criminology and the causes of crime, (3) law enforcement, (4) law adjudication, and (5) corrections. Birzer and Palmiotto went beyond the ACJS recommendations and argued that criminal justice education—in order to prepare effective practitioners for the future—should include a broad-based curriculum, eclectic approaches covered in coursework, and an urban and social competencies prong that complements this curriculum and coursework.[71] They made the following recommendations[72]:

1. *Broad-based curriculum.* In line with the ACJS recommendations, this curriculum would include the subjects of juvenile justice, crime, criminological theory, police organization, police discretion, police subculture, law and adjudication, criminal law, court systems, and corrections.

2. *Eclectic approaches in coursework.* In line with a liberal arts orientation, coursework would be offered in sociology, social work, psychology, minority and women studies, ethics, macro problem solving, social justice, and human services. Criminal justice coursework should stress the interrelatedness in these disciplines, particularly in solving societal problems.

3. *Urban and social competencies.* Criminal justice coursework should increasingly reflect multicultural issues both on the domestic and international fronts. This multicultural flavor should include an exploration of issues pertaining to racial/ethnic group contacts, social power and group conflict, social problems, diversity issues in the 21st century, and discrimination and racism in the United States.

 ## SUMMARY

In this chapter, we have discussed the role and importance of police training. It is said that training is the lifeblood of a police organization, and police executives face tremendous liability for failing to properly train their personnel. There are usually two types of training in police organizations: preservice or recruit training and in-service training. Many states now require that police officers receive a specific number of in-service training hours annually to maintain their law enforcement certificate.

Many police academy environments are very militaristic in orientation, but there is evidence that suggests this is not the best environment for effective learning to take place. Police academies are increasingly moving toward an environment that incorporates adult learning principles and that deviates from the military training model. The theory of andragogy is one such adult learning theory that holds promise in training both neophytes and veteran police officers.

What police are taught in the academy is evolving to support new police strategies and philosophies. This curriculum change, in part, is being nurtured because of community-oriented policing strategies, which many police departments have adopted in their operations. Subjects such as cultural diversity, ethics, problem solving, interpersonal communication, and community organizing skills are increasingly being offered at police academies.

Once a recruit graduates from a police academy, he or she enters the field training officer program, which is one of the most crucial programs in the police agency. The field training officer program bridges the gap between the academics of the classroom and actual police practices. Field training officers are specially trained to instruct new officers and are highly skilled, both in their knowledge of law enforcement and in their ability to be teachers. Officers who are accepted into the field training officer program are selected on the basis of their experience, knowledge, and exemplary work performance.

In many states, police officers are required to maintain a certain number of in-service training hours per year to maintain their law enforcement certificate. In-service training is designed to provide veteran officers with new skills and to update them regarding changes in technology, law, procedures, department policies, and the like.

The question of whether police officers should have a college degree has been the topic of scrutiny and debate for some time. Much of the research suggests that police officers who possess college degrees typically perform better on the job compared to police officers without a college degree; however, some have argued that requiring police to possess a college degree when hired will jeopardize minority recruiting because many minorities have not had the opportunity to attend college. Nonetheless, police executives should strive to develop recruitment plans that seek college-educated police officers, especially minorities.

QUESTIONS IN REVIEW

1. Discuss the traditional nature of police training and the problems it creates in the training of new police officers.
2. Discuss evolving themes in the police training curriculum.
3. What is the purpose of in-service training?
4. How does the legal environment impact police training?
5. Identify and discuss the arguments for and against college education requirements for police officers.
6. Discuss how the adult education theory of andragogy can be adapted in the police academy.

POLICE RESOURCES ON THE WEB

American Society of Law Enforcement Trainers Home Page
http://www.aslet.org/i4a/pages/index.cfm

FBI Academy
http://www.fbi.gov/hq/td/academy/academy.htm

National Law Enforcement Training Center
http://www.nletc.com/index.php

New Jersey Division of Criminal Justice Police Training Commission
http://www.state.nj.us/lps/dcj/njptc/home.htm

University of Illinois at Urbana Police Training Academy
http://www.pti.uiuc.edu

Western New Mexico University Police Academy
http://www.wnmu.edu/academic/applied/academypage.html

REFERENCES

1. THE PRESIDENT'S COMMISSION ON LAW ENFORCEMENT AND ADMINISTRATION OF JUSTICE, *Task Force Report: The Police* (Washington, DC: GPO, 1967), p. 137.

2. MICHAEL L. BIRZER and RON TANNEHILL, "A More Effective Training Approach for Contemporary Policing," *Police Quarterly* 4, no. 2 (2001): 233–252.

3. KENNETH R. MCCREEDY, "Entry Level Police Training in the 1980s." *The Police Chief* (October 1983): 32–37.

4. PAUL M. SATTERFIELD, *The Police Academy: A Practical Approach* (San Clemente, CA: Quick-Code, Inc., 1986).

5. ROBERT A. LORINSKAS and JOSEPH C. KULIS, "The Military Model and Policing: A Misunderstood Ideology," *Police Studies* 9, no. 4 (1986): 184–193.

6. WILLIAM H. MCNEILL, *The Pursuit of Power: Technology, Armed Forces, and Society Since A.D. 1000* (Chicago: University of Chicago Press, 1982).

7. RONALD W. GLENSOR, KENNETH J. PEAK, and LARRY K. GAINES, *Police Supervision* (Boston: McGraw-Hill, 1999).

8. PETER B. KRASKSA and VICTOR E. KAPPELER, "Militarizing American Police: The Rise and Normalization of Paramilitary Units," *Social Problems* 44, no. 1 (1997): 1–18.

9. DAVID C. WEBER, *Warrior Cops: The Ominous Growth of Paramilitarism in American Police Departments* (Washington, DC: The Cato Institute, 1999).

10. Ibid.

11. PAUL J. ORTMEIER, "Leadership for Community Policing: A Study to Identify Essential Officer Competencies," *The Police Chief* (October 1997): 88–85.

12. WILLIAM W. BENNETT and K.M. HESS, *Management and Supervision in Law Enforcement* (Belmont, CA: Wadsworth Publishing Co., 2001), p. 261.

13. KEN J. PEAK and RON W. GLENSOR, *Community Policing and Problem Solving: Strategies and Practices,* 3rd ed. (Upper Saddle River, NJ: Prentice Hall, 2002).

14. WILLARD OLIVER. "The Third Generation of Community Policing: Moving Through Innovation, Diffusion, and Institutionalization," *Police Quarterly* 3, no. 4 (2000): 314–317.

15. DAVID L. CARTER and LOUIS A. RADELET, *The Police and the Community,* 6th ed. (Upper Saddle River, NJ: Prentice Hall, 1999).

16. QUINT C. THURMAN and JIHONG ZHAO, "Community Policing: Where Are We Now?" *Crime and Delinquency* 43, no. 3 (July 1997): 17–21.

17. MICHAEL J. PALMIOTTO, MICHAEL L. BIRZER, and N. PRAHBA UNNITHAN, "Training in Community Policing: A Suggested Curriculum," *Policing: An International Journal of Police Strategies and Management* 23, no.1 (2000): 8–21.

18. TERRY D. EDWARDS, "State Police Basic Training Programs: An Assessment of Course Content and Instructional Methodology," *American Journal of Police* 12 (2002): 23–45.

19. MICHAEL L. BIRZER, "Police Training in the 21st Century," *FBI Law Enforcement Bulletin* 68, no. 7 (1999): 16–19.

20. STEVEN M. RAMIREZ, "The Need for a New Learning Culture in Law Enforcement," *The Police Chief* 63 (November 1996): 24–26.

21. PAUL J. ORTMEIER, "Leadership for Community Policing: A Study to Identify Essential Officer Competencies," *The Police Chief* (October 1997): 85–88.

22. BUREAU OF JUSTICE STATISTICS, "Report to the Nation on Crime and Justice," (Washington, DC: GPO, 1983).

23. PALMIOTTO, BIRZER, & UNNITHAN, 2000, pp. 15–16.

24. MICHAEL L. BIRZER, "Applying the Theory of Andragogy to Police Training," *Policing: An International Journal of Police Strategies and Management* 26, no. 1 (2003): 29–42.

25. Ibid.

26. MALCOLM S. KNOWLES, *The Modern Practice of Adult Education: From Pedagogy to Andragogy* (Chicago: Follett, 1980).

27. MALCOLM S. KNOWLES, *The Adult Learner: A Neglected Species* (Houston, TX: Gulf Publishing Co., 1990), p. 57.

28. Ibid., p. 60.

29. MALCOLM S. KNOWLES, *The Modern Practice of Adult Education: Andragogy Versus Pedagogy* (New York: Association Press, 1970), pp. 83–84.

30. K.D. CODISH, "Putting a Sacred Cow out to Pasture," *The Police Chief* 63, no. 11 (November 1996): 40–44.

31. BIRZER and TANNEHILL, 2001.

32. BIRZER, 2003.

33. VICTOR J. MARSICK, "Case Study," in *Adult Learning Methods,* 2nd ed., ed. M.W. Galbraith, (Malabar: FL: Krieger Publishing Co., 1998), pp. 241–243.

34. P. PIGORS, "Case Method," in *Training and Development Handbook: A Guide to Human Resource Development*, ed. R.L. Craig (New York: McGraw-Hill Book Co., 1976), pp. 173–175.

35. Ibid.

36. MICHAEL L. BIRZER and RON TANNEHILL, 2001.

37. WILLIAM A. GELLER, *Local Government Police Management* (Washington, DC: International City Management Association, 1991).

38. WILLIAM J. STEPIEN, and STEVEN A. GALLAGHER, "Problem-Based Learning: As Authentic as It Gets," *Educational Leadership* 50, no. 7 (1993): 25–28.

39. OFFICE OF COMMUNITY ORIENTED POLICING SERVICES, "First New Post Academy Police Officer Field Training Program in 30 Years Emphasizes

Community Problem Solving Skills Over Traditional Response Methods." Accessed April 25, 2004 at http://www.cops.usdoj.gov/Default.asp?Item=1021.

40. RENO POLICE DEPARTMENT, "Police Training Officer Manual," 2004.

41. Ibid.

42. Ibid.

43. GLENSOR, PEAK, and GAINES, 1999.

44. Ibid.

45. MARK W. MOORE and DARYL W. STEVENS, *Beyond Command and Control: The Strategic Management of Police Departments* (Washington, DC: Police Executive Research Forum, 1991).

46. MASSACHUSETTS POLICE TRAINING COMMISSION, "Annual Professional Training for Veteran Officers." Web posted at http://www.mass.gov./mptc/inservice.htm. Accessed April 14, 2004.

47. VICTOR E. KAPPELER, *Critical Issues in Police Civil Liability*, 2nd ed. (Cincinnati, OH: Anderson Publishing Co., 1997).

48. ROLANDO V. DEL CARMEN, *Civil liabilities in American Policing* (Englewood Cliffs, NJ: Brady, 1991).

49. CYRIL D. ROBINSON, *Legal Rights, Duties, and Liabilities of Criminal Justice Personnel* (Springfield, IL: Charles C. Thomas Publisher, 1992).

50. CHARLES R. SWANSON, LEONARD TERRITO, and ROBERT W. TAYLOR, *Police Administration,* 5th ed. (Upper Saddle River, NJ: Prentice Hall, 2001).

51. *City of Canton* v. *Harris* 489 US 378, 390, n. 10 (1989).

52. Ibid.

53. *Greason* v. *Kemp,* 891 F2d 829, 836–837 (11th Cir 1990).

54. *Cooper* v. *Merrill,* 736 F.Supp. 552 (D Del 1990).

55. *Cooper* v. *Merrill* at 567–568 (1990).

56. WILLIAM G. DOERNER and MARK L. DANTZKER, *Contemporary Police Organization and Management* (Boston, MA: Butterworth-Heinemann, 2000).

57. EDWARD THIBAULT, LAWRENCE M. LYNCH, and R. BRUCE MCBRIDE, *Proactive Police Management,* 3rd ed. (Englewood Cliffs, NJ: Prentice Hall, 1995).

58. GLENSOR, PEAK, and GAINES, 1999.

59. STAN SHERNOCK and GAIL D. DANTZKER, "Education and Training: No Longer Just a Badge and a Gun," in *Contemporary Policing: Personnel, Issues, and Trends,* ed. Mark L. Dantzker (Newton, MA: Butterworth-Heinemann, 1997), pp. 75–98.

60. MICHAEL J. PALMIOTTO, *Policing: Concepts Strategies and Current Issue in American Policing* (Durham, NC: Carolina Academic Press, 1997).

61. *Report of the National Advisory Commission on Civil Disorders* (Washington, DC: GPO, 1968).

62. U.S. President's Commission on Campus Unrest, (Washington, DC: GPO, 1968), p. 154.

63. NATIONAL ADVISORY COMMISSION ON CRIMINAL JUSTICE STANDARDS AND GOALS, *The Police* (Washington, DC: GPO, 1973), p. 369.

64. BRIAN A. REAVES, *Local Police Officers* (Washington, DC: U.S. Department of Justice, 1996).

65. DAVID L. CARTER, ALLAN D. SAPP, and DARYL W. STEPHENS, "Higher Education as a Bonafide Occupational Qualification (BFQ) for Police: A Blue Print," *American Journal of Police* 7, no. 2 (1988): 16–18.

66. B.E. SANDERSON, "Police Officers: The Relationship of College," *The Police Chief* (August 1977): 62–63.

67. Ibid.

68. DAVID L. CARTER and ALLEN D. SAPP, *Police Education and Minority Recruitment: The Impact of a College Requirement* (Washington, DC: Police Executive Research Forum, 1991).

69. Ibid, pp. 4–5.

70. MICHAEL L. BIRZER and MICHAEL J. PALMIOTTO, "Criminal Justice Education: "Where Have We Been? And Where Are We Headed?" *Justice Professional* 15, no. 3 (2002): 203–211.

71. Ibid.

72. Ibid., p. 208.

Women and Minorities in Policing: Mirroring Society

Key Terms

Affirmative action
Alice Stebbins Wells
Authoritarian personality
Civil Rights Act
Consent decree
Crime prevention model
Discrimination
Normative theory

Protection movement
Reverse discrimination
Scapegoating
Self-fulfilling prophecy
Sexual harassment
Stereotyping
Title VII
White slave scare

Outline

Introduction
Women in Policing
Women Police: Critical Issues
Women on the Move
Minorities in Policing
Discrimination Against Minority
  Police Officers

Theoretical Explanations for
  Discrimination
Discrimination in Context
Affirmative Action
Reverse Discrimination

Learning Objectives

After reading this chapter, you should be able to:

1. Discuss the evolution of the role of women and minorities in the police profession.
2. Explain what the early roles of women and minority police officers were.
3. List and describe critical issues that both women and minority police officers face.

4. Discuss factors that may result in steering women away from a police career.
5. Describe incidents of discrimination and their impact on the larger police profession.
6. Explain the role that the Supreme Court and the various commissions have had in minimizing discrimination against women and minority police officers.
7. Identify the various theories of prejudice and discrimination.

INTRODUCTION

Today women and minorities can be found in virtually all areas of police employment; they are represented not only in patrol functions but also in specialized investigative functions and command and control positions within police agencies. It is common in most communities to see women and minority officers performing the police function, but crossing the gender and color lines has not been an easy road for them. Throughout history equal opportunity for women and minority police officers has sometimes been resisted, and many of these officers have suffered discrimination in forging an identity in the policing profession.

In this chapter, we discuss the status of women and minorities in the policing occupation. Specifically, we will focus on historical issues pertaining to women and minority police and their current status in policing as well as examining some critical issues. We begin the chapter with an examination of the status of women police; in the second half of the chapter, we examine minority police officers. We conclude the chapter with a discussion of a few theories of prejudice and discrimination as well as affirmative action.

WOMEN IN POLICING

In 1910, the first policewoman was employed by the Los Angeles Police Department (LAPD). **Alice Stebbins Wells,** a social worker, was appointed by the LAPD and given the limited responsibilities of supervising dance halls, skating rinks, penny arcades, movie theaters, and places of recreation and searching for missing persons.[1] For more than half a century after the appointment of Wells, women police officers were selected according to different criteria from those for men. These women police were assigned to work as jail matrons, to work with children and abused women, and to do various clerical duties.[2]

Policewomen's role in the early 20th century was perceived as a "preventive role." Women police officers had the same authority as male officers and could make arrests and enforce criminal laws; however, neither the women nor male officers considered their tasks to be similar. During this period, the acceptable practice in policing was that the male officers would make the arrests and the women officers would provide counseling and guidance to women and children.

During the second decade of the 20th century, the **crime prevention model** of policing was initiated, and it preceded the crime control model that was developed in the 1930s. The crime prevention model accentuated two key points: First, it emphasized the social work aspect of policing; second, it stressed that women were better than men at preventing crime.[3] During this time frame, the role of women police consisted largely of social service functions, which included working with juveniles, doing clerical duties, working in the jail as matrons, and in some cases carrying out vice work.

Between the years 1910 and 1940, there was a middle-class movement to expand the role of women in public affairs, and policing was one of the public arenas that women began to permeate. This evolution of women in policing had its roots in the **protection movement,** initiated by police organizations to protect the rights and welfare of women and children.[4] Another concern during the 1910s and 1920s was the **white slave scare,** a publicized concern that women were being abducted and sold into prostitution. In 1915, the National Association of Police Women was formed as a clearinghouse for the compilation and dissemination of information on the work of women police officers. This organization also had as a goal the promotion of prevention and protective services by police departments.[5]

Under the crime prevention model of policing, which appears to have been followed at least until around 1940, women police officers were considered to be more effective as crime prevention specialists than their male counterparts. In the 1930s, the crime control model, with its emphasis on managerial efficiency, technological sophistication, and crime fighting, began to replace the crime prevention model. With this emphasis on the crime control model and a deemphasis on the crime prevention model, the policewomen's movement became stagnant and lost institutional support.[6]

Contemporary Development of Women's Role in Policing

It has been only in the last 30 or so years that the status and role of women in policing have changed significantly. In 1968, the Indianapolis Police Department made history by assigning the first two female officers to patrol on an equal basis with their male colleagues. Since that time, women have entered the field of law enforcement in increasing numbers and played a critical role in the development of modern policing, yet the number of women in law enforcement has remained small.

The opportunities for women to serve in police operations and in administration on an equal footing with their male counterparts are now greater than ever. Much of this progress is the result of the Equal Employment Opportunity Act of 1972 as well as the amendment to Title VII of the Civil Rights Act of 1964, which subsequently assisted women to more fully gain an entry into policing by making **discrimination** (different treatment based on something other than merit) illegal. **Title VII** of the **Civil Rights Act** of 1964 (as amended) prohibits individual and class discrimination in the federal government on the basis of race, color, sex, national origin, or religion. Title VII applies to employers with 15 or more employees and includes

PIONEERS IN POLICING

Alice Stebbins Wells

Alice Stebbins Wells, a social worker, joined the Los Angeles Police Department (LAPD) as the nation's first sworn policewoman in 1910 and was assigned to work with juveniles. Her duties were later extended to include enforcing laws concerning dance halls, skating rinks, penny arcades, movies, and other places of recreation populated by women and children. She searched for missing persons and provided information to women within the scope of her police duties. The LAPD's present-day juvenile bureaus and crime prevention units can be traced directly to the foundation Wells laid. Wells felt strongly about women in police work, and she toured more than 100 cities in the United States and Canada to promote the cause of female officers, and as a result, many cities began to appoint policewomen. New York and Massachusetts went so far as to enact statutes requiring towns with populations in excess of 20,000 to employ at least one policewoman. In 1915, Wells founded the International Association of Police Women and served as its president. Today the International Association of Police Women continues to provide a forum for exchanging ideas and encouraging the use of women in important law enforcement roles. By the time Wells retired in 1940, she had served as a policewoman for 30 years.

state and local governments. It also applies to employment agencies and to labor organizations as well as the federal government. Even given the opportunities engendered by civil rights legislation and the enhanced status of women in policing, it cannot be denied that women entering the male-dominated police profession have faced many obstacles.

Currently it is estimated that there are more than 50,000 sworn female police officers serving in law enforcement agencies at both the state and local levels.[7] However, one disturbing trend was that by the end of the 1990s, increases in the employment of women police officers slowed down considerably. The National Center for Women and Policing found that women make up 13 percent of all law enforcement personnel nationwide and that employment for sworn women police officers has risen only 3.2 percent from 1990 (when women made up about 10.6 pecent of officers).[8]

It is particularly troubling that the number of women police officers has been slow to rise even in light of the facts that equal employment legislation prevents discrimination and that a significant number of women have entered the general labor force. What is even more perplexing is the minimal number of women who hold supervisory and top command positions in police organizations. Recent data from the National Women in Policing organization indicate that women hold 7.4 percent of top command positions nationwide and 8.8 percent of supervisory positions.[9] Overall, women are still underrepresented in American law enforcement.

WOMEN POLICE: CRITICAL ISSUES

There are a number of factors that may explain why women are employed in such small numbers in the policing profession and why the profession has attracted few women to serve in law enforcement. We discuss a few of these in the sections that follow.

Sexual Harassment

The headlines of the *Los Angeles Times* newspaper screamed the sobering news: "Sexual Harassment Lawsuit Settled." Two lawsuits from numerous sexual harassment complaints by three female police officers against the Glendale, California, Police Department were settled for a total of $4 million.[10] Included was testimony from a sergeant, who admitted to owning an Internet pornography site that he accessed while on duty as a supervisor, and from a longtime secretary, who claimed another sergeant exposed himself to her and harassed her for years.

Studies have found that 60 to 70 percent of women police officers have experienced sexual harassment.[11] **Sexual harassment** is a form of sex discrimination that violates Title VII of the Civil Rights Act; unwelcome sexual advances, requests for sexual favors, and other verbal or physical conduct of a sexual nature constitute sexual harassment when the conduct explicitly or implicitly affects an individual's employment, unreasonably interferes with an individual's work performance, or creates an intimidating, hostile, or offensive work environment.[12]

Warrior Image

The National Center for Women and Policing cites that one reason police agencies have a difficult time recruiting and retaining larger numbers of women is due to the male-dominated "warrior image."[13] This warrior image is typically that of a beefy male police officer, often with a paramilitary background, who defuses a situation by using a number of masculine physical traits. Whether it is the Dirty Harry character from Hollywood, the *Top Cops* television series, or the toy action figures, they all glamorize an outdated and dangerous image of policing as a he-man occupation, with the primary requirements for success being a thick neck and a taste for physical violence.[14]

The National Center for Women and Policing argues that the policing profession uses this image to draw the wrong type of people into policing, which subsequently restricts the field primarily to males. In contemporary policing, this image does not support the needs of the community, nor does it support the philosophy of community-oriented policing, which stresses outreach, victim assistance, community partnerships, problem solving, and collaboration. Moreover, the warrior image may be a contributor to police brutality and to claims of excessive force against the police. The effects of this warrior image manifest themselves in many ways in the recruiting and retention of not only qualified female police officers but in some cases qualified male officers.

Entrance Standards

Police agencies often rely on antiquated and unnecessary entrance standards in order to reduce the pool of applicants. Many of these entrance standards test physical attributes, which give men a biological advantage; subsequently many female applicants are weeded out during the selection process. These standards include physical fitness and agility tests, which are used by many departments as part of the application process. Physical agility tests focus on attributes of upper-body strength and speed. The problem is that, in some cases, physical fitness and agility tests have been found to discriminate against females and members of certain minority groups, and some of these tests have been found to be non-job-related.[15]

The National Center for Women and Policing advocates elimination of or at least reduced dependency on the physical fitness part of the entrance test in order to get better-qualified officers and to increase female representation. The organization claims the physical agility test is one reason women constitute only about 13 percent of sworn officers in the United States.[16] Furthermore, those authorities responsible for developing physical agility tests should carefully and thoroughly evaluate the physical duties to be performed by law enforcement officers.

Discrimination

The President's Commission on Law Enforcement and Administration of Justice issued the 1967 *Task Force Report: The Police* that stated, "[I]n 1960, there were 5,617 female police officers and detectives in the United States. Of these, all but 400 served in urban areas."[17] Since the commission gave its report, the role of women in policing has stayed essentially the same up to the present. The *Task Force Report: The Police* further stated, "[Q]ualified women should be utilized in such important staff service units as planning and research, training, intelligence gathering, inspection, public information, community relations and legal advisors."[18] The task force explicitly commented that women police officers could and should be given the opportunity to perform the same tasks as their male counterparts. These operational activities included serving in the patrol unit, in vice, and in the investigative division; in addition, qualified women officers should have the opportunity to advance to administrative positions in police agencies. The President's Crime Commission laid the foundation for equality for women in policing, but there is no doubt that women (and other minorities) have been discriminated against in policing.

Historically, there have been many reasons why women are discriminated against in policing. One reason is that police work was perceived as too dangerous and much too violent for women to handle. This paternalistic ideology is grounded in the notion that policing is a man's profession and that women do not possess the physical strength of men, facts which inherently make women incapable of performing on an equal level as men.

Another area in which women police officers were discriminated against in the past was in department educational requirements. Generally, male police officers were only required to be high school graduates or to have a GED, while female officers were required to have a college education.[19] This was common practice until at least the 1970s. In the first half of the 20th century, female officers were considered to be crime prevention specialists; their duties included counseling and guidance, while the male police officer would make arrests.[20] It should also be noted that female officers' duties were often confined to internal operations within the department, so they had minimal contact with the public. These positions included police dispatchers, evidence technicians, and research and development specialists. When women were given positions involving public contact, their responsibilities were in general public relations positions involving schools, neighborhoods, or traffic control.[21]

The prevailing warrior image promoted by police has to a certain degree perpetuated discrimination against women recruits, and this covert use of predominately male traits may drive women away from the police occupation. This very image may keep the number of women officers in the policing profession low.[22] The warrior image is most conspicuous in advertising literature, which primarily reflects the crime-fighting aspects of the profession while ignoring the helping aspects of the job. Recruiting and advertising literature that depicts only the crime-fighting or masculine aspects of a police career may deter women from applying for sworn police positions.

Skills, Traits, and Competencies

The emphasis in recruitment and selection of police should be on specified skill sets or characteristics while at the same time reducing the warrior image. The application and selection process should increasingly focus on communication, problem solving, empathy, and the ability to successfully interact with members of diverse cultures. These skills are more important for the 21st-century police officer than the warrior skills that were glamorized during the past in policing. These more contemporary skills are necessary to develop sound police leaders, irrespective of gender, who can manage assets and lead their personnel through these changing times.

Police leaders today should recruit and retain officers who are capable of carrying out multiple functions during their career. It is no longer a given that an officer will serve in the same capacity throughout his or her career; he or she must be capable of doing many diverse assignments. The key to leadership success is to develop a team attitude and avoid the police mob mentality. Only when this is fully indoctrinated into the prevailing police culture will the gender of the officer no longer matter.

WOMEN ON THE MOVE

It cannot be denied that discrimination against females in policing still exists today, nor can it be denied that the profession has suffered from poor decision making regarding women police and sexual discrimination in the past. It may be that many of these problems can be attributed to a culture created by police leadership that was rooted in the traditional policing model.

With the rising number of single females with children entering the police profession, police leaders must increasingly be sensitive to issues of childcare, flex hours, and perhaps part-time employment in order to draw qualified female applicants. One study pointed out that the failure of police agencies to be sensitive to these issues was one of the primary reasons females leave the police occupation.[23]

In order to attract and retain larger numbers of females in law enforcement, the prevailing traditional warrior image and its culture will have to give way to a culture of service, collaboration, and problem solving that is more in line with community-oriented policing. Likewise, obstacles should be removed that traditionally have been barriers for women police.

Performance

Evaluations have shown that women perform just as well as their male colleagues in the law enforcement profession.[24] For example, research has found that female police officers are the subject of fewer citizen complaints compared to male police officers; that women police officers may exhibit better communication skills, field tactics, initiative, and self-confidence; and that policewomen are more adept at public relations compared to their male counterparts.[25]

Additional evaluations have found that although men and women are equally likely to use force in their routine duties as law enforcement officers, women are less likely to engage in excessive force.[26] Other research has shown that women police officers (compared to male officers) more often use a communication style consistent with the principles of community policing and respond more sympathetically to violent crime victims.[27]

Male police officers typically see police work as involving control through authority, while female police officers see it as a public service.[28] Some have even gone as far as suggesting that in some respects women are better suited for police work.[29] Because women police officers perform just as well as male police officers and may be more likely to exhibit the demeanor and traits desired for community-oriented policing, police leaders should design and use effective marketing strategies that carry a compelling message targeted to reach women.

Leadership

Women continue to be underrepresented in supervisory and executive positions in law enforcement.[30] Women hold 7.4 percent of top command positions nationwide and only 8.8 percent of supervisory positions. This may suggest that women are leaving the police service before they are eligible for promotion to leadership positions, or it may be that the glass ceiling restricts them from lateral mobility within the organization and prevents them from obtaining experience in other core areas of the police organization. Without having this wider base of experience, women are less likely to have opportunities for advancement.

Women not only possess the traits desired in community-oriented police strategies, but they also exhibit those traits typically sought in leaders. Some evaluations have shown that women police leaders as a group exhibit more strength in leadership-associated personality traits than do male police executives as a group.[31] Research has pointed out a number of workplace-specific gender differences that may give women a significant advantage in leadership positions: Men tend to be competitive whereas women tend to be more collaborative; men's creativity tends to focus on the scientific approach compared to women's systems-oriented approach; and men tend to be more company-oriented whereas women are more entrepreneurial.[32] These traits that women exhibit are desired in 21st-century policing, especially under the axiom of community policing.

Opportunities

Police managers need to increasingly widen their recruiting net to secure women. A police department that does not actively recruit women or that lacks women in its ranks gives the impression that the organization is not open to women or to diversity. Women police convey a feeling of openness and inclusion, and their presence demonstrates that the police organization mirrors the society it serves. In order to avoid dire consequences, police organizations should be aware of their possible shortcomings of not employing women and work to achieve truly equal opportunities.

Police managers should experiment with various approaches to foster advancement for women police; an approach such as using internship programs to attract, retain, and train women for a police career may assist in securing qualified women. Women currently employed in police organizations could be given the opportunity for rotational assignments to provide them with professional development opportunities and exposure to larger police organizations. Likewise, police executives can hold recruiting authorities accountable by tying merit pay increases or performance evaluation criteria to attainable goals for securing qualified women applicants for police careers. Law enforcement agencies that hire and retain more women enjoy six advantages[33]:

1. Women officers are proven to be as competent as their male counterparts. Research studies show no meaningful differences between male and female officers in their activities or productivity on patrol, their commitment to law enforcement organizations, their response to violent confrontations, and their performance evaluations received both at the academy and on the job.

2. Women officers use a style of policing that relies less on physical force, and they are less likely to become involved in incidents of excessive force.

3. Women officers bring skills and abilities to the job that help implement community-oriented policing, which facilitates cooperation and trust between police officers and citizens.

4. More women officers will improve a law enforcement agency's response to domestic violence against women, the largest single category of calls to local police departments.

5. Increasing the presence of female officers reduces the prevalence of sex discrimination, underutilization, and sexual harassment in an agency by reducing the numeric underrepresentation of female officers.

6. The presence of women in a law enforcement agency can bring about beneficial changes in policy for all officers. For example, one scholar noted that the introduction of women will create an incentive to examine many management practices that are less acceptable now that they must be applied to men and women alike. This may result in the development of improved selection criteria, performance standards, and supervision for all officers.[34]

While the number of women in law enforcement continues to grow, police leaders must address the problems of limited female applicants, bias by fellow officers, gender discrimination, glass ceilings, and sexual harassment. Police leadership must articulate gender-neutral hiring as an important goal. Effective strategies for recruiting women within police departments, as well as training and equipping women police to succeed in the field, should be pursued. Once a new female officer joins the force, programs for mentoring and support should be initiated to assist in the transition from recruit to officer.

MINORITIES IN POLICING

Although minority police officers have had a rich history working in various capacities in policing, the job of police officer was for many years reserved almost exclusively for white males.[35] Despite the Civil Rights Act of 1964, a study found that more than 30 years later almost 80 percent of all sworn police officers were still white males.[36]

In the 21st century, the term "minority" continues to include a wide variety of people: African Americans, Hispanics, Asians, women, and homosexuals (gay males and lesbians). Many police agencies are making a concentrated effort to recruit females, blacks, Hispanics, Asians, and other groups.

African Americans

African Americans (compared to other minority groups) have the longest history in the field of policing.[37] For example, the New Orleans City Council in 1805 passed a city ordinance allowing "free men of color" to serve as police officers as long as white officers commanded them. These "free men of color" performed tasks that white police officers did not want to perform, were used as slave catchers, and had to enforce laws in segregated African-American communities. By 1830, the "free men of color" had lost their positions on the New Orleans Police Department because new immigrants, especially the Irish, had taken their positions.[38] In 1839, African-American men were deputized as special police officers by the mayor of Pittsburgh specifically to allow the African-American community to defend itself against a white mob.[39] Both of these situations were unique because prior to the Civil War the majority of African Americans were slaves and legally could not be considered for police service, even in the role of special police for a temporary period of time.[40]

After the Civil War, racial tensions manifested themselves in several Southern cities in which whites attacked African Americans, and law enforcement officers in these cities were often incapable or unwilling to protect African Americans from white violence. To some scholars, it became apparent that in order to obtain fair and equitable policing, African-American communities would need to be served by police officers of their own race.[41] In response to this, the city of New Orleans initiated the appointment of black officers in 1867; in 1868, the first African-American captain was appointed by the New Orleans Police Department.[42] As a group, however, African-American police officers in many Southern cities were restricted to policing African-American residential areas and to arresting only African Americans. When white Southerners were able to regain political control after the Reconstruction period, the white Southern establishment worked to eliminate African-American law enforcement officers.[43]

In 1872, the city of Chicago appointed its first African-American police officer in what may be the first appointment of an African-American police officer anywhere outside the South. This was followed by the appointment of African Americans in Philadelphia and Cleveland (Ohio) in 1881, in Columbus (Ohio) in 1885, in Detroit in 1890, and in St. Louis (Missouri) in 1893.[44] During the 20th century, African Americans were appointed to many large and small American cities as police officers; more often than not, their numbers did not reflect the proportion of African Americans in the population they served. To be specific, their numbers on the police force generally represented 1–2 percent of the total number of sworn police personnel. Typically, African-American police officers were denied access to choice assignments, promotions were difficult for them to obtain, and they were generally not given command positions. Although African-American officers' opportunities increased after World War II, it was not until the social movements of the 1960s that African-American officers began to make visible strides in policing.

During the 1960s, there was a great deal of unrest reflected in disturbances and riots in American communities. As a result of these disturbances in American cities, studies and commissions were established to examine the causes for urban unrest and to find solutions to prevent further disturbances and riots in American cities. President's Commission on Law

Enforcement and Administration of Justice, in its *Task Force Report: The Police* (published in 1967), recommended that police forces with a considerable minority population need to vigorously recruit black and other minority police officers. The commission explained that a police department dominated by white officers policing a black neighborhood caused annoyance and resentment among black residents. The *Task Force Report* also stated that police departments should reflect the ethnic composition of the city and that black police officers policing black neighborhoods would have an understanding of the language and subculture of those communities. The commission's *Task Force Report: The Police* stated:

> In short, in every city, county, and State where statistics are available, Negroes are under represented, usually substantially, on police forces. Although the number of Negroes in police departments has been increasing, in some places rapidly, there is indication that the percentage of Negroes on police forces may level off well below their percentage of the population unless police departments are more effective in recruiting.[45]

In 1973, the report of the National Advisory Commission on Criminal Justice Standards and Goals titled *The Police* reemphasized that qualified blacks should be recruited as police officers in communities with black residents. Because there is often distrust between blacks and the police, it is extremely important that blacks and other minorities be recruited to help overcome the community's distrust of the police. The commission's report recommended the following five steps[46]:

1. Every police agency should engage in positive efforts to employ ethnic minority groups. When a substantial ethnic minority population resides within the jurisdiction, the police agency should take affirmative action to achieve a ratio of minority group employees in approximate proportion to the makeup of the population.
2. Every police agency seeking to employ members of an ethnic minority group should direct recruitment efforts toward attracting large numbers of minority applicants. In establishing selection standards for recruitment (in addition to height and weight requirements), special abilities such as knowledge of a foreign language, strength, agility, or any other compensating factor should be taken into consideration.
3. Every police agency seeking to employ qualified ethnic minority members should research, develop, and implement specialized minority recruitment methods.
4. Every police chief executive should ensure that hiring, assignment, and promotional policies and practices do not discriminate against minority group members.
5. Every police agency should evaluate continually the effectiveness of specialized minority recruitment methods so that successful methods are emphasized and unsuccessful ones discarded.

Government commissions have influenced the recruitment of blacks and other minorities by police departments, and many cities have established recruitment programs to attract minority candidates. As we discussed in Chapter 7, these programs include posting billboards along highways and using television, radio, and newspaper advertisements. Some police agencies have offered cash incentives to employees who have recruited minority officers. Strides have been taken in recruiting, promoting, and increasing the number of blacks on America's police forces. There are more black officers in command positions than ever before in American history.[47]

A study of the 50 largest cities in the United States found that police departments still fell below desirable levels in employing African Americans and Hispanics: Only 2 of the 50 police departments achieved population representation for both blacks and Hispanics. Two reasons given for not achieving adequate representation were budgetary constraints and police layoffs.[48]

Throughout the 1990s, blacks and Hispanics still seemed to be playing catch-up in many American cities. For example, while New York City has a black population of approximately 29 percent, its police department has a black police representation of 11 percent; 39 percent of Chicago's population is black, but black police officers total only 25 percent of the city's police force; and in Philadelphia, which has a black population of 40 percent, only 25 percent of its police force is black.[49] A U.S. Justice Department report stated, "Black officers accounted for 18.4 percent of the total in 1990, compared to 20.1 percent in 2000. The percentage of Hispanic officers was 9.2 percent in 1990, and 14.1 percent in 2000."[50] Table 9–1 shows female and minority full-time sworn personnel in large city police departments as of the year 2000.

TABLE 9–1

Female and Minority Full-Time Sworn Personnel in Large City Police Departments, 2000[1]						
Population Served	Female	Any Minority	Black (Non-Hispanic)	Hispanic (Any Race)	Asian-Pacific Islander	American Indian
Total	16.3	38.1	20.1	14.1	2.8	0.4
1,000,000 or more	16.8	37.6	16.9	17.5	2.1	0.3
500,000 – 999,999	16.1	41.1	27.0	7.7	5.3	0.5
350,000 – 499,999	14.4	36.4	20.4	12.7	2.1	1.0
250,000 – 349,999	15.8	32.7	20.9	10.4	0.7	0.4

[1]Expressed in percentages.

Source: U.S. Department of Justice, Bureau of Justice Statistics, *Police Departments in Large Cities,* Special Report NCJ 175703 (Washington, DC: U.S. Department of Justice, May 2002), p. 3.

Detroit Police Officers' Association v. City of Detroit

May a city institute an affirmative action program that discriminates against nonminority police officers?

It was undisputed that in 1968 the total black component of the Detroit police force was between 4 and 5 percent, and the percentage of black sergeants and higher-ranking officers was even less. In the wake of tragic civil disturbances in Detroit in July 1967, the community's attention turned to improving race relations in Detroit.

Widespread alienation of black residents from the Detroit Police Department was one problem identified by city leaders. Two groups, a mayor's task force and a police advisory group, were formed to recommend changes in personnel policies that could contribute to the solution of this problem. The advisory group, the Vickery Committee, was composed of personnel administrators and psychologists from private industry. Believing that "any incident involving the police might serve to incite a civil disturbance of the kind experienced in July, 1967," the Vickery Committee recommended to the department the abandonment of certain qualifications for police employment it found "non-relevant to the actual requirements" of police work.

The U.S. District Court, 446 F.Supp. 979 (E.D. Mich.1978), permanently enjoined (stopped) the city from continuing the operation of an affirmative action program by the Detroit Police Department. The plaintiffs were an association of police officers and a number of white Detroit policemen who were passed over for promotion to the rank of sergeant when black officers with lower numerical standings on the eligibility list received promotions. The district court found that the affirmative action program offended the equal protection clause of the Fourteenth Amendment and violated 42 U.S.C. §1981, Section 601 et seq. (Title VI) of the Civil Rights Act of 1964, 42 U.S.C. §2000d et seq. (1976), and Section 703(a) and (j) (Title VII) of the 1964 Act, 42 U.S.C. §2000e-2(a) and (j) (1976).

The U.S. Court of Appeals, Sixth Circuit, reversed the judgment of the district court and vacated the injunction entered by it. The court dismissed all claims of the plaintiffs based on the contention that the affirmative action program for promotion to sergeant violates Title VI, Title VII, and Section 1981. The case was remanded for further consideration of the constitutional issues. The remand required a determination by the district court of whether it had been established that the Detroit Police Department engaged in intentional discrimination against blacks, and if not, whether the affirmative action plan was justified under the alternative claim of operational needs.

The appellate court stated that if the court concluded that prior acts of the Detroit Police Department did deprive blacks of rights guaranteed them under the equal protection clause, it must then determine whether the affirmative action plan, with its 50/50 ratio, was a reasonable remedial response. The appellate court stated that it was clear that a case involving a claim of discrimination against members of the white majority was not a simple mirror image of a case involving claims of discrimination against minorities. One analysis was required when those for whose benefit the Constitution was amended or a statute enacted claim discrimination. A different analysis must be made when the claimants are not members of a class historically subjected to discrimination. When claims are brought by members of a group formerly subjected to discrimination, the case moves with the grain of the Constitution and national policy. A suit that seeks to prevent public action designed to alleviate the effects of past discrimination moves against the grain, and the official actions complained of must be subjected to the analysis prescribed in the plurality opinion in *Bakke* (*Regents of University of California* v. *Bakke,* 438 U.S. 265), which the appellate court found was controlling. The appellate court stated that in the event the district court concluded that the affirmative action plan may remain in force, it will be necessary to determine a formula for its eventual termination.

Homosexuals

Another group that has been added to the list of minorities in policing is homosexuals. The acceptance of homosexuals in policing has been slow to evolve; as a result, many openly gay and lesbian police officers have been subjected to harassment. Consider the case of Sergeant Mitchell Grobeson, an openly gay officer in the Los Angeles Police Department, who returned to work recently after winning a harassment suit in which he was awarded $770,000. As part of the settlement, every city department has been ordered to make more of an effort to recruit homosexuals. Los Angeles Police Department officials have also assured Grobeson that they will not permit the harassment of homosexuals.[51]

To date, the few studies that have analyzed antigay discrimination in the workplace report substantial fear of discrimination among lesbians and gay men as well as accounts and incidence rates of various forms of sexual-orientation-based discrimination.[52] Many states still use sodomy laws to disqualify law enforcement candidates who are openly gay or lesbian or who are discovered to be homosexual during a background investigation. In those states, agencies use these laws to point out that homosexuals' propensity to violate the law due to their orientation makes them unsuitable as officers.[53]

Gays and lesbians cannot be denied the opportunity to be police officers; in some cities homosexual police officers are "coming out of the closet," while in others they are remaining quiet. While gay and lesbian police officers are still in the silent minority, many are no longer willing to conceal their sexual orientation. In the 1990s, cities such as Atlanta, Boston, Los Angeles, Madison (Wisconsin), Minneapolis (Minnesota), New York, San Francisco, and Seattle actively recruited homosexuals to become police officers.[54]

In the last decade, there have been attempts to open law enforcement positions to homosexuals. Government officials working with the homosexual community have confronted difficulties in police organizations regarding the hiring of homosexuals. For example, the International Association of Chiefs of Police (IACP) openly came out against hiring homosexuals as police officers. Police unions and fraternal police organizations in several cities have opposed recruiting homosexuals as police officers. For example, the

Patrolman's Benevolent Association in New York City strongly opposed the hiring of homosexuals.[55]

Sources of homophobia may be traced to what some individuals consider to be the unnatural nature of the homosexual lifestyle, privately held religious beliefs, and the spreading of AIDS by homosexual men. Homosexual police officers reported that causes of hostility toward them ranged from the fear of catching AIDS from them to the belief that their sexual preference was "sick," "sinful," or "immoral."[56]

Discrimination against homosexuals (gay men and lesbians) appears to be a major issue in many police departments. Recently a group of homosexual police officers sued the New York City Police Department alleging bias. The homosexual officers felt that their police organization, the Gay Officers' Action League (GOAL), had not received treatment equal to that of other fraternal organizations. GOAL accused the NYPD of discrimination by not allowing the league use of a department van during the Gay and Lesbian Pride Parade down Fifth Avenue and by not allowing the department's marching band to participate in the event (the NYPD does allow the band to participate in the St. Patrick's and Columbus Day parades).

DISCRIMINATION AGAINST MINORITY POLICE OFFICERS

Incidents of Discrimination

The city of Los Angeles recently agreed to pay $3.5 million to a Japanese-American police officer who alleged that he was discriminated and retaliated against because of his race. The officer stated that when he was assigned to the Los Angeles Police Department's canine unit as a dog handler, other officers refused to respond to his backup calls and he received threats; in addition, a police sergeant made a derogatory remark about an Asian American and forced the officer, who is Japanese-American, to sign a complaint form written in Korean as his supervisors laughed. The officer was then shunned and investigated for two alleged excessive-use-of-force complaints, which were dismissed. Also, someone posted copies of the officer's complaint in the K-9 Unit offices and stuffed pink women's underwear into his work mailbox.[57]

Recently 200 African-American and Hispanic police officers in Chicago filed a federal lawsuit contesting a controversial sergeant's examination that the plaintiffs maintain will turn back the clock to the discrimination of 1973. In the lawsuit, the officers charge that the city relies too heavily on the written portion of the test, promotes on the basis of rank, refuses to ease past discrimination by using affirmative action, and uses a biased consultant. Only 5 minority officers (3 blacks and 2 Hispanics) were among the 114 officers promoted within a ten-month period since the promotional exam. More than 75 percent of the remaining minority officers failed the exam, a rate twice that of white officers, the suit stated.[58]

In Hartford, Connecticut, cultural sensitivity training was ordered for all police supervisors following a complaint from an officer who claimed his lieutenant had issued him racially charged instructions during a roll call.[59] In another case, a former special agent, who served 16 years with the U.S. Secret Service, is suing the 135-year-old agency for discrimination concerning a denied promotion. The former African-American agent, who worked on numerous top-security presidential details, was overlooked for the position of leading a White House protection squad; the job went to a white special agent with no experience in the area. Consequently, the agent and nine other former and current African-American agents filed a federal lawsuit in Washington, D.C., accusing the federal police agency of racial discrimination dating back to 1974. Members of the Secret Service are reportedly shocked by this episode, according to one spokeswoman, and Secret Service Director Brian Stafford has commented that the service tolerates no discrimination.[60]

A Louisiana Appellate Court recently upheld a jury's award of $1 million for two African-American officers who faced racial harassment and other discrimination in a major city police department. The officers reported that they were subjected to frequent racist comments in their department and over the police radio from white officers. Furthermore, these officers presented evidence that they had been denied promotions because they were black and that, at some point during their career, white officers openly displayed Ku Klux Klan logos and a hangman's noose.[61]

Discrimination against racial and ethnic minorities has been a major problem throughout American history. Minority and ethnic groups had to organize and fight to obtain equality in the American workforce and in society. The blocking of minorities from eligibility to employment opportunities has occurred in all professions and vocations, including public safety positions such as policing. The following statement represents the attitude of the majority toward minorities:

> Members of the majority group tend to act toward the minority individual on the basis of the former's informal assumptions about someone with those wrong characteristics. Thus, women and blacks who enter the occupations in which a majority of workers are male or white face difficulties as a result of others' tendency to focus on their salient status and thus treat them as women or blacks. This interferes with their ability to function effectively in the occupational role.[62]

Historically, police departments (as in other fields of employment) have had a long tradition of discrimination in their recruitment and hiring process and their assignment practices. Until the last decades of the 20th century, most African-American men were denied employment because of their race; those who were employed as police officers were often denied choice assignments based on their race. As we discussed earlier, in some cases black officers were not allowed to work in white neighborhoods or to arrest whites. They were specifically assigned to maintain order only in black neighborhoods.

United States v. *Paradise*, 480 U.S. 149 (1987)

Was a district court correct in ordering that one minority be promoted in the Alabama Department of Public Safety for every nonminority promoted?

In 1972, based on the finding that for almost four decades the Alabama Department of Public Safety had systematically excluded blacks from employment as state troopers in violation of the Fourteenth Amendment, the U.S. District Court issued an order imposing a hiring quota and requiring the department to refrain from engaging in discrimination in its employment practices, including promotions. By 1979, no blacks had attained the upper ranks of the department. The court therefore approved a partial consent decree in which the department agreed to develop within one year a procedure for promotion to corporal that would have no adverse impact on blacks and would comply with the Uniform Guidelines on Employee Selection Procedures (Guidelines), and thereafter to develop similar procedures for the other upper ranks (1979 Decree).

As of 1981, however, more than a year after the 1979 Decree's deadline, no black troopers had been promoted. The district court approved a second consent decree in which the parties agreed that the department's proposed corporal promotion test would be administered to applicants, that the results would be reviewed to determine any adverse impact on blacks under the Guidelines, that the determination of a procedure would be submitted to the court if the parties were unable to agree thereon, and that no promotions would occur until the parties agreed or the court ruled on the promotion method to be used (1981 Decree). Of the 60 blacks to whom the test was administered, only 5 (8.3 percent) were listed in the top half of the promotional register, and the highest-ranked black was number 80. The department then declared that it had an immediate need for between 8 and 10 new corporals and stated its intention to elevate between 16 and 20 individuals before constructing a new list.

The United States objected to any use of the list in making promotions. In 1983, the district court held that the test had an adverse impact on blacks and ordered the department to submit a plan to promote at least 15 qualified candidates to corporal in a manner that would not have an adverse racial impact. The department proposed to promote 4 blacks among the 15 new corporals, but the court rejected that proposal and ordered that "for a period of time," at least 50 percent of those promoted to corporal must be black, if qualified black candidates were available, and imposed a 50 percent promotional requirement in the other upper ranks, but only if there were qualified black candidates, if a particular rank were less than 25% percent black, and if the department had not developed and implemented a promotion plan without adverse impact for the relevant rank.

The department was also ordered to submit a realistic schedule for the development of promotional procedures for all ranks above the entry level. Subsequently, the department promoted 8 blacks and 8 whites under the court's order and submitted its proposed corporal and sergeant promotional procedures, at which time the court suspended the 50 percent requirement for those ranks. The United States appealed the court's order on the ground that it violated the Fourteenth Amendment's equal protection guarantee. The U.S. Court of Appeals affirmed the order.

Justice Brennan, joined by Justice Marshall, Justice Blackmun, and Justice Powell, concluded that even under a strict scrutiny analysis, the one-black-for-one-white promotion requirement was permissible under the equal protection clause of the Fourteenth Amendment.

The Court stated that the race-conscious relief ordered by the district court was justified by a compelling governmental interest in eradicating the department's pervasive, systematic, and obstinate discriminatory exclusion of blacks. The contention that promotion relief was unjustified because the department had been found to have committed only hiring discrimination was without merit, since promotion, like hiring, had been a central concern of the district court since the action's commencement. The department's intentional hiring discrimination had a profound effect on the force's upper ranks by precluding blacks from competing for promotions; moreover, the record amply demonstrated that the department's promotional procedure was itself discriminatory, resulting in an upper-rank structure that totally excludes blacks.

The district court's enforcement order was also supported by the societal interest in compliance with federal court judgments. The department had a consistent history of resistance to the district court's orders, and relief was imposed only after the department failed to live up to its court-approved commitments. The Court concluded that the one-for-one promotional requirement was narrowly tailored to serve its purposes, both as applied to the initial corporal promotions and as a continuing contingent order with respect to the upper ranks.

THEORETICAL EXPLANATIONS FOR DISCRIMINATION

The literature that addresses prejudice, discrimination, and racism is framed around many theoretical constructs. We discuss four of these in the following sections: scapegoating, authoritarian personality, stereotyping, and normative theory.

Scapegoating

Scapegoating contends that prejudiced people believe they are society's victims. This theory suggests that individuals, rather than accepting responsibility for some failure, transfer the responsibility for failure to some susceptible group. This is often seen when unsuccessful applicants assume that a woman or a minority candidate got the job that they were denied.[63]

Authoritarian Personality

The **authoritarian personality** centers on an adherence to conventional values, uncritical acceptance of authority, and a concern for power and is, in turn, aggressive toward persons who do not conform to conventional norms or authority structures. In essence, a person who is raised in an authoritarian environment will then later treat others as he or she had been raised. Authoritarian personality theory views prejudice as an isolated incident that anyone may experience. Discrimination would then be acted out against persons or groups who celebrate customs or cultures that are different from the conventional ones.[64]

Stereotyping

Stereotyping is the process of assuming a person or a group has one or more characteristics because most people or members of that group have (or are thought to have) the same characteristics. It is a simplification and generalization process that helps people categorize and understand their world, but at the same time it often leads to errors. Stereotyping is not only harmful in its own right, but it does damage by fostering prejudice and discrimination. An example of a stereotype that is often wrong is that women are weak and submissive while men are powerful and domineering. This may be true for some women and some men, but it is not true for all. When stereotypes are inaccurate and negative (as they often are between groups in conflict), they lead to misunderstandings, which make resolving the conflict more difficult. Stereotypes can be either positive ("Black men are good at basketball") or negative ("Women are bad drivers"), but most stereotypes tend to make us feel superior in some way to the person or group being stereotyped. Stereotypes ignore the uniqueness of individuals by painting all members of a group with the same brush.

Stereotyping and discrimination often go hand in hand, but it is also possible to have one without the other. When an ethnic group is stereotyped with a neutral or positive attribute such as family-oriented, prejudice and discrimination may not be involved. Similarly, a generalized prejudice against "foreigners" or "amputees" may not include specific stereotypes or acts of discrimination. There are even times when discrimination takes place without prejudice or stereotyping, either intentionally or unintentionally.

Gender stereotypes occur when you apply generic attributes, opinions, or roles, for example, toward either gender, and these stereotypes are apparent everywhere in our society, especially in the media. Companies display ads and commercials geared toward common gender stereotypes. They portray women in housecleaning and child-rearing roles to sell cleaners and baby products; they sell beer and garden tractors to men by showing women in revealing outfits or a sweating man out in the yard working hard on his lawn. These gender stereotypes are used to sell products to people advertisers think would most often use them by showing these people in situations advertisers believe they would most likely be in. Table 9–2 provides an

TABLE 9–2

Stereotypes	
Stereotypes Associated with Females	**Stereotypes Associated with Males**
Submissive	Aggressive
Emotional	Unemotional
Quiet	Loud
Neat/clean	Messy
Clumsy	Athletic
Artsy	Math- and science-oriented
Domestically oriented	Leadership-oriented
Child-rearing-oriented	Moneymaking-oriented
Weak	Brutish

example of typical stereotypes of males and females. Reflecting on the table contents, ask yourself how often you are guilty of stereotyping. Do you think gender stereotyping is common in policing?

Normative Theory

Normative theory, as advocated in the classical work of Professor Thomas Pettigrew, contends that prejudice and discrimination are influenced by societal norms and are found in situations that serve to encourage or discourage tolerance or intolerance of minority groups.[65] Social norms provide the generally shared rules of what is acceptable and nonacceptable behavior; thus, by learning and accepting the prevailing prejudices or discriminatory practices, the individual is conforming to those norms. In essence, the normative theory contends that there is a direct relationship between the degree of conformity and the degree of prejudice and discrimination. There is research that supports this view. For example, Professor Thomas Pettigrew found that Southerners in the 1950s became less prejudiced against blacks when they interacted with them in the U.S. Army, where the social norms were less prejudicial.[66] Similarly, Professor Jeanne Watson's classical study found that people moving into an anti-Semitic neighborhood in New York City became more anti-Semitic.[67] Explicit normative theories of prejudice and discrimination are not advocated frequently today; however, based on past research, these explanations are in part conducive to, if not directly related to, discrimination.[68]

DISCRIMINATION IN CONTEXT

In analyzing discrimination (as exhibited in prejudice and racism) from an organizational approach, sociologists have delineated a structural perspective, based on the racial and ethnic dominance that exists in and is reproduced by systems through the formulation and application of rules, laws, regulations, and, ultimately, access and allocation of resources. These practices are a process because structures and ideologies do not exist outside the everyday practices through which they are created and confirmed. These practices both adapt and contribute to changing social, economic, and political conditions in society.[69]

There are a number of historical dynamics that have contributed to both racial and sexual discrimination in hiring and promotional practices in law enforcement; these dynamics must be analyzed at both the macro and micro levels of cultural properties of discriminatory practices within the policing system. Based on anecdotal accounts from white police officers, it appears that there is a lack of understanding and education regarding power and privilege in the United States. In this regard, we take into account the constraining impact of entrenched ideas and practices within each policing agency while also acknowledging that each organization is itself continually construed based on everyday life.[70]

Macro Level

Investigating the organization of policing at the macro level of sociological reality, we argue that it is composed of aggregates of micro situations. Yet traditional sociological approaches have defined macro structures as more or less independent of the practices in daily life; instead, discriminatory practices are defined as systemic structural inequalities created and re-created through historical policies indicative of routine cultural practices. From a micro point of view, specific practices—whether their consequences are intentional or unintentional—can be evaluated in terms of racism only when they are consistent with our knowledge of existing macro structures of racial inequality in the system. In other words, structures of racism do not exist external to agents; they are made by agents, but specific practices are (by definition) racist only when they activate existing structural racial inequalities in the system.[71]

Micro Level

At the micro level, discriminatory practices as group power exist only because they are created and perpetuated by the individuals within the group. In this regard, the domination of African Americans and women in law enforcement could be compared to systemic domination. Hence, it is at the individual level that cultural stereotypical views of both African Americans and women as "the other" evolve into patterns of treatment within an organization as a whole and that dominance is reproduced. Thus, whites within these systems can dominate African Americans and women without necessarily being aware that their cultural "blinders" are transformed into organizational practices; then these practices are structured in the interest of maintaining group power rather than being inclusive.[72]

Racial and ethnic domination can be implemented as interlocking forces of oppression and repression, coordinated and unified. These interlocking forces represent, at the same time, micro and macro dimensions of racism. From a micro point of view, oppression can be implemented as structures of racial and ethnic inequalities through situated practices. These inequalities can only be maintained when other forces operate to secure compliance and to prevent, manage, or break oppression. Seen from this point of view, the macro structures of domination are contextualized in racial ideologies implicitly or explicitly. Uniformity of oppressive and repressive practices is coordinated ideologically through socialization and the constant actualization (through the media and other channels of communication) of images, opinions, and versions of reality legitimizing the status quo of groups. The firm interlocking of forces of domination operates in a way that makes it difficult to escape the impact of these forces on everyday life.[73]

There have been many major structural and ideological forces that have operated to relegate African Americans and women to a secondary status in the field of law enforcement. This status is rooted in the historical treatment and perceptions of these two groups in the United States. We see a conceptual framework that views racism and discriminatory practices as a matter of extensive everyday experiences that are institutionalized and systemic across all institutions. These systemic practices are centuries old and encompass widespread discriminatory practices targeting women, African Americans, and other Americans of color. These ideologies and attitudes generate an underlying grid of discriminatory practices through social in-groups, networks, and institutions.[74] For discriminatory practices to occur systemically, there must be attitudes and ideological rationalizations that stimulate and legitimize discriminatory practices over the short and long term. Sociologist Howard Becker's "Outsiders" contextualize discriminatory practices when stereotypes are utilized as measures of performance, a practice which can ultimately become a self-fulfilling prophecy.[75]

Self-fulfilling prophecy is a phenomenon in which people's expectations about future events lead them to behave in particular ways that, on occasion, can cause the expected events to occur. People tend to find what they are looking for; more than that, they may even tend to unwittingly create what they seek. For example, prejudice is the belief that other people are less capable than we are. If we are managers and we think other people are less capable, then we will establish a management policy that reflects that belief. Through employee turnover and self-fulfilling prophecy, our opinion will be proven right.

AFFIRMATIVE ACTION

One of the remedies to correct past gender and racial discrimination, as well as an effective way to increase the number of women and minority police officers, is **affirmative action.** In 1965 President Lyndon Johnson, in Executive Order 11246, required federal contractors to take affirmative action to ensure that applicants are employed without regard to race, creed, color, or national origin. In 1967, Executive Order 11246 was amended to include affirmative action requirements to benefit women. Affirmative action programs seek to remedy past discrimination against minorities, women, and others by increasing the recruitment, promotion, retention, and on-the-job training opportunities in employment and by removing barriers to admission to educational institutions. Because of the long history of discrimination based on race and gender, affirmative action programs have been directed toward improving employment and educational opportunities for minorities and women.

Affirmative action strategies include expanding the pool of job applicants through recruitment strategies that reach outside the traditional channels, such as posting job notices in places where women and minorities are more likely to see them. In employment, affirmative action programs also have sought to increase on-the-job training opportunities that are related to job mobility within workplaces.

In some cases in which discriminatory actions on the part of an employer have been found to exist, a **consent decree,** which is an agreement between involved parties submitted in writing to a court, is negotiated. Once approved by the judge, it becomes legally binding. Since the parties worked out the details of the agreement, it is final and cannot be appealed. Consent decrees are often granted when the government has sued in order to have a corporation comply with the law, and the government may agree not to pursue criminal penalties in return for the corporation's agreement to a consent decree.

The Los Angeles Police Department recently entered into a consent decree with the U.S. Department of Justice (DOJ), which stipulated that 25 percent of all incoming sworn employees were to be women. The strategy was to continue until the LAPD stabilized the number of women police officers at 20 percent.[76]

Also in the city of Los Angeles, following the discovery and disclosure of the Rampart corruption incident by the LAPD, the U.S. Department of Justice notified the city that it intended to file a civil suit alleging that the LAPD was engaging in a pattern or practice of excessive force, false arrests, and unreasonable searches and seizures. Subsequently the LAPD entered into a consent decree. Whenever the DOJ has reasonable cause to believe such violations have occurred, it may obtain a court order to eliminate the pattern or practice.[77] The consent decree in the LAPD is intended to promote police integrity within the department and to prevent conduct that deprives individuals of any rights, privileges, or immunities protected by the Constitution of the United States.

The Department of Justice's consent decree with the city of Los Angeles places emphasis on the following nine major areas[78]:

1. Management and supervisory measures to promote civil rights integrity
2. Critical incident procedures, documentation, investigation, and review
3. Management of Gang Units
4. Management of confidential informants
5. Program development for response to persons with mental illness
6. Training
7. Integrity audits
8. Operations of the Police Commission and Inspector General
9. Community outreach and public information

In a landmark case involving the University of Michigan's affirmative action policies (one of the most important rulings on this issue in 25 years), the Supreme Court decisively upheld the right of affirmative action in higher education.[79] In the Michigan case, the Supreme Court ruled that although affirmative action was no longer justified as a way of redressing past oppression and injustice, it promoted a compelling state interest in diversity at all levels of society.

In recent years, affirmative action programs have become controversial. Some think that American society has made great strides in the elimination of discrimination and that minorities and women now have equal opportunities in the workplace. Some critics argue that both employment decisions and promotion decisions that are made based on race violate the 1964 Civil Rights Act; these critics base their opposition to affirmative action on reverse discrimination, the topic of the next section.

REVERSE DISCRIMINATION

Lawsuits based on **reverse discrimination,** which is used to describe policies or habits of social discrimination against members of a historically dominant group (with an implication of unfairness), are a relatively new phenomenon that police management has to be concerned with. Consider that seven Dallas police officers are suing the city for reverse discrimination. The officers claim they were denied transfers or promotions because they are white or do not speak Spanish, and they accuse the Dallas police of promoting less qualified minority officers. Each officer is seeking $1 million in damages.[80]

Two former white police officers in Inglewood, California, were awarded $2.4 million as the result of a reverse discrimination suit. The award came after the two police officers were disciplined by the city for the (videotaped) rough arrest of a handcuffed black teenage youth at a gas station. A superior court civil jury voted 11-1 to award one of the officers $1.6 million, finding that the fired white officer was treated more harshly than a black colleague who allegedly hit the 16-year-old youth with a flashlight. The jury found that because of the white officer's race, he had suffered an adverse employment decision. The officer had been tried twice in criminal court, but neither jury could reach a unanimous decision. The officer claimed that he reacted when the suspect grabbed the officer's testicles, something a bystander's videotape of the encounter did not capture. Prosecutors eventually dismissed the felony case. The same civil panel awarded $811,000 to the officer's former white partner; he had been suspended for 10 days for his role in the encounter with the black teenager.[81]

In Charlotte, North Carolina, a U.S. District Court awarded nine white police officers $3,000 each for mental and emotional distress; the officers said less qualified black officers were promoted to sergeant. The city is appealing the ruling, stating that the officers aren't entitled to damages because they would not have been promoted anyway. The reverse discrimination suit stems from a U.S. District Court ruling that ordered Charlotte to stop using race as a factor when making sergeant promotions.[82]

Reverse discrimination suits can arise under either Title VII or the Fourteenth Amendment to the U.S. Constitution, which basically provide that no state can deny equal protection of its laws to its citizens. The suits may also arise under the equal protection clauses of state constitutions that bar preferential treatment of certain individuals or groups based on categories such as race, sex, color, and ethnicity. Reverse discrimination suits are usually treated as an equal protection issue.[83] Under reverse discrimination, if an employee is not getting the same benefits that another employee in another group is getting on the basis of his or her race or gender, then the deprived employee has been discriminated against.

▲ SUMMARY

The entry of minorities and women into police organizations has evolved slowly. The 1960s was a time of great changes aided by various crime commissions, such as the President's Commission on Law Enforcement and Administration of Justice, which recommended that the numbers of both women and minority police officers be increased. The commissions of the 1960s (and later) advocated that women and minorities be given the same opportunities as white male police officers.

Federal laws, such as Title VII of the Civil Rights of 1964 and the Equal Employment Act, were passed to eliminate discrimination in America. The federal laws not only applied to the private sector in the United States but also applied to local and state police agencies. Women and minorities have filed class action suits, which have assisted in eliminating discrimination in police forces. Although discrimination against women and African Americans in police agencies has not been completely eliminated, it must be recognized that some improvements have been made. We submit that the lowering of discrimination may be attributed to presidential executive orders, various governmental commissions, federal legislation, and court decisions.

Affirmative action levels the playing field so that women and people of color have the chance to compete in education and in business. Despite the enormous gains made in civil rights, women and people of color still face unfair obstacles in business and education. Police organizations should establish affirmative action policies to recruit and advance qualified minorities and women.

Recently there has been a considerable backlash against affirmative action; as a result, many in the majority class have begun to file reverse discrimination lawsuits. "Reverse discrimination" is a term that describes policies or habits of social discrimination against members of a historically dominant group, with an implication of unfairness. Sometimes reverse discrimination can result from policies created to decrease discrimination against minority employees.

Regardless of which group or class of people is in the minority, police departments should not practice discrimination because it has no place in law enforcement. The mission of police agencies is to be enforcers of the law, not violators of the law. Police agencies should have a reputation of integrity and trustworthiness and should operate as an equal opportunity employer. The police organization of the 21st century should set an example of decency and civility. If the police in the 21st century can be that kind of example, then they will do something that police agencies preceding them were unable to accomplish.

QUESTIONS IN REVIEW

1. Discuss the role of women in early American police departments.
2. Identify and describe factors that were crucial for women to begin to make advances in policing.
3. Why should police departments make an effort to recruit and retain women and minority police officers?
4. List and discuss some of the theoretical explanations for discrimination.
5. Explain the role of minorities in early American police departments.
6. Do you think affirmative action programs in police departments are still viable to ensure adequate representation of minorities and women? Why or why not?

POLICE RESOURCES ON THE WEB

Hispanic American Police Command Officers Association
http://www.hapcoa.org/index.php

Hispanic National Law Enforcement Association
http://www.angelfire.com/md2/hnlea/index.html

International Association of Women Police
http://www.iawp.org

National Asian Peace Officers Association
http://www.napoa.org

National Black Police Association
http://www.blackpolice.org

National Center for Women and Policing
http://www.womenandpolicing.org/ncwpadvbd.html

National Native American Law Enforcement Association
http://www.nnalea.org/links.htm

National Organization of Black Law Enforcement Executives
http://www.noblenational.org/program_grants.htm

U.S. Equal Employment Opportunity Commission
http://www.eeoc.gov

REFERENCES

1. M.J. PALMIOTTO, *Policing: Concepts, Strategies, and Current Issues in American police Forces* (Durham, NC: Carolina Academic Press, 1997), pp. 227–245.

2. S.E. MARTIN, "Women Officers on the Move: An Update on Women in Policing," in *Critical Issues in Policing*, 3rd ed., ed. R.G. Dunham and G.P. Alpert (Prospects Heights, IL: Waveland Press, 1997), pp. 363–384.

3. J. APPIER, "Preventive Justice: The Campaign for Women Police, 1910–1940," *Women and Criminal Justice* 4, no. 1 (1992): 3–9.

4. Ibid., p. 3.

5. PETER HORNE, *Women in Law Enforcement*, 2nd ed. (Springfield, IL: Charles C. Thomas Publisher, 1980).

6. Ibid.

7. HARRY W. MORE, *Special Topics in Policing*, 2nd ed. (Cincinnati, OH: Anderson Publishing Co., 1998), pp. 117–147.

8. J. ZHAO, L. HERBST, and N. NICOLAS, "Race, Ethnicity and the Female Cop: Differential Patterns of Representation," *Journal of Urban Affairs* 23, no. 3 (2001): 243–257.

9. "Future of Women in Policing," *The Police Chief* (March 1999): 53–54.

10. STEVE HYMON, "Glendale Settles Suits," *Los Angels Times* November 15, 2004, part B, p. 3.

11. JOSEPH POLISAR and DONA MILGRAM, "Recruiting Women Police Officers: Strategies That Work," *The Police Chief* (October 1988): 42–53.

12. The United States Equal Employment Opportunity Commission, "Title VII of the Civil Rights Act." Web posted at: http://www.eeoc.gov/policy/vii.html. Accessed March 3, 2005.

13. K.A. LONSWAY, "Dismantling the Warrior Image," *Community Links*, September 2001, pp. 31–33.

14. Ibid., p. 16.

15. MICHAEL L. BIRZER and DELORES E. CRAIG, "Gender Differences in Police Physical Selection Methodologies," *American Journal of Police* 15, no. 2 (1996): 93–108.

16. "IACP Study Identifies Obstacles, Defines Strategies, the Future of Women in Policing: Mandates for Action," *The Police Chief* (March 1999): 53.

17. THE PRESIDENT'S COMMISSION ON LAW ENFORCEMENT AND ADMINISTRATION OF JUSTICE, *Task Force Report: The Police* (Washington, DC: GPO, 1967), p. 167.

18. Ibid, p. 168.

19. PALMIOTTO, 1997, p. 230.

20. Ibid.

21. RALPH KNOOHUIZEN and RICHARD GUTMAN, *Women in Police Work in Chicago* (Chicago, IL: Chicago Law Enforcement Study Group, 1974), p. 15.

22. LONSWAY, 2001, p. 111.

23. BELINDA CRAWFORD SEAGRAM and CONNIE STARK-ADAMS, "Women in Canadian Urban Policing: Why Are They Leaving?" *The Police Chief* (October 1992): 120–127.

24. MORE, 1998, p. 127.

25. K.G. HICKMAN, "Measuring Job Performance Success for Female Officers of the Los Angeles Police Department," Unpublished Doctoral Dissertation, Claremont Graduate School, 1983.

26. K.A. LONSWAY, "Police Women and the Use of Force," *Law and Order* 49, no. 7 (July 2001): 109–114.

27. D. PRUSSEL and K.A. LONSWAY, "Recruiting Women Police Officers," *Law and Order* 49, no. 7 (July 2001): 91–96.

28. J. BALKIN, "Why Policemen Don't Like Policewomen," *Journal of Police Science and Administration* 16, no. 1 (1988): 29–38.

29. Ibid., 37.

30. BARBARA RAFFEL PRICE, "Female Police Officers in the United States," National Criminal Justice Resources Center, 1996. Web posted at http://www. ncjrs.org/policing/fem635.html. Accessed March 5, 2005.

31. BARBARA RAFFEL PRICE, "A Study of Leadership Strength of Female Police Executives," *Journal of Police Science and Administration* 2, no. 2 (1974): 219–226.

32. W.W. BENNETT and K.M. HESS, *Management and Supervision in Law Enforcement*, 3rd ed. (Belmont, CA: Wadsworth Publishing Co., 2001), p. 205.

33. BARBARA RAFFEL PRICE, "Female Police Officers in the United States," National Criminal Justice Resources Center, 1996. Web posted at http://www. ncjrs.org/policing/fem635.html. Accessed March 5, 2005.

34. Ibid.

35. DAVID E. BARLOW and MELISSA HICKMAN BARLOW, *Police in a Multicultural Society: An American Story* (Prospect Heights, IL: Waveland Press, 2000), p. 206.

36. Ibid., p. 206.

37. SAMUEL WALKER, *Popular Justice: A History of American Criminal Justice*, 2nd ed. (New York: Oxford University Press, 1998).

38. W. MARVIN DULANEY, *Black Police in America* (Bloomington, Indiana: University Press, 1996), pp. 8–10.

39. Ibid., p. 4.

40. BARLOW and HICKMAN BARLOW, 2000, p. 23.

41. Ibid.

42. W. MARVIN DULANEY, 1996, pp. 1–13.

43. Ibid., p. 15.

44. Ibid. pp. 18–19.

45. THE PRESIDENT'S COMMISSION ON LAW ENFORCEMENT AND ADMINISTRATION OF JUSTICE, *Task Force Report: The Police* (Washington, DC: GPO, 1967), p. 168.

46. NATIONAL ADVISORY COMMISSION ON CRIMINAL JUSTICE STANDARDS AND GOALS *Police* (Washington, DC: GPO, 1973), pp. 121–124.

47. PALMIOTTO, 1997, pp. 240–241.

48. SAMUEL WALKER, "Employment of Black and Hispanic Police Officers," *Review of Applied Urban Research*, 11, no. 6 (October 1983): 17–23.

49. PAUL GLASTRIES, "The Thin White Line," *U.S. News and World Report*, 117, no. 7 (August 15, 1994): 241–244.

50. BUREAU OF JUSTICE STATISTICS, *Local Police Departments, 2000* (Washington, DC: U.S. Department of Justice 2001).

51. PHILLIP WHITE, "Gay Police Officer Back at Work," *New York Times* late edition, August 14, 1993, p. 6.

52. MARY BERNSTEIN and CONSTANCE KOSTELAC, "Lavender and Blue," *Journal of Contemporary Criminal Justice* 18, no. 3 (August 2002): 302–328.

53. ROBERT M. SHUSTA, DEENA R. LEVINE, PHILLIP R. HARRIS, and HERBERT Z. WONG, *Multicultural Law Enforcement* (Upper Saddle River, NJ: Prentice Hall, 2002).

54. STOPHEN H. LEINEN, *Gay Cops* (New Brunswick, NJ: Rutgers University Press, 1993).

55. Ibid., p. 8.

56. Ibid.

57. The Associated Press State and Local Wire, "Jury Orders LAPD to Pay $3.5 Million in Discrimination Suit." Accessed online December 8, 2004 at lexis-nexis.com.

58. SYLVIA P. FLANAGAN, "192 Minority Police Officers File Suit in Chicago Alleging Bias in Sergeants Examination," *Jet* 86, no. 23 (1994): 19–21.

59. NANCY EGAN, "Hartford Takes Another Crack at Cultural-Sensitivity Training," *Law Enforcement News* 30, no. 625 (2004): 1.

60. BRUCE FRANKEL, "Black Agent Files Discrimination Law Suit Against Secret Service," *People Weekly* 53, no. 20 (May 22, 2000): 163–164.

61. KENNETH BOLTON JR. and JOE R. FEAGIN, *Black and Blue* (New York: Routledge, 2004).

62. SUSAN E. MARTIN, "Policewomen and Policewomen: Occupational Role Dilemmas and Choices of Female Officers," *Journal of Police Science and Administration* 7, no. 3 (1979): 314–323.

63. BRUNO BETTELHAM and MORRIS JANOWITZ, *Social Change and Prejudice* (New York: Free Press, 1964).

64. THOMAS.W. ADORNO, EDWARD FRENKEL-BRUNSWIK, DANIEL J. LEVINSON, and R.N. STANFORD, *The Authoritarian Personality* (New York: Wiley, 1950).

65. THOMAS T. PETTIGREW, "Personality and Socio-cultural Factors in Intergroup Attitudes: A Cross National Comparison," *Journal of Conflict Resolution* 2 (March 1958): 29–42.

66. THOMAS T. PETTIGREW, "Regional Differences in Anti-Negro Prejudice," *Journal of Abnormal and Social Psychology* 59 (July 1959): 28–36.

67. JEANNE WATSON, "Some Social and Psychological Situations Related to Change in Attitude," *Human Relations* 3 (1950): 15–56.

68. MICHAEL L. BIRZER and RICHARD B. ELLIS, "Perceived Discrimination in Topeka, Kansas," *Free Inquiry in Creative Sociology* 31, no. 2 (2003): 133–142.

69. BOLTON JR. and FEAGIN, 2004, p. 213.

70. YOLANDA ST. JEAN and JOE R. FEAGIN, *Double Burden: Black Women and Everyday Racism* (New York: Armonk, 1998).

71. K.A. MYERS and PASSION WILLIAMSON, "Race Talk: The Perpetuation of Racism Through Private Discourse," *Race and Society* 4 (2001): 3–26.

72. BOLTON JR., and FEAGIN, 2004, p. 214.

73. Ibid.

74. LAWRENCE D. BOBO, "Inequalities That Endure? Racial Ideology, American Politics, and the Peculiar Role of the Social Sciences." Paper presented at conference; The Changing Terrain of Race and Ethnicity, University of Illinois, Chicago, October 26, 2001.

75. HOWARD S. BECKER, *Outsiders* (New York: Free Press, 1962), pp. 47–50.

76. GEORGE T. FELKENES and JEAN R. SCHROEDEL, "A Case Study of Minority Women in Policing," *Women and Criminal Justice* 4, no. 2 (1993): 65–89.

77. Los Angeles Police Department Consent Decree, November 2, 2000. Web posted at http://www.lapdonline.org/inside_lapd/cd/consent_decree.htm. Accessed March 3, 2005.

78. Ibid.

79. *Grutter* v. *Bollinger*, 539 U.S. 306, 156 L. Ed. 2d 304, 123 S. Ct. 2325 (2003)

80. CBS The Morning Show, Dallas Police Officers Suing for Reverse Discrimination, *CBS, The Morning Show*, July 7, 2004. Web posted at http://web.lexis-nexis.com/universe/document. Accessed March 5, 2005.

81. HECTOR BECERRA, "Case May Haunt Cities: A $1.6-Million Jury Award for an Inglewood Officer Fired over a Taped Beating Could Lead to Reluctance to Discipline Officers, Experts Say," *Los Angeles Times*, Part B, June 12, 2004, p. 1.

82. JOE CAMPBELL, "Ruling Appealed in Officers' Reverse-Discrimination Case," *Greensboro News & Record*, February 12, 1995, p. B2. Web posted at http://infoweb.newsbank.com. Accessed March 2, 2005.

83. GEORGE RIVAS, "The Reverse Discrimination Trap," *Employment Digest*, June 3, 2003. Web posted at http://www.xtremerecruiting.org/blog/archives/ss/000110.html. Accessed on March 2, 2005.

Police Operations

Key Terms

Aircraft patrol
Automated Fingerprint
　Identification System (AFIS)
Bicycle patrol
Detective
Differential police response
Directed patrol
DNA
Follow-up investigation

Foot patrol
Hot spots
Motorcycle patrol
Motorized patrol
Mounted horse patrol
Patrol
Preliminary investigation
Specialization
Water/marine patrol

Outline

Introduction
Patrol Function
Patrol Officers
Patrol Methods
Patrol Deployment

Traffic Function
Detective Operations
Specialized Functions
Developments in Police
　Operations

Learning Objectives

After reading this chapter, you should be able to:

1. List and discuss the occupational tasks specific to police patrol.
2. Explain the police patrol officer job.
3. Identify and discuss the methods of police patrol.
4. Describe differential response and directed police patrol strategies.

5. Discuss the duties of the traffic officer.
6. Discuss the evolution of the modern detective.
7. Describe the general duties of detectives.
8. Discuss what studies have discovered regarding the general effectiveness of detectives.
9. List and discuss developments in police operations.
10. Identify specialized police operational functions.

INTRODUCTION

Many years ago police reformer O. W. Wilson wrote that the patrol force is the backbone of the police department.[1] In the 21st century, this assumption has not changed; if anything, police patrol has become more and more the focal point of police operations. In fact, with the evolving community policing strategy that is taking shape across American communities, the roles and functions of police patrol are increasingly becoming more complex and challenging.[2] Within a police organization, **patrol** is usually the largest police division and is responsible for performing the primary police mission; police patrol operations cover 24 hours a day, 7 days a week. In essence, the police patrol function is one of the few government agencies that you can call 24 hours a day and almost be assured of a response.

One other part of police operations is the investigation function. As you probably know (after reading this far in the textbook), the job of a police investigator, or **detective,** is primarily to investigate crimes. According to Wilson, the basic purpose of the detective function is not only to investigate crimes but also to gain enough information to arrest and convict the perpetrator and to recover stolen property.[3]

Many of our impressions of the American police detective have been shaped by television. For example, you may remember the long-running detective television series *Columbo*. Columbo, a detective lieutenant, was a shabby and apparently slow-witted police detective, although (as criminals always eventually learned), appearances can be deceiving. Columbo solved his cases through close attention to tiny inconsistencies in suspects' stories, hounding them until they confessed. Columbo's signature technique was to start exiting the scene of an interview, invariably stopping in the doorway to say "Just one more thing" and then posing a question to a suspect that always brought to light the key inconsistency.

Detectives, like patrol officers, are considered an operations or frontline component of the department. In many police departments, the patrol and investigation divisions share many of the investigative functions. For example, patrol officers are usually given the responsibility to conduct preliminary investigations of crimes; then detectives carry out a follow-up investigation at some later time. A **preliminary investigation** starts when the patrol officers try to find out who was involved in the incident, what happened, why the incident occurred, when the incident happened, where the incident occurred, and how the incident occurred. The **follow-up investigation** begins when the case is assigned to a detective after patrol has conducted its preliminary investigation, and during the follow-up investigation, detectives usually contact witnesses and victims regarding the case, with the goal of identifying a suspect or uncovering evidence that will be used to later secure the guilt of the suspect.

In this chapter, we examine police operations. Our coverage will mostly focus on those units with duties performed in operations or with frontline services delivered to the community. These units primarily include patrol and investigative functions.

PATROL FUNCTION

As you will recall from the discussion of community-oriented policing in Chapter 3, police departments became highly reactive under the traditional model of policing. Patrol was traditionally performed by officers assigned to specific geographical areas for the purpose of maintaining a mobile (usually visible) police presence. Law enforcement responded to calls for service from citizens and focused primarily on arresting offenders after crimes had been committed. Under the axiom of community policing, police patrol operations focus not only on enforcement activities but also on crime prevention while addressing the root causes of crime and disorder. The community actively engages in collaborating on crime prevention and problem-solving activities, with the goal of reducing victimization and fear of crime.

With the challenges that community policing presents, police patrol operations will not only have to adapt to new strategies required for successful community policing, but since the 9-11 terrorist attacks, they must also use strategies that deal effectively with the threat of terrorism (these strategies are discussed in detail in Chapter 13). The fact of the matter is that police patrol operations are very complex and demanding, and the uniformed men and women patrolling our communities have an awesome responsibility.

Police patrol officers keep order in their communities, make sure that people follow laws, and protect people and property. They patrol areas by walking or riding through them, some officers riding horses or bikes. While on patrol, officers watch for signs of criminal activity and talk to residents and businesspeople, trying to build relationships in their community. Officers are also called to respond to accidents, crimes in progress, fights, and other events. Officers evaluate the information they receive and determine the best way to respond.

Uniformed police officers make up the majority of the police patrol. Those who work in municipal police departments of various sizes, in small communities, and in rural areas have general law enforcement duties including maintaining regular patrols and responding to calls for service. They may direct traffic at the scene of a fire, investigate a burglary, or give first aid to an accident victim. In large police departments, officers usually are assigned to a specific type of duty. As discussed throughout this book, many urban police agencies are becoming more involved in community policing, a practice in which an officer builds relationships with the citizens of local neighborhoods and mobilizes the public to help fight crime.

The word "patrol" in early English meant to "walk or paddle in muddy water." There are several versions of how the word became associated with law enforcement. One popular version is that the police are "walking in muddy water" when they patrol the community looking for the dirty (criminal) aspects of its citizens. Patrolling is the most visible part of police work, and many of our opinions of the quality of the local police department are based on our observations of police patrols in the community.

As previously pointed out, the largest and most visible component of any municipal law enforcement agency is the patrol section. It consists of officers working in uniform 24 hours a day, 365 days a year. They handle calls for service from the public in motor vehicles, on horseback, or on foot. Patrol is the heart of the police mission.[4] Although all aspects of the police organization have the responsibility of meeting the organization's mission, patrol usually takes the lead in this effort due to its size and visibility.

An integral part of the patrol function is the response to noncriminal calls for service. Depending on community expectations, noncriminal calls for service range from conducting vacant home checks while homeowners are on vacation to contacting homebound senior citizens daily to see if they are in need of assistance. Police will often respond to medical aid calls even if paramedic assistance is available, and traffic control for churches as well as security for high school sporting events and dances may be provided. However, with decreasing budgets and resources, it has become necessary for law enforcement to reevaluate the role of patrol and streamline its functions in order to concentrate on its primary mission.

Police officers in Lawrence, Kansas conducting a sobriety checkpoint.

Photo courtesy of Kansas Highway Patrol

Generally the major activities of police patrol involve law enforcement issues. Studies indicate, however, that the police officer on patrol averages less than one felony arrest a week. Most experts now agree that the great majority of police patrol activities are devoted to order maintenance or peacekeeping.

Studies indicate that the average patrol time is divided into four parts[5]:

1. *Calls for service (25 percent)*. This refers to the percentage of time the officer assigned to patrol spends answering or responding to requests from citizens for help.
2. *Preventive patrol (40 percent)*. This is the percentage of time the officer spends on patrol while attempting to prevent crime.
3. *Officer-initiated activities (15 percent)*. This means the percentage of time the officer is actively involved in officer-initiated activities, such as stopping and talking to juveniles in the area.
4. *Administrative tasks (20 percent)*. This is the time the officer spends completing reports and other doing administrative tasks.

PATROL OFFICERS

Patrol officers maintain order in society by enforcing laws and ordinances. Their duties vary, depending on what level of police work they are involved in. Those working as city police or county law enforcement officials direct traffic, issue traffic tickets, and apprehend, arrest, and process prisoners. Most patrol officers spend a great deal of their time patrolling the area they are assigned to, normally in a police car. While patrolling, they monitor any activity in the area and look into any activity that seems out of the ordinary or that is a violation of the law. When they receive calls from citizens about a disturbance, they must respond promptly and try to resolve the problem. In these situations, they often inform or recommend to citizens those available services that might provide a longer-term solution to the problem; for example, they might recommend that a couple who are arguing seek marital counseling.

As we pointed out in the introduction to this chapter, the job of a police officer in the 21st century can be complex yet enjoyable and rewarding. Police officers are expected to do extraordinary things in what can be very chaotic and at times dangerous situations. Police officers may spend hours with little or no activity and then suddenly and without warning have to face an armed robbery in progress, a suspect with a gun, a death scene, a serious traffic accident, or a child abuse situation. The following list of occupational tasks is specific to patrol officers[6]:

- Patrol areas on foot, horses, or bikes or in vehicles.
- Evaluate requests for service to determine how to respond.
- Arrest people who break laws.
- Monitor traffic to make sure motorists obey laws.
- Write citations or tickets for drivers who violate traffic laws.

- Investigate traffic accidents to determine which drivers are at fault.
- Photograph or draw diagrams of crime or accident scenes.
- Interview witnesses to gather more information.
- Give first aid to people who are injured.
- Review facts to determine if criminal acts were committed.
- Prepare reports about accidents and arrests.
- Direct traffic flow and reroute traffic in case of emergencies.
- Testify in court to present evidence.

Police officers who work the busy sections of their patrol beats are expected to be familiar with businesses, schools, and habits of individuals. In the late 1960s, a university research team reported a list of essential behavioral requirements that a patrol officer must possess to be successful, and this listing is as valid in the 21st century as it was in the 1960s. According to the university research team, a patrol officer must do the following[7]:

1. Endure long periods of monotony in routine patrol yet react effectively (and almost instantaneously) to problem situations observed on the street or to orders issued by the radio dispatcher (in much the same way that a combat pilot must react to interception or a target opportunity).
2. Gain knowledge of his or her patrol area, not only of its physical characteristics but also of its normal routine of events and the usual behavior patterns of its residents.
3. Exhibit initiative, problem-solving capacity, effective judgment, and imagination in coping with the numerous complex situations he or she is called on to face, such as a family disturbance, a potential suicide, a robbery in progress, an accident, or a disaster. Police officers themselves clearly recognize this requirement and refer to it as "showing street sense."
4. Make prompt and effective decisions, sometimes in life-and-death situations, and be able to size up a situation quickly and take appropriate action.
5. Demonstrate mature judgment, as in deciding whether an arrest is warranted by the circumstances or a warning is sufficient or in facing a situation where the use of force may be needed.
6. Demonstrate critical awareness in discerning signs of out-of-the-ordinary conditions or circumstances that indicate trouble or a crime in progress.
7. Exhibit a number of complex psychomotor skills, such as driving a vehicle in normal and emergency situations; firing a weapon accurately under extremely varied conditions; maintaining agility, endurance, and strength; and showing facility in self-defense and apprehension, as in taking a person into custody with a minimum of force.
8. Adequately perform the communication and record-keeping functions of the job, including oral reports, preparation of formal case reports, and completion of departmental and court forms.
9. Have the facility to act effectively in extremely divergent interpersonal situations. A patrol officer constantly confronts persons who are acting in violation of the law; these people range from curfew violators to felons. He or she is constantly confronted by people who are in trouble or who are victims of crimes. Besides these dealings with criminals, he or she has contact with

Image unavailable

para-criminals, informers, and people on the border of criminal behavior and must also be streetwise. At the same time, the patrol officer must relate to the people on his or her beat—businesspeople, residents, school officials, visitors, etc. Interpersonal relationships must range up and down a continuum defined by friendliness and persuasion on one end and by fairness and force at the other.

10. Endure verbal and physical abuse from citizens and offenders (as when placing a person under arrest or when facing day-in, day-out race prejudice) while using only necessary force in the performance of the patrol function.

11. Exhibit a professional, self-assured presence and a self-confident manner when dealing with offenders, the public, and the courts.

12. Be capable of restoring equilibrium to social groups, such as restoring order in a family fight, in a disagreement between neighbors, or in a clash between rival groups of youths.

13. Be skillful in questioning suspected offenders, victims, and witnesses of crimes.

14. Take charge of situations (such as a crime or accident scene) yet not unduly alienate participants or bystanders.

15. Be flexible enough to work either under loose supervision, as in most day-to-day patrol activities (either alone or as part of a two-man team), or under the direct supervision of supervisors, as in situations where large numbers of officers are required.

16. Tolerate stress in a multitude of forms, such as dealing with the violent behavior of a mob, rousing people in a burning building, coping with the pressure of a high-speed chase or a weapon being fired at him or her, or dealing with a woman bearing a child.

17. Exhibit personal courage in the face of dangerous situations that may result in serious injury or death.

18. Maintain objectivity while dealing with a host of special-interest groups, ranging from relatives of offenders to members of the press.

19. Maintain a balanced perspective in the face of constant exposure to the worst side of human nature.

20. Exhibit a high level of personal integrity and ethical conduct (for example, refraining from accepting bribes or favors and providing impartial law enforcement).

Do you think police operations have changed all that much from the activities police performed 20, 30, or even 50 years ago? Some police writers say no. According to Professor Samuel Walker, the basic purposes of police patrol have not changed since 1829: deterrence of crime, maintenance of a feeling of public security, and 24-hour availability for service to the public.[8]

PATROL METHODS

In order to effectively take care of and protect communities, police departments utilize many different types of patrol. In the next few sections, we examine the various types of patrol that are used in American police departments.

Motorized Patrol

Motorized patrol is by far the most commonly used type of police patrol. The use of the patrol car dates back to the 1930s when police reformer O. W. Wilson advocated replacing foot patrols with motor vehicle patrols because, Wilson reasoned, patrol cars create a sense that the police are omnipresent in the community, present a way of responding to calls in a more rapid manner, and allow police officers to patrol in less routine patterns. Officers in a motor vehicle can carry more emergency equipment, such as a fire extinguisher, blankets, traffic cones, and extra tactical weapons. Motorized patrol also allows police officers some protection from the elements (snow, rain, sleet, cold, and heat) while patrolling their beats.

One key advantage to automobile patrol is the cost, since patrol officers are a police department's biggest expense.[9] For example, it takes fewer officers to cover a geographical area by automobile, compared to those needed for foot patrol or bicycle patrol, because they can cover a larger area (and do it more quickly) when operating in a motor vehicle.

One-Officer/Two-Officer Patrol

Generally, a patrol vehicle occupied by one officer is more cost-efficient than one occupied by two officers, so from a cost standpoint, it is apparent that in most cases funding two officers in a vehicle is not economically practical. The debate between one-officer and two-officer patrol techniques has always taken place within law enforcement agencies. Unions or associations, which represent the field officer, tend to support two-officer patrol vehicles; however, cost-conscious police administrators have generally favored the single-officer patrol vehicle concept.

Unions present the issue of officer safety in their argument, with the contention that two officers riding together will provide immediate support to each other in a crisis and that the alternative of bringing in a backup unit takes additional time and is less safe. Unions also argue that two officers can be watching for activity on both sides of the vehicle, making the patrol effort more effective.

Many police executives agree with the officer safety issue, particularly in certain cases. Some cities contain neighborhoods that are unsafe for a lone officer on patrol, and sections of some larger, older cities present a real danger to law enforcement officers. For example, Chicago, Detroit, New York, and Philadelphia have tremendous inner-city crime problems that often require two-officer vehicles. Violent criminals are less likely to assault two police officers as opposed to a single officer.

There are many police departments, however, that advocate one-officer patrol units. Criminal justice scholar Larry Nichols, writing on the subject of one-officer versus two-officer patrol units, argued that one-officer units are better than two-officer units for the following reasons[10]:

1. Reliance on a partner becomes a crutch that allows individual performance to suffer.
2. A high degree of admiration by one partner for another can cause the first officer to take unnecessary risks.
3. Resentment, jealousy, or fear of the partner can cause negative conduct by one or both partners.
4. Overzealous activity by one partner can result in the other's withdrawal and ineffectiveness.
5. One partner may cover up for another who is engaged in unethical, immoral, or possibly illegal conduct.
6. It is difficult for supervisors to give credit or blame for good or bad performance to the proper partner.
7. The productivity of a two-person unit is half that of a one-person unit while the cost of operation is almost doubled.
8. The additional costs of vehicles and their maintenance to provide one-person unit coverage are offset by the increased productivity.
9. Nine out of ten calls for police service can be effectively handled by one-person units.
10. That one call in ten requiring more than one officer almost always allows enough time for the second officer to arrive.
11. One-person units encourage each officer to become observant and subsequently less susceptible to accident or sudden attack.
12. One-person units make quicker and wiser decisions, and the officer assumes more personal responsibility for his or her actions and decisions.
13. More and better care of vehicles and equipment is seen in one-person units.
14. One-person units tend to develop more accurate and detailed investigations and stronger court cases.

Foot Patrol

You will recall that in Chapter 3 we discussed foot patrol thoroughly, so in this section we only summarize foot patrol as a police patrol method. If you desire additional information or simply wish to refresh your memory, we encourage you to return to Chapter 3.

Foot patrol is the oldest patrol method, one that has received much attention through the years yet has proven to be valid.[11] Before the advent of motor vehicle patrol, foot patrol was the single most popular method of patrol; when automobiles became the most popular method of patrol for police departments, foot patrol increasingly lost its popularity.

Foot patrol has recently been reintroduced to major population centers such as Newark, New Jersey, and Houston, Texas, which has resulted in a number of findings[12]:

1. With the presence of foot patrols in neighborhoods, fear levels decrease significantly.
2. Withdrawal of foot patrols causes fear levels to increase significantly.
3. Citizen satisfaction with police increases with the presence of foot patrols in neighborhoods.
4. Police who patrol on foot have a greater appreciation for the values of the neighborhood residents than do police in automobiles.
5. Police who patrol on foot have greater job satisfaction, less fear, and higher morale than do officers who patrol in automobiles.

You may recall from our discussion in Chapter 3 that more and more police departments are using foot patrols. A recent Department of Justice survey revealed that 62 percent of departments (including 86 percent of those serving 250,000 residents or more) routinely used foot patrol.[13]

Foot patrols are useful for special events such as parades, large community celebrations, dignitary protection, and public relations. Officers on foot can observe more than officers in vehicles can. By being on the street, an officer's senses of smell and hearing are also improved. Foot patrol officers provide an effective method of improving face-to-face communication between community residents and police officers, and this increased communication can cultivate the exchange of information needed to prevent and solve crime.[14]

Motorcycle Patrol

Motorcycle patrol has traditionally been used for traffic enforcement activities because motorcycles are agile and can be maneuvered through traffic and in areas where a vehicle could not travel. For example, let's suppose that a community has several large manufacturing plants employing thousands of people, that during shift changes the main streets and throughways around the plants have traffic tie-ups, and that there have been many incidents in which motorists have disobeyed traffic laws, resulting in an increase in traffic accidents. Motorcycle units are ideal to enforce traffic laws in this situation due to their maneuverability. Also, in the case of an auto accident, it may take a police vehicle several minutes to get through heavy traffic while a motorcycle can maneuver through the highly congested area and get to the scene of the accident more quickly.

There are some disadvantages of motorcycle units. One disadvantage is that motorcycles leave the police officer vulnerable in traffic; one accident involving a police motorcycle could injure and prematurely end the officer's career due to medical disability. Other major disadvantages of motorcycles are that they lack protection from the elements, they limit the amount of equipment that can be carried, and they cannot transport any prisoners. This last situation results in the motorcycle officer having to call for a motor vehicle unit to transport any prisoners, which ties up three officers (if the motorized unit is a two-officer unit).

Bicycle Patrol

Putting police officers on bicycles is actually a very old idea that has made a strong comeback in the past decade. Units on **bicycle patrol** provide an alternative method of patrol, and experience has shown that bike officers are an important tool in improving police-community relations because the officers are more accessible to citizens. Bike officers can provide a proactive, highly visible police service, along with giving officers a "stealth" advantage when desired. Bicycles also allow officers access to areas not normally patrolled by motorized units.

Historically, bicycle patrol can be traced back to the 19th century when it was started by the New York Police Department (over 100 years ago) in an attempt to find a less expensive alternative to the mounted horse patrol. Bicycles were less expensive than vehicles and did not have the high maintenance cost of horses. Like foot patrol, bicycle patrol was discontinued with the advent of motorized patrol. Recently, however, many police departments have returned to the use of bicycle patrol.[15] A recent report revealed that an estimated 94 percent of police departments in the United States make use of bicycle patrol.[16]

Bicycles now come in a number of styles and models that can be used in a variety of geographical areas and terrains. A few uses for bicycle patrols include patrolling college campuses, community events, areas inaccessible by motor vehicles, parks, congested downtown areas, off-road terrain, and parking lots and garages at large shopping and event centers. Furthermore, bicycle patrols are an excellent tool for use in community relations and in crime prevention and detection.

Mounted Horse Patrol

Mounted horse patrol has a long history in policing and can be traced back to the 19th century. Many police departments cannot afford horses, due to the special care that goes into stabling them and maintaining their diet and health. Mounted horse patrols are useful for patrol at large community events, for crowd control, and for traffic patrol. Horse patrol units are also excellent public relations tools; for example, during the 1990s the Sedgwick County Sheriff's Department (a medium-sized urban department located in Wichita, Kansas) made use of horse patrols in high-crime areas and as part of their community policing strategy.[17] Research of 25 police departments that made use of mounted horse units revealed that the most common uses for these patrols were riot control, visibility (crime repression), community relations, crowd control (movement and circulation of people), general law enforcement (arrest, citation, etc.), and traffic control, as well as the public demand for the units.[18]

Aircraft Patrol

Many law enforcement agencies utilize **aircraft patrol,** which provides assistance to ground patrol units by observing areas that ground units cannot view. Aircraft can also be used for picking up and transporting prisoners over great distances. For example, if a suspect is picked up in California and is wanted in Wichita, Kansas, for homicide, a sheriff's department pilot would fly the department aircraft to Los Angeles and transport the suspect back to Kansas. An aircraft unit may be either an airplane (fixed wing or rotary wing) or a helicopter, depending on the needs of the agency. The helicopter has a few advantages over aircraft: It is able to travel at slower speeds, to hover when necessary, and to land in otherwise inaccessible places because of its vertical take-off and landing capabilities.[19] One major drawback to aircraft patrol is that it is the most expensive form of patrol and requires highly trained personnel.

Water/Marine Patrol

Communities that are near large bodies of water or beaches, shorelines, and inland waterways often use **water/marine patrol** to control crime. In some cases, a separate waterway patrol or harbor patrol may have its own unit. Marine patrols are also used to control water safety violations and to carry out search and rescue missions, as well as a variety of traditional law enforcement functions. There are a number of crimes that can occur along our nation's coastlines; crimes such as drug smuggling and other serious types of predatory crimes make marine patrol an ideal law enforcement tool. Marine patrol tends to be very expensive and requires special training on the part of police officers. The size and type of boat that a police department may use will depend on factors such as the size of the waterway or coast and how often the boats will be used (just during the summer months or all year).

PATROL DEPLOYMENT

Policing a community is more than just assigning officers to various parts of the community for the purpose of crime reduction, so police departments rely on different types of patrol methods to detect and prevent crime. With the evolving community policing strategy, police agencies have begun to experiment with different types patrol deployment in an effort to support problem-solving functions and to increase crime prevention.

Directed Patrol

Directed patrol is a program that provides patrol officers with specific duties to perform during a specified time period when they are freed from normal 911 dispatches.[20] Directed patrol tactics use accurate and timely information to predict where and when crimes are most likely to be committed, thus helping to allocate uncommitted patrol resources rationally and effectively.[21] Typically patrol officers are assigned to specific activities, such as patrolling a highcrime area that was chosen based on an analysis of specific crime patterns. Officers in a community may spend time in high-crime areas known as **"hot spots,"** which are usually discovered as a result of analysis of 911 call data. Minneapolis experimented with heavy patrol in hot spots by using a crackdown/back-off technique in which patrol officers intensively patrolled hot spots for short, intermittent periods of time. The assumption was that the impact of a short-term police presence would carry over because of residual deterrence.[22] The goal of directed patrol is to increase the patrol unit's effectiveness and the productivity of the department. There is some evidence that suggests that directed patrol may reduce some targeted crimes in specific areas, but more research is needed to fully determine whether crimes are actually being prevented or merely being displaced to other locations.[23]

One of the key research findings of the last 10 to 15 years has been the discovery of the importance of hot spots of crime. Researchers have discovered that even within high-crime areas, there are specific locales that generate the majority of calls for police service and response to crime.[24] This discovery informs important theoretical work on problem-oriented policing, the community policing movement, and situational crime prevention.[25] Hot-spot analyses also have become increasingly important for police departments as they seek to move from a reactive to a proactive model of policing. Perhaps most reflective of this orientation is the New York City Police Department's COMPSTAT program, which systematically utilizes hot-spot computerized statistical analyses in regular crime analysis meetings involving strategic planning and managerial benchmarking.

Differential Police Response

Some police agencies have abandoned the notion that every call for police service should be responded to as quickly as possible; likewise, some agencies have attempted to manage the calls for service. **Differential police response** to calls for service is a policy that deviates from the traditional practice of responding to all calls for service, and responses to citizens' calls to 911 are matched to the importance and severity of the calls.[26] Calls receive (1) an immediate response by police, (2) a delayed response by police, or (3) no police response, with citizens' reports being taken over the telephone or by mail or by having citizens come to the police station in person.[27] Conditions that are appropriate for delayed or alternative responses may include burglaries, larcenies or other thefts, lost property, past assaults, and auto accidents at which there are no injuries or property damage.

Research has revealed that differential response strategies have proven to show promise. For example, some departments that have implemented differential response strategies have diverted up to 50 percent of their calls to alternative responses without suffering any reduction in citizen satisfaction levels.[28]

Kansas City Police Department's Approach to Firearm-Related Crime

In 1992, the Kansas City Police Department, as part of its Weed and Seed program, implemented a directed patrol initiative in a police beat with very high levels of homicide and firearm-related violent crime.

The Kansas City Gun Experiment used intensive police patrols directed to an 80-block hot-spot area where the homicide rate was 20 times the national average. Patrol officers seized guns by frisking individuals who were arrested and by making plain view sightings of firearms during routine traffic violation or safety stops. Traffic stops were most effective in locating illegal guns, with 1 gun found per 28 stops. Gun crimes, including drive-by shootings and homicides, declined significantly during the 29-week experimental period between July 1992 and January 1993. Drive-by shootings dropped from 7 to 1 in the target area while increasing from 6 to 12 in a comparison area. Overall gun crimes dropped 49 percent (169 to 86) and criminal homicide declined 67 percent (30 to 10) from the 29 weeks before the patrols to the 29-week experiment period. However, there was no effect on other crime indicators, including calls for police service, calls about violence, property or disorder crimes, and total offense reports within the target area. Significantly, there did not appear to be a displacement effect (that is, gun crimes did not increase in any of the seven surrounding patrol beats).

Based on a statistical comparison with a control area, directed patrols were three times more cost-effective than traditional patrols in removing firearms from the streets in hot-spot areas. Active involvement of community and religious leaders in developing the program resulted in broad community support, even among those who had objected to previous police crackdowns on guns. However, the program was not institutionalized in the city budget after federal funding ended. The program was replicated in Indianapolis between April 1995 and September 1997. Directed patrols are now used in Indianapolis as the front end of a more comprehensive Weed and Seed effort directed at reducing crime and stabilizing the community.[29]

TRAFFIC FUNCTION

Imagine you are driving to campus early one morning for your 8:00 A.M. introduction to law enforcement class. You glance down at your watch and notice you are running behind, so you gently push the accelerator down a bit; before you know it, a police car pulls up behind you with red lights flashing and siren blaring. You think to yourself, "It's too early for this." You maneuver your car over to the side of the road, and the officer approaches your car and asks for your driver's license and proof of insurance. He then tells you that you were clocked on radar traveling 45 miles per hour in a 30-mile-per-hour zone. You tell the officer that you are sorry and that you are running late for school. You notice right away that the officer shows no empathy for your situation. The officer tells you that he will be back with you in a moment and returns to the patrol car; in a few moments (though it seemed like hours), the officer returns and issues you a citation for speeding. As you drive away, you have a terrible feeling inside of you and are somewhat embarrassed because passing motorists go by and stare at you as if you just robbed a bank. Enforcing speeding laws is part of the police traffic control function.

Traffic control is an important patrol operations component. More citizens have contact or interaction with the police because of traffic control problems than any other reason. Why and how traffic laws are enforced can have a significant effect on how the community views the police. Since traffic control is a complex activity with thousands of contacts with the public, selective enforcement is necessary in the maintenance of traffic laws. It would be impossible to strictly enforce every traffic regulation or law.

Many police agencies have a traffic section within the patrol division. This section consists of patrol officers whose primary responsibility is traffic-related duties; they do not have to respond to the other law enforcement and service-related calls. In other police agencies, the regular patrol officers are responsible for the majority of traffic-related duties. Whether a police agency has a separate traffic section is usually dependent on the size of the agency as well as the need.

Duties of Traffic Officer

The duties of officers assigned to traffic control include the following[30]:

- Obtaining the best possible movement of vehicles and pedestrians
- Ensuring compliance with various regulations and traffic laws from as many motorists and pedestrians as possible
- Assisting at traffic accidents
- Investigating the causes of traffic accidents
- Assisting lost or stranded motorists and pedestrians
- Helping to educate the public regarding traffic laws and safety

Accident-Causing Violations

According to the National Safety Council, certain traffic violations are more likely to cause serious accidents.[31] In most jurisdictions, the traffic officer is expected to concentrate on these violations, which include driving under the influence of drugs or alcohol, speeding, following too close to other vehicles, passing other vehicles improperly or in an unsafe manner, failing to stop at stop signs, failing to yield the right-of-way, and driving over center lines.

San Antonio, Texas, Police Department's Traffic Unit

The Traffic and Emergency Operations Section of the San Antonio Police Department has administrative responsibilities for the units that provide traffic safety through prevention, education, and enforcement. The unit also has operational planning responsibilities for special events and unusual occurrences.

Traffic control is divided into three shifts, each under the supervision of a lieutenant. Each shift has the responsibility of managing the traffic flow over 250 miles of expressways within the city limits. Included in the management of traffic is the responsibility for the detection and arrest of DWI (driving while intoxicated) suspects, traffic crash investigation, traffic assistance, haz-mat (hazardous materials) spills, and critical incidents. This detail also takes the lead in traffic planning for special events such as Fiesta, Spurs games, and the NCAA Final Four basketball games at the Alamodome. The white covers on their regulation police caps distinguish traffic officers from patrol officers assigned to the Patrol Division.

The Traffic Control Unit utilizes a variety of special vehicles and equipment. Some of the vehicles used by the Traffic Control Detail are 22 Honda GL 1500 Goldwing motorcycles, 72 marked police units, and 1 marked police pickup truck (used to conduct Department of Transportation truck inspections).

DETECTIVE OPERATIONS

The investigation of crimes is an important police function. Detectives are plainclothes investigators who gather facts and collect evidence for criminal cases; they conduct interviews, examine records, observe the activities of suspects, and participate in raids or arrests. Some detectives are assigned to interagency task forces to combat specific types of crime, and these detectives usually specialize in one of a wide variety of violations such as homicide or fraud. They are assigned cases on a rotating basis and work on them until an arrest and conviction occur or the case is dropped.

According to Professors Charles O'Hara and Gregory O'Hara, the modern detective or criminal investigator is a person who collects facts to accomplish a threefold aim: to identify the suspect, to locate the guilty party, and to provide evidence of his guilt.[32] Most police departments (regardless of size) either have full-time personnel who devote their attention to investigative functions or have a detective division. Once the patrol division has conducted the preliminary investigation of a criminal matter, the case is then sent to the detectives for follow-up criminal investigation. In the case of a serious crime such as a homicide or assault, detectives usually travel to the scene and conduct an on-site investigation. In some cases such as a homicide investigation, detectives may spend days or even weeks looking for clues at the scene of the crime.

Whenever possible, it is wise to allow patrol officers to conduct the follow-up criminal investigation of some crimes in lieu of referring all cases to detectives, and under the community policing strategy, this has become more common. Three conditions favor assigning some cases to patrol officers: Many crimes are committed by persons who do not travel far from where they live; uniformed officers are very familiar with the people living, working, and hanging out in their patrol area; and the techniques or skills needed to investigate many crimes are relatively easy to acquire, either with formal training or with experience. But if patrol officers are to handle the investigation of some crimes, they should have ready access to support and clerical assistance because patrol cars and squad rooms do not make good offices.[33]

The work environments of police detectives vary according to their duties. For most, their time is split between the office setting and whatever locations their investigations take them to (such as streets, businesses, or private homes) in order to look over crime scenes and question witnesses. Some work regular hours while others work irregular hours. Travel may be involved to complete investigations in the area where crimes occurred, and safety hazards are involved when dealing with suspects or witnesses who become defensive or abusive.

Development of the Modern Detective

The first detective bureau was established in 1841 by the London Metropolitan Police. Today we tend to see the police investigator as a romantic figure portrayed in movies and novels, someone usually pictured as a loner who often breaks departmental rules (such as Hunter and Dirty Harry). Unlike a detective portrayed in the movies, the criminal investigator is likely to be an experienced veteran civil servant who has worked his or her way up to the detective division. Detectives are usually considered the elite of the police department; they are paid more, wear civilian clothes, and have more freedom in accomplishing their duties.

Some scholars have studied the American detective and have been able to identify the various stages of development. Table 10–1 presents what police scholar Jack Kuykendall identified as the three stages of development in the detective's role: secretive rogue, inquisitor, and bureaucrat.

Functions of the Modern Detective

Detectives have a wide variety of techniques available in conducting investigations, but the majority of cases are solved by interrogation of suspects and witnesses, which takes time. Because of the time spent as a uniformed police officer and then as a police detective, a detective develops an intuitive sense of the plausibility of suspect and witness accounts; this intuition may fail at times but usually is reliable. In addition to interrogations, a detective may rely on a network of informants he or she has cultivated

TABLE 10–1

Stages of Development of the American Police Detective		
Role	Dates	Description
Detective as secretive rogue	1850s–1920s	1. Detective used stool pigeons to obtain information about crimes.
		2. Crimes by stool pigeon were usually tolerated in order to obtain information about crimes.
		3. Identity of detective was usually kept secret.
		4. Investigative work was clandestine (secretive).
		5. Detective was concerned with crimes such as pickpocketing, gambling, and nuisance crimes.
Detective as inquisitor	1890s–1960s	1. Detective was concerned with scientific evidence.
		2. Scientific laboratory was developed.
		3. Physical evidence was viewed as important.
		4. Detective began to use the Bertillon system of identification (fingerprints, physical evidence).
		5. Use of *modus operandi* (method of operation) and files was initiated.
		6. Detective commonly used third degree (physical abuse) to secure confession from suspect.
Detective as bureaucrat	1940s–1980s	1. Detective spent time gathering, organizing, and using information.
		2. Paperwork (reading, writing reports) was big part of detective's job.
		3. Case management and case screening were initiated.
		4. Screening factors included looking for solvability factors.
		5. Detective focused on cases that were most solvable.

Source: Jack Kuykendall, "The Municipal Police Detective: An Historical Analysis," *Criminology* 24, no. 1 (1986): 179–193.

over the years, and these informants often have connections with persons a detective would not be able to formally approach.

The general duties of detectives are to investigate the causes of crime and attempt to identify the individual(s) responsible for committing particular crimes. After patrol officers have made initial contacts, detectives usually enter the case. Often they investigate the cases on their own; in

TABLE 10–2

Typical Units in the Detective Division		
Crimes Against Property	**Crimes Against Persons**	**Other Units**
Burglary Unit	Homicide Unit	Narcotics Unit
Polygraph Unit	Missing Persons Unit	Vice Unit
Economic Crimes Unit	Family Violence Unit	Crime (Forensic) Laboratory
Evidence Technicians	Robbery Unit	Photo Lab
Fingerprint Unit	Traffic Homicide Unit	
	Auto Theft Unit	
	Sex Crimes Unit	
	Exploited and Missing Children Unit	

addition, they follow up on initial police reports through leads and informants. Detective bureaus are generally subdivided into sections or bureaus such as homicide, vice, robbery, or rape. The general mission of an investigator is to establish that a crime has been committed; to locate and take statements from witnesses; to establish the identity and whereabouts of the offender; to collect, preserve, and transport evidence; and to testify at court.

In medium-sized and larger police agencies, the detective division consists of many areas: Homicides are assigned to the homicide section or unit, burglaries to detectives investigating crimes against property, and assaults to the crimes against persons section. In smaller police organizations, one detective may handle both crimes against persons and property crimes. Table 10–2 depicts the areas of the detective division.

Effectiveness of the Modern Detective

The effectiveness of detectives has been the center of much debate. A study by the RAND Corporation concluded that a great deal of a detective's time was spent in nonproductive work and that a detective's expertise did little to solve cases.[34] For a thorough discussion on the RAND study, please refer back to Chapter 3.

A similar study by the Police Executive Research Forum (PERF) found that if a time lapse of more than 15 minutes occurs between when the crime is reported and the criminal is identified, there is only a 5 percent chance of solving the crime; accordingly, by the time the case is transferred to an investigator, there is only a 5 percent chance that the criminal will be identified and arrested. The PERF study did, however, conclude that detectives do make meaningful contributions to the solution of criminal cases.

To increase the effectiveness of investigation efforts, the trend in most law enforcement agencies is to give patrol officers greater responsibilities to conduct on-site investigations of the crime. Old-fashioned detective divisions have been replaced by specialized units; in addition, the use of technological advances in areas such as DNA and fingerprint identification has increased investigative effectiveness. Sophisticated computer identification systems, which allow the investigator to develop computer-assisted drawings of suspects, are now being used to help witnesses identify suspects. Other methods to improve investigative effectiveness include the careful screening of cases referred to the division, monitoring of case flow and activity, and use of targeted investigations in which the focus is on certain individuals who are known to be engaged in criminal behavior on a continuing basis.

Tools of the Modern Detective

DNA Technology. Over the past two decades in the field of ever-changing technology, the most significant advances have been in the analytical (laboratory examination of physical evidence) fields.[35] Analysis of **DNA** (short for deoxyribonucleic acid, the molecular basis of heredity) allows scientists to match genetic material from a sample taken from a victim or crime suspect with another sample. It is important for the crime scene investigator or evidence recovery technician to be well read and to keep abreast of these ever-changing techniques and methods in technology.

Genetic samples (evidence) such as blood, hair, tissue, saliva, and semen left by a suspect at the scene of a crime can be analyzed using DNA matching. Any type of organism can be identified by examination of DNA sequences unique to that species. Identifying individuals within a species is less precise at this time, although as DNA sequencing technologies continue to improve, direct comparison of very large DNA segments (and possibly even whole genomes) will become feasible and practical, which will allow precise individual identification.

DNA profiling is a process that begins when a minute sample of genetic material (DNA) is taken from human tissue and ends when the sample is given a computerized numeric value in the form of a bar code.[36] Comparing a person's DNA profile with a DNA sample retrieved from the scene of a crime can eliminate innocent people but can also provide a strong indication of guilt. The experience acquired by countries already using DNA profiling in their crime investigations shows that there are several important advantages[37]:

1. Rapid and absolute elimination of innocent suspects
2. Rapid identification of offenders with a very high degree of certainty
3. Reliability of evidence produced in court
4. Better administration of justice
5. Increased public confidence in the criminal justice system
6. Deterrent effect on offenders, with a concomitant decrease in crime
7. Cost-effectiveness (in terms of investigation time saved)

To identify an individual, forensic scientists scan 13 DNA regions that vary from person to person and use the data to create a DNA profile of that individual (sometimes called a DNA fingerprint). There is an extremely small chance that another person has the same DNA profile for a particular set of regions. The use of DNA will advance forensics in many different areas[38]:

- Identifying potential suspects whose DNA may match evidence left at crime scenes
- Exonerating persons wrongly accused of crimes
- Identifying crime and catastrophe victims
- Establishing paternity and other family relationships
- Identifying endangered and protected species as an aid to wildlife officials (information could be used for prosecuting poachers)
- Detecting bacteria and other organisms that may pollute air, water, soil, and food
- Matching organ donors with recipients in transplant programs
- Determining pedigree for seed or livestock breeds
- Authenticating consumables such as caviar and wine

Recently the company Orchid BioSciences, in cooperation with the New York City Police Department, conducted a pilot program to identify burglary suspects by matching DNA from crime scene evidence to DNA databases of convicted criminals.[39] DNA testing methods now enable advanced forensic labs to obtain DNA from the minute amounts of evidence that burglars may leave at the crime scene, such as a cigarette butt, perspiration, skin cells on clothing, or a partial fingerprint. This NYPD pilot program is based on the fact that a large proportion of burglaries are committed by repeat offenders whose DNA is already on file in state and federal criminal databases. Orchid Cellmark isolates DNA profiles from evidence recovered at the scene of the burglary; the profiles are then compared to these criminal databases to identify potential suspects.

Automated Fingerprint Identification System (AFIS). An **Automated Fingerprint Identification System (AFIS)** is a storage, search, and retrieval system for fingerprint and palm print electronic images and demographic data. AFIS is a high-speed, high-capacity image-processing system that enhances the ability of the latent fingerprint examiners to search and identify crime scene evidence against ever-increasing pools of fingerprint records; it is designed to replace manual fingerprinting ID systems still used by many law enforcement agencies.[40]

AFIS utilizes specialized software and powerful computer hardware configurations to create unique mathematical maps (algorithms) based on relationships between the characteristics present in the fingerprint (or palm print) and its friction ridge skin structures. A modern AFIS rapidly extracts information from a fingerprint to establish the pattern type, fine points, and axis of the image. The use of mathematical algorithms enables a fingerprint to be compared with millions of file prints within a matter of seconds, so AFIS has the potential to assist law enforcement investigators in the identification of a suspect in an expedient manner.[41]

Specialized Functions

The term **"specialization"** is used in two different ways: a division of labor among units of the organization (the division of the organization into specialized units, each of which has a particular task to perform), and a division of labor among the individual workers in the organization (each individual is a specialist in a particular type of work). We use specialization in the first sense because many components of police operations are specialized in order to deal with specific crises and problems.

Many police departments have specialized operational units that have the responsibility for handling technical or specialized tasks; often these specialized or tactical units are formed to address a particular problem. For example, on March 31, 1999, the Federal Bureau of Investigation (FBI) established 164 Safe Streets Task Forces in 52 FBI field offices throughout the United States, and of these, 45 focus totally or primarily on gangs. Safe Streets is an initiative designed to allow the special agent in charge of each FBI field office to address street, gang, and drug-related violence through the establishment of FBI-sponsored long-term proactive task forces. These task forces team up 785 FBI special agents with 142 other federal agents and 1,255 state and local law enforcement participants. Together, they focus on violent gangs, drug-related violence, and apprehension of violent fugitives.[42]

Other specialized operational groups have different targets and areas of responsibility:

- *SWAT team*. The SWAT (Special Weapons and Tactics) team is a highly trained police unit equipped to handle everything from unusual entry cases to hostage situations. Most SWAT units maintain a variety of specific weapons, including chemical agents, for any circumstance that might arise.

- *Narcotics unit*. Personnel in a narcotics unit consist of uniquely trained individuals who have extensive knowledge of the narcotics trade and specifically investigate violations of controlled substances laws; they specialize in the recognition, apprehension, and prosecution of persons involved in illegal drug activity. These units use state-of-the-art equipment to conduct surveillance and undercover operations and focus on the interdiction and seizure of illegal drugs and drug assets. Many communities maintain task forces that comprise local, state, and federal law enforcement personnel. Most task forces investigate the larger and more highly organized narcotics distribution networks.

- *Vice unit*. A vice unit investigates sundry criminal enterprises including prostitution, illegal weapons, gambling, massage parlors, escort services, and alcohol beverage violations.

- *K-9 unit*. A K-9 unit is designed to enhance the ability of police officers to locate and apprehend criminals who run and hide from them. The dogs are tightly controlled and serve as important tools for police officers as they strive to reduce crime. Dogs that are specially trained may also be used to sniff out and detect drugs and bombs. The use of dogs greatly enhances law enforcement's ability to locate missing children, elderly Alzheimer's patients, and lost or missing property; in addition, studies have shown that criminal suspects who are known flight risks are less likely to run in the presence of these fleet-footed animals.[43]

- *Crisis negotiation team.* The crisis negotiation team usually works closely with the SWAT unit to assist in the safe outcome of situations involving hostages and barricaded suspects. This team may also be utilized for crisis intervention and suicide prevention.
- *Bomb squad.* Personnel assigned to a bomb squad or bomb disposal unit respond to incidents in which a suspected explosive device is found, and they handle, transport, and/or render safe any explosive device. Bomb units are increasingly relying on robots to take over the dangerous task of finding and defusing bombs.
- *Computer crimes unit.* Increasingly, criminals are using computers to commit crimes or to keep track of their illegal business dealings. In some cases when officers serve a search warrant, some of the most important evidence may be stored on a suspect's computer. Retrieving the computer records necessary to solve these crimes is complex and highly technical, so it must be done in a manner that ensures that the evidence can be used in court. In response to the increasing demand for specialized assistance in this field, many police agencies have created a specialized computer crimes unit; investigators assigned to these units use specialized equipment and extensive training to successfully extract evidence from a suspect's computer. Once a computer is seized, investigators follow specific procedures to ensure that the evidence can be presented successfully in court, where the investigators may testify as experts in computer forensics.

DEVELOPMENTS IN POLICE OPERATIONS

In the future, police departments will rely more heavily on new technologies for investigation efficiency, but these new technologies will also place new demands on police officers. Recall our previous discussion of the advancements in DNA testing and how those advancements have made the careful collection and preservation of bodily fluids critical. Computer-based record-keeping and electronic surveillance devices will increasingly be used in police operations. In addition, with more communities implementing community-oriented and problem-oriented policing strategies, police will be more focused on public well-being and security than on efforts to simply control crime. In light of the dwindling budgets that many police agencies are experiencing, the police will be challenged to do more with fewer resources.

The transfer of certain traditional police functions to private police would reduce the demand on law enforcement. For example, one possible strategy is to transfer burglar alarm responses to the private sector. This is important to consider given that the number of homes and businesses with private security systems has grown rapidly in recent years. Subsequently, there will also be an increase in the number of false alarms of these systems; we have heard anecdotal accounts from many police commanders who have estimated that up to 50 percent of alarm calls are false alarms in their communities.

Each year, more is expected of our police officers. The average police officer needs to be a sidewalk sociologist to fix community and individual problems, and they are no longer primarily crime fighters but civil problem solvers. This duty of solving civil problems has been placed by default on police departments because the police are available 24 hours a day, 7 days a week, and no other social service is as readily available. Many of the calls to the police for assistance have nothing to do with crime. For example, when a cat is stranded in a tree, the normal reaction is to call the police, or if an elderly person has not been seen for several days, often the police will be contacted to check on that person.

Computers

Computers have become standard in many police agencies and greatly enhance the operations component of police agencies. The uses for computers in police work seem to be endless yet are still expanding. For example, mobile data terminals installed in patrol cars are linked to the computer-aided dispatching systems, which provide prioritized car-to-car and car-to-dispatcher messaging services. These terminals allow patrol officers to query driver's license files as well as the National Criminal Information Center. Furthermore, mobile data computers electronically transmit reports completed by officers in the field directly to the records section or to the police supervisor for approval. The use of computers and other technologies in policing will continue to increase, which will assuredly make the detection and prevention of crime more attainable goals.

Geographical Assignment

Police administrators for years organized detectives by specialized function (burglary, larceny, assault, homicide, etc.). With this assignment protocol, a detective working in burglaries may have cases assigned from many different geographical areas of the community; the problem with this assignment method is that detectives have a tendency to become too specialized by crime area and ignore other important factors that may be beneficial in solving crimes. Suppose one detective is assigned an assault case involving a known suspect, and another detective is assigned a burglary case involving the same suspect. It is possible that these two detectives are not aware they are working on two separate cases involving the same suspect because the incidents occurred in two different locations in the same community.

As an alternative to this assignment method, some departments are beginning to use geographical assignments of detectives in which detectives are assigned all cases within a certain district or beat area. For example, detectives may be assigned cases involving both crimes against persons and crimes against property in a specific geographical area. With this approach, detectives become more generalist in orientation. The advantages, which appear to go hand in hand with the community policing strategy, are many:

1. Detectives become familiar with the specific geographical area within which he or she is assigned cases.
2. Detectives develop detailed knowledge of the criminal operations within that geographical area.
3. Detectives become more aware of potential problems within that geographical area and can use this knowledge for problem-solving endeavors and crime prevention efforts while working with the citizens and patrol officers.
4. Detectives develop a better rapport with the citizens living within that geographical area.
5. Detectives develop closer working relationships with patrol officers working within that geographical area.

There is some evidence to suggest that decentralizing detectives' functions by using geographical districts or precincts improves performance.[44] Such evaluations should be viewed with caution, however, in light of the fact that there have been no rigorous studies of centralized detective functions for comparison purposes.[45]

▲ SUMMARY

This chapter focused on police operations, which make up those units that deliver the frontline services to the citizenry. Operational components include a variety of units that operate within the patrol and investigations divisions or bureaus. Police patrol is considered the backbone of policing; it may consist of one-officer or two-officer units, but research suggests that one-officer units are more efficient and may be more effective than two-officer units. Likewise, police patrol may be carried out by motorized patrol, foot patrol, motorcycle patrol, bicycle patrol, mounted horse patrol, aircraft patrol, or water/marine patrol.

The traffic function is a vital part of patrol. Many medium and large police departments have special traffic units whose functions include traffic law enforcement; collision prevention and investigation; citation of impaired drivers; traffic control at civic functions, sporting events, processions, parades, and for visiting dignitaries; responses to high-priority patrol calls; community traffic complaint investigations; and community functions such as speeches to driver education classes, promotion of the use of vehicle child restraints, and other traffic-related training.

The purpose of the investigations unit is to identify, apprehend, and secure evidence to convict criminal offenders. Detectives usually perform follow-up criminal investigation, which occurs when patrol has not solved the case and the case is forwarded to the investigations division. For serious crimes, detectives may actually travel to the scene, conduct the investigation, and collect physical evidence left at the scene.

Many medium and large police agencies divide operations components into specialized units such as tactical (SWAT) units, narcotics and vice units, K-9 units, crisis negotiation units, bomb recovery and disposal units, and computer crimes units. The purpose of specialized units is to assist the police agency in operating more efficiently and more effectively.

REFERENCES

1. O.W. WILSON and ROY C. MCLAREN, *Police Administration*, 4th ed. (New York: McGraw-Hill, 1977), pp. 73–76.
2. CARL B. KLOCKARS, *The Idea of the Police* (Beverly Hills, CA: Sage, 1985).
3. WILSON and MCLAREN, 1977, p. 364.
4. CHARLES D. HALE, *Patrol Administration, Local Government Police Management* (Washington, DC: GPO, 1982), p. 115.
5. STEPHEN SCHACK, THEODORE H. SCHELL, and WILLIAM G. GAY, *Specialized Patrol: Improving Patrol Productivity*, vol. 2 (Washington, DC: GPO, 1977).
6. "Career: Police Patrol Officers." Web posted at http://www.iseek.org/sv/13000.jsp. Accessed October 29, 2005.
7. CHARLES B. SAUNDERS Jr., *Upgrading the American Police* (Washington, DC: Brookings Institute, 1970), pp. 19–21.
8. SAMUEL WALKER, *The Police in America: An Introduction* (New York: McGraw-Hill, 1983), p. 118.
9. MICHAEL J. PALMIOTTO, *Policing: Concepts, Strategies and Current Issues in American Police Forces* (Durham, NC: Durham Academic Press, 1997).
10. LARRY D. NICHOLS, *Law Enforcement Patrol Operations: Police Systems and Practices*, 2nd ed. (Berkeley, CA: McCutchan, 1995), pp. 27–28.
11. PALMIOTTO, 1997, p. 243.
12. GEORGE KELLING, *Foot Patrol* (Washington, DC: National Institute of Justice, 1987).
13. MATTHEW J. HICKMAN and BRIAN A. REEVES, *Law Enforcement Management and Administrative Statistics, Local Law Enforcement Departments, 2000* (Washington, DC: U.S. Department of Justice, Bureau of Justice Statistics, 2003), p. 3.
14. PALMIOTTO, 1997, p. 245.
15. CARL ENT, "Bicycle Patrol: A Community Policing Alternative," *The Police Chief* 58 (1991): 58–59.
16. HICKMAN and REEVES, 2003, p. 3.
17. Based on author Michael Birzer's knowledge as a former commander of community policing activities for the Sedgwick County Sheriff's Department in Wichita, Kansas.
18. WILLIAM E. CANFIELD, "Comparative Analysis of Twenty-Five Horse Mounted Police Units in the United States," Unpublished publication.

19. THOMAS F. ADAMS, *Police Field Operations*, 5th ed. (Upper Saddle River, NJ: Prentice Hall, 2001).

20. SAMUEL WALKER, *The Police in America* (New York: McGraw-Hill, 1998).

21. WILLIAM H. BIECK, WILLIAM SPELMAN, and THOMAS J. SWEENY, "The Patrol Function," in *Local Government Police Management*, 3rd ed., ed. William Gellers (Washington, DC: International City Managers Association, 1991), pp. 59–95.

22. LAWRENCE W. SHERMAN and DAVID WEISBURD, "General Deterrent Effects of Police Patrol in Crime 'hot spots': A Randomized Control Trial," *Justice Quarterly* 12 (December 1995): 617–623.

23. GARY W. CORDNER and ROBERT C. TROJANOWICZ, "Patrol," in *What Works in Policing? Operations and Administration Examined*, ed. Gary W. Corder and Donna C. Hale (Highland Heights, KY and Cincinnati, OH: Academy of Criminal Justice Sciences and Anderson, 1992), p. 11.

24. LAWRENCE SHERMAN, "Hotspots of Crime and Criminal Careers of Places," in *Crime and Place*, ed. John Eck and David Weisburd (Monsey, NY: Criminal Justice Press, 1995).

25. HERMAN GOLDSTEIN, *Problem Oriented Policing* (New York: McGraw-Hill Books, 1990).

26. MICHAEL T. FARMER, "Differential Police Response Strategies," *Police Executive Research Forum Report* (Washington, DC: GPO, 1981).

27. WALKER, 1998.

28. MICHAEL E. CAHN and JAMES M. TIEN, *An Alternative Approach in Police Response: The Wilmington Management of Demand Program* (Cambridge, MA: Public Systems Evaluation, 1981), pp. 217–234.

29. LAWRENCE W. SHERMAN and D.P. ROGAN, "Effects of Gun Seizure on Gun Violence: 'Hotspots' Patrol in Kansas City," *Justice Quarterly* 12, no. 4 (1995): 218.

30. Duites of traffic officer based on experiences of author Michael Birzer, a former sheriff's lieutenant.

31. "Driver Saftey." Web posted at http://www.nsc.org/issues/drivsafe.htm. Accessed October 29, 2005.

32. CHARLES E. O'HARA and GREGORY L. O'HARA, *Fundamentals of Criminal Investigation,* 7th ed. (Springfield, IL: Charles C. Thomas Publisher), p. 5.

33. JOHN ECK and GERALD L. WILLIAMS, "Criminal Investigations," in *Local Government Police Management*, 3rd ed., ed. William Gellers (Washington, DC: International City Managers Association, 1991), pp. 132–158.

34. JOHN ECK, *Solving Crimes* (Washington, DC: Police Executive Research Forum, 1984).

35. MIKE BYRD, "DNA, the Next Generation Technology Is Here." Web posted at http://www.crime-scene-investigator.net. Accessed November 12, 2004.

36. INTERPOL DNA MONITORING GROUP, "Frequently Asked Questions About DNA Profiling." Web posted at http://www.interpol.int/public/forensic/dna/dnafaq.asp.

37. Ibid.

38. DNA FORENSICS, "How Does DNA Matching Work?" Web posted at http://www.ornl.gov/sci/techresources/human_genome/elsi/forensics.shtml#1. Accessed March 3, 2005.

39. ORCHID BIOSCIENCES, "Company Helps Police Department Use DNA to Track Burglary Suspects." *Medical Devices and Surgical Technology Week.* Web posted at http://www.newsRx.com. Accessed December 12, 2004.

40. P.J. ORTMEIER, *Policing the Community: A Guide for Patrol Operations* (Upper Saddle River, NJ: Prentice Hall, 2002), p. 245.

41. CRISTOPHER J. LENNARD and TREVOR PATTERSON, "Automated Fingerprint Identification System," *The Thin Blue Line.* Web posted at http://www. policensw/info/fingerprints/finger15/html. Accessed December 14, 2004.

42. Federal Bureau of Investigation Violent Crimes and Major Offenders Section, "Safe Streets Violent Crimes Initiatives." Web posted at http://www.iir.com/nygc/youthGangDoc/7_justice3.htm. Accessed December 14, 2004.

43. WALKER, 1998, p. 147.

44. TIMOTHY OETTMEIER and LEE P. BROWN, "Developing a Neighborhood-Oriented Policing Style," in *Community Policing: Rhetoric or Reality*, ed. Jack R. Greene and Stephen D. Mastrofski (New York: Praeger, 1988).

45. ECK and WILLIAMS, 1991.

CHAPTER 1

Police Organization and Management

Key Terms

Administrative management
Bureau
Bureaucracy
Chain of command
Classical theory
Contingency management
Division
Division of labor
Field services
Fredrick Winslow Taylor
Functions of management
Incident-driven policing
Learning organization

Luther Gulick
Lyndall Urwick
Max Weber
Organization
Organizational reengineering
Professional model of policing
Scientific management
Section
Span of control
Units
Unity of command
Watch

Outline

Introduction
Definition of an Organization
Traditional Police Organization
Organizational Structure

Organizational Terminology
Levels of Management and
    Supervision
Organizational Change

Learning Objectives

After reading this chapter, you should be able to:

1. Discuss features of the traditional police organization.
2. List and discuss the seven primary goals of the professional model of policing.

3. Explain scientific management.
4. Identify and discuss the paramilitary features of police organization.
5. Identify the various organizational terminology.
6. Discuss the roles of the various levels of management.
7. List and discuss the factors that are driving organizational change in American policing.
8. Explain total quality management.
9. Explain the learning organization.
10. Identify and discuss the benefits of flattening the police organizational structure.

> No significant change will occur unless it's driven from the top. There is no point in starting unless the CEO is on board. Nothing will happen without top management buy in.
>
> *—Peter Senge, Leading Learning Organizations, 1995*

INTRODUCTION

The management of a police department, an organization that is directed by specialized administrators, is a complex process involving human resources from varying levels within the organization. We use the term "administrators" interchangeably with the word "managers." Within any police department, there are persons (usually the chief of police, deputy chief, and perhaps majors) who have specific top administrative duties and responsibilities that encompass ensuring that the department's resources are managed so that its objectives are achieved economically and effectively. Then there are those personnel in middle-management positions (usually captains and lieutenants) who carry out specific responsibilities that support the mission and goals of the organization and those directives passed down from top administrators. There are also men and women at the supervisory level (usually sergeants) who oversee the day-to-day activities of police officers performing the police function.

As you have probably discovered in this book, many of the changes taking place in policing center on the community-oriented policing philosophy. Recall from previous chapters that community policing is based on the premise that proactive partnerships between police and citizens will help increase public safety and minimize or solve crime and disorder problems. While partnerships and problem-solving efforts are important elements in community policing, the equation is not complete without the reengineering of organization and management. Reengineering, as we will discuss later in the chapter, occurs when the organization redesigns the processes that are crucial to citizen satisfaction, or put another way, reengineering means changing the way a police organization works, what tasks are performed, and how information flows across functional areas and departments. Police administrators are responsible for ensuring that their departments adequately respond and adapt to citizen concerns and to the ever-changing conditions in society.

A police substation in Haco, Costa Rica.
Source: Cliff Roberson

This chapter is about police organization and management because it is important for students of the police to have an understanding of the general organization and management strategies of American police departments. It is also critical that students be exposed to the exciting yet complex changes in organization and management that are happening in the police profession. The objective of this chapter is twofold. First, we introduce you to the philosophical background of police organization and management; second, we take a look at the evolving police organization and management strategies that more appropriately support community-oriented and problem-oriented policing. Specifically, we examine the traditional model of police organization, which is sometimes referred to as the **professional model of policing,** that reflects the classical theory and paramilitary model of organization, which police departments are rooted in. We conclude the chapter with a discussion of new and evolving models of management and organization. After reading this chapter, you will be familiar with some organizational terminology, such as span of control, unity of command, division of labor, chain of command, that is frequently used in police organizations.

DEFINITION OF AN ORGANIZATION

An **organization** is "a consciously coordinated social entity, with a relatively identifiable boundary, that functions on a relatively continuous basis to achieve a common goal or set of goals."[1] Put another way, an organization is a structure through which people work as a group.[2] If we take a moment to come up with examples of organizations, it would not take us too long. A police department is an organization, so are churches, colleges and universities, sports teams, the military, hospitals, the local utility company, even your favorite neighborhood grocery store. They are all organizations because they share three common elements: a distinct purpose, a deliberate structure, and a group of people working together to accomplish a desired goal.

Police organizations serve a distinct purpose. For example, the police arrest lawbreakers, investigate crimes, regulate the safe movement of traffic, maintain order, prevent crime, and respond to many noncriminal service-related calls anytime day or night. In fact, the police are one of the few government organizations that you can call anytime and be assured of a response. Most police departments express their distinct purpose in the form of goals that the organization wishes to accomplish, a goal being an unmet objective that usually has some measurable characteristic.[3] Suppose, for instance, that the captain of the patrol division believes that the most important goal at present is to reduce the number of alcohol-related accidents. To accomplish this goal, the captain arranges for massive community education campaigns and aggressive enforcement of laws regarding driving under the influence. This goal can then be measured at some future time to see if education and aggressive enforcement efforts have reduced the number of alcohol-related accidents. We can say, then, that an organization has a distinct purpose to work toward accomplishing some unmet objective.

Police departments also have a deliberate structure so that the organization's members can perform their tasks. An organizational structure is the formal framework by which jobs are divided, grouped, and coordinated.[4] The organizational structure may be open and flexible, allowing for much problem solving and self-direction, or it may be a more traditional structure, setting out carefully defined rules, regulations, standard operating procedures, and job descriptions.

All police departments are composed of a group of people who work toward a common goal or goals. People who work in a police department consist of both sworn and nonsworn personnel: Sworn personnel are police officers in the department who have taken an oath of office and have the power of arrest; nonsworn personnel are usually employees who have not taken an oath and are not authorized to make an arrest.

A police organization also has to have some kind of organizing function whose purpose is to make the best use of the organization's resources to achieve organizational goals. Formalization—the extent to which the units of the organization are explicitly defined and its policies, procedures, goals, and objectives are clearly stated—is an important aspect of structure. The official organizational structure is conceived and built by top police administrators, and this formal organization can be seen and represented in a chart, which displays the organization's structure and

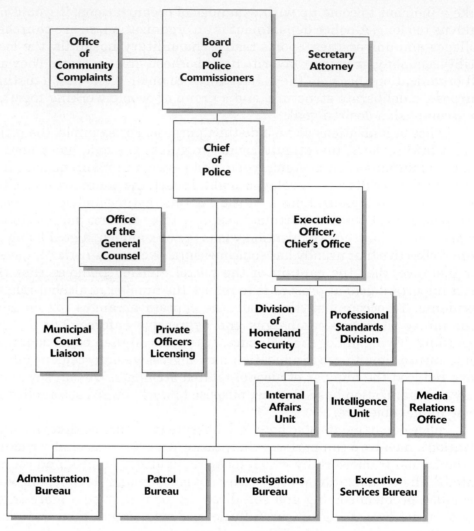

FIGURE 11–1   Organizational Structure of the Kansas City, Missouri, Police Department

shows its job titles, its lines of authority, and the relationships among its divisions.

The following is a list of terms used when discussing organization and management:

Goal. Unmet objective toward which effort is directed.

Policy. Broad statement of principle.

Procedure. Method of operation. It is more specific than a goal or a policy but still allows some flexibility (within limits). Instructional materials or manuals are composed largely of procedural directives.

Rule or regulation. Authoritative order dealing with situations in which no deviations or exceptions are included, making it more restrictive than a policy or procedure.

Police manual. Booklet containing statements of goals, permanent policies, procedures, and rules or regulations. Police employees usually receive a copy during recruit training or new employee orientation.

Fiscal plan. Information on matters such as budget preparation and use or control of funds allotted for personnel, equipment, and supplies.

TRADITIONAL POLICE ORGANIZATION

If we take a critical look at the history of American policing, we find there was an early-20th-century movement to professionalize the police and to eliminate the corruption and brutal methods that were plaguing policing at that time. This movement, which came to be known as the reform movement, resulted in a professional model of policing.

Professional Model of Policing

The professional model of policing became dominant during the period between the early 1900s and the early 1960s when reformers enjoyed remarkable success in altering the public conception of what the police ought to do and how they ought to be organized. This period of reform witnessed the displacement of patronage with civil service, divestiture of regulatory services (licensing and inspections) that allowed greater focus on law enforcement, and both technological and organizational innovations that made it possible to centralize police command and control.[5] Professor Samuel Walker described the seven primary goals of the professional model of policing[6]:

1. Eliminating political influence
2. Appointing qualified chief executives
3. Establishing a mission of nonpartisan public service
4. Raising personnel standards
5. Introducing principles of scientific management
6. Emphasizing military-style discipline
7. Developing specialized units

Using this professional model, police reformers sought both to insulate the police from political interference while retaining local government control and to change the role of the police in American society. In the 19th century, American police enforced health and building codes, secured housing for the homeless, built and supervised playgrounds for children, and even found jobs for ex-convicts. Reformers believed that these duties provided too many opportunities for political favoritism and squandered too many resources that could be better spent fighting crime, so they called for the police to give up social work and concentrate on law enforcement.[7] It is no coincidence that the main function of the police during the professional model increasingly became that of crime fighters.[8]

Despite its many positive aspects, the professional policing model also had some significant shortcomings. As Professor Robert Langworthy pointed out, "The reformers' success also spelled their failures."[9] One problem with the professional model is that over time police became less directly involved with the communities they served. Much of this was deliberate in order to avoid some of the political problems that developed with the political model (which reformers sought to move away from). Also, policing continued to be largely incident-driven. **Incident-driven policing** (or reactive policing) has police officers responding to crimes after they occur.

The professional model of policing is grounded in the classical theory of organization, which comprises three types of management models: scientific, administrative, and bureaucratic. Scientific management focuses on the one best way to do a job; **administrative management** emphasizes the flow of information in the operation of the organization; and bureaucratic management relies on a rational set of structuring guidelines such as rules and procedures, a hierarchy, and a clear division of labor. This classical school of thought, with its three management models, began around 1900 and continued into the 1920s. Aspects of all three models can be found in some form in each police organization.

Scientific Management

Few law enforcement officers know the name **Fredrick Winslow Taylor** (1856–1917), but nearly every officer sworn in during the past 75 years has served under the organizational structure he advocated.[10] Taylor's theory of **scientific management** indoctrinated officers along traditional lines; it was highly centralized, bureaucratic, and designed on the premise of divisions of labor and unity of control. This was the enduring model of organizational command and control adopted by law enforcement agencies across America for most of the 20th century.[11]

Scientific management focuses on worker and machine relationships. Under scientific theory, it is thought that organizational productivity can be raised by increasing the efficiency of production processes; this efficiency perspective is concerned with creating jobs that economize on time, human energy, and other productive resources. Jobs are designed so that each worker has a specific well-controlled task that can be performed as instructed. Specified procedures and methods for each job must be followed—with no exceptions. Taylor concluded[12] that supervision should be divided according to tasks and that a subordinate should report to a number of different supervisors, each of whom is responsible for the various tasks subordinates perform. For example, in a police department, a traffic sergeant is responsible for the supervision of traffic officers, a patrol sergeant supervises patrol officers, a records sergeant is responsible for records personnel, and a detective sergeant supervises detectives.

The scientific management approach strives to achieve these five objectives[13]:

1. Replace rules of thumb with science (organized knowledge).
2. Obtain harmony rather than discord in group actions.
3. Achieve the cooperation of human beings rather than cultivate chaotic individualism.
4. Work for maximum output rather than restricted output.
5. Develop all workers' capabilities to the fullest extent possible for their company's highest prosperity.

Administrative Management

The theory of administrative management is based on the work of **Luther Gulick** (1892–1993) and **Lyndall Urwick** (1891–1983) and is concerned with the organizational problems of the departmental divisions of work and coordination. While Frederick Tayor's scientific management theory was more concerned with operations at the bottom of the organizational hierarchy, the administrative management theorists were more concerned with operations at the middle and upper levels of the structure.

Gulick is best known for his work as a member of President Franklin D. Roosevelt's Committee on Administrative Management. The committee's report, *Papers on the Science of Administration*, led to the most thoroughgoing changes in the executive branch since the adoption of the Constitution. Gulick's own *Theory of Organization* became an instant classic, anticipating the direction of later research while establishing benchmarks for future theorists. He coined the acronym POSDCORB, which has become a classic in the administration and management literature. POSDCORB describes seven functions of management[14]:

1. *P (planning)*. Working out in broad outline the things that need to be done and the methods for doing them to accomplish the purpose set for the enterprise.
2. *O (organizing)*. Establishing the formal structure of authority through which work subdivisions are arranged, defined, and coordinated for the defined objective.
3. *S (staffing)*. Bringing in and training the staff and maintaining favorable conditions of work for all the personnel.
4. *D (directing)*. Making decisions and continually embodying them in specific and general orders and instructions and serving as the leader of the enterprise.
5. *CO (coordinating)*. Carrying out the duty of interrelating the various parts of the work divisions.
6. *R (reporting)*. Keeping those to whom the executive is responsible informed as to what is going on, which includes keeping himself or herself and his or her subordinates informed through records, research, and inspections.
7. *B (budgeting)*. Overseeing all that goes in the budget process, including fiscal planning, accounting, and control.

In the POSDCORB functions of management, Gulick and Urwick believed that within organizations there should be a unity of command and a clearly defined division of labor, and most police departments today follow this administrative management model. For example, they are organized according to clearly defined divisions of labor (such as patrol, investigations, warrant service, traffic functions, and training functions), and there is a clear unity of command, with each line officer knowing the supervisor to whom he or she is accountable in a given situation.[15]

The most famous administrative management theorist was Henri Fayol (1841–1925), a French industrialist who developed a framework for studying management. His writings are based largely on his personal experiences as a manager, and his famous book, *General and Industrial Management* (1916), has become a management classic. According to Fayol, the five **functions of management** are (1) planning, (2) organizing, (3) commanding, (4) coordinating, and (5) controlling. These functions are goal-directed, interrelated, and interdependent. Planning involves devising a systematic process for attaining the goals of the organization and prepares the organization for the future. Organizing encompasses arranging the necessary resources to carry out the plan through the process of creating structure, establishing relationships, and allocating resources to accomplish the goals of the organization. Commanding is the guiding, leading, and overseeing of employees to achieve organizational goals, whereas coordinating is the act of arranging the resources so that the plan can be carried out. Controlling involves verifying that actual performance matches the plan; if performance results do not match the plan, corrective action is taken.

In his book, Fayol also laid down 14 principles of management that have become the underpinning of most organizations[16]:

1. *Division of work.* Specialization.
2. *Authority and responsibility.* Right to give orders and power to extract obedience regardless of who exercises authority or has responsibility.
3. *Discipline.* Obedience, application, energy, behavior, and outward marks of respect in accordance with standing agreement between the firm and its employees.
4. *Unity of command.* Each employee receiving orders from only one supervisor.
5. *Unity of direction.* One head and one plan for a group of activities having the same objective (unity of command cannot exist without unity of direction).
6. *Subordination of individual interests to general interests.* Interests of an individual or a group of employees not prevailing over concerns of the firm.
7. *Remuneration of personnel.* Monetary fairness to both employee and employer.
8. *Centralization.* Natural order of things (but centralization or decentralization is a question of proportion, finding the optimum degree for the particular concern).
9. *Scalar chain.* Chain of superiors ranging from the ultimate authority to the lowest ranks, often referred to as **chain of command.**
10. *Order.* Issue of there being a place for everyone and everyone being in his or her place.
11. *Equity.* Combination of kindness and justice.

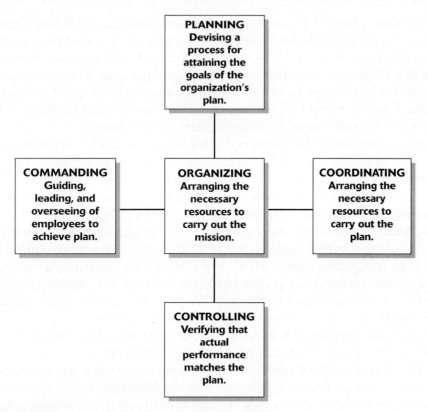

FIGURE 11–2 Functions of Management

12. *Stability of tenure of personnel.* Employees becoming familiar with their jobs and being productive (a mediocre manager who stays is infinitely preferable to outstanding managers who come and go).

13. *Initiative at all levels of the organization.* Great source of strength for the business.

14. *Esprit de corps.* Harmony and unity of personnel (this is also seen as a great strength, and efforts should be made to establish this mind-set).

Bureaucratic Management

Max Weber (1864–1920), a German sociologist considered by some to be the father of modern sociology, analyzed **bureaucracy** as the most logical and rational structure for large organizations. Weber was the first to observe and write on bureaucracies that developed in Germany during the 19th century. He considered them to be efficient, rational, and honest—a big improvement over the haphazard administration they replaced. The purpose behind bureaucracies is to ensure efficient and methodical social organization.[17] Bureaucracy has emerged as a dominant feature of the contemporary world, and most modern police departments are bureaucracies.[18]

What does bureaucracy mean to you? If your professor in your introduction to law enforcement class asked you to stand in front of the class and describe a bureaucracy, how would you describe it? What examples would you use? What do you think of when you envision a bureaucracy? If you are like many, you may have vivid thoughts of red tape, slow movement, layers of authority, waste, and inefficiency, and perhaps a large company or the government comes to mind. Virtually everywhere one looks in both developed and developing nations, economic, social, and political spheres are extensively influenced by bureaucratic organizations.

Bureaucracies in their own right are better suited for some tasks than others. For example, bureaucracies are not well suited to industries in which technology changes rapidly or is not yet well understood; on the other hand, bureaucracies excel at businesses involving routine tasks that can be specified in writing and that do not change quickly. In policing, this is a double-edged sword. Technology and equipment are changing rapidly and police departments can barely keep up; nevertheless, police are increasingly using technology in fighting crime. Much of police work is routine, however, and the way police do business is slow to change (in fact, the policing profession as a whole is very resistant to change). We point to the slow implementation of community policing as one example of this resistance.

The main purpose of a bureaucracy is to develop lines of authority, to delineate divisions of labor, and to create productive workers and job efficiency. Bureaucracies are founded on legal or rational authority, which is based on laws, procedures, rules, and so on.[19] Modern police departments are notorious for having manuals of rules and regulations, policies and procedures. These manuals spell out how police officers will react to specific situations such as a crime scene, mass public disorder, or a traffic accident; dictate what equipment is authorized and what uniform is to be worn during certain times of the year; and list the chain of command, the rational authority structure, and the organizational structure.

Since police departments are bureaucracies, the term "authority" is used often in the procedures manual and the rules and regulations manual. Positional authority of a superior over a subordinate is based on legal authority whereas charismatic authority stems from the personal qualities of an individual.

Efficiency in bureaucracies comes from clearly defined and specialized functions, use of legal authority, hierarchical forms, written rules and procedures, technically trained bureaucrats, appointment to positions based on technical expertise, promotions based on competence, and clearly defined career paths.[20]

The 20th century saw the perfection of the bureaucracy, a form of organization that has been enormously successful as a result of thousands of years of trial and error. Management expert Warren Bennis described the six basic principles of a bureaucracy[21]:

1. Division of labor by functional specialization
2. Well-defined hierarchy of authority
3. System of rules covering the rights and duties of employees

TABLE 11–1

Police Divisions Based on Tasks		
Operations or Field Services	**Staff Services**	**Auxiliary Services**
Patrol	Personnel	Records
Traffic	Training	Communications
Investigations	Planning	Property
Vice	Budget	Laboratory
Organized crime	Legal	Booking/jail
Youth	Clerical	Identification
Crime prevention	Inspections	Equipment
Community relations	Maintenance	

4. System of procedures for dealing with work situations
5. Impersonal relations between people
6. Promotion and selection based on technical competence

As bureaucracies, police departments are organized along a specific division of tasks. As Table 11–1 depicts, these are usually divided among operations or field services, staff services, and auxiliary services. Those police officers in operations or **field services** deliver the product of policing to the citizenry. The term "operations" embraces the traditional (or primary) functions for which the agency was established—patrol service, criminal investigation, traffic control, vice enforcement, and various other activities having a direct effect on crime prevention and law enforcement.[22] Line operations are the most visible within the police department, that is, men and women working in a line operations function are on the front line answering crime calls, responding to service calls, arresting law violators, investigating traffic accidents, performing crime scene investigations, and assisting citizens.

Staff and auxiliary services are sometimes referred to as support services and assist the department in developing better personnel. For example, police officers who work in recruitment, selection, training, and development are typically part of staff services; also, those police personnel who are involved in budgeting and clerical positions are considered to be part of staff services. Auxiliary services provide the technical support and facility services for the organization, which include but are not limited to work in the records division, detention or lockup, communications center, and equipment and maintenance services.

Chain of Command

Police departments are bureaucracies marked by hierarchical structures with a clearly delineated chain of command, important for proper order. The chain of command is the succession of commanding officers, from a superior to a subordinate, through which command is exercised. In a police department, the chain of command is critical during times of mass social disorder or other volatile situations that threaten public peace because police officers need to know quickly who is in command. The chain of command functions largely along the lines of the military command structure: Patrol officers are responsible to their sergeants, sergeants to lieutenants, lieutenants to captains, captains to majors, majors to deputy chiefs, and deputy chiefs to the chief.

Most interagency communication in a police department also operates on the principle of chain of command. For example, if a sergeant wishes to communicate with the captain regarding a certain divisional policy or procedure, the sergeant must first receive approval from the lieutenant before talking with the captain; likewise, if the lieutenant wishes to communicate with the deputy police chief about an operational issue, the lieutenant must first receive permission from the captain.

Criticisms of the Classical Theory

The **classical theory,** modified and refined during implementation by professional model-era police executives such as August Vollmer and O. W. Wilson, represented a reaction to the rampant corruption and other inequities that had plagued American policing since its early days.[23] To reduce the contaminating effects of local ward politics on line officers, the classical model centralized authority in police headquarters, and to alleviate favoritism and petty corruption in neighborhoods, the classical model established beats and revolving assignments for patrol officers.[24] Using the classical theory, police leaders moved to routinize and standardize police work, especially patrol work.[25] Police work became a form of crime fighting in which police enforced the law or arrested criminals when the opportunity presented itself. Attempts were made to limit discretion in police work, resulting in a generation of police officers being raised with the idea that they merely enforced the law.[26]

To ensure officers performed their assigned duties, the classical model instituted a military-style structure of authority and discipline; to encourage personnel to follow the rules established by headquarters, proponents of the classical model (most notably O. W. Wilson) believed that line-level officers should adhere to a rigid chain of command and be supervised closely through the use of massive amounts of written policy pronouncements.[27]

For the most part, police departments have remained amenable to the classical theory of organization, command, and supervision that dictates a rigid manual of procedures for employees. Unfortunately, adherence to these procedures prevents personnel, in many instances, from solving problems in the communities they serve. For line officers, the strict pyramid-like control structure of the classical model severely limits use of officers' discretion when they are carrying out their duties. Historically, central headquarters has full and final authority in all police matters.[28]

At one time, a rigid centralized command structure represented the best prescription to deter corruption and misconduct; however, as policing evolves with newer strategies, this centralized command-and-control structure will require redefinition. Police operations must become decentralized (through substations, neighborhood stations, satellite offices in storefronts) and move into the communities being served.

Management expert Chris Argyris noted that classical principles of formal organization result in certain kinds of employees in a work environment[29]:

- They have minimal control over their working lives.
- They are expected to be subordinate, passive, and dependent.
- They work from a short-term perspective.
- They are induced to perfect and value the frequent use of a few surface or shallow abilities.
- They are in working conditions conducive to psychological failure because they are treated more as infants than as competent human beings.

ORGANIZATIONAL STRUCTURE

The police organizational structure is pyramidal in design and has many bureaucratic layers that separate the top command and administration from line-level personnel. This is sometimes referred to as the line organization or the military-type organization. In the line organization, channels of authority and responsibility extend in a direct line from top to bottom within the structure.

An organizational structure is a mechanical means of depicting, by an arrangement of symbols, the relationships that exist among individuals, groups, and functions within the organization.[30] Some conclude that the steep hierarchical structure found in many police organizations often makes them dysfunctional and that police organizations should be restructured or flattened in order to become more efficient, more effective, and more responsive to the community.[31] However, there are advantages to the line organization: Quick decisions can be made because of the direct lines of authority, and each member in the chain of command knows to whom he or she is accountable and who is accountable to him or her.[32]

There are some differences among organizational structures, but there are many similarities that enable them to be classified. One widely used classification is the twofold system (mechanistic versus organic forms of organizational structure) developed by Tom Burns and G. M. Stalker in their study of electronics firms in the United Kingdom.[33]

The mechanistic structure is reflected in the traditional or classical bureaucratic design, common in many medium-sized and large police organizations; they are somewhat rigid in that they consist of very clearly delineated jobs, have a well-defined hierarchical structure, and rely heavily on the formal chain of command for control. Bureaucratic organizations, with their emphasis on formalization, are the primary form of mechanistic

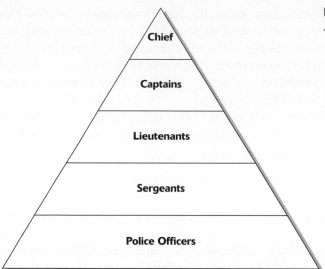

FIGURE 11–3 Hierarchy of Authority

structure, and in this type of structure, people become relatively confined to their own area of specialization. Mechanistic bureaucracies are driven by a top-down or command-and-control approach in which managers provide much direction and have considerable control over others.

On the other hand, the organic structure is more flexible, more adaptable to a participative form of management, and less concerned with a clearly defined structure. The organic organization is open to the environment in order to capitalize on new opportunities. Because of this, organic organizations operate with a flatter structure, with only one or two levels of management. Flat organizations emphasize a decentralized approach to management that encourages high employee involvement in decisions.

Differentiation

Vertical differentiation is based on levels of authority or positions holding formal power within the organization. For example, an organizational chart that shows the chief at the top and the officers at the bottom would demonstrate vertical differentiation between the chief and the officers. Horizontal differentiation is the way a police department groups organizational activities into functions, departments, or divisions. For example, within the patrol division there may be several functions or sections such as the traffic unit, gang unit, and bicycle unit. Horizontal differentiation may be based on activity (patrol division and detective division), on clientele (senior citizens detail and gang squad), on geography (precinct one and precinct two), or on time (day shift and night shift).

The level of complexity within a police agency is determined by the amount of vertical and horizontal differentiation that exists in the organization.[34] In police agencies, the differentiation process generally occurs in two basic ways. First is the synthesis approach, which focuses on combining tasks into larger and larger sets of tasks. This approach is often referred to as the bottom-up approach and is used by agencies that are declining in size and that need to consolidate jobs or units.

The second approach is the analysis approach, which considers the overall work of the agency from the top and splits the work assignments into increasingly more specialized tasks as one moves down the organization from the top to the bottom. The latter approach is often referred to as the top-down approach and is used in growing organizations because it is easy to visualize the sets of tasks to be accomplished and to break those sets into subsets.

Military Model

In 1829 Sir Robert Peel, "father" of the London Metropolitan Police, proposed the Metropolitan Police Act, in which he noted that police should be efficient and organized along military lines. As a result, police agencies in Great Britian are grounded in a paramilitary and hierarchical composition.[35] The paramilitary orientation was later adopted by American police agencies and for the most part remains in place today.

Despite the widespread adoption of community policing principles, the number of police departments that use the equipment, training, rhetoric, and tactics of warfare is on the rise nationwide. According to a study by Professor Peter Kraska, there are more than 30,000 heavily armed, militarily trained police units in the United States.[36] His study found that the number of paramilitary police missions quadrupled between 1980 and 1995.[37]

The term "paramilitary" means that the police have borrowed certain aspects from the military and applied them to police organizations. Police organizations are modeled after the military: Police departments use military-style rank designations (sergeant, lieutenant, captain), police wear identifiable uniforms similar to those of the military, police are organized along strict lines of authority and reporting relationships, police officers (and military personnel) are trained to respond quickly to orders, and police (and military personnel) carry weapons and are authorized to use force when necessary.

Characteristics of Paramilitary Police Model

- Centralized command structure
- Rigid differences among ranks
- Terminology similar to that of military
- Frequent use of commands and orders
- Rules, regulations, and discipline strongly enforced
- Individual creativity not encouraged
- System resistant to challenge[38]

While the police and the military do possess many similar features, there are many differences. Probably the most significant difference is their respective roles. The job of the police is to react to the violence of others, to apprehend criminal suspects, and to deliver them over to a court of law. A soldier, on the other hand, does not think; he or she initiates violence on command and doesn't worry about the Bill of Rights.[39] The police are trained to use the minimum amount of force necessary when dealing with a situation; this principle is nonexistent in military war operations. The police are not trained to fight a foreign enemy (as soldiers are) but to protect and serve the citizenry, prevent crime, and enforce criminal laws. When the police attempt to operate as paramilitary forces, they usually alienate the population they are attempting to serve; the military considers doing police-like activities to be a distraction from their primary goal of fighting an enemy.

There are numerous concepts or doctrines within the military that support and encourage a war-fighting mentality that are almost completely missing from policing. The military actively employs concepts such as combined arms, which views successful fighting as the highly coordinated employment of every organizational function or specialty in a mutually supportive manner; likewise the military actively integrates all the actions, resources, and personnel of its organization to the best operational advantage.[40]

While American police departments may appear somewhat like the military, there are more dissimilar features than similarities. O. W. Wilson, who perhaps is the greatest reformer in the history of American policing, saw the need some years ago for the police to move away from military rank designation, observing that the usual designation of police ranks is not completely satisfactory because of the inevitable comparison with military titles.[41] The rank of sergeant in the military service is traditionally noncommissioned, but in modern police service, the commissioned versus noncommissioned concept does not exist. Wilson proposed a system in which all police personnel are referred to as officers, using grade numbers to identify rank for internal and administrative purposes.[42] Wilson thought that conventional insignia, such as chevrons, bars, and gold leaves, should be eliminated and proposed that rank be indicated by simple pins, with grade numbers depicted by Arabic or Roman numerals.[43]

ORGANIZATIONAL TERMINOLOGY

There are a number of organizational terms commonly used in police departments, and new police officers usually become familiar with these terms after a short time on the job. In the following sections, we present you with some of the more common organizational terms that are indigenous to police departments.

Unity of Command

Imagine for a moment that you are a police officer assigned to second watch (3:00 P.M.–11:00 P.M.) in the field patrol section. As you are patrolling on your beat, your police radio beacons your call number and the communications dispatcher relays that you are to report to a homicide scene and assist. You arrive at the scene and notice people standing everywhere; it appears that everyone in the neighborhood has gathered to see what is going on. You also notice that your sergeant and one other police officer have already arrived at the scene. Your patrol sergeant notices that you are now on the scene and directs you to stand at the front door of the crime scene (in this case, a house) and keep everyone out of the crime scene who does not belong there. After about 10 minutes, a detective sergeant arrives at the scene and directs you to leave your post and go talk with the neighbors to see if they heard or saw anything. If you leave your post, your patrol sergeant will most assuredly be upset with you, but if you don't, the detective sergeant may accuse you of not following a direct order. What would you do if faced with this situation? The management principle unity of command which is used in police organizations minimizes the likelihood of a situation such as this from occurring.

The purpose of **unity of command** is to ensure singleness of effort by having each person report to only one responsible supervisor for every objective. Efficiency is supposed to be enhanced by arranging the members of the organization in a determinate hierarchy of authority in order to preserve unity of command.[44] Unity of command means that all organizational personnel operate under a single commander with the requisite authority to direct all personnel employed in pursuit of a common purpose, which ensures that conflicting orders are not issued to the same police officers by several supervisors. In the above situation, the police officer could have brought the conflicting order to the attention of the detective sergeant.

In multiagency law enforcement operations, which may be necessary during times of mass public disorder or other large community events, unity of command may not be possible, but unity of effort becomes paramount. Unity of effort—coordination through cooperation and common interests—is an essential complement to unity of command.

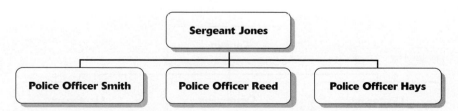

FIGURE 11–4 Unity of command is the principle under which subordinates report to one and only one supervisor. In this example, Officers Smith, Reed, and Hays report to Sergeant Jones.

Span of Control

Span of control refers to the number of persons that one person can effectively supervise. The span of control is often limited unknowingly by administrators and supervisors who are trying to control too much of the work or trying to supervise too many people. Two factors may cause administrators to make such an error: an overestimation of their own ability and an inability or unwillingness to delegate authority because of a desire or real need to exercise close control over operations.[45] Efficiency is supposed to be enhanced by limiting the number of subordinates who report directly to one supervisor to a small number.[46]

The principle of span of control is routinely taught in management schools and widely employed in large organizations such as the military, government agencies (including police departments), and educational institutions. As a general rule, the span of control is usually three to five at the top level of the organization and often broader at the lower levels, depending on factors such as the capacity of the supervisor and those persons supervised, the time needed to perform the tasks, and the types of persons served.[47] Within a police agency, the more levels in the pyramid, the smaller is the span of control.[48]

Division of Labor

Division of labor, or work specialization, is the degree to which tasks in an organization are divided into separate jobs. Work process requirements and employee skill level determine the degree of specialization. The placing of capable people in each job ties in directly with productivity improvement, so to maximize both efficiency and effectiveness, supervisors match employees' skill levels with task requirements. In a police department, the tasks of the organization are divided according to personnel, area, time, and function or purpose. For example, a police department with 100 police officers will probably be broken down into several divisions of labor: 60 may be field patrol officers assigned across three shifts, each working in different geographical areas of the city; 20 are investigators; 5 are administrators; 5 are assigned to the training unit; 2 are Internal Affairs officers, etc. Each of these represents a division of labor, with police officers in their respective areas performing a specialized job function.

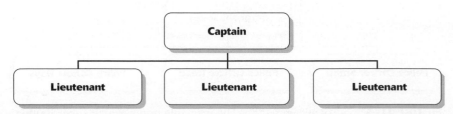

FIGURE 11–5 Span of Control. In this example, only three lieutenants report to one captain.

The division of labor is usually reflected in an organizational chart, a pictorial representation of reporting relationships in an organization. A well-thought-out and well-designed organizational chart should allow anyone, after viewing the chart, to have an accurate idea of the structure of the organization, the various functions and specialization, and the chain of command (who reports to whom within the organization).

Department

A department is the primary organizational unit within a governmental structure. For example, the Los Angeles Police Department is a primary organizational unit within the governmental structure of the city of Los Angeles, and the Los Angeles County Sheriff's Department is a primary organizational unit within the governmental structure of Los Angeles County.

Bureau

A **bureau** is the largest unit within a police department. Some police departments have as few as two bureaus while others may have three or more bureaus. For example, a police agency may have a patrol bureau, an investigations bureau, a staff and support bureau, and a technical services bureau. The title of each bureau will vary by the organization, and the number of bureaus in a police department is dependent on the size of the organization (large organizations will usually have more bureaus than small or medium-sized organizations).

Division

A **division** is a subdivision of a bureau. Within the patrol bureau, for example, you may find the patrol division, the traffic division, and the tactical division; within the investigations bureau, you may find the criminal investigations division and the special investigations division.

Section

A **section** is a subdivision of a division. The patrol division may have several sections covering traffic, crime prevention, and community liaison. The crimes against persons section and the crimes against property section may fall within the detective division.

Unit

When further specialization is needed, a section can be divided into **units,** which are subdivisions of a section. For example, the investigations division houses the detective section, and that section may have a number units including the vice unit, narcotics unit, license unit, sex crimes unit, intelligence unit, bomb unit, auto theft unit, and missing and exploited children unit.

Watch

A **watch** (or shift) is a time division of the day for purposes of police assignment; it is usually eight hours in duration. There are some shifts (usually referred to as fourth shifts) that overlap other shifts to meet unusual or peak loads. For example, a police department may have four patrol watches: first, 7:00 A.M. to 3:00 P.M.; second, 3:00 P.M. to 11:00 P.M.; third, 11:00 P.M. to 7:00 A.M.; and fourth, 7:00 P.M. to 3:00 A.M. Notice how the fourth watch overlaps second and third watch.

Beat

A beat is a geographical area assigned to a police officer, whether on foot or in a motor vehicle, for patrol purposes. The size of the community, crime factors, and general call load in a city or town will usually determine the number of beats as well as the size of a particular beat. A beat in some jurisdictions is referred to as a zone or response area.

LEVELS OF MANAGEMENT AND SUPERVISION

Police departments have various levels of management and supervision that are largely determined by the size of the police department. In a small police department, a sergeant may perform many of the duties that a lieutenant or captain performs in a large department. Police departments typically have three layers of management and supervision: top management, middle management, and line-level supervision.

Top Management

At the top of the organizational structure are those police managers who are primarily involved in administration. Top managers spend most of their time on the functions of planning and organizing, and they determine the mission and set the goals for the organization, so their primary function is long-range planning. Top management is accountable for the overall direction of the organization. The specific rank of those personnel in top management may range from police chief to deputy police chief to major. Police managers have an awesome responsibility for planning the department's mission, implementing programs, planning ways the department will carry out programs, budgeting and procuring funds from the appropriate governmental entity, and planning and directing the department's future.

Middle Management

Middle management implements top management's goals. In large police departments, those in middle management usually hold the rank of captain or lieutenant; in smaller police departments, the rank of sergeant may be included in middle management. Those police personnel in middle management positions have the responsibility of commanding bureaus or divisions. For example, in some police organizations the captain may be a patrol division commander and a lieutenant the patrol watch commander, and the latter might be responsible for field patrol activities in a specific geographical area or precinct during the second watch. In other words, the patrol lieutenant, who answers directly to the patrol captain, is usually responsible for administering a particular patrol watch.

The captain, on the other hand, is responsible for managing the entire patrol division, which would include developing goals and objectives for the division, budgeting, ensuring that the mission and directives passed down from the chief of police are carried out, and managing all activities within the patrol division.

Line-Level Supervision

Supervisors, those persons who direct and control the work of employees in order to achieve the departmental goals, are the only level of management managing nonmanagers, so most of a supervisor's time is allocated to the functions of directing and controlling. Sergeants are the frontline supervisors in most police organizations. The job of police sergeant differs from that of police officer in that while they both perform essentially the same law enforcement duties, the police sergeant has full supervisory responsibility for subordinates and in a staff capacity assists management with the development and implementation of specialized programs. In some departments, sergeants may be involved in coordinating training programs.

Police sergeants have the most day-to-day contact with the men and women performing the police job. In one sense, it can be said that they hold one of the most important management positions in the department. It is usually through a sergeant that orders and directives are given to those police officers at the bottom of the hierarchy; therefore the sergeant plays an instrumental role in gaining the support of police officers to carry out the chief's programs, mission, and goals set for the department. Police sergeants are responsible for preparing written performance evaluations on subordinates, recommending commendations and disciplinary action when appropriate to division commanders or the chief of police, responding to grievances at the first level, training new police officers, observing police officers' performance in the field, recording the performance of subordinates, demonstrating leadership and decision making in emergency situations, and carrying out other supervisory functions.

ORGANIZATIONAL CHANGE

Organizational change, which is also referred to as **organizational reengineering** or organizational transformation, is usually provoked by some major outside driving force. Change in policing (as in any field) has been driven by a wide range of factors[49]:

- Increases in crime in a particular area and/or the fear of crime
- Budgetary concerns (a need to do more with less)
- Citizens' greater expectations of the police
- An increase in specific types of crimes (for example, juvenile crimes and domestic violence)
- Technological changes affecting the nature of police work

As discussed in Chapter 3, community policing is a response to the complexities listed above. Community policing strategies require that the police become proactive problem solvers in the communities they serve, and they are expected to become resource catalysts and direct links to the many public and private agencies that foster the problem-solving process. For community policing change to last in a law enforcement organization, the nature of the organization itself must change, so how effectively change is implemented will in large part determine whether that organization sustains community policing as a new policing model or retrenches to a more traditional style of policing.[50]

Typically, the concept of organizational change refers to organization-wide change rather than smaller changes such as adding a new employee or modifying an existing program. Examples of organization-wide change might include a change in mission, restructuring operations (for example, to reflect community-oriented policing or problem-oriented policing), new technologies, consolidation, major collaborations, or new programs such as total quality management. Often the term "organizational change" designates a fundamental and radical reorientation in the way the organization operates.

Change is complicated, and never more so than in hierarchical and bureaucratic organizations such as a police department. Aligning a law enforcement agency's resources, processes, and systems with the community policing philosophy can be a taxing undertaking. As Victor Strecher pointed out, "The status quo is easier, it is easier to defend (people who know it; they're more comfortable with a predictable, known quantity) and it is less risky."[51]

Typically in police departments, there is strong resistance to change. People are afraid of the unknown, and many think things are already just fine and do not understand the need for change. Others are inherently cynical about change, particularly after reading about the notion of change as if it were a mantra, while still others doubt there are effective means to accomplish major organizational change. Nevertheless, organizational change must be initiated and should be the first of many steps, especially in those departments that are implementing community policing.

Total Quality Management (TQM)

Total quality management (TQM) was a system initially devised by W. Edwards Deming (1900–1994) to combat the stagnation of American-operated businesses and governmental institutions resulting from a bureaucratic management style. Since the early 1980s, TQM has been adopted by many companies, such as the Ford Motor Company and the Florida Power Company, as well as colleges and universities, the military, and some police departments, such as the Madison, Wisconsin, Police Department.[52]

TQM means different things to different people. What first captured the attention of American managers was a Japanese "import" called quality circles, whose idea was to have workers meet occasionally to discuss work problems, with the end result that workers developed ideas about how to solve problems. Between 1962 and 1980, there were over 100,000 quality circles in operation in Japan, and American corporations began to use quality circles in the mid-1970s.

Total quality management means that the organization's culture is defined by and supports the constant attainment of satisfaction through an integrated system of tools, techniques, and training involving the continuous improvement of processes and resulting in high-quality products and services.[53] As popularized by Deming, TQM's premises center on intrinsic quality control, removal of adversarial relationships, constancy of purpose, continual in-service training, and attention to customer preferences.[54] It holds that change is inevitable, desirable, and welcome and that it must be planned for with participation by the greatest number of constituencies.[55] Deming's management is based on what are called the 14 points[56]:

1. Create constancy of purpose in improvement of product and service, with the aim to become competitive, to stay in business, and to provide jobs.
2. Adopt the new philosophy. We are in a new economic age. Western management must awaken to the challenge, must learn their responsibilities, and take on leadership for change.
3. Cease dependence on inspection to achieve quality. Eliminate the need for inspection on a mass basis by building quality into the product in the first place.
4. End the practice of awarding business on the basis of price tag; instead, minimize total cost. Move toward a single supplier for any one item, building a long-term relationship of loyalty and trust.
5. Improve constantly and forever the system of production and service, to improve quality and productivity, and thus constantly decrease costs.
6. Institute training on the job.
7. Institute leadership. The aim of supervision should be to help people and machines and gadgets to do a better job. Supervision of management is in need of overhaul as well as supervision of production workers.
8. Drive out fear so that everyone may work effectively for the company.

9. Break down barriers between departments. People in research, design, sales, and production must work as a team to foresee problems of production and product use that may be encountered with the product or service.

10. Eliminate slogans, exhortations, and targets for the workforce that ask for zero defects and new levels of productivity. Such exhortations only create adversarial relationships, as the bulk of the causes of low quality and low productivity belong to the system and thus lie beyond the power of the workforce.

11. Eliminate work standards (quotas) on the factory floor. Substitute leadership. Eliminate management by objectives. Eliminate management by numbers or numerical goals. Substitute leadership.

12. Remove barriers that rob the hourly worker of his or her right to joy of workmanship. The responsibility of supervisors must be changed from sheer numbers to quality. Remove barriers that rob people in management and in engineering of their right to joy of workmanship. This means abolishment of the annual merit rating and of management by objectives.

13. Institute a vigorous program of education and self-improvement.

14. Put everybody in the company to work to accomplish the transformation. The transformation is everybody's job.

Although Deming's 14 points appear to be geared toward the private sector, their major premises can be applied by police administrators as well. The orientation to continually improving service, the replacement of quantitative goals (quotas) with qualitative goals, the emphasis on the crucial feedback of line personnel, the enlargement of the roles of lower-level employees through increased training, and the use of diverse cross-unit teams to analyze the production/service delivery process fit in well with the new police strategies of problem-oriented and community-oriented policing.[57]

Learning Organization

One vision of organizational change in the management literature is the concept of the learning organization. Peter M. Senge, in his book *The Fifth Discipline: The Art and Practice of the Learning Organization*, describes the **learning organization** as one "where people continually expand their capacity to create the results they truly desire, where new and expansive patterns of thinking are nurtured, where collective aspiration is set free, and where people are continually learning how to learn together."[58] Senge proposed a systems approach to doing business, one that encourages a continuing flow of feedback from the external environment and through and among organizational units to promote the learning necessary for the organization to adapt to changing conditions.

A system is a collection of parts that interact with each other to function as a whole.[59] Thus, police organizations have a collection of divisions, sections, and units that make up the whole, with each area of the organization having a direct relationship to other areas. One area that does not function properly will ultimately affect other areas in the organization.[60]

TABLE 11–2

Traditional Management Versus Total Quality Management (TQM)	
Traditional Management	**Total Quality Management (TQM)**
Needs of users of products and services defined by specialists	Customer focus, where users of products and services define what they want
Errors and waste tolerated if they do not exceed standards	No tolerance for errors, waste, or work that does not add value to products and services
Products and services inspected for problems and then fixed	Prevention of problems
Many decisions governed by assumptions and gut feelings	Fact-based decisions using hard data and scientific procedures
Short-term planning based on budget cycle	Long-term planning based on improving mission performance
Product or service designed sequentially by isolated departments	Simultaneous design of total product or service life cycles by teams from many functions
Control and improvement by individual managers and specialists	Teamwork among managers, specialists, employees, vendors, customers, and partnering agencies
Improvement focused on onetime break-throughs such as computers and automation	Continuous improvement of every aspect of how work is done
Vertical structure and centralization based on control	Horizontal and decentralized structure based on maximizing value added to products and services
Short-term contracts awarded on price	Vendor partnership of long-term buyer/seller obligations, based on quality and continuous improvement

Source: David K. Carr and Ian D. Littman, *Excellence in Government: Total Quality Management in the 1990s.* (New York: Dutton, 1995), pp. 129–131.

The learning organization requires that all employees in all areas of the police department understand how they are linked to one another, an idea that is conspicuously absent in many police organizations. For example, in the traditional police organization, patrol officers are taught to take reports in an expedient manner, write them up, send them through the bureaucracy to the detectives, and check back into service on their beats as quickly as possible, yet paradoxically many divisions and sections in police organizations work relatively independently of each other. The reason police organizations were created in this traditional manner was to ensure the implementation of operational decisions and the following of orders.[61] Managers should focus on the system or organization as a whole but often are deterred from successfully doing so by "workplace learning disabilities," such as the natural tendency for territoriality in the workplace and the tendency to put the blame on nonexistent third parties for things amiss.[62]

A learning organization is one able to adapt and respond to change, which empowers employees because they acquire and share knowledge and then apply this learning to decision making and because they are pooling collective intelligence and stimulating creative thought to improve performance. Supervisors facilitate learning by sharing and aligning the organization's vision for the future and sustaining a sense of community and strong culture.

The challenge issued by the learning organization is to use knowledge as a basis for its strategy and to use organizational learning as bedrock for its ability to be proactive. According to one author, learning organizations possess several characteristics:

> Learning organizations are skilled at five main activities: systematic problem solving, experimentation with new approaches, learning from the experiences and best practices of others, and transferring knowledge quickly and efficiently throughout the organization. . . . Many companies practice these activities to some degree. But few are consistently successful because they rely largely on happenstance and isolated examples. By creating systems and processes that support these activities and in integrating them into the fabric of daily operations, companies can manage their learning more effectively.[63]

Most organizations learn poorly regarding the way they are designed and managed, the way people's jobs are defined, and (more importantly) the way we have all been taught to think. In police organizations, learning problems persist despite the best efforts of bright and committed people, and often the harder they try to solve problems, the worse the results.[64] This situation may be perpetuated by the hierarchal and paramilitary structure of policing, which does not usually encourage creativity or innovative problem solving. One advantage of a police learning organization is that it fosters an organizational culture that encourages continual learning. A continual learning culture in a police organization may involve creating a research and development division that actually does empirical research and development, developing a structure or process to foster learning (for example, crime analysis that spans work units); developing a process to foster learning involving senior police officials, which may reduce battles between departmental units, and taking a talent inventory of sworn and civilian personnel; and fostering learning around problem solving and instituting a bottom-up performance appraisal of organizational performance to continue to enhance police-researcher partnerships.[65]

A learning culture allows the police organization to more effectively adapt and transition in a changing environment. For example, the idea that police organizations establish a research and development unit that actually performs research will allow the police to make more informed and fiscally responsible decisions. A police department, in order to provide a more effective service, should know if there is a relationship between foot patrol activities and decreases in crime in specific areas or if there is a correlation with community policing activities and decreases in crime in the community. Further, police executives may desire to know the level of citizen satisfaction or fear of crime in various areas when different patrol methodologies are employed.

Imagine a police organization that allows officers the opportunity to participate in group processes with the objective of identifying new and improved methodologies aimed at improving police service. This is a stark deviation from the traditional police organizational environment in which most decisions are made at the top of the organizational pyramid and filter down to those employees in the bottom ranks. Line-level police officers deal with problems on a daily basis and may be in the best position to offer solutions and recommend new or improved procedures to adapt to the ever-changing environment.

A police organization that evolves into a learning organization may raise the morale of police employees. Employees could examine processes and recommend changes without fear of reprisal and could be given more leeway for their problem-solving talents; such developments would fit in well with the community policing model. Under the traditional command-and-control structure, managers are not sufficiently challenged and stimulated by detailed and truthful feedback from lower levels.

Contingency Management

In an ever-changing society, police working under the axiom of community policing are now asked to solve crime and disorder problems working in concert with citizens. Under the classical theory of organization, this is a difficult task because the police respond to community problems in one uniform way and usually in accordance with a set of standard operating procedures or rules or regulations that are rarely deviated from. Effective problem-solving and community policing strategies will be deficient in organizations that are still largely dependent on the classical theory of organization. Police deal with a variety of problems each day in any given community, and each of these problems may require a different problem-solving approach; in other words, problems experienced in one part of a community may be totally different from problems experienced in another part of the community and thus require different solutions and approaches.

Contingency management (sometimes called the situational approach) is a viable management tool when dealing with many complex problems and issues that police encounter. The contingency perspective underscores and emphasizes the fact that organizations are different, face varying circumstances (contingencies), and thus may require different ways of managing, that is, different managerial decisions and actions.[66] The contingency perspective recognizes that managers must read and attempt to interpret the situational contingencies facing them before deciding the best way to coordinate and integrate work activities. The contingency approach—like TQM and the learning organization—seems to be a natural complement to community-oriented policing.

It was in the mid-1960s that the contingency view of management, which emphasizes the fit between organizational processes and the characteristics of the situation, first emerged. It calls for fitting the structure of the organization to various possible or chance events, it questions the use of universal management practices and advocates using behavioral and systems viewpoints independently or in combination to deal with various circumstances, and it assumes that managerial behavior is dependent on a wide variety of situations.

Flattening of the Organization

Modern police organizations are dominated by the use of bureaucratic systems of control whose organizational structures tend to be characterized by high levels of vertical and horizontal differentiation. A steep vertical organizational structure often makes police organizations dysfunctional because responding to crime problems in the community requires a flexible structure that allows officers to make necessary adjustments both quickly and efficiently.[67] The most obvious side effect of the burdensome hierarchy is the slow speed of decision making—if every decision has to be filtered down through six or seven levels of hierarchy, which is common in many police departments, no decision is likely to be quick. Professor David Bayley has criticized the traditional police organizational structure on several grounds[68]:

1. The traditional structure cannot support new, more democratic leadership styles.
2. Today's police officers are very different from the officers of just 20 years ago. They want and need to ask questions about issues affecting them in the work environment. The traditional structure of police command and control is in direct conflict with this new mentality.
3. The traditional structure creates impediments to the adoption of new ideas. The traditional emphasis is on rules and regulations, which can mean that when ideas run counter to policy, accepted practice, or tradition, they are labeled "unworkable" and discarded before they have a chance. Further, the requirement that line-level personnel's suggestions make their way up a steep chain of command means that the transmission of good ideas may be delayed, distorted, or prematurely stopped.
4. The traditional top-down structure is far too centralized. Resources are allocated according to generic plans drawn up at headquarters, and the officers who are in closest contact with operational problems have little opportunity to shape policy.

In his book *The Third Wave*, noted futurist Alvin Toffler examined many of the forces that will shape society in the 21st century and predicted that to survive in the 21st century, organizations will become significantly less top-heavy.[69] Flattened hierarchies will, in turn, vastly alter the traditional bureaucratic pyramid structure common in most organizations, including law enforcement agencies. Toffler also speculated that successful organizations will become more flexible, capable of interchanging two or more structural shapes as conditions warrant.[70]

If we apply Toffler's ideas to police agencies, the advantages of such structural flexibility become clear. In times of riots or other mass disorder, the police must quickly become a rigid central unit of operation, and a clearly defined and strict chain of command becomes critical to applying force efficiently and to initiating a quick response to social upheaval. When relative tranquility prevails, however, the rigid command structure must give way to a flexible response to specific community problems.[71]

Structural duality requires that police supervisors operate flexibly under both systems. In one circumstance, this means adapting to a situation that demands strict command and control for the sake of public and officer safety; in another, it calls for allowing patrol personnel more accountability, control, and input in their daily beat work. A flattened, decentralized, and more horizontal structure allows an organization to react to the changing environment more effectively. When the organizational structure is flattened, employees at lower levels will make more decisions, including some decisions that have traditionally been made by middle management or (in some cases) upper command.[72]

Flat organizations will have shorter lines of communication between top and bottom levels of the organization, so the communications are more likely to be faster and have less chance of distortion.[73] In addition, individuals working in organizations with flat structures tend to have higher morale and job satisfaction when compared to those in organizations with more hierarchical structures. Organizations with flat structures, however, tend to place more stress and pressures on supervisors and require high-caliber managers.

In sum, the benefits of flattening the organizational structure are many[74]:

1. Communication enhancement (fewer layers of the chain of command to send information through)
2. Empowerment of employees at the bottom of the organization to make more decisions
3. Increased participation in the problem-solving process of those employees closest to the problems
4. Improved service delivery (the police officers at the bottom of the pyramid being closest to the customers, meaning citizens, and being in an advantageous position to identify methods to improve service delivery)
5. Enhanced bottom-up input on policy development
6. Improved coordination of services internally in the police department
7. Reduced bureaucracy, red tape, and time delays

◢ SUMMARY

Police organizations are made up of many persons performing a number of tasks to accomplish the mission and goals of the organization. Traditional police departments are paramilitary in style and are organized according to the classical theory of organization. Traditional or classical management focuses on efficiency and includes bureaucratic, scientific, and administrative management: Bureaucratic management relies on a rational set of structuring guidelines (such as rules and procedures), a hierarchy, and a clear division of labor; scientific management focuses on the one best way to do a job; administrative management emphasizes the flow of information in the operation of the organization. No single theory is used exclusively in a police department; instead, it may use a constellation of approaches in order to accomplish its mission.

Managers create and maintain an internal environment, commonly called the organization, so that others can work efficiently in it. A manager's job consists of planning, organizing, directing, and controlling the resources of the organization. In a police department, there are various levels of management and supervision—top management, middle management, and line-level supervision—each of which performs distinct duties to accomplish the mission of the organization.

Police departments across the nation are increasingly engaging in organizational reengineering (or organizational change) in order to more appropriately guide organizations in the era of community-oriented and problem-oriented policing. Organizational reengineering means changing the way people work—what tasks are performed and how information flows—across functional areas and departments. Organizational approaches such as total quality management (TQM), the learning organization, contingency management, and flattening of the organizational structure appear to complement the changes required in community-oriented and problem-oriented policing environments.

▣ QUESTIONS IN REVIEW

1. What are the criticisms of the classical theory on which police departments are modeled?
2. Discuss the principles of the learning organization.
3. What is meant by the terms "chain of command" and "span of control"?
4. What are the advantages of flattening the police organizational structure?
5. What is contingency management?
6. Discuss the criticisms of the paramilitary nature of police departments.
7. What are the objectives of the professional model of policing?

◆ POLICE RESOURCES ON THE WEB

FBI Futures Working Group
http://www.fbi.gov/hq/td/fwg/residence.htm

Fredrick Taylor and Scientific Management
http://www.netmba.com/mgmt/scientific

International Association of Chiefs of Police
http://www.theiacp.org

Max Weber Profile
http://cepa.newschool.edu/het/profiles/weber.htm

National Institute of Justice Publications
http://nij.ncjrs.org/publications/pubs_db.asp

Peter Senge and the Learning Organization
http://www.infed.org/thinkers/senge.htm

Police Futurists International
http://www.policefuturists.org

Police Institute, Rutgers University, Newark
http://policeinstitute.org/index.htm

Southern Police Institute
http://www.louisville.edu/a-s/ja/spi

REFERENCES

1. STEPHEN P. ROBBINS, *Organizational Theory: Structure, Design, and Applications* (Englewood Cliffs, NJ: Prentice Hall, 1987), p. 3.
2. NATHAN F. IANNONE and MARVIN P. IANNONE, *Supervision of Police Personnel*, 6th ed. (Upper Saddle River, NJ: Prentice Hall, 2001), pp. 210–215.
3. CHARLES R. SWANSON, LEONARD TERRITO, and ROBERT W. TAYLOR, *Police Administration: Structures, Processes, and Behavior*, 5th ed. (Upper Saddle River, NJ: Prentice Hall, 2001).
4. STEPHEN P. ROBBINS and MARY COULTER, *Management*, 6th ed. (Upper Saddle River, NJ: Prentice Hall, 1999).
5. ROBERT H. LANGWORTHY, "Organizational Structure," in *What Works in Policing: Operations and Administration Examined*, ed. Gary Cordner and Donna C. Hale (Cincinnati, OH: Anderson Publishing, 1992).
6. SAMUEL WALKER, *The Police in America: An Introduction* (New York: McGraw-Hill, 1990).

7. JEFFREY PATTERSON, "Community Policing: Learning the Lessons of History," *FBI Law Enforcement Bulletin* (November 1995), p. 17.

8. LANGWORTHY, 1992, pp. 88–89.

9. Ibid., p. 90.

10. MICHAEL L. BIRZER, "Police Supervision in the 21st Century," *FBI Law Enforcement Bulletin* (June 1996): 31–35.

11. Ibid.

12. Ibid.

13. HAROLD KOONTZ, CYRIL O'DONNELL, and HEINZ WEIHRICH, *Essentials of Management*, 4th ed. (New York: McGraw-Hill, 1986), p. 10.

14. LUTHER GULICK, "Notes on the Theory of Organization," in *Papers on the Science of Administration*, ed. L. Gulick and L. Urick (Reprinted 2001, New York: August M. Kelly, 1969), p. 13.

15. MICHAEL L. BIRZER, "Organizational Change and Community Policing," in *Community Policing: A Policing Strategy for the 21st Century*, ed. M.J. Palmiotto (Gaithersburg, MD: Aspen Publishing, 2000).

16. HENRI FAYOL, *General and Industrial Management*. Translated from the French by Constance Storrs; with a foreword by L. Urwick (London, New York: Pitman, 1949), pp. 19–41.

17. JAY M. SHAFRITZ and J. STEVEN OTT, *Classics of Organizational Theory* (Fort Worth, TX: Harcourt College Publishers, 2001).

18. J. STEVEN OTT, *Classic Readings in Organizational Behavior* (Pacific Grove, CA: Brooks/Cole, 1989).

19. DAVID SCHUMAN, *Bureaucracies, Organizations, and Administration: A Political Primer* (New York: Macmillan, 1976).

20. TALCOT PARSONS (ed.), *Max Weber: The Theory of Social and Economic Organization* (New York: Free Press, 1947).

21. WARREN BENNIS, *Beyond Bureaucracy: Essays on the Development and Evolution of Human Organization* (New York: McGraw-Hill, 1966), p. 5.

22. O.W. WILSON and ROY C. MCLAREN, *Police Administration*, 4th ed. (New York: McGraw-Hill, 1977).

23. JEFFREY PATTERSON, "Community Policing: Learning the Lessons of History," *FBI Law Enforcement Bulletin* (November 1995), p. 5.

24. BIRZER, 1996.

25. GEORGE L. KELLING and MARK H. MOORE, "The Evolving Strategy of Policing," *Perspectives on Policing* 4 (Washington, DC: National Institute of Justice, 1988): 1–15.

26. Ibid.

27. W.J. BOPP, *O.W. Wilson and the Search for a Police Profession* (Port Washington, NY: Kennikat Press, 1977), p. 5.

28. BIRZER, 1996.

29. CHRIS ARGYRIS, *Personality and Organization: The Conflict Between System and the Individual* (New York: Harper, 1957), pp. 24–29.

30. IANNONE and IANNONE, 2001, p. 211.

31. MICHAEL J. PALMIOTTO, *Policing: Concepts, Strategies, and Current Issues in American Police Forces* (Durham, NC: Carolina Academic Press, 1997).

32. IANNONE and IANNONE, 2001, p. 213.

33. TOM BURNS and G.M. STALKER, *Management of Innovation* (London: Tavistock Publications, 1961), p. 19.

34. BILLY J. HODGE and WILLIAM P. ANTHONY, *Organizational Theory: An Environmental Approach* (Boston, MA: Allyn & Bacon, 1979), p. 249.

35. PALMIOTTO, 1997.

36. PETER B. KRASKA, "Grounded Research into U.S. Paramilitary Policing: Forging the Iron Fist Inside the Velvet Glove," *Policing and Society* 7, no. 4, (1997): 253–270.

37. Ibid.

38. DIANA CECILIA WEBER, *Warrior Cops: The Ominous Growth of Paramilitarism in American Police Departments* (Washington, DC: The Cato Institute, 1999), p. 10.

39. JAMES H. AUTEN, "The Paramilitary Model of Police and Police Professionalism," in *The Ambivalent Force*, 3rd ed., ed. Abraham S. Blumberg and Elaine Niederhoffer (New York: Holt, Rinehart and Winston, 1985), pp. 122–123.

40. TOMAS J. COWPER, "The Myth of the Military Model of Leadership in Law Enforcement," in *Contemporary Policing: Controversies, Challenges, and Solutions*, ed. Q.C. Thurman and J. Zhao (Los Angeles, CA: Roxbury, 1999), pp. 113–125.

41. WILSON and MCLAREN, 1977.

42. Ibid.

43. Ibid.

44. HERBERT A. SIMON, "The Proverbs of Administration," *Public Administration Review* 6 (Winter 1946): 53–67.

45. Ibid., pp. 292–293.

46. SIMON, 1946, p. 64.

47. NATHAN F. Iannone, *Supervision of Police Personnel*, 5th ed. (Englewood Cliffs, NJ: Prentice Hall, 1994).

48. WAYNE W. BENNETT and KAREN M. HESS, *Management and Supervision in Law Enforcement,* 3rd ed. (Belmont, CA: Wadsworth, 2001).

49. BIRZER, 2000, p. 229.

50. ANDREA SCHNEIDER, *Community Policing in Action: A Practitioners View to Organizational Change* (Washington, DC: United States Department of Justice, Office of Community Oriented Policing, 2003).

51. VICTOR G. STRECHER, *Planning Community Policing: Goal Specific Cases and Exercises.* (Prospect Heights, IL: Waveland, 1997), p. 12.

52. BIRZER, 2000.

53. MARSHALL SASHKIN and KEN KISER, "What Is TQM?" *Executive Excellence* 9, no. 5 (May 1992): 11.

54. W. EDWARDS DEMING, *Out of Crisis* (Cambridge, MA: Massachusetts Institute of Technology, Center for Advanced Engineering Study, 1986), pp. 48–52.

55. SASHKIN and KISER, 1992, p. 12.

56. DEMING, 1986.

57. BIRZER, 2000.

58. PETER M. SENGE, *The Fifth Discipline: The Art and Practice of the Learning Organization* (New York: Doubleday, 1990), p. 3.

59. DRAPER L. KAUFFMAN, *Systems I: An Introduction of Systems Thinking* (Minneapolis, MN: S.A. Carlton Publisher, 1980), pp. 201–211.

60. MICHAEL L. BIRZER, RONALD TANNEHILL, and MICHAEL PALMIOTTO, "Police Organizational Change: Learning Principles That Apply," *Law Enforcement Executive Forum* 4, no. 7 (2004): 87–101.

61. DAVID H BAYLEY, *Police for the Future* (New York: Oxford University Press, 1994).

62. PETER M. SENGE, "All Systems Are Go: The Model of the Learning Organization Integrates Psychological Realism in Understanding and Modify the Organization, *Management Today* (November, 1997): 137–138.

63. D. GARVIN, "Building a Learning Organization," *Harvard Business Review* (August 1993): 231–241.

64. SENGE, 1990.

65. WILLIAM A. GELLER, *Local Government Police Management*, 3rd ed. (Washington, DC: International City/County Manager's Association, 1991), p. 21.

66. ROBBINS and COULTER, 1999, pp. 231–232.

67. ROBERT A. JOHNSON, "Police Organizational Design and Structure," *FBI Law Enforcement Bulletin* (June 1994): 5–7.

68. BAYLEY, 1994, p. 88.

69. ALVIN A. TOFFLER, *The Third Wave* (New York: Bantam Books, 1981).

70. Ibid., p. 263.

71. BIRZER, 1996.

72. BIRZER, 2000.

73. JOHNSON, 1994, p. 231.

74. Ibid., p. 234.

Critical Issues in Policing

Key Terms

Burnout
External stress
Hair analysis
Internal stress

Operational stress
Police stressors
Stress
Urinalysis

Outline

Introduction
Police Stress and Burnout
Police Suicide
Police Alcoholism and Drug Abuse

Biohazards in Policing
Reduction and Prevention of Stress
   in Policing

Learning Objectives

After reading this chapter, you should be able to:

1. Discuss the causes of stress for police officers.
2. Explain why police officers commit suicide.
3. Identify and describe the problems involving alcoholism and drug abuse
   by law enforcement personnel.
4. List and describe the biohazards in policing.
5. Discuss the various methods that can be used to reduce police stress.

INTRODUCTION

A growing body of evidence indicates that in any police department a small percentage of officers are responsible for a disproportionate share of citizen complaints. The 1991 Rodney King incident heightened national awareness of the phenomenon of the problem officer.[1]

This chapter focuses on several critical issues in policing that are not covered elsewhere in the text. The issues include police stress and burnout, police suicide, alcoholism and drug abuse among police officers, and biohazards in policing. While the issues are not closely related, they all provide serious problems for law enforcement agencies.

POLICE STRESS AND BURNOUT

As discussed in Chapter 4, police work is full of stress, **stress** being defined as physical or mental tension. As one researcher noted,[2] whether it's police stress or police burnout, the results are the same—a broken individual. How the officer breaks can vary. It may be physical: heart attack, chronic ulcers, diabetes, severe dermatitis, or a host of other health-related problems induced by and resulting from extreme stress. At times it is psychological: alcoholism, suicide, pronounced depression, debilitating phobic reactions, excessive anxiety. Frequently the results are both physical and psychological. Remember, the vast majority of police officers do not suffer extreme burnout or excessive stress and suffer a breakdown; for every officer who breaks down to the point of no return, there are at least ten others who are not that severely affected but who are painfully affected nevertheless.

Burnout refers to a state of extreme psychophysical exhaustion that is usually work-related. Authors Schaufeli and Enzmann suggested that a single all-encompassing definition of burnout may be elusive.[3] They developed the following definition of burnout:

> Burnout is a persistent, negative, work-related state of mind in "normal" individuals that is primarily characterized by exhaustion, which is accompanied by distress, a sense of reduced effectiveness, decreased motivation, and the development of dysfunctional attitudes and behaviors at work. The psychological condition develops gradually but may remain unnoticed for a long time by the individual involved. It results from a misfit between intentions and reality in the job. Often burnout is self-perpetuating because of inadequate coping strategies that are associated with the syndrome.[4]

Their definition encompasses four general symptoms: (1) distress (affective, cognitive, physical, and behavioral), (2) a sense of reduced effectiveness, (3) decreased motivation, and (4) dysfunctional attitudes and behaviors at work. The definition also suggests that burnout may be self-perpetuating. There are some physical results of police burnout:

- Physical exhaustion
- Viral sicknesses
- Diarrhea or constipation
- Stomach disorders
- Chest pains
- Hyperventilation
- Trouble breathing
- Pains in arms

There are also emotional results of police burnout:

- Substance abuse
- Negative attitudes
- Depression
- Inability to sleep (or too much sleep) accompanied by feelings of tiredness
- Proneness to accidents both on and off the job
- Constant warring attitude regarding the department and continual trouble at work
- High frequency of citizen complaints
- Unhappy family life
- Thoughts of going "crazy" (and fear of letting anyone know)
- Suicidal ideation (and fear of discussing it, not wanting to appear weak)
- Desire to quit and run away
- Attitude of counting the days to retirement

Stress researcher Kroes grouped **police stressors** into four broad categories:

1. **Internal stress** caused by organizational practices and characteristics. Internal stress generally includes functional duties, policies, and procedures that have been implemented as part of an organization's standard operating procedures. According to Kroes, stress develops when such policies are implemented without input from officers and when there are insufficient organizational resources available to meet the requirements of the policies.[5] The productivity of officers also suffers from shift rotations and the resulting alterations to body rhythms. Other internal stressors include poor supervision, lack or perceived lack of support by administrators, no recognition for tasks performed, insufficient training, lack of adequate career ladders, and excessive paperwork.
2. Stress caused by system practices and characteristics. For example, officers' court testimony is scheduled at times other than their regular work schedule, adding more stress to court appearances; in addition, the mandatory court appearances tend to interfere with officers' personal time, which could be spent with their family. Also, officers are often harassed in court and made to appear incompetent.

1

3. **External stress** caused by public practices and characteristics. This type of stress is caused by the perception of lack of general public support for police officers. Also included under this category is the social stress caused by the dissimilarity between officers' socioeconomic status and that of their constituency.

4. **Operational stress** caused by police work itself. Operational stress results from the tragedies of life on the street, daily confrontations with life-and-death situations, and dealings with drug pushers, prostitutes, murderers, thieves, and the like on a regular basis. There are dangerous times threatening an officer's safety interspersed with periods of boredom, resulting in alternating levels of alertness and energy.

J. F. Dietrich identified what he considered the five progressive career stages of police stress and burnout.[6] During the first period of an officer's career (0–5 years), the officer suffers alienation from the nonpolice world;

Terminate Deputy Sheriff Whose Misconduct Was Allegedly Caused by Job-Related Stress?

When Gregory Nicolini was 21 years of age, he was hired as a deputy sheriff for Tuolumne County, California. During his 9 years with the department, he was neither disciplined nor recommended for discipline. His personnel file contains references to his outstanding job performance, favorable evaluations, regular merit increases, and letters of appreciation, and he was promoted to the rank of sergeant and certified as a paramedic.

The incident resulting in his termination started when a pharmacist called the sheriff claiming that Nicolini had just filled a questionable prescription and appeared to be "on" something. When questioned, Nicolini admitted injecting himself with drugs during work hours and falsifying a prescription. He claimed he injected himself with a painkilling prescription drug to combat a migraine headache caused by the stress of his job. He was fired for being dishonest and for discrediting the county by conduct unbecoming an officer.

By way of a petition for a writ of administrative mandate, Nicolini sought to reverse the county sheriff's and board of supervisors' decision to terminate him from his deputy sheriff's job. Nicolini contended that the sheriff and the board refused to consider evidence that the alteration of the Valium prescription was unlikely to recur, was stress-related, and was due to a transitory medical condition that would not affect his future job performance. To support this argument, he relied on the testimony of a clinical psychologist specializing in police stress who examined him and presented the opinion that the Valium prescription alteration was a "lapse of judgment" that "sounds like a once-in-a-lifetime event up to that time." The doctor testified that when people experience a serious life-threatening event or a major loss, it is common for the individual to experience the same emotions or become "a little crazy" on or about the anniversary of the event. The doctor then hypothesized that the altered Valium prescription was part of this "anniversary reaction" due to an incident in which an unknown assailant repeatedly shot at Nicolini but was never apprehended.

Would you reinstate former officer Nicoline to his position as deputy sheriff?[7]

in the second period (5–10 years), the officer suffers emotional shutdown and tends to block out everything but the police world. An emotional uncertainty is experienced during the third period (10–15 years), and an officer becomes unsure of how to start to express his or her emotions again to avoid experiencing the alienation and emotional shutdown of the early years on the force. The namelessness stage occurs in the fourth period of the officer's career (15–20 years) when an officer often finds a safe administrative niche and tries to perform useful service but is unable to fight the system. In the last period of a career (20–35 years), the officer attempts to maintain the status quo: The officer has a stake in not changing because there is too much that needs changing, the officer does not want to admit that he or she has failed, and the officer does not want to let the new officers down.

POLICE SUICIDE

The numbers of deaths of law enforcement officers due to suicide are two to three times the number of line-of-duty deaths in law enforcement agencies and among emergency workers. In one 1992 study it was noted that the suicide rate among New York City Police Department (NYPD) officers was about 29 per 100,000 annually, which was considerably higher than that of the general U.S. population (11.7 per 100,000).[8] Many of these suicides were attributed to the high stress level of the profession and a lack of awareness of suicidal signs or symptoms and suicide prevention techniques.

Common Myths About Suicide

The National P.O.L.I.C.E. Suicide Foundation lists common myths regarding suicide[9]:

- People who talk about suicide rarely commit suicide.
- The tendency toward suicide is inherited and passed on from one generation from another.
- The suicidal person wants to die and feels there is no turning back.
- Everyone who commits suicide is depressed.
- There is very little correlation between alcoholism and suicide.
- A person who commits suicide is mentally ill.
- A suicide attempt means that the attempter will always entertain thoughts of suicide.
- If you ask someone directly, "Do you feel like killing yourself?" this will lead him or her to make a suicide attempt.
- Suicide is more common among lower socioeconomic groups than elsewhere in our society.
- Suicidal persons rarely seek medical help.

The National P.O.L.I.C.E. Suicide Foundation was established to provide suicide awareness and prevention training programs as well as support services to meet the psychological and spiritual needs of emergency workers and their families. The foundation's goals are many: to provide suicide-related counseling and support for families and officers (including law enforcement, paramedics, IRS agents, firemen, and other emergency workers); to offer encouragement and hope to families of suicide victims by helping them to understand and deal with their anger and guilt; to provide educational seminars to educate the general public and government employees on suicide awareness; and to establish a network of communication among suicide survivors.

POLICE ALCOHOLISM AND DRUG ABUSE

Most studies of alcoholism and drug abuse by law enforcement personnel suggest that alcohol and drug abuse are as frequent or more frequent than in the general population. One national study of 2,000 plus police officers concluded that about 23 percent of the officers had serious alcohol problems and 10 percent had serious drug problems. This number is substantially higher than the number estimated for the general population. Alcohol abuse has been implicated as a significant factor in officer suicides. A study of 6,182 Canadian police officers revealed that 11 percent drank more than five drinks per day and an additional 13 percent drank more than three drinks per day, so a total of 24 percent drank at a frequency that, if maintained over an extended period, can be predicted to cause physical damage.[10] With regard to drugs, 37 percent reported using illicit drugs in their lifetime, 14 percent said they had used illicit drugs in the past year, and 7 percent reported illicit drug use in the past 30 days. A questionnaire administered to police officers in Chicago revealed that 40 percent drank while on duty. In a study of officers in a major Midwestern state, data revealed that 53 percent came to work with a hangover and that an "average" officer drank alcohol on the job almost eight days every half year.[11] Another report estimated that alcohol abuse was present in approximately 60 percent of the police suicides in the Chicago Police Department.[12] Alcoholism may also lead to other problems such as absenteeism and traffic accidents, as well as intoxication on duty.

Drug-Testing Regulations, Hawaii Police Department

Appendix A to the text contains Hawaii Police Department's Drug Testing General Order No. 529. A careful examination of the appendix will provide the reader with an understanding of the complexity of this issue.

Testing Methods for Drug Use

Urinalysis.   **Urinalysis,** the most commonly used method of testing for drug use, is an old drug-testing technology whose problems have been exploited by drug users. Urinalysis can generally detect drug use for the previous two to three days for most drugs, but after that, the body flushes out the substance. Drug users can simply abstain (from drug use) for a short period of time, drink water, take the urine test, and pass; also, they can substitute clean samples or tamper with urine specimens. Information about beating urine tests is widely available, and advertisements for "clean urine" and urine-adulterating products are seen on the Internet. Beating a urine test is not that difficult for an experienced drug user. The act of collecting a urine sample is intrusive and unpleasant. To decrease a person's ability to tamper with the sample, urine collection must be observed, a situation that creates uneasiness (especially for women) due to the lack of privacy.

Blood Testing.   The period for drug detection in blood testing is short, usually only hours. Because of people's fear of blood-borne infectious diseases, drug testing using blood is not a preferred method. Blood testing is the least-used and least-recommended form of drug testing due to the invasiveness of the collection procedure, the need for skilled phlebotomists (those who take blood samples), and the extremely short drug detection period.

Hair Testing.   **Hair analysis** can detect drug use for approximately 90 days, and temporary abstention won't beat the test. It cannot be evaded (as happens in urinalysis) because the drug residue remains permanently entrapped in the hair. A cosmetically undetectable snip of hair is easily collected without causing embarrassment and can be done in-house, saving the time, inconvenience, and cost of having someone visit a urine collection site.

BIOHAZARDS IN POLICING

Most discussions and research regarding biohazards in policing are concerned with those associated with terrorism, especially since September 11, 2001. Prior to that date, the law enforcement community had significant problems dealing with individuals who were (or were suspected to be) carriers of infectious diseases such as AIDs. Since 9/11 the police have been confronted with an entirely new set of concerns regarding safety and security; in addition to earlier hazards, the police now need to deal with terrorist threats of attack using biochemical hazards that could mean the potential destruction of an entire community. Since most alleged terrorists have been identified as individuals from a variety of countries, the police must also pay attention to preventing harassment and discrimination based on national origin and religion.

Each law enforcement agency is required to develop policies for its officers on how to handle situations that may involve a biohazard threat. For example, the U.S. Postal Service has developed warning signs for suspicious mail[13]:

- Mail that is unexpected or that is from someone unfamiliar to you
- Mail that is addressed to someone no longer with your organization and/or that contains misspelled names or otherwise outdated information (such as improper title)
- Mail that bears no return address or that has one that can't be verified as legitimate
- Mail whose postmark is from a city different from the return address
- Mail that has unusual weight (given its size) or that appears to be lopsided
- Mail that is marked with restrictive endorsements such as "Personal" or "Confidential" and letters or packages that exhibit powder or dust, protruding wires, strange odors, or stains

The U.S. Postal Service directs its employees to promptly separate suspicious mail and put it in a zippered plastic bag, after which they are directed to contact the appropriate law enforcement officials immediately. Anyone who comes in contact with an unknown substance should immediately wash it off with soap and water and then seek medical attention.

REDUCTION AND PREVENTION OF STRESS IN POLICING

The material for this section was taken from a report issued by the *NIJ Journal* in January 2000 that was coauthored by Peter Finn, Vincent Talucci, and Jennifer Wood.

Police officers and members of their families consider their jobs to be one of the most stressful. It is hard to disagree with that assessment, as officers themselves report high rates of divorce, alcoholism, suicide, and other emotional and health problems. No job is immune from stress, but for the law enforcement officer, the strains and tensions experienced at work are unique, often extreme, and sometimes unavoidable. Fortunately, many law enforcement agencies, recognizing the high toll exacted by stress on officers and their families, are tackling it with an array of creative prevention and reduction strategies. Through the Corrections and Law Enforcement Family Support (CLEFS) program of the National Institute of Justice, several of these agencies are receiving support.

This article summarized an NIJ report that documented the causes and effects of job-related stress affecting law enforcement officers and their families. Much of the information was drawn from interviews (conducted as part of the study) with officers themselves and their family members. Also included in this article were highlights both of some stress prevention and reduction programs reported in the study and of some CLEFS projects.

Sources of Stress

Exposure to violence, suffering, and death is inherent to the profession of law enforcement officers. There are other sources of stress as well: Officers who deal with offenders on a daily basis may view some sentences as too lenient, they may perceive the public's opinion of police performance to be unfavorable, they often are required to work mandatory rotating shifts, and they may not have enough time to spend with their families. Police officers also face unusual, often highly disturbing, situations, such as dealing with a child homicide victim or the survivors of vehicle crashes.

The nature of the organizations in which officers work may also be a source of stress. Police departments historically have been structured along military lines and as a result often have been rigidly hierarchical and highly bureaucratic, with management styles that can be inflexible. Although in many instances police culture is changing, in many others the leadership remains predominately white and male, opportunities for advancement are limited, and despite the ubiquity of the personal computer, a large amount of paperwork still is required.

Is Stress Getting Worse?

Officers may increasingly view stress as a normal part of their job, but they also see themselves as being under considerably more pressure than they or their colleagues were 10 or 20 years ago. They see new sources of stress in the high level of violent crime and in what they perceive as greater public scrutiny and adverse publicity. They also feel that police camaraderie has declined, they fear contracting air- and blood-borne diseases such as tuberculosis and HIV/AIDS, and they see themselves as having to deal with such relatively new issues as cultural diversity and the imperative of political correctness.

Even widely accepted changes in law enforcement can lead to more stress for some officers. Although community policing may mean more job satisfaction, greater overall departmental efficiency, and higher morale, the transition to it can cause apprehension on the part of the officers who on a day-to-day basis must operationalize this fundamental shift in the philosophy of policing.

Performance expectations are new and perhaps not fully understood by all officers. Whether or not stress is increasing, identifying the causes is a first step toward reducing and preventing it.

Effects of Stress

The physical and emotional effects of stress are numerous and often severe, and any one of them can impair job performance. Police officers commonly reported many consequences of job-related stress:

- Cynicism and suspiciousness
- Emotional detachment from various aspects of daily life

- Reduced efficiency
- Absenteeism and early retirement
- Excessive aggressiveness (which may trigger an increase in citizen complaints)
- Alcoholism and other substance abuse problems
- Marital or other family problems (for example, extramarital affairs, divorce, or domestic violence)
- Posttraumatic stress disorder
- Heart attacks, ulcers, weight gain, and other health problems
- Suicide

According to many counselors who work with police officers, difficulties with intimate relationships are the most common problem they treat.

Do Families Feel Stress, Too?

If the effects on officers are severe, they can be similarly serious for officers' family members. In one survey of the spouses of police officers, a very large percentage said they experienced unusually high levels of stress because of their spouse's job.[14]

Stress felt by spouses is a concern in and of itself and also because a stressful home environment can adversely affect the officer's job performance. Even conditions, situations, or incidents that may not trouble the officers themselves—or that they may even enjoy (such as shift work or undercover work)—can mean severe problems for their families.

Many sources of stress were commonly cited by officers' spouses[15]:

- Shift work and overtime
- Concern over the spouse's cynicism, his or her need to feel in control in the home, or his or her inability or unwillingness to express feelings
- Fear that the spouse will be hurt or killed in the line of duty
- Officers' and others' excessively high expectations of their children
- Avoidance, teasing, or harassment of the officer's children by other children because of the parent's job
- Presence of a gun in the home
- Officer's 24-hour role as a law enforcer
- Perception that the officer prefers to spend time with coworkers rather than with his or her family
- Too much or too little discussion of the job
- Family members' perception of the officer as paranoid or excessively vigilant and overprotective of them
- Problems in helping the officer cope with work-related problems
- "Critical incidents" or the officer's injury or death on the job

Because stress affects family members, they are often the first to recognize the officer's need for help, and they can play a crucial role.

When the Baltimore Police Department decided to seek the sources of stress in the agency, it turned for assistance to public health researchers at nearby Johns Hopkins University. With the Fraternal Order of Police as the third partner, the department created Project SHIELDS to take on this task as well as to develop response strategies.

The sources of stress were identified by means of a survey conducted by the researchers among line officers and spouses/life partners. Some of the results were surprising[16]: Fully two-thirds of the officers said they considered media reports of alleged police wrongdoing to be stressful to them; the same proportion said that what they view as lack of administrative support for officers in trouble was a major source of stress; and almost one-fourth reported low energy or chronic back pain, which they believed was related to job stress.

After the Johns Hopkins researchers complete their analysis of the survey data, they and the project's advisory board (officers and family members) will help the department develop a response. Total quality management (TQM) teams will be established to focus on selected issues drawn from the research findings. Consisting of officers from all ranks, the TQM teams will develop strategies to address aspects of organizational stress identified in the survey as particularly problematic.[17]

Encouraging an individual to seek assistance before the problem becomes worse is the concept behind the Spousal Academy, a component of the comprehensive officer and family support program offered by the Collier County, Florida, Sheriff's Office. The academy offers training to spouses and other domestic partners of deputies and recruits who are enrolled in the sheriff's office's training academy. The ten-hour program involves an introduction to the nature of law enforcement work and an opportunity to discuss expectations about the effect the spouse's occupation will have on family life.

Participants learn about the structure of the sheriff's office, about such human resources issues as employee benefits (health insurance, for example), and about stress management and conflict resolution.

Two related programs in the development stage are peer support groups for spouses and life partners and for deputies' adolescent children. Soliciting feedback from participants is part of the program, and several noted the program's effectiveness in conveying the reality of what an officer does on the job. In the words of one spouse, "I now realize some of what my husband goes through."[18]

One of the comments heard most frequently concerns the value of simply meeting and interacting with other spouses. As one participant characterized the spouse's role, "Sometimes, this can be a lonely job."[19]

Stress and Domestic Violence

Some people believe that a relatively large proportion of law enforcement officers may be involved in domestic violence, in part because of the stressful nature of the job.[20] Many law enforcement agencies have begun to turn their attention to this issue and devise ways to respond. One agency, the Los Angeles (County) Sheriff's Department (LASD), has adopted a zero-tolerance policy toward domestic violence, with a full range of disciplinary actions that could include dismissal from the force. To reduce the number of domestic violence incidents among the LASD's 8,000 sworn officers, the department bolstered its policy with a training program for all supervisory personnel; a vigorous information dissemination campaign (which included development of an educational video to be shown to all staff); and counseling services for individuals, couples, and families. The department has trained more than 1,200 supervisors to spot signs of stress and domestic violence.[21]

Stress Reduction Programs

Why should law enforcement agencies spend time and money on (and perhaps set aside space for) a law enforcement stress reduction program? The answer has to do with the implications of stress for the department: Essentially, stress reduces the quality of departmental performance.

The cumulative negative effects of stress on officers and their families typically affect the agency through impaired officer performance and the related problems of tardiness, absenteeism, and low morale, with the departmental consequence of lower productivity. Stress-related performance inadequacies may generate labor-management friction and lead to civil suits, and there may also be adverse public reaction as a result of stress-related incidents, such as an officer's suicide or a case of police brutality. Even problems that are confined to only a few individuals or that occur rarely can have major repercussions; for instance, a single incident in which a handful of officers abuse alcohol or other drugs can lower public confidence in the entire agency.

Though establishing and operating a stress reduction program requires a financial outlay, it can mean cost savings over the long term because stress affects the bottom line. Agencies can find stress enormously costly when employee turnover increases as a result of stress-related early retirement or long-term disability.

Robert Peppler, Assistant Sheriff of the San Bernardino (California) Sheriff's Department, noted the cost to his agency: "We have a tremendous investment in cops," he said, "and if they leave after one traumatic incident, we have lost a tremendous amount. A dollar in psychological services now can save us hundreds of thousands down the road."[22]

Employee Assistance Programs (EAPs). Many agencies have access to city or countywide employee assistance programs (EAPs). Law enforcement staff and their families may be eligible for services from additional providers, including police chaplains, wellness programs, support groups, and local private service providers. This prompts the question: Why shouldn't an agency rely on other existing programs rather than develop its own stress reduction program?

The fact that a service is available does not necessarily mean it is meeting—or can meet—the distinctive needs of police officers. When asked about city or county EAPs, mental health practitioners, police administrators, and others said police officers do not use them because these programs do not provide enough confidentiality, because EAP staff usually do not understand law enforcement, and because the officers feared the stigma that might be attached to using an EAP.

Types of Stress Reduction Programs. Approaches to reduce or prevent stress can take many forms: services provided by a private mental health practice or an individual therapist working with one or more law enforcement agencies; peer support and referrals from specially trained police officers; psychological services set up in the agency through the union, chaplaincy, or employee assistance program; or some combination of these arrangements. Almost all programs are geared primarily to line officers because they constitute the largest group in any law enforcement agency, they deal with the public on a day-to-day basis, they are widely believed to experience high levels of stress, and they may have limited means to pay for extended counseling. Most programs also provide at least minimal services (that is, referral to other treatment providers) to nonsworn personnel and former employees as well as to officers' and other employees' family members and close friends. Services typically include assessment and referral to mental health or other practitioners; critical incident debriefing; intervention for other types of crises; short-term counseling for both individuals and families; and long-term counseling and other services, including treatment for substance abuse.

Most mental health practitioners emphasize the importance of involving family members, when possible, in all these services. To varying extents, all programs include referrals to outside sources of assistance; for some programs that operate with limited resources, referral to outside services is the primary component, and that is often the case with programs staffed largely by peers.

Stress Prevention

The most common method for preventing stress is to train officers to recognize its signs and sources and to develop individual coping strategies. Training both helps encourage officers and nonsworn personnel to use stress reduction techniques and services and dispels the stigma frequently attached to seeking assistance.

One period during which officers could be taught about stress is when they are at the academy, according to most of the police officers, program administrators, and independent mental health practitioners who were asked about this issue. They felt that the initial training period was a possibility because recruits are a captive audience and because the information may remain with them throughout their entire police career. There is some thinking that "inoculation" during recruit training is not the best approach because most recruits are preoccupied with other information they are receiving.

Sometimes it takes a tragedy or critical incident to prompt a law enforcement agency or related organization to develop or expand a stress reduction program for police officers. That was the case in New York City, where 26 police officers committed suicide in the two-year period from 1994 through 1995; the unusually high number was the result of such factors as perceived pressure from the media and allegations of corruption. The crisis spurred the Patrolmen's Benevolent Association, supported by the city council, to establish a peer support program by officers for officers. The Members Assistance Program (MAP) trained 150 officer volunteers to aid fellow officers and an additional 26 to aid their families. The peer support officers staff a 24-hour hotline, serve as a point of first contact and screening for officers who report stress-related difficulties, and encourage individuals who need more intensive help to seek it.

MAP also trained 60 mental health practitioners in law enforcement stress, and these practitioners began taking referrals from the peer support officers. Between 1996 (the year the program started) and 1998, the hotline received some 1,500 calls that resulted in more than 650 referrals.[23]

Some agencies offer in-service training not only for line officers but also for mid-level managers and command staff, prospective retirees, and nonsworn personnel. Because, as noted above, the structure and management of the agency can be a significant source of stress, mental health professionals should consider working with departmental management and unions to plan and implement organizational change. This can be done in a number of ways, all of which fall within the domain of management:

- Train command staff in effective supervision.
- Train field training officers to constructively supervise rookies.
- Eliminate rotating shift work.
- Improve the match between officers' capabilities and the demands of specific assignments.

NIJ Stress Reduction Efforts

The issue of job-related stress for law enforcement officers and their families has received attention at the highest levels of government. In the 1994 Omnibus Crime Act, the U.S. President and Congress recognized the severity of the problem and mandated a federal government response. The National Institute of Justice (NIJ) was assigned the task of sponsoring research, establishing pilot programs, and conducting program evaluations in stress reduction.

Since the start of the Corrections and Law Enforcement Family Support program, NIJ has sponsored research and program development in some 30 agencies and related organizations (labor unions and employee professional organizations, for example). These projects include

---

Law Enforcement and Corrections Resources

- *Developing a Law Enforcement Stress Program for Officers and Their Families,* by Peter Finn and Julie Esselman Tomz (Washington, DC: U.S. Department of Justice, National Institute of Justice, March 1997) (NCJ 163175).
- "Fighting the Enemy Within: Helping Officers Deal with Stress," by Rebecca Childress, Vincent Talucci, and Jenifer Wood, *Corrections Today* (December 1999): 70.

---

the development of innovative treatment and training programs as well as research into the nature and causes of stress. In one study now underway, NIJ is exploring the nature and extent of job-related stress for police in a single geographical region.

To improve access to service, NIJ provided support to the Metro Nashville Police Department in creating an online resource of information for the families of law enforcement officers, particularly those in underserved communities. Available on the Internet, the resource is a new type of service delivery system. The Web site contains, among other things, materials developed by psychologists for preparing workshops on stress, message boards, a chat room, links to related Web sites, recommended readings, and postings from police psychologists and consultants. To view this or any of NIJ's other programs, visit www.ojp.usdoj.gov/nij/clefs.

 ## SUMMARY

Police work is stressful. Whether it is police stress or police burnout, the results are the same—a broken individual. How an officer breaks can vary. It may be physical: heart attack, chronic ulcers, diabetes, severe dermatitis, or a host of other health—related problems induced by and resulting from extreme stress. At times it is purely psychological: alcoholism, suicide, pronounced depression, debilitating phobic reactions, excessive anxiety. Frequently, the results are both physical and psychological. The vast majority of police officers, however, do not suffer excessive stress or extreme burnout and suffer a breakdown.

Burnout is a common metaphor for a state of extreme psychophysical exhaustion that is usually work-related. It encompasses four general symptoms: distress (affective, cognitive, physical, and behavioral), sense of reduced effectiveness, decreased motivation, and dysfunctional attitudes and behaviors at work. The definition also suggests that burnout may be self-perpetuating.

Internal stress generally results from functional duties, policies, and procedures that have been implemented as part of an organization's standard operating procedures. External stress is caused by public practices and characteristics, including stress caused by the perception of lack of general public support for police officers. Operational stress is that stress caused by police work itself.

The numbers of deaths of law enforcement officers due to suicide are two to three times the number of line-of-duty deaths among law enforcement agencies and emergency workers. The National P.O.L.I.C.E. Suicide Foundation was established to provide suicide awareness and prevention training programs as well as support services to meet the psychological and spiritual needs of emergency workers and their families.

Most studies of alcoholism and drug abuse by law enforcement personnel suggest that alcohol and drug abuse are as frequent as or more frequent than in the general population. Alcohol abuse has been implicated as a significant factor in officer suicides.

Urinalysis is the most commonly used method of testing for drug use, but it has problems that have been exploited by drug users. Urinalysis can generally detect drug use for the previous two to three days for most drugs; after that, the body flushes out the substance. The period of drug detection in blood testing is short, usually only hours. With the fear of blood-borne infectious diseases, drug testing using blood is not a preferred method. Blood testing is the least-used and lest-recommended form of drug testing because of the invasiveness of the collection method, the need for skilled phlebotomists (those who take blood), and the extremely short drug detection period.

QUESTIONS IN REVIEW

1. What are the causes of stress in law enforcement officers?
2. What steps may be taken to reduce stress and burnout?
3. What are the most common reasons given for police suicides?
4. Why is it important to consider the stress that law enforcement families face?
5. What is the NIJ doing regarding the issue of law enforcement stress?

POLICING ON THE WEB

Help for Police Families
http://policefamilies.com, a Web site developed by the Metropolitan Police Department of Nashville and Davidson County, with funding from the National Institute of Justice.

National Institute of Justice Stress Program (CLEFS)
http://www.ojp.usdoj.gov/nij/clefs

REFERENCES

1. SAMUEL WALKER, GEOFFREY P. ALPERT, and DENNIS J. KENNEDY, "Responding to the Problem Police Officer: A National Study of Early Warning Systems, Final Report," *NCJRS* Document 184510 (September 20, 2000), p. 13.

2. Ibid., p. 17.

3. WILMAR SCHAUFELI and DIRK ENZMANN, "The Burnout Companion to Study and Practice: A Critical Analysis," *Issues in Occupational Health* (London: TAYLOR & FRANCIS, 1998), pp. 43–45.

4. Ibid., p. 36.

5. WILLIAM H. KROES and J. J. HURRELL, *Job Stress and the Police Officer: Identifying Stress Reduction Techniques* (Washington, DC: GPO, 1976), pp. 21–23.

6. DIETRICH, J.F., "Helping Subordinates Face Stress," The *Police Chief* (November 1989): 44–46.

7. That question was addressed in *Nicolini* v. *County of Tuolumne*, 190 Cal. App. 3d 619. The court refused to order his re-instatement.

8. J.J. HURRELL and R. KLIESMET, *Stress Among Police Officers* (Cincinnati, OH: National Institute of Occupational Safety and Health, 1984), p. 11.

9. National P.O.L.I.C.E. Suicide Foundation website accessed on December 14, 2004 at http://www.psf.org/about.htm.

10. H. BASOWITZ, *Anxiety and Stress* (New York: McGraw-Hill, 1955), p. 7.

11. Ibid., p. 11.

12. PETER FINN AND JULIE ESSELMAN TOMZ, "Developing a Law Enforcement Stress Program for Officers and Their Families," *Issues and Practices* (Washington, DC: U.S. Department of Justice, National Institute of Justice, March 1997) (NCJ 163175).

13. SCHAUFELI and DIRK ENZMANN, 1998, p. 171.

14. The survey was conducted as part of a study by Leanor Boulin-Johnson, professor of African-American Studies and Family Studies at Arizona State University. See "On the Front Lines: Police Stress and Family Well-Being," testimony of Leanor Boulin-Johnson before the Select Committee on Children, Youth, and Families, U.S. House of Representatives, 102nd Congress, 1st Session, May 20, 1991 (Washington, DC: GPO, 1991), p. 32.

15. R. BORUM and C. PHILPOT, "Therapy with Law Enforcement Couples: Clinical Management of the 'High-Risk Lifestyle,'" *American Journal of Family Therapy* 21 (1993): 122–135.

16. Progress report of Law Enforcement Work Stress and Family Support (Project SHIELDS), Johns Hopkins University School of Hygiene and Public Health, Baltimore (1999). Reprinted by the National Institute of Justice, U.S. Department of Justice, by Robyn Gershon, Principal Investigator, March 31, 1999. *National Institute of Justice Journal* (January 2000).

17. Unpublished program evaluations by participants in Spousal Academy, Collier County (Florida) Sheriff's Office, no date.

18. "On the Front Lines: Police Stress and Family Well-Being," testimony of B.J. Anderson before the Select Committee on Children, Youth, and Families, U.S. House of Representatives, 102nd Congress, 1st Session, May 20, 1991 (Washington, DC: GPO, 1991), pp. 61–63.

19. Ibid.
20. Unpublished progress report of the Family Violence Prevention and Recovery Project (FVPRP), Los Angeles County Sheriff's Department, submitted to the National Institute of Justice, U.S. Department of Justice, by Audrey L. Honig, Principal Investigator, FVPRP, and Steven E. Sultan, Project Coordinator, FVPRP, for period September 1, 1998, through March 3, 1999.
21. Ibid.
22. PETER FINN and JULIE TOMZ, Developing a Law Enforcement Stress Program for Officers and Their Families (Washington, DC: NIJ, 1997), p. 3.
23. NYC Patrolmen's Benevolent Association Members Assistance Program: Program for the Reduction of Stress for New York City Police Officers and Their Families, final report submitted to the National Institute of Justice, U.S. Department of Justice, grant 96-FS-VX-007, December 1998, pp. 91–93.

Policing and Terrorism

Key Terms

Outline

Learning Objectives

After reading this chapter, you should be able to:

1. Explain the difficulty of defining terrorism.
2. Discuss what constitutes a terrorist act.
3. Describe the problems and duties placed on local law enforcement agencies because of terrorists.
4. Define threat assessment.
5. Define international terrorism.
6. Explain the concept of intelligence disconnect.

INTRODUCTION

> The enemies of freedom have no regard for the innocent, no concept of the just and no desire for peace. They will stop at nothing to destroy our way of life, and we, on the other hand, we stop at nothing to defend it.
>
> —*Former Secretary Tom Ridge, Department of Homeland Security (in his remarks celebrating the 213th birthday of the U.S. Coast Guard)*

This chapter will focus on how terrorism has and will continue to affect local law enforcement. The chapter and the text conclude with the keynote address of Marc H. Morial, President and Chief Executive Officer of the National Urban League, at the 2004 National Community Policing Conference titled "Community Policing for America's Future." Morial addressed several major issues including terrorism and the future of law enforcement.

DEFINITION OF TERRORISM

Clifford Simonsen and Jeremy Spindlove pointed out that the task of defining terrorism is difficult and cautioned that the term must be carefully constructed so that it projects the intended meaning.[1] The first general use of the term "terrorism" is considered as having taken place in France during the French Revolution (1792–1794). For many individuals, **terrorism** is the systematic application of violence to promote or maintain a political or religious system. While a rape victim feels that she is the victim of an act of terrorism, that type of violent act is not included in the general definition of terrorism because most definitions of terrorism exclude acts of violence in which the terror component is incident or secondary to other primary objectives. For example, kidnapping for the purpose of obtaining money for personal use is not considered a terrorist act. Merely because someone is labeled a terrorist does not preclude also considering that individual as a criminal, madman, or murderer.

Alex Scmid surveyed about 100 scholars and researchers regarding their definition of terrorism and concluded that a definition of terrorism will have two general characteristics[2]: First, an individual is being threatened; second, the meaning of the terrorist act is derived from the choice of targets and victims. Scmid noted that certain elements were common to all the varied definitions of terrorism[3]:

- Terrorism is an abstract concept with no essence.
- A single definition does not account for all the possible uses of the term.
- Many different definitions share common elements.
- The meaning of terrorism derives from the target or victim.

The FBI uses the definition of terrorism that is set forth in the Code of Federal Regulations: Terrorism is "[t]he unlawful use of force and violence against persons or property to intimidate or coerce a government, the civilian population or any segment thereof, in furtherance of political or social objectives."[4]

According to a Department of Homeland Security definition, terrorism is the use of force or violence against persons or property in violation of the criminal laws of the United States for purposes of intimidation, coercion, or ransom. The U.S. Code, Title 22, Section 2656f(d), provides that the term "terrorism" means premeditated, politically motivated violence perpetrated against noncombatant targets by subnational groups or clandestine agents, usually intended to influence an audience. The U.S. Code also describes **international terrorism** as terrorism involving citizens or the territory of more than one country and the term **terrorist group** to mean any group practicing (or that has significant subgroups that practice) international terrorism.

Since there is a lack of definitional consistency, it is important to list some major characteristics of terrorism:

- Terrorist groups adapt as times change.
- The majority of terrorist groups are unsuccessful in their long-term goals.
- Terrorist groups network and pool resources.
- Terrorist groups work with other organizations, including organized crime groups, to finance activities and mobilize resources.
- Terrorist groups are creative in their tactics and leave open the possibility that anything can happen.

THREAT ASSESSMENT

"**Threat assessment**" is a phrase commonly used in counterterrorism and refers to the evaluation of a potential terrorist act—whether it will happen, where it will happen, and what the expected damages or injuries would be if it happens. Threat assessment is a developing field pioneered by the U.S. Department of the Treasury's Secret Service, which is charged with protecting the President of the United States and other U.S. and foreign leaders; with the creation of the Department of Homeland Security, threat assessment became one of its major duties. Threat assessment measures involve investigation and analysis of situations and individuals who may pose threats to the public.

EFFECTS OF TERRORISM ON POLICE OPERATIONS

Local police agencies must now investigate suspected terrorists and suspicious acts and work to prevent acts of terrorism on areas considered target-rich, such as airports, athletic events, shopping malls, water reservoirs, and utilities centers. Unprecedented new demands are placed on local law enforcement agencies, mostly without any appreciable increase in funds or personnel.

Lois Pilant concluded that the burden of preventing terrorist acts is hardest on local law enforcement agencies; along with efforts to detect vulnerabilities in the critical infrastructure and to make targets more difficult to hit, local agencies are charged with finding ways to gather intelligence and investigate potential threats.[5] According to Pilant, counterterrorism and antiterrorism are difficult tasks made even harder by the operational style that exists at almost every level of policing and in nearly every agency, that of withholding rather than sharing information; she claimed that the intelligence disconnects also exist between state and local agencies and those at the federal level.[6]

INTELLIGENCE DISCONNECT

One problem in fighting terrorism is to prevent the intelligence disconnect that exists between agencies tasked with combatting terrorism. By **intelligence disconnect,** we are referring to the failure of an agency to share intelligence information with other agencies. The creation of entities such as Los Angeles County's counterterrorism program is considered an effective way to reduce the intelligence disconnect. The program uses a terrorism early warning (TEW) group, a Los Angeles-based regional multiagency, multidisciplinary task force that cuts across jurisdictional and disciplinary boundaries. TEW attempts to remedy many of the problems inherent in gathering, analyzing, and sharing information among agencies that have unrelated missions and diverse operating styles.

The early warning group was the brainchild of two Los Angeles County deputy sheriffs, John Sullivan and Larry Richards, who started work on the concept in August 1996 when a then-little-known Islamist radical named Bin Laden issued his first fatwa urging his followers to conduct terrorist attacks against the United States. The two officers concluded that the only way to deal with terrorists was to create a counterterrorism network and that information sharing among public agencies was the key to preventing or reacting to terrorist attacks. The Los Angeles TEW had its first meeting in October 1996, and by the end of 1996, the group included representatives from sheriff's departments, the FBI, police departments, public health, public works, fire services, and neighborhood law enforcement agencies.[7]

The Los Angeles TEW identified several challenges[8]:

- Ability to recognize attack (or outbreak)
- Lack of weapons of mass destruction (WMD) knowledge/experience
- Lack of personal protection equipment (PPE) and doctrine for its use
- Security/crowd control issues
- Issues of quarantine
- Staffing/resources
- Speed of decision cycle

This TEW group monitors trends and assesses threats that could result in terrorist attacks in Los Angeles County by evaluating media accounts, information from other state, local, and federal agencies, and other open source data and then determining their credibility. During an actual incident, TEW provides information to incident commanders.

Although this TEW group existed in Los Angeles County before 9/11, since then its concept has been duplicated in other states, with the support of the Office of Domestic Preparedness.

HOMELAND SECURITY ACT

In January 2003, the Department of Homeland Security (DHS) became the nation's 15th and newest Cabinet department, consolidating 22 previously disparate agencies in a unified organization; prior to the creation of DHS, no single federal department had homeland security as its primary objective. Its most important job is to protect the American people and the American way of life from terrorism. It is expected that DHS—through partnerships with state, local, and tribal governments and the private sector—will work to ensure the highest level of protection and preparedness for the country and the citizens it serves.

The Homeland Security Act, passed in 2002, was a direct result of the terrorist acts of September 11, 2001. The act was perhaps the biggest change management challenge in the United States since the establishment of the Constitution.[9] The primary mission of DHS, as set forth in Section 102(a) of the act, is to prevent terrorist attacks within the United States; reduce the vulnerability of the United States to terrorism; and minimize the damage, and assist in the recovery, from terrorist attacks that do occur within the United States.

The Department of Homeland Security absorbed many different law enforcement resources and organizations, including customs enforcement, Federal Law Enforcement Training Center (FLETC), Federal Protective Service, immigration-related law enforcement and Border Patrol, maritime enforcement, and drug interdiction.

Cliff Mariani listed the general duties of police officers, as the first responders, after a terrorist event[10]:

- Observe, witness, and report.
- Provide ample information to dispatcher.
- Request supervisor and backup personnel.
- Recognize signs and symptoms of biological, chemical, and radiological poisoning.
- Request presence of appropriate agencies.
- Protect life and property.
- Evacuate injured and endangered persons.
- Minimize personal risk and contamination.

Heart of America Joint Terrorism Task Force

One task force that has been created to combat terrorism is found in Kansas City, Missouri. The Counterterrorism Executive Board (Kansas City Division) was established by Kevin Stafford, Kansas City Special Agent in Charge (SAC). On December 16, 2001, the FBI's Kansas City Division (KCD) officially created the Heart of America Joint Terrorism Task Force (HOA JTTF).

This task force was created to effectively and efficiently develop, analyze, and disseminate intelligence and to work cases involving domestic and international terrorism matters in Kansas and western Missouri. Consistent with FBI national priorities, the primary mission of HOA JTTF is to prevent acts of terrorism and to respond to, investigate, and prosecute individuals or groups involved in acts of terrorism. HOA JTTF comprises FBI Special Agents and full-time task force officers from 19 different federal, state, county, and municipal law enforcement/intelligence agencies. HOA JTTF personnel are located in the Kansas City headquarters office as well as in several resident agencies. On February 4, 2002, SAC established the Counterterrorism Executive Board (CEB), which initially was composed of agency heads from 19 federal, state, county, and municipal law enforcement organizations, with each assigning one full-time investigator to HOA JTTF. As it has evolved, membership in CEB has been modified to include individuals who bring unique subject-matter expertise that enhances CEB's tactical and strategic capabilities.

Currently representatives from 8 federal agencies, 5 state agencies (including the Directors of Homeland Security for both Kansas and Missouri), and 10 local agencies constitute the CEB. Also included on the board is Dr. Joseph Waeckerle, a nationally recognized medical expert on weapons of mass destruction and emergency medicine. CEB was created to ensure that federal, state, county, and municipal law enforcement officials receive critical terrorism threat intelligence concerning their territorial responsibilities in the most thorough and expeditious manner and, most importantly, that they are given the opportunity to provide operational input on how those threats could be addressed. CEB meets on an as-needed basis, but no less than quarterly.

Classified information is disseminated personally by SAC or through agency investigators assigned to JTTF, who then brief their agency head. All members of CEB maintain a secret or top secret security clearance. CEB addresses the concerns that many Police Executive Research Forum (PERF) executive session participants voiced—that local law enforcement chief executives wanted more direct and substantive briefings and more effective mechanisms to contribute to the work of their JTTF and coordinate their efforts with federal and state agencies.

To address investigative matters that will arise in the event of hostilities, CEB developed (and is in the process of implementing) satellite command posts to handle unclassified investigative leads that KCD receives or develops. These command posts, referred to as Intelligence Integration and Regional Operation Centers (IIROICs), will support KCD's Crisis Management Center (CMC) by providing more human resources (including staffing for additional telephone banks) and handling unclassified leads. As this goes to press, the FBI anticipates that all investigative activities conducted by the IIROICs will be assigned and coordinated through Rapid Start, operated at KCD's CMC. The IIROICs are based in different locations. Rapid Start is a computer database designed to organize a large volume of case information that includes tracking of leads, subjects, victims, and witnesses. Reports—such as how many leads are assigned or unassigned, how many leads are outstanding, and to whom the leads are assigned—can be obtained through Rapid Start. Rapid Start also has full-text search capability, and searching in the database assists in preventing the duplication of leads.

There are 865 federal, state, county, and municipal law enforcement agencies in the KCD territory, which includes all of Kansas and the western two-thirds of Missouri. These centers will provide appropriate coordination of intelligence and will pool area resources and address future leads in a timely manner. Leads are documented in the Rapid Start database, which will facilitate coordination among law enforcement agencies within the territory.

All law enforcement agencies that have provided full-time task force members need to be included in CEB; additionally, it should include individuals who are capable of providing unique tactical and strategic expertise to assist in the development of JTTF investigative strategies. The overall effectiveness and efficiency of law enforcement counterterrorism efforts can be significantly enhanced by involving a select group of federal, state, county, and municipal law enforcement executives in the operational decisions of select JTTF investigation initiatives rather than making them merely the passive recipients of intelligence information.

The level of cooperation among CEB members in sharing intelligence and participating in operational decisions on counterterrorism cases has significantly improved JTTF's strategic and tactical capabilities. CEB integrates and enhances the intelligence and operational capabilities of all federal, state, county, and municipal law enforcement agencies and provides a unique forum for the exchange of ideas as well as the sharing of information and personnel resources.[11]

- Be alert for secondary attack or device.
- Isolate and contain area.
- Preserve crime scene.
- Detour pedestrian and vehicular traffic.
- Apprehend violators.
- Cooperate with other agencies working at scene.
- Keep dispatcher informed of developments.

HOMELAND SECURITY ADVISORY SYSTEM

In 2003, the Office of Homeland Security established a Homeland Security Advisory System that is based on five threat conditions or stages. Each of these represents a different type of alert:

- *Green*. Low-level threat.
- *Blue*. Guarded threat level.
- *Yellow*. Mid-level threat.
- *Orange*. High-level threat.
- *Red*. Severe threat level.

The authority to name a specific threat condition lies with the U.S. Attorney General, who is to consult with the members of the Homeland Security Council.

DOMESTIC TERRORISM

While our nation has focused on international terrorism since 9/11, home-grown terrorists have plotted and carried out attacks that were completely unrelated to international terrorism. The 1995 bombing of the Oklahoma City federal building killed 168, as of this date the deadliest act of terrorism against our nation by a U.S. citizen. Domestic terrorists range from white supremacists, antigovernment types, and militia members to eco-terrorists and people who hate big business. Domestic terrorist acts have also been committed by violent antiabortionists as well as black and other ethnic nationalists.

A Texas man who was arrested in 2002 had stockpiled enough sodium cyanide to gas everyone in a 30,000-square-foot building, the size of a high school gymnasium; he also had 9 machine guns and 100,000 rounds of ammunition. Clayton Waagner of Pennsylvania was convicted of mailing hundreds of threat letters containing bogus anthrax to abortion clinics in 24 states. During his trial, prosecutors documented that Waagner had ties to the Army of God, an extremist group that believes violence against abortion providers is an acceptable way to end abortion.

Law enforcement officials must assess and prioritize steps for preventing, preparing for, and responding to domestic terrorism while retaining the gains made through community policing. Working with other public officials, law enforcement agencies must begin by determining their community's risk of and vulnerabilities for potential terrorist attacks—an overwhelming endeavor exacerbated by competing demands for police services and limited resources. To help local law enforcement agencies in combatting bioterrorism, the Police Executive Research Forum has published a multivolume manual titled *Protecting Your Community from Terrorism* in the Strategies for Local Law Enforcement series. Volume 3, *Preparing for and Responding to Bioterrorism*, was published in September 2004 and may be obtained from the U.S. Department of Justice's Office of Community-Oriented Policing Services.

FUTURE OF POLICING

This section is a reprint of a speech given on June 21, 2004, by Marc H. Morial, President and CEO of the National Urban League, before the Office of the U.S. Attorney General's Annual COPS Conference in Washington, D.C.[12] Morial is a former New Orleans Chief of Police and Mayor whose speech highlighted issues that need to be considered when examining the future of policing.

I just want to take a few minutes this morning to talk to you on three areas. First, I think we just acknowledge, think and strategize on how community-oriented policing is indeed a tool, an indispensable tool on the fight against terrorism in this nation. Local law enforcement is our citizens' first line of defense. You indeed know that. But in this new environment in the 21st century, we must think creatively, strategically, and practically about the appropriate role of local law enforcement allied with our national law enforcement agencies in the fight against terrorism.

What is painfully obvious is that the war against terror is going to be a very long war that could last a generation or two, or even longer. And I think it is very important that not only local law enforcement but people who make policies at the national level recognize how critical and how meaningful the partnership is in communicating, in balancing interests, in making sure that law enforcement at every level understands what, in fact, is going on in this very important fight. This area provides many opportunities and many challenges, and also many pitfalls. It's an opportunity to put the weight of hundreds of thousands of local law enforcement personnel behind a very important fight for safety and security in our nation. It's also a great challenge because of the necessity of balancing the interests of civil liberties with the interests of public safety and security. Something that is going to take a lot of work and a lot of struggle for us to get the balance just right, because in fact, the fight against terrorism is a work to preserve our civil rights and our civil liberties here in this country, and for all who embrace that notion abroad.

Second, I want to talk to you this morning about what I call a 21st-century model of law enforcement. And I recall just 10 years ago being with some of you, and some who may not be here, in the great hall at the Department of Justice, with the then president, with bipartisan leadership in Congress, with police chiefs and leadership throughout this country, as the Community-Oriented Policing Act was signed. And it represented at that time a highly ambitious commitment in dollars and ingenuity by the nation to assist local law enforcement at a time when the country was reeling from rising crime rates, rising rates of violence, in cities big and small throughout the country. That commitment has yielded great success. I think we can be proud 10 years later that the COPs Act has made a difference, that the COP staff has made a difference, that local law enforcement has been augmented and enhanced, new offices paid for, new technology, new training, and new strategy. But we are now at a proverbial crossroads. Ten years later it is important that we think about the future of law enforcement, the future of Community-Oriented Policing in this country.

And I want to just share with you some thoughts about that. Policing has come a long way in America. In the old days, the emphasis was on the beat cop, the cop who walked the streets, who knew the neighborhood, who knew the shopkeepers, the shop owners, who knew the priests, the ministers, and the rabbis, who knew the community leaders, who walked the streets and ferreted out crime because they knew exactly what was going on in communities. Then as technology, particularly community communications technology began to change, policing began to evolve. Policing became supported substantially by the use of automobiles and also both handheld radios and radios inside of automobiles. As a former Chief of

The Honorable Marc H. Morial, Chief Executive Officer, National Urban League.

Photo courtesy of National Urban League

Police in New Orleans, Joseph Giarrusso told me we turned a lot of beat cops into what he called "radio cops," who rode around waiting for a call on the radio to go to spot A or indeed spot B. I even heard yesterday on the radio in New York City how the original radio technology was one-way technology. You all probably remember, or still in some communities they have the old call boxes. What would happen is that headquarters would radio out to an officer, or put a call out on the radio, and the police officer would have to stop at a call box to call in to do a 2-way communications transmission. The point is that policing became changed in the 1960s, the 1970s, and the 1980s to more of a rapid response system, where officers would indeed respond to calls for service to a 911 system to a telephone system by citizens, indicating where in fact and indeed there was a problem where law enforcement's help was needed. And we put a great premium on that.

As community policing evolved in the 1980s and the 1990s, there was sort of a shift back to the notion that simply radio responding, responding to 911 calls, was not effective, especially when it came to preventing crime, preventing the advent of violence in our communities. And I think the movement more towards community-oriented policing became a shift to the past, but a shift with perhaps the tools and the advantages of 21st-century technology. New communications now, mobile data terminals in vehicles, all of the new types of things, computerized crime mapping and COMPSTAT-type systems that New York pioneered and that we brought to New Orleans when I was mayor. And I think what it calls for or what it suggests is that we need a new model of policing here in the 21st century. While crime and violence have decreased in some communities, it is still too high in most communities. And I think we can never be in a mode of accepting any level or any statistics of crime or violence in our community. Our goal must be zero crime, zero violence, no murders, no advent of crime in our communities, and that ought to be a continuing goal.

But I think a 21st-century model of law enforcement is going to require a number of things. First, it is going to require a steadfast commitment to how we hire new police officers and law enforcement officers, and here is why. The marketplace is much more competitive than it has ever been. And I think what community-oriented policing strategies of the 1990s and the early 21st century have shown is that higher standards are a necessity, and as all of the law enforcement executives in this audience know, to be a good police officer requires not just brawn, not just courage, but requires a lot of brains, a lot of savvy, and a whole lot of judgment. And we must imbue those needs into how we hire. So I think in the 21st century, I certainly advocate increasing emphasis on better training, increasing emphasis on higher educational standards for the people we encourage to become law enforcement officers. We must affirm and reaffirm at every turn that being a police officer, being in law enforcement, being a sheriff, is a profession. It's a profession with dignity and with honor. It's not just a job. But it's a place where you make a commitment to not only public safety but also to public service.

Second, in the 21st century, we hear this a lot, but more now than ever, this concept of diversity is a must. And it's a must because trust is a must. I say that police departments, sheriff's departments that mirror the communities that they serve are ultimately going to be more trusted and more accepted. And in the 21st century, that brings into challenge so many new aspects of diversity. It's not only racial diversity, but gender diversity. In many communities, it requires language diversity and cultural diversity. Where I reside now in New York City, the most diverse community in America, or whether you look at Washington, D.C., you see a new and emerging diversity within diversity. The "black community" in New York City is a community of African Americans, people from the Caribbean, and people from Africa. The Latino community in New York City, which was once dominantly Puerto Rican, now has a large Dominican population. The traditional European communities in New York, which were dominated by people of Irish and Italian descent, now have a growing population of people from Eastern and Southern Europe. And such is the case in other large cities, Los Angeles, Chicago, Washington, D.C., Philadelphia, Houston, Dallas. This new diversity within diversity. We must, as we hire new officers, as we train officers, must pay attention to diversity, because diversity, I believe, is inextricably linked to the idea of trust. So diversity must be a cardinal principle of a 21st-century model of law enforcement.

Third, partnerships. Partnerships. As you work in every partnerships in every beat cop, every community policing unit, every sergeant, every district commander knows the value of partnerships. Building partnerships with churches, synagogues, and mosques. Building partnerships with business organizations, neighborhood organizations, community organizations. Building partnerships with community-based organizations. I think we've got to focus much more on that in the 21st century, and focus on it by helping to train officers and train police departments, if you will, on the appropriate way to build these partnerships as an important tool in fighting crime and in increasing public safety. I would say that these partnerships help build a foundation of trust, but not only that, they also assist officers in placing a heavy and high emphasis on prevention, on preventing crime from occurring before it takes place. These partnerships, I think, are why the community-oriented policing office of the Department of Justice has emphasized on the webcast that will take place tomorrow the involvement of mayors, community organizations, in the almost 100 communities that are going to participate in the tabletop exercise tomorrow. The partnerships are key to a 21st-century model.

Fourth, I think we have to think long and hard in the 21st century about things like allowing law enforcement officers sabbaticals and early retirement options. What you know and what people don't always recognize is that being a law enforcement person or police officer is a highly stressful job with heavy demands. Yesterday I was on the elevator in the subway stop in Brooklyn. My family, my wife and my son and I going to church. And as we went to church, we got on the elevator, and there was an officer who was on the elevator, on the beat, doing his duty. And I sat there and thought to myself, I said, "This is Father's Day and he's working." And I said, "I wonder how many other holidays this officer has to routinely work." He looked like a young officer, and you know what kind of shifts you all give young officers. They're not always the best shifts, and they've got to pay their dues and earn their dues. But the stress of the profession, the demands of the profession, I think require that for many law enforcement officers and many police officers, we have to look at policing maybe in the 21st century as what may be the first of two careers, or the first of three careers, to make the work attractive, to say that you can do 15 years or maybe 20 years and be able to retire and go on to a second career. I think that we've got to do that in recognition of the stress, the long hours, the heavy physical, emotional, and mental demands that policing places on officers. And I think we have to be open to, and I think that people should be open to that notion in the 21st century. And some communities have much more attractive retirement opportunities for officers. Many treat officers similar to the way they might treat other municipal personnel, not completely recognizing the heavy stresses of the profession.

The third thing in the 21st-century model is the idea that we must work very, very hard, particularly in this climate of terrorism to ensure that racial profiling ends and does not expand. This is a sensitive, very difficult issue, but this is where I think partnerships between law enforcement and community

organizations, frank conversations and discussions can play a very important role. In every job you have, it is important for people to understand how
the customer sees you. And I think it's important for law enforcement personnel to understand how the community that they serve sees them, so that
work can be done to improve that relationship. There is nothing more important in this area than for there to be diverse police forces. But in addition to
that, and it goes beyond that, there must be intensive training and a fundamental acknowledgment that there had been racial profiling practices in the
past. But not to dwell on it, but to focus on trying to ferret it out and certainly
correct it. And I think that means a focus on intensive training at every single
level, intensive retraining on a mandatory basis of officers on an ongoing
basis. I think it requires a commitment by every law enforcement department
in this country to an early warning system that ferrets out and identifies
problems where they indeed exist. And certainly, it requires a very strong
role by the United States Department of Justice in assisting with the training side, but also in assisting with the enforcement of civil rights laws on the
other side of the equation. Both are important as we face the 21st century.

This nation is changing. It's going to change in the 21st century in new
and exciting ways. How is it going to change? We will soon be a nation that
no longer has a majority ethnic group. And that will be America by 2050.
What does that mean? This great country will stand unique in history as the
only democracy in recorded history not to have a majority ethnic group, to
truly be a diverse society. I think it's exciting that this nation, with its
prosperity, can face this exciting future. But I do think that it will require
the leaders of this generation, whether you are in public life or in the private
sector, in law enforcement or wherever you sit, to face the challenge of what
this means in local communities, and what this means for your profession.
It's not the first time that the United States has faced true demographic
and swift demographic change in a short period of time. Indeed, we faced it
in the early 20th century, when America's northern and western communities were transformed by European immigration and black migration from
the south to America's cities. Those two forces changed America, and I would
submit to you changed America indeed for the better. And I think as we face
this new change, I think we should face it and relish it as the challenge for
this generation. A challenge that will not be without pain, but a challenge
with a whole lot of hope and opportunity.

I share this model of 21st-century policing with you this morning with
the hope that it is going to guide our thinking and guide our thoughts. We
need the people who represent us in Congress on both sides of the aisle to
understand that the Community-Oriented Policing program has worked
and we need their continued support. We need people at the local level to
not only understand that it has worked, but that this is a subject and this
is a set of strategies that require a long-term commitment by the nation.
The federal government must be a partner with local law enforcement in
making our community safe, by balancing public safety with civil liberties
and constitutional rights. The federal government's role can be dynamic.

It can be one of intellectual capital. It has to be one of funding. It has to be one of leadership and guidance. And I want to thank Carl and Tim, and the entire COPs office, because I think they've brought this measure of thinking about the 21st century to their very important work.

We at the National Urban League through our affiliates at the local level want to be allies with all of the police chiefs, all of the sheriffs, and all of the law enforcement executives who are out there.

▲ SUMMARY

The task of defining terrorism is difficult. The term must be carefully constructed so that it projects the intended meaning. Most definitions of terrorism exclude acts of violence in which the terror component is incidental or secondary to some other primary objectives. Merely because someone is labeled a terrorist does not preclude also considering that individual as a criminal, madman, or murderer. The FBI uses the definition of terrorism that is set forth in the Code of Federal Regulations. According to that definition, terrorism is "[t]he unlawful use of force and violence against persons or property to intimidate or coerce a government, the civilian population or any segment thereof, in furtherance of political or social objectives."

Since there is a lack of definitional consistency, it is necessary to mention some important characteristics of terrorism: Terrorist groups adapt as times change; the majority of terrorist groups are unsuccessful in their long-term goals; terrorist groups network and pool resources, and they work with other organizations, including organized crime groups, to finance activities and mobilize resources; and terrorist groups are creative in the tactics and leave open the possibility that anything can happen.

"Threat assessment" is a phrase commonly used in counterterrorism and refers to the assessment of a potential terrorist—whether it will happen, where it will happen, and what the expected damages or injuries would be if it happens.

Local police agencies must now investigate suspected terrorists and suspicious acts and work to prevent acts of terrorism in areas considered target-rich, such as airports, athletic events, shopping malls, water reservoirs, and utilities centers. Unprecedented new demands are placed on local law enforcement agencies, mostly without any appreciable increase in funds or personnel.

One problem in fighting terrorism is to prevent the intelligence disconnect that exists between agencies tasked with combatting terrorism; by intelligence disconnect we are referring to the failure of an agency to share intelligence information with other agencies.

The Department of Homeland Security (DHS) is the nation's 15th and newest Cabinet department, consolidating 22 previously disparate agencies under a unified organization; prior to DHS, no single federal department had homeland security as its primary objective. Its most important job is to protect the American people and the American way of life from terrorism. It is expected that DHS, through partnerships with state, local, and tribal governments and the private sector, will work to ensure the highest level of protection and preparedness for the country and the citizens it serves.

QUESTIONS IN REVIEW

1. Define the term "terrorism."
2. What is meant by the phrase "intelligence disconnect"?
3. What is the role of local law enforcement in combatting terrorism?
4. What issues does Marc Morial advocate as being necessary to improve 21st-century policing?

POLICING ON THE WEB

Department of Homeland Security
http://www.dhs.gov

Iowa Homeland Security and Emergency Management
http://www.iowahomelandsecurity.org

Missouri Homeland Security Education Program
http://www.ready.missouri.gov

Nevada Homeland Security
http://www.homelandsecurity.nv.gov

Pennsylvania Homeland Security
http://www.homelandsecurity.state.pa.us

Texas Homeland Security
http://www.texashomelandsecurity.com

REFERENCES

1. CLIFFORD E. SIMONSEN and JEREMY R. SPINDLOVE, *Terrorism Today: The Past, the Players, the Future*, 2nd ed. (Upper Saddle River, NJ: Prentice Hall, 2004), pp. 3–5.
2. ALEX P. SCMID, *Political Terrorism* (Cincinnati, OH: Anderson, 1983), pp. 107–109.

3. Ibid.

4. 28 C.F.R. Section 0.85.

5. LOIS PILANT, "Strategic Modeling," *Police Magazine* 28, no.5 (May 2004): 34–39.

6. Ibid., p. 34.

7. GREG KRIKORIAN, "Terrorism Early Warning Group Works to Keep L.A.'s Guard Up," *Los Angeles Times* Online, November 7, 2004.

8. Online briefing by TEW at http://www.markletaskforce.org/documents/TEW.pdf.

9. As reported in remarks by Secretary of Homeland Security Tom Ridge at the American Association of Port Authorities Spring Conference, Washington, DC, March 23, 2004.

10. CLIFF MARIANI, *Terrorism Prevention and Response* (Flushing, NY: Loose-leaf Law Publications, 2003), pp. 1–2.

11. Information taken from NIJ Publication "Protecting Your Community from Terrorism: Strategies for Local Law Enforcement," Vol. 1: Local-Federal Partnerships NCJ 207078 (Washington, DC: GPO, 2003), pp. 52–54.

12. This was the keynote address at the U.S. Department of Justice's "Community Policing for America's Future," Conference in Washington, DC, June, 2004.

Appendix A

Hawaii Police Department–Drug Testing General Order No. 529

I. Purpose

The purpose of this document is to establish departmental policy, define responsibilities, and outline procedures for administering the drug urinalysis screening program for police personnel of the Hawaii County Police Department.

II. Definitions

  A. Confirmation Test. A secondary test required when the initial urine sample tests positive.

  B. Confirmed Text. Any specimen that has been confirmed positive by secondary testing.

  C. Drug. All dangerous, harmful, and detrimental substances, marijuana, hallucinogens, and prescription drugs that are not properly prescribed for medical use.

  D. Drug Abuse. Intentional misuse of controlled or illegal substances or the use of such substances to an extent deemed deleterious or detrimental to the user, to others, or to society.

  E. Drug Urinalysis Testing. Sequence of tests for certain metabolites in the urine samples submitted by employees.

  F. Employee. Any sworn employee of the Hawaii Police Department, and any Reserve Police Officers.

    1. Regular Employee. Any sworn employee who is not on initial probationary status.

    2. Probationary Employee. Any sworn employee who is on initial probationary status.

    3. Initial Screening. Preliminary test to detect the presence of prescribed drugs. An indicated positive sample at this level will be labeled confirmation pending.

  G. Memorandum of Agreement. Written understanding between this department and collective bargaining agents for Unit 12 regarding policies, practices, and procedures pertaining to the drug urinalysis screening program.

H. Random Test Group.   Employees who are subject to random drug testing.

I. Required Test Group.   Employees who are subject to regular or frequent drug testing.

III. Program

The Hawaii Police Department shall institute a drug urinalysis screening program designed to detect and deter the use of dangerous, harmful, and detrimental substances, hallucinogens, and marijuana.

IV. Policy

The Hawaii County Police Department recognizes that drug abuse represents one of the most serious threats to the stability of our society and that the police department is responsible for dealing with drug abuse. Furthermore, that the public expects that all members of this department possess the integrity, physical coordination, and clear judgment necessary to provide police services. It is therefore the policy of the Hawaii County Police Department that drug abuse by any employee will not be tolerated and is expressly prohibited.

A. Sworn employees who are found to be in violation of this policy shall be relieved of police powers.

B. The maximum disciplinary penalty for any employee for violation of the department's policy on drug abuse is termination of employment.

V. Responsibilities

A. The Assistant Police Chief of the Administrative Bureau shall:

1. Retain under his/her control all records, reports, and official confidential correspondence relating to the program.

2. Coordinate drug urinalysis testing for Staff Officers with the Deputy Police Chief.

B. The Major of Administrative Services shall:

1. Coordinate, control, and maintain the operation of the Drug Testing Program.

2. Promptly report all confirmed positive test results to the Police Chief.

3. Notify the Captain of Internal Affairs to investigate any confirmed positive test results.

4. Notify the appropriate Division Commander about any confirmed positive test.

5. Ensure that all Divisions are in compliance with the Drug Testing Program.

C. The Lieutenant of Administrative Services shall:

1. Ensure the monitoring and security of all drug testing sites.

2. Maintain all supplies and materials necessary to conduct the tests.

D. The Captain of Internal Affairs shall:

1. Investigate all confirmed positive test results and report the results of the investigation to the Administrative Review Board.

2. Report all instances of refusals to submit a specimen or failure to appear for the urinalysis test to the Major of the Administrative Services Division.

3. Review all misconduct reports on employees who have refused to submit a specimen or who failed to appear for the urinalysis test, and forward these reports to the Administrative Review Board.

E. The Administrative Review Board shall:

1. Review the investigative findings of the Internal Affairs Unit.

2. Make recommendations for appropriate action to the Police Chief.

F. The Division Commanders shall:

1. Ensure that all affected employees in their command are in compliance with the Drug Testing Program.
2. Promptly report all instances of noncompliance to the Major of the Administrative Services Division and the Internal Affairs Unit.
3. If any employee refuses to take or appear for a drug screening test, initiate an investigation for violation of:

   a. General Order 300 III-I, Obedience to Laws, Written Orders, Policies, etc.; and
   b. General Order 300 III-J, Orders of Superior Officers.

4. Forward the completed report of violations of General Orders to the Captain of the Internal Affairs Unit for review.
5. Upon notification of a confirmed positive test result:

   a. Notify the affected employee of the confirmed positive test result and recover the employee's badge and issued firearm(s).
   b. Assign the affected employee to a position where a gun and badge are not essential, pending the completion of the internal investigation.

VI. Drug Screening Test Groups

A. Required Test Group

The following employees shall be required to submit to a drug screening test on a regular basis:

1. All Staff Officers, to include the Police Chief, Deputy Chief, all Assistant Chiefs, Majors, and Captains.
2. Officers assigned to the following:

   a. Internal Affairs and Criminal Intelligence Units.
   b. Administrative Services Division, to include the Training Section, Community Relations, and D.A.R.E.
   c. HIPAL and the Traffic Enforcement Unit.
   d. Vice Sections.
   e. Probationary employees.
   f. Employees with a first confirmed positive test result.
   g. Employees who refuse to submit to a drug screening test administered to their Random Test Group assignment.

3. Employees who fail to submit to or are in noncompliance with drug testing procedures may be assigned to this group.

B. Random Test Group

1. All employees shall be subject to random drug tests.

C. Mandatory Test Group

1. In addition to random testing, all employees not subject to required testing shall be subject to mandatory testing to ensure that all employees are tested at least once every fiscal year.

   a. Employees shall be subject to mandatory testing once per prescribed time period.

2. The requirement to undergo a mandatory drug test by an employee is not precluded by a previous random drug test.

VII. Procedures for Scheduling Drug Testing

A. The Assistant Chief of the Administrative Bureau shall coordinate drug urinalysis testing for Staff Officers, with the Deputy Police Chief, and notify the Major of the Administrative Services Division to schedule and coordinate such tests.

B. The Major of the Administrative Services Division or designee shall:

1. Coordinate the testing of all employees within the test groups, with the exception of Staff Officers.
2. Determine the testing dates.

   a. For the Random Test Group, the order of testing shall be by use of a computerized random selection process under direct control of the Major of the Administrative Services Division.

3. Coordinate the drug urinalysis test with the Division Commander of the group to be tested within forty-eight (48) hours of the test date.
4. Notify a SHOPO Representative of the group to be tested within forty-eight (48) hours of the test date.
5. Notify the drug testing laboratory to report to the test site to conduct the specimen collection and drug urinalysis.
6. Have screening staff report to the designated test site on the selected day and time.

C. The Lieutenant of the Administrative Services Section or designee shall:

1. Coordinate and schedule mandatory pre-employment drug testing for Police Officer I applicants.
2. Notify applicants to report to the Hilo Police Station.
3. Notify the drug testing laboratory to report to the test site to conduct the specimen collection and drug urinalysis.

VIII. Test Site Procedures

A. For Staff Officers, the Assistant Chief of the Administrative Bureau on the selected day and time shall:

1. Ensure that all on-duty Staff Officers report to the test site and comply with the test procedures.
2. Initiate a Misconduct Report and investigation if any employee from the designated test group refuses to submit to a specimen or fails to appear as ordered.

B. With the exception of Staff Officers, the Division Commander of the group being tested on the selected day and time shall:

1. Ensure that all on-duty employees in the test group report to the test site and comply with the test procedures.
2. Initiate a Misconduct Report and investigation if any employee from the designated test group refuses to submit to a specimen or fails to appear as ordered.

C. The Lieutenant of the Administrative Services Section or designee, on the selected day and time, shall:

1. For mandatory pre-employment drug testing, ensure that the test procedures are reviewed with all applicants. This review shall cover:

   a. That security procedures shall be enforced during the test period.
   b. That the subject shall have four hours to render an acceptable sample.
   c. That the subject shall remain at the location to be determined by the site supervisor or informed to return to the site within the four-hour time frame.
   d. That if the temperature strip has been removed or tampered with or has an unacceptable reading, the subject has within the four-hour period from when first summoned to render a sample.
   e. Procedures that shall be followed when a test subject is unable to void before or after entering the test site, providing the

amount of specimen required, contamination of the specimen cups, etc.

    f. That subjects are instructed not to flush the toilets before, during, or after the test unless instructed to do so.

2. Assure the test subjects that every attempt has been made to maximize their privacy while maintaining the integrity of the samples submitted.
3. Secure the test site restrooms for the group being tested.
4. Monitor the test site.
5. Control the master log, and control numbers at the test site.

D. The Captain of the Internal Affairs Unit or designee, on the selected day and time, shall:

  1. Review the test procedures with all employees. This review shall cover:

    a. Security procedures that shall be enforced during the test period.
    b. That the subject shall have four hours to render an acceptable sample.
    c. That the subject shall remain at the location to be determined by the site supervisor or informed to return to the site within the four-hour time frame.
    d. That if the temperature strip has been removed or tampered with or has an unacceptable reading, the subject has within the four-hour period from when first summoned to render a sample.
    e. Procedures that shall be followed when a test subject is unable to void before or after entering the test site, providing the amount of specimen required, contamination of the specimen cuts, etc.
    f. That subjects are instructed not to flush the designated toilet before, during, or after the test unless instructed to do so.

  2. Assure the test subjects that every attempt has been made to maximize their privacy while maintaining the integrity of the samples submitted.

E. All on-duty employees and applicants within the designated test group, on the selected day and time, shall:

  1. Report to the test site when ordered to do so, and submit the urine specimens within the scheduled four-hour time period.
  2. Be required to submit a urine specimen, which shall be split into two samples, Sample A and Sample B.

    a. After the specimen is split, the specimen cups shall be sealed and secured in the presence of the test subject; the test subject shall initial the specimen cups.
    b. Both samples shall be turned over to the laboratory personnel of the certified screening laboratory.
    c. Laboratory personnel shall maintain appropriate chain of custody processing after the collection process is completed and the specimens are transported to the laboratory.

  3. If failing to submit a specimen within the four-hour period, immediately notify the Division Commander or the Internal Affairs Officer at the site as to the reason(s) for noncompliance.

IX. Procedures for Failure/Refusal to Submit to Drug Urinalysis Test or Noncompliance with Drug Testing Procedures

A. Any failure or refusal by an employee to submit to drug testing or noncompliance with any of the testing procedures may subject the employee to disciplinary action, including possible termination.

  1. The employee may be placed on suspension pending investigation, in compliance with Hawaii County Civil Service Rule #12A.3.

B. The following shall apply when a regular employee refuses/fails to submit to the drug urinalysis test or is in noncompliance with drug testing procedures:

    1. The Internal Affairs Unit shall immediately notify the employee's Division Commander.

    2. The Division Commander shall:

        a. Recover the employee's badge and issued firearm(s), if any, and assign the employee to administrative (nonenforcement) duties.

        b. Initiate a Misconduct Report, and forward the completed report to the Administrative Review Board via the Internal Affairs Unit and the Deputy Police Chief.

        c. Notify the Major of the Administrative Services Division about the action initiated.

    3. The Major of the Administrative Services Division shall serve written notice to the employee, informing the employee that refusal to obey lawful regulations or orders may result in dismissal.

    4. The Major of the Administrative Services Division shall arrange for the employee to be tested within five days of the first test and shall notify the employee to report for the scheduled test.

        a. Appropriate testing procedures listed under Paragraph VII of this document shall apply.

    5. The Captain of the Internal Affairs Unit shall notify the employee's Division Commander if the employee refuses/fails to submit to the second drug urinalysis test or is in noncompliance with drug testing procedures.

    6. The Division Commander shall initiate a Misconduct Report, and forward the completed report to the Administrative Review Board via the Internal Affairs Unit and the Deputy Police Chief.

    7. The Major of the Administrative Services Division shall arrange for the employee to be tested within five days of the second test and shall notify the employee to report for the scheduled test.

        a. Appropriate testing procedures listed under Paragraph VII of this document shall apply.

    8. The Captain of the Internal Affairs Unit shall notify the employee's Division Commander if the employee refuses/fails to submit to the third drug urinalysis test or is in noncompliance with the drug testing procedures.

    9. The Division Commander shall initiate a Misconduct Report, and forward the completed report to the Administrative Review Board via the Internal Affairs Unit and the Deputy Police Chief.

C. The following shall apply when a probationary employee refuses/fails to submit to the drug urinalysis test or is in noncompliance with drug testing procedures:

    1. The Internal Affairs Unit shall immediately notify the employee's Division Commander.

    2. The Division Commander shall:

        a. Recover the employee's badge and issued firearm(s), if any, and assign the employee to administrative (nonenforcement) duties.

        b. Initiate a Misconduct Report and forward the completed report to the Police Chief via the Internal Affairs Unit.

        c. Notify the Major of the Administrative Services Division about the action initiated.

    3. The Major of the Administrative Services Division shall serve written notice to the employee, informing the employee that refusal to obey lawful regulations or orders may result in dismissal.

4. Upon conclusion of the investigation and review by the Police Chief, the employee's initial probation may be terminated.

D. The following shall apply to the assignment of employees to the Required Test Group:

1. Any employee who refuses to undergo drug testing shall be assigned to the Required Test Group for a period not to exceed twelve (12) months from the date of the first refusal.

2. Any employee who fails to submit to drug testing or is in noncompliance with drug testing procedures may be assigned to the Required Test Group for a period not to exceed twelve (12) months from the date of failure of noncompliance.

E. The following shall apply to an applicant on the Civil Service Certified List of Eligible Applicants for Police Officer I positions who has been given a conditional Offer of Employment and who fails/refuses to submit to the third drug urinalysis test or is in noncompliance with drug testing procedures.

1. The applicant will be informed that the Conditional Offer of Employment provided by the Department is being withdrawn, and the Department will be requesting the removal of the applicant's name from the Certified List.

2. A memorandum from the Police Chief specifying the reasons will be sent to the Department of Civil Service and requesting the removal of the applicant's name from the Certified List.

X. Analysis of Test Results

A. The appropriate laboratory shall forward the results of any drug urinalysis testing to the Major of the Administrative Services Division.

B. All Sample A specimens identified as positive on the initial test shall be confirmed using gas chromatography/mass spectrometry (GC/MSP) techniques on Sample B. Sample B specimens shall be confirmed with additional samples from the same testing group in a ratio of five (5) negative samples for each positive sample.

1. A nonconfirmation of a positive test sample shall nullify the results of the original test.

2. When a drug screening test is confirmed positive by the second test, the licensed Medical Review Officer (MRO) of the State shall notify the subject employee of the results. The MRO shall have discussions with the employee to make final determinations of the drug testing results.

   a. If the employee reports to the MRO that the positive test result is a prescribed drug, the MRO shall:

      (1) Ask the subject employee for the name of the physician who issued the prescription and necessary authorization for the release of medical information.

      (2) Contact the physician who issued the prescription to the subject employee to verify that the drug was in fact prescribed for the employee.

   b. If the MRO determines that the metabolite level of the controlled drug is consistent with the attending physician's prescription, the test will be determined to be negative and no further action will be taken.

   c. If the positive test result is found to be unsubstantiated, the MRO shall terminate the inquiry and no further action shall be taken. The MRO shall notify the subject employee of this determination.

   d. If the positive test result is confirmed by the MRO, the MRO shall inform the Major of the Administrative Services Division of his/her findings.

XI. First Confirmed Positive Test Results

A. For any Regular Employee:

1. The Major of the Administrative Services Division shall notify the Police Chief, the Captain of the Internal Affairs Unit, and the affected employee's Division Commander of all confirmed positive test results. Information on any positive result shall be otherwise restricted and confidential.

2. The Division Commander shall notify the employee of the test results and recover the employee's badge and issued firearm(s).

   a. The employee shall be assigned to a position where a gun and badge are not essential, pending completion of an internal investigation.

3. The Internal Affairs Unit shall initiate an investigation based on the final determination of a confirmed positive test result by the MRO and forward the completed investigation to the Administrative Review Board via the Deputy Police Chief.

4. Pursuant to Memorandum of Agreement (MOA) with the State of Hawaii Organization of Police Officers (SHOPO), effective February 4, 2001, upon conclusion of the investigation and the disciplinary review process, and with the concurrence of the Police Chief, Regular Employees shall be subject to termination of employment for a first confirmed positive drug test result for the following illicit drugs:

Initial Test	Level (ng/ml)
Cocaine metabolites	300
Phencyclidine	25
Opiate metabolites	300*
Amphetamines	1,000
Methaqualone	300**

0.25 ng/ml if immunoassay specific for free morphine.

**Test level in accordance with State Department of Health Administrative Roles.

   a. Article 57, Sections G.2 and 3, of the SHOPO collective bargaining agreement relating to first confirmed positive test results shall not apply.

5. For all other first confirmed positive test results, upon conclusion of the investigation and the disciplinary review process, and with the concurrence of the Police Chief, the Regular Employees with a first confirmed positive test result shall be subject to disciplinary action up to and including termination of employment, with any discipline being held in abeyance and not imposed if the employee:

   a. Complies with a written directive served by the Major of the Administrative Services Division to participate in and satisfactorily complete a department-approved drug/substance abuse treatment program whose cost shall be at the expense and responsibility of the employee. Conditions:

      1. The employee shall take no longer than two calendar weeks to enter a departmentally approved drug/substance abuse treatment program or demonstrate an effort to start treatment.

   b. A Regular Employee with a first confirmed positive test result shall not be allowed limited or modified duty while undergoing treatment.

The employee may apply for Leave Without Pay, Vacation, Sick Leave, or Compensatory Time Off to comply with the treatment program requirements.

c. The affected Regular Employee shall remain on leave status until:

1. Satisfactorily completing the departmentally approved drug/substance abuse treatment program, and,
2. Obtaining an approved negative drug urinalysis test, and,
3. Obtaining a clearance from the County Physician to return to full duty.

d. A Regular Employee with a first confirmed positive test result, upon returning to full duty after complying with the aforementioned requirements, shall be placed in the Required Test Group for a period of one year.

B. For any Probationary Employee:

1. The Major of the Administrative Services Division shall notify the Police Chief, the Captain of the Internal Affairs Unit, and the affected employee's Division Commander of all confirmed positive test results. Information on any positive result shall be otherwise restricted and confidential.
2. The Division Commander shall notify the employee of the test results and recover the employee's badge and issued firearm(s).

   a. The employee shall be assigned to a position where a gun and badge are not essential or place on leave in compliance with the SHOPO collective Bargaining Agreement pending completion of an Internal Investigation.

3. The Internal Affairs Unit shall initiate an investigation based on the final determination of a confirmed positive test result by the MRO and forward the completed investigation to the Administrative Review Board via the Deputy Police Chief.
4. Upon conclusion of the investigation and the disciplinary review process, and with the concurrence of the Police Chief, Regular Employees shall be subject to termination of employment.

C. For applicants on Civil Service Certified List of Eligible Applicants for Police Officer I positions:

1. The Major of the Administrative Services Division shall notify the Lieutenant of the Administrative Services Section of the confirmed positive test results. Information on any positive result shall be otherwise restricted and confidential.
2. The Lieutenant of the Administrative Services Section shall notify the applicant that the Conditional Offer of Employment provided by the Department is being withdrawn, and the Department will be requesting the removal of the applicant's name from the Certified List.
3. A memorandum from the Police Chief specifying the reasons will be sent to the Department of Civil Service and requesting the removal of the applicant's name from the Certified List.

Index